The EVERYTHING™ PASTA COOKBOOK

The Everything™ Series:

The Everything™ Baby Names Book

The Everything™ Bartender's Book

The Everything™ Bicycle Book

The Everything™ Cat Book

The Everything™ Christmas Book

The Everything™ College Survival Book

The Everything™ Games Book

The Everything™ Home Improvement Book

The Everything™ Study Book

The Everything™ Wedding Book

The Everything™ Wedding Checklist

The Everything™ Wedding Etiquette Book

The Everything™ Wedding Vows Book

The Everything™ Pasta Cookbook

The EVERYTHING™ PASTA COOKBOOK

Over 300 delicious recipes—many created by great chefs—that will have pasta lovers begging for more!

Edited by

Jane Resnick

ADAMS MEDIA CORPORATION
Holbrook, Massachusetts

An Everything™ Series Book. The Everything™ Series is a trademark of Adams Media Corporation.

Published by Adams Media Corporation
260 Center Street, Holbrook, MA 02343

ISBN: 1-55850-719-1

Printed in the United States of America.

J I H G F E D C B A

Library of Congress Cataloging-in-Publication Data
  Resnick, Jane Parker
    The everything pasta cookbook / edited by Jane Parker Resnick.
        p.   cm.
    Includes index.
    ISBN 1-55850-719-1
    1. Cookery (Pasta) 2. Pasta products. I. Resnick, Jane Parker.
    TX809.M17E88   1997
    641.8'22—dc21   97-477
                                          CIP

Permissions were given for the following recipes: The recipe for "Orecchietti with Peas and Onions" is reprinted with the permission of Simon & Schuster from *Moosewood Restaurant Cooks at Home* by The Moosewood Collective. Copyright ©1994 by Vegetable Kingdom, Inc. The recipe for "Thai Noodle Salad" is reprinted with the permission of Simon & Schuster from *Sundays at Moosewood Restaurant* by The Moosewood Collective. Copyright ©1990 by Vegetable Kingdom, Inc. The recipe for "Herb Ravioli with Basil Oil and Tomato Coulis" from *Cooking with Daniel Boulud* by Daniel Boulud. Copyright ©1993 by Daniel Boulud. Reprinted by permission of Random House, Inc. The recipe for "Ramatuelle Pasta Sauce" is excerpted from *New Recipes from Moosewood Restaurant*. Copyright ©1987 by Vegetable Kingdom, Inc. with permission from Ten Speed Press.

Illustrations by Barry Littmann

This book is available at quantity discounts for bulk purchases. For information, call 1-800-872-5627 (in Massachusetts, call 617-767-8100).

Visit our home page at http://www.adamsmedia.com

Dedication

For Paul, for whom books were food.

Acknowledgments

I would like to thank Lois Ringelheim, for her expertise and unerring eye for a recipe; Wendy Philcox and Molly Collins of the American Culinary Federation for their help in contacting their members; all the chefs who so generously contributed; and my editor, Pam Liflander, for her great good work in bringing both Gabrielle and this book into the world at the same time.

CONTENTS

Introduction:
The History of Pasta vii

Chapter 1: Pasta Shapes and Sizes . . . 1

Chapter 2: Pasta on the Table 17

Chapter 3: The Freshest *Pasta Fresca*:
Making Pasta at Home 23

Chapter 4: Basic Sauces
and Beyond 41

Chapter 5: Great Beginnings:
Appetizers 57

Chapter 6: Stock Pot:
Pasta in Soups 73

Chapter 7: Adding Greens to Pasta:
Vegetables 87

Chapter 8: White Meat:
Pasta and Poultry 105

Chapter 9: A Full Plate:
Pasta and Meat 125

Chapter 10: Ocean Abundance:
Pasta and Seafood 143

Chapter 11: Inside/Outside:
Pasta Stuffed and Layered 167

Chapter 12: Ancient Noodles:
Asian Pastas 197

Chapter 13: The Global Village:
Ethnic Pastas 227

Chapter 14: Cool Noodles:
Pasta Salads 243

Chapter 15: Salt of the Earth:
Pasta and Beans 261

Chapter 16: The Thin Line:
Low Fat Pasta 275

Chapter 17: Pasta on the Run:
Quick and Easy Pasta 293

Chapter 18: Sweet Tooth Pasta:
Dessert 307

Index 322

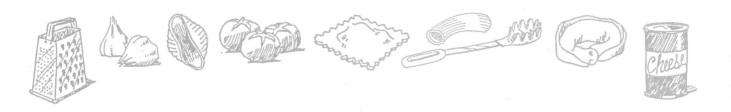

INTRODUCTION:
The History of Pasta

History tells us that food travels. Pasta, however, has galloped across continents in bold explorations, bloody conquests, and the passionate intermingling of peoples. Wherever there was flour, people created pasta: German *spaetzle*, Polish *pierogi*, Japanese *udon*, Chinese *mein*, Indian *sevika*, and French *nouilles* name merely a few incarnations. But the country that is undeniably the spiritual home of pasta is Italy, birthplace of macaroni.

Legend credits Marco Polo for bringing pasta from China to Italy. They say that he dined on pasta in the court of Kubla Khan and returned to Italy from the Orient in 1292 with a stash of dried spaghetti. That may be true, but only proves that pasta was abroad in the world, not that the Italians had never seen a noodle. Indeed, by the third and fourth centuries B.C., campfires of many early cultures were cooking a dough or paste (*pasta* means paste in Italian) made by mixing together flour and liquid. And, the Etruscans, the ancient people who first settled on Italian soil, left a giant culinary footprint: A fourth-century B.C. Etruscan tomb outside of Rome reveals carvings of all the tools necessary for producing pasta five thousand years ago—and today.

Basic pasta has not been a victim of progress. But it has been embellished by history. The Italian peninsula has always been at the matrix of cultural cross currents. For centuries, pasta accrued the permutations of conquering and developing civilizations. While building an empire, the Romans invented *gnocchi* and stacked flat noodles into the form of *lasagna*. The Arabs swept through Sicily and left behind the technique of making pasta in the form of hollow threads, which they called *itriyah*. Contemporary Sicilians call these "little strings" *trii*, an echo of their original name, and make dishes with eggplant and raisins and cinnamon, legacies of their Middle Eastern interlopers.

During the Renaissance, pasta took hold in Italy both as an aristocratic repast and a staple of the people. The country that emerged from the dark Middle Ages as Europe's most advanced society was, in the fifteenth century, a composite of city-states. This fractious situation, which caused no end of competitive strife, was a boon to the evolution of pasta, for each region developed its own characteristic cuisine, complete with pasta shapes, local produce, and idiosyncratic

spices. These separate entities remained distinct until the mid-nineteenth century, when Italy became a united country and pasta became the nation's emblematic dish. Today the regional cuisines remain intact and are the basis for the marvelous diversity and range of flavors that make pasta dishes so infinitely various.

Dried, or *pasta secca*, was a phenomenon that came to Italy from the nomadic peoples of the East and eventually sailed the Atlantic to America. It was made commercially in Italy, though on a small scale, as early as the sixteenth century, and blossomed in Naples in the 1700s where the seacoast breeze offered the perfect drying environment. Sheets of pasta hung everywhere in the city, like delicious laundry, and piqued the enthusiasm of America's well-traveled statesman Thomas Jefferson. Not only did he ship home quite a bit more than a single serving, he even investigated purchasing a pasta machine.

At the time of Jefferson's visit, the streets were dotted with *maccheronaros*, macaroni vendors, selling pasta, cooked and sauced. These stalls were so popular in the mid-eigh-teenth century among English tourists that the young men were called "macaronis," which meant "fop" or "dandy." The word also implied a certain elegant perfection and grew into the slang, "that's Macaroni!" for "terrific," which explains why Yankee Doodle stuck a feather in his hat and called it "Macaroni!"

But, to begin with, why macaroni or *maccheroni* for a generic term for pasta? There is, not surprisingly, a legend with an Italian flourish. The story goes that the inventive cook of a thirteenth-century nobleman created little boiled tubes of flour and water and served them with sauce and cheese. The novelty of the dish entranced the nobleman. Tasting the diminutive morsels, he exclaimed, "*Ma, che carini!*, Ah, little darlings!"

Little darlings in Italy, bean threads in Vietnam, wontons in Hong Kong, rice noodles in Bangkok, dumplings in Budapest, spaghetti with tomato sauce in New York, and American as apple pie, some form of pasta is being served for every meal all over the world. Pasta is indigenous to and has been embraced by more cultures than any other food in the world. Pasta travels well.

TAKE ME TO YOUR LINGUINI

CHAPTER 1

PASTA SHAPES AND SIZES

Entrées, appetizers, soups, and side dishes, pasta roams the menu like a quick-change chameleon. Part of the reason for its amazing versatility is the number of shapes pasta can be found in. The names, whimsical and sometimes silly, are a reflection of the earthy, exuberant gusto of its inventors. Indulging their flair for the dramatic and comical, the Italians created "little ears and "hats," "radiators," and even "worms." But playfully named pastas aren't merely amusing. Each shape has a role to play in its relation to its complements, thereby enhancing flavors and textures and intensifying the experience of every meal.

There are a few Italian root words that are useful in recognizing variations. *Bucati* means "with a hole," and so is applied to pastas that are hollow. *Bucatini*, or "little hole," is a tubed pasta thinner than spaghetti. *Lisci* is "smooth," as distinguished from *rigati*, pastas that are "ridged."

Long Pastas

The strand that started it all was spaghetti. This "little string" is the simple tune on which a great symphony was composed. In time, the strands became narrower and wider, and then narrower and wider still, and then flatter and fatter and curled and twisted. The same and yet different, the small, appealing variations are emblematic of what makes pasta so endlessly alluring.

Italian Name	English	Description	Comments
spaghetti	little strings	long, slim solid pasta	The most common form used for a variety of sauces
spagellini		short, thin pieces of *spaghetti*	
spaghettini	fine strings	slim *spaghetti*	Used with garlic and oil sauce, fish and clam sauces
spaghetti all chitarra	guitar string	thin cut strand	

Italian Name	English	Description	Comments
fedelini	little faithfuls	very thin strands	
capellini or *capelli d'angelo*	fine hairs or angel hair	thinner than *fedelini*	Used for very delicate sauces. Sometimes sold as a ring for soups
vermicelli	little worms	thinner than *spaghettini*	Thicker than angel hair. Used for tomato, butter and cheese sauces
linguine	small tongues	flat or oval strands	Often used with seafood sauces
liniguine fini	little tongues	narrower than *linguine*	Also used with thin oil-based sauces like clam sauce
bavettine		very narrow *linguine*	
fusilli lunghi	long springs	curly strand	Excellent for chunky sauces that cling

Ribbons

Smooth, slippery ribbons run along the tongue with a silky feel. Most are made with eggs in addition to the basics, flour and water. They taste best either homemade or bought fresh. Their porous nature makes them fabulous partners for cream- and butter-based sauces, the most famous being *fettuccine Alfredo*. While herbs permeate these shapes, bits of medium-fine sauces adhere to them, creating a complexity of taste and texture.

Italian Name	English	Description	Comments
tagliatelle	from the verb "to cut"	1/3 inch wide, fresh egg pasta	Classically paired with meat
fettuccine	ribbons	1/5 inch wide, medium width	Best for cream sauces; available available in many flavors, especially spinach
fettucce	ribbons	wider than *fettuccine*	

Italian Name	English	Description	Comments
fettucelle	little ribbons	narrower than *fettuccine*	
tagliolini or *taglierini*		extremely narrow fresh egg pasta	Mostly used in broth
tonnarelli		$1/16$ inch square ribbons	
pappardelle		$3/4$ inch wide, ripple or plain edged	
pizzoccheri		earthy, brown color, medium wide, 3" or 4" lengths	Buckwheat flour added to eggs and white flour
malfade		wide ribbon with frilly edges	
paglia e fieno	straw and hay	green and white *linguine* or *fettuccine* mixed together	

Tubes

Tubes are muscular pastas that can stand deliciously alone with a little butter and cheese. But tubes are also welcoming receptacles for every nuance a sauce has to offer.

Italian Name	English	Description	Comments
maccheroni	"macaroni" general term for tubed pasta	slightly curved tubes	
penne	pens or quills	1" long, $1/4$" wide, slanted	Available in smooth (*lisce*) or ridged (*rigate*)
perciatelli	small pierced	hollow tube like a straw	Good for thicker sauces
bucatini	from bucato "with a hole."	heavier tube than *perciatelli*	

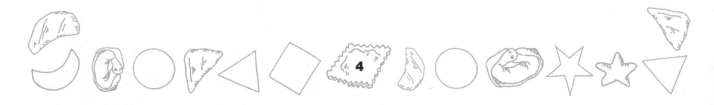

Italian Name	English	Description	Comments
penne piccoline	little quills		All forms of *penne* are good for meat, vegetable and cheese sauces
mostaccioli	mustache	same as *penne*	
ziti	bridegrooms	wider than *penne*, straight edged	Often used in backed dishes Good for thick sauces
zitoni	husky bridgegrooms	thicker than *ziti*	Excellent for heavy ragu sauces
rigatoni	big ridges	large slightly curved tubes with ridges	Excellent for meat sauces or delicious barely adorned with butter and cheese
gnocchetti rigati	thin *rigatoni*		Fine for hearty tomato sauces
millerighe	thousand lines	straight-sided large tube with many ridges	Good for meat sauces
gigantoni	super giants	very large tubes	Suited only for baking
elicoidali	helixes	straight-edged tubes with wrap-around ridges	Excellent for cheese and ricotta sauces
sedani	celery stalks	long, ridged like celery than *penne*	Longer and thinner
chifferi or gomiti	short, bent tubes		Good for light cheese sauces
cavatappi	corkscrews	snake-shaped tubes	Holds sauce very well. Good for vegetable sauces
manicotti	little muffs	large tube	Similar to *cannelloni* Used filled or baked
candele	candles	pipes of 1/2" to 3/4" diameters	

Italian Name	English	Description	Comments
canneroncini	narrow pipes	1/2" long tubes	
canneroni	pipes	longer than *canneroncini*	
garganelii		squares rolled diagonally	The only tube made by hand from egg pasta

Soup Shapes

The general term for a small pasta used in soup is *pastina*. Many are variations on the same theme, and others are individual diminutive works of art.

Italian Name	English	Description	Comments
acini di pepe	peppercorns	tiny beads	
anelli	little rings	small circles	
anelli rigati	little ridged rings	small circles with ridges	
funghetti	little mushrooms	mushroom shaped	
conchigliette	little shells	small snail shells with ridges	
farfalline	little butterflies	small bow ties	
semi di melone	melon seeds		
orzo	barley	rice-shaped	Also known as *pasta a riso*
orzi piccoli		thinner than *orzo*	

Italian Name	English	Description	Comments
alfabetini	little alphabet	pasta to spell with	
tubetti	little tubes	short and stubby pipes	
perline	little pearls	small beads	
stelline	little stars	small stars	
ditalini	little thimbles	tiny tubes, smaller than *ditali*	
quadretti	small squares		
salamini	tiny sausages		

Stuffed Shapes

Ever since the awareness of stuffed pastas has broadened beyond meat-filled ravioli in a can, their popularity has soared. And no wonder. Filled with vegetables and cheese, meat and seafood, and any combination thereof, stuffed pastas are interesting and endlessly variable. The very best balance pasta, stuffing, and sauce so that the integrity of each is not compromised.

Italian Name	English	Description	Comments
cannelloni	from *canna*, "hollow cane"	4" tube made by rolling a rectangle of pasta	
agnollotti or angolotti		crescent shaped	Also called *raviolini*
agnolini		smaller than *ravioli*	

Italian Name		English	Description	Comments
tortellini			circles stuffed, then folded in half and pinched into a ring	Usually stuffed with meat or cheese
cappelletti		little hats	similar to *tortellini*, but made from a square so that a "peak" forms into a hat shape	
tortelloni			similar to *cappeletti*, but smaller	Also a square usually stuffed with riccota. Also called *tortelli*.
ravioli		stuffed squares		Shapes may differ according to regions
pansotti		little bellies	stuffed triangles	
lasagna			wide strips of pasta	Layers of *lasagna* with filling created the dish that bears their name

Special Shapes

These fancy shapes were most likely regional specialties or simply the result of singular imaginations—with a sense of humor. No one could name a pasta "radiators" without a smile. And who can explain the impetus for an Italian wagon wheel, more a symbol of the American Wild West than its Sicilian home territory? Each appeals to the eye as well as to the taste buds, an important element in any culinary effort.

Italian Name		English	Description	Comments
ruote		cartwheels	wheels complete with spokes	*Ruote* can be ridged or smooth
rotelle		wagon wheels	another name for *ruote*	*Rotelle* can also refer to spirals

Italian Name	English	Description	Comments
conchiglie	shells	snail shell design	Middle-sized *conchiglie* are for sauces
conchiglioni	large shells		Used for stuffing
radiatori	radiators	shaped like small heaters	
gnocchi		pasta shaped like the "real" potato version	
gnocchetti		smaller than gnocchi	
gemelli	twins	one ½" length, folded and curled to look like two pieces	
casareccia	twists	curved ½" lengths of "S" shaped pasta	
fusilli	springs	short, telephone cord pieces	Sometimes called *fusilli corti*, meaning "short springs"
fusilli bucati		fusilli made from a tube	
orecchiette	little ears	circles pressed between fingers	less than 1 inch
cavatelli		cylinder bent into a "C"	less than 1 inch
farfalle	butterflies or bow ties	ridged squares pinched in the center	Also made with egg pasta
campanelle	bells	small cones with frilled edges	
lumache	snails	snail-like shape	*Lumanchine* is the smallest size
lumachone	fat snail		

Italian Name	English	Description	Comments
cappelli de pagliaccio	clown's hats		
capelvenere	maidenhair fern	fine noodles for soup	

Colored and Flavored Pastas

Italians are apt to think of colored and flavored pastas as a gimmick that has crashed somewhere off the culinary track. Spinach and tomato are the traditional classics and you can serve them knowing that a noble history is behind them. But it seems very stodgy to reject innovation without experimenting, so here is a list of some pastas, new and old, that, at first, seem strange, but may be wonderful. Except for the squid, which would seem to have a natural affinity for seafood, most of these would best be served with simply butter, oil, or light cream sauces.

Color	Added Ingredients
Red	Tomato; tomato paste
Deep Pink	Beets
Pale to deep orange	Saffron
Beige to brown	Mushroom; *porcini*, for Italian, *champignon*, for French
Black	Squid's ink
Orange tint	Carrots
Green	Spinach Peas Broccoli Asparagus
Speckled	Finely chopped herbs; basil is the most common
Yellow	Corn

Buying the Best Pasta

Semolina

Semolina and water are the only true ingredients for *pasta*, which is the general term used for all the many shapes and sizes—from teeny dots to curly ribbons. Semolina is the flour ground from the heart (or endosperm) of durum wheat, the hardest of all wheats. Durum is especially high in gluten, which accounts for its elasticity. Dried, commercial, and fresh pastas are simply the result of combining the right amounts of semolina and water. Some pastas and noodles have the added ingredient of eggs.

Dried, fresh, and frozen pasta all have places on a good cook's table. Choices depend on when and how the pasta will be used, of course, and personal preference. Fresh pasta is not necessarily superior to dried, and indeed, dried is better suited to chunky and strong-flavored sauces.

Dried pasta, *pasta secca*, is a machine made staple that looks down on us from supermarket shelves like old friends. Most of us slurped up "alphabet soup" as children and take as much comfort from our favorite shapes in the cupboard as we do milk in the refrigerator. Commercial brands made in the United States are acceptable and some are quite good, but others contain soft wheat flour and will not hold their firmness in cooking. The best list durum wheat flour or semolina

in their ingredients. Those imported from Italy hold the promise of being better because of their insistence on fine quality semolina.

Nutty in taste and chewy in texture, good dried pasta has a flavor all its own, as important to any dish as the sauce. Most dried pastas, like spaghetti, are made without eggs, but some, like fettuccine, are egg noodles. Avoid shapes that look broken or marbled. Store in as dry a place as possible in the original wrapping or a tightly covered container.

Fresh pasta, *pasta fresca*, must be refrigerated and kept tightly covered. It is made with ordinary white flour and usually contains eggs. Note the smoothness of the surface when buying. It should be dry, but not parched and free of any apparent moisture or water droplets.

Frozen pasta, which tends to be shaped like tortellini or ravioli, must be kept frozen until use. When purchasing, make sure that the pieces are not clumped together or covered with ice crystals.

Equipping the Kitchen

It may seem too basic to mention a big pot, but you can't even begin to cook pasta without it. A standard sized 5-quart pot that most kitchens have will just suffice for one pound of spaghetti for a family of four. Beyond that, your pasta will not have enough room to swim. Invest in a good 10-quart pot—

it will make all the difference in the texture of larger quantities—or use two pots if you are going to cook more than two pounds of pasta.

Cheese Grater Small cylindrical cheese graters are simplicity itself, a reminder to always use fresh-grated cheeses.

Colander A good stainless steel one is best, one large enough for at least 2 pounds of pasta.

Drying Rack A folding pasta rack for homemade pasta is handy. A long 2-inch round pole is even better, but only if space is available.

Dough Scraper This stainless steel square with a handle works well for gathering dough into a ball.

Food Chopper All of us chop garlic and onion and herbs in some habitual way. An Italian cook has the flair, and good reason, to use a crescent shaped, double-bladed tool called a *mezzaluna*.

Food Mill For puréeing tomatoes, there is nothing newfangled that outperforms a food mill. Unlike food processors, it separates rather than grinds seeds and thus produces a much smoother purée.

Pastry Board For rolling out homemade pasta, a large board, wooden, marble, or plastic is essential.

Pasta Machine The basic pasta machine is fitted with smooth rollers that knead and thin pasta dough, and cutters that trim a sheet of dough into ribbons. The rollers adjust to make the dough thinner and thinner, and the cutters create noodles of various sizes. The classic machines are hand operated and are quite adequate. Optional motor attachment can free your hands to handle the dough more easily.

Electric Pasta Machines mix the ingredients, knead, and extrude the dough in a variety of shapes. It is not a tool for purists, but, needless to say, a great time-saving device.

Pasta Wheels Both a straight-edged and fluted wheels are needed for different pasta shapes.

Ravioli Forms The choice of using ravioli forms or rolling out a strip of dough and cutting the ravioli by hand is purely individual. Experimenting is the only way to decide.

Rolling Pin The choices here are wooden, ceramic, glass, or marble and the *feel* is the criterion. You should be comfortable with the heft and glide in your hands. The size should be about two feet long.

Slotted Spoon Small and stuffed pastas like ravioli need a slotted spoon to be removed from water. A large skimmer is also excellent.

Spaghetti Fork This large, pronged fork is designed to lift pasta from boiling water. A wooden one is best. A wooden fork should be used to stir pasta as well.

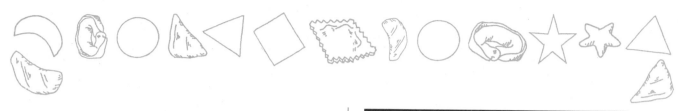

Cooking *al Dente,* or "to the Tooth"

If you can boil water, you can cook pasta. First, bring a large amount of water to rolling boil in a pot big enough to give the pasta plenty of room—at least 4 quarts of water to a pound of pasta—6 quarts of water if you have a big enough pot.

When the water is at a boil (not before), add one or two tablespoons of salt. Adding salt before the water boils seems to cause an odor that affects the pasta. Salt adds flavor to the pasta and helps it retain its shape. Adding a tablespoon of oil at this point will keep the water from boiling over, but it may also prevent the sauce from properly adhering to the pasta.

Add the pasta when the water is at a rolling boil, small shapes all at once; longer strands in bunches. Never break long strands. If the pot is not tall enough, as the pasta softens push it down with a wooden fork.

Keep things moving. Using a pasta fork for strands or a slotted spoon for solid shapes, start stirring the minute the pasta hits the water. Gently separate any pieces that seem determined to cling together. Be aware that dense shapes may stick to the bottom of the pot. Carefully rustle up the water until it reaches a boil and the pieces are cooked enough so they don't stick to each other.

Personal Pasta

If cooking is creative, then pasta shapes are one place to express yourself. Homemade pasta offers the chance to be as original with shapes as the dough allows. Remember, though, simpler is probably better when designing your own stuffed shapes. So, why not try heart shapes for Valentine's Day? The pasta, tinted pink with the addition of a little beet, can be stamped out with a heart-shaped cookie cutter. These little valentines can be used in a main course or a dessert recipe, and are the makings of a lovefest far beyond flowers. For Christmas, stars are wonderful (and easier than Christmas trees). Color them green or red (spinach or tomato) and your holiday meal will be spectacular.

Test often for doneness. The length of time any pasta needs to cook depends on its shape and thickness. Precision is impossible, but the "feel" can be pretty exact. *Al dente,* "to the tooth," is the ideal tenderness: not stiff, not soft, but pliable, a texture that

engages the mouth with firmness. The pasta will be just cooked through with no white-center core. This occurs at a sublime, but fleeting moment and there's no way to capture it, but to take a bite of the pasta. In fact, you will have to take several bites to check the pasta as it cooks. Each time, look for the white dry core and let your teeth assess the amount of resistance. As the *al dente* moment approaches, check and check again. This is not a perfect science, but it is the only method that works.

The length of cooking time depends on the type of pasta. Dried pasta takes longer to cook than fresh and it is better to rely on your own judgment than the directions on the box. Homemade pastas can cook in less than minutes, so you have to test for doneness in a matter of seconds after it hits the boiling water. Because it is more porous and softer in texture to begin with, homemade pasta is *al dente* when it feels softly springy—never mushy. Store-bought fresh pastas need to cook a little longer. And stuffed pastas need to cook the longest.

As soon as the pasta is done, pour into a colander and gently shake the colander to strain. Pasta must remain moist, so it is important not to overdrain. A good idea is to retain some of the cooking water in a measuring cup and keep it on hand in case the pasta becomes too dry. A little water is preferable when the pasta meets its sauce.

Never rinse, if the pasta is to be served immediately. The only time to rinse pasta is when making pasta for a salad.

Saucing the Pasta

Pasta pieces can't remain together unadorned for very long without becoming glued to each other. The next step must be speedy. The simplest method is to place the pasta in a large, warm bowl, add the sauce, and toss. Or, transfer the pasta to the pan with the sauce and combine. If pasta is added to the pan, it should be just a bit undercooked because it will cook further in the skillet. *All* the pasta should be tossed with sauce at once. Pasta should never be naked with sauce on top. Every strand or curl should convey the taste of the whole dish. Note too, the emphasis on *warm* for the bowl. A bowl warmed on the lowest setting in the oven will make the difference between eating pasta lukewarm or properly hot. Even better, also warm the dishes the pasta will be eaten in.

These simple saucing procedures can be slightly altered for particular pastas and sauces:

If the pasta is strands, combine most of the pasta and sauce in a large warm bowl. Transfer to individual warm dishes and top with *only* two or three tablespoons of sauce. Do not oversauce.

If the pasta is grooved, curled, or tubed, mix all the sauce with the pasta in the large warm bowl so the ridges and crevices will have a chance to grasp the ingredients.

If the sauce is cream and vegetables, combine it fully with the pasta in the saucepan and crown each serving with more of the vegetables.

There are other possibilities, all designed to prevent the pasta from becoming mushy or sticking together:

When the pasta is *al dente*, quickly drain in a colander and place in a warm bowl with butter (about two tablespoons to a pound) or oil, if the sauce is based on oil. Toss with the butter. Quickly add the sauce and toss with the pasta. Transfer to warm plates and serve.

A technique used by many professional chefs is to skip the colander and straining entirely. Instead, place a large bowl near the boiling pasta. The bowl should be warm and have butter or oil in it. When the pasta is *al dente*, lift batches out of the water with a pasta fork (or slotted spoon for short shapes), shake off the water, and transfer to the bowl. When all the pasta is shifted, toss with the butter or oil to coat and then combine with the sauce.

Lasagna noodles, slippery and large, require special treatment for easy handling. Since they will be further cooked in the casserole, they should only be boiled for one minute. If they are poured into a strainer, they are bound to stick. Instead, bring the pot to the sink and add cold water until you can grab each noodle with your hands. Gently shake, and place on a paper towel or cloth to blot. Manicotti squares, before being rolled, can be handled in the same way.

Reheating pasta is anathema to serious cooks, but practically speaking, the demands of convenience are paramount. There are a few ways to give pasta a second life:

Microwave pasta in a tightly covered bowl with just a little water for up to 3 minutes, depending on the amount and shape.

Gingerly, give the pasta a 2 minute dip in boiling water. Or pour boiling water over pasta in a colander. Drain and serve.

Wrap the pasta in tinfoil and place in a 350° oven for fifteen minutes or until it is hot.

Sauce Repair

There are times, almost always at the last minute, when the perfect medium between a sauce that's too thick or too thin eludes us. Here are a few methods of emergency repair that should work. Remember that if you dilute a sauce, taste to correct the seasoning.

Tomato Sauce

If a tomato sauce is too thick, it can be thinned with $1/2$ cup of the hot water in which

the pasta was cooked. Heat the sauce through to smooth the texture. A little juice reserved from canned tomatoes can also be used. If the sauce is too thin, add a few tablespoons of grated Parmesan and stir over heat to thicken.

Cream Sauce

If a cream sauce is too thick, thin it with at least ½ cup of the hot water in which the pasta was cooked. Stir gently over a low heat to combine. If a cream sauce is too thin, add a little warm cream. Do not use half-and-half or milk because they will ruin the consistency.

What Sauce for What Pasta

When marrying sauce to pasta, shapes count. Sauces that are thick or thin, chunky or buttery, made with meat or vegetables tend to blend better with shapes that complement them. No matter what the sauce, the nutty, chewy, comfort taste of the pasta should never be drowned out. A sauce is an enhancement. Of course, pasta preferences are personal. Going against 200 years of tradition and choosing whatever we like is one of the pleasures of cooking. Whatever combination you enjoy the most is perfect, but here are some suggestions.

Pastas with nooks and crannies or holes, like rigatoni or *rotelle*, *rotini*, spirals or shells, have surfaces that capture pieces of meat or ham or small vegetables.

Thin strand pastas like vermicelli and *cappelini* are blended best with lighter sauces, especially those made with broth and olive oil or butter.

Heavier strands like spaghetti have more surface for absorbing satiny sauces like a tomato sauce.

Ribbon shapes like fettuccine or flatter like *orecchiette* have wider surfaces that creamy sauces can cling to.

Sturdy shapes like *ziti*, *penne*, or *mostaccioli* stand up to heftier sauces.

Homemade pastas with their softer surfaces are ideal for hugging the flavor of cream and cheese sauces.

Some pastas and sauces truly do marry. The long tubes like *perciatelli* should be allowed a brief, covered honeymoon with their sauce so that the taste permeates all the surfaces inside and out.

CHAPTER 2

PASTA ON THE TABLE

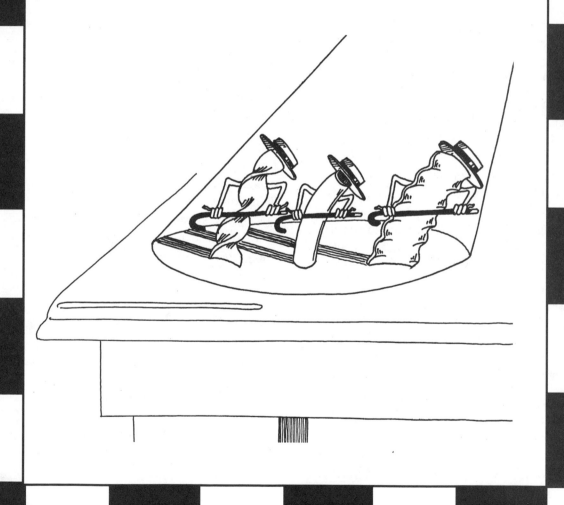

Who has not been guilty of cooking too much pasta? The tiniest shapes *grow* as soon as you turn your back. Most pastas increase to three times their size in cooking. Two ounces of pasta will mushroom into 1½ cups of cooked pasta, depending on the shape and size. In general, a pound of pasta serves four people as a main course, six as a first course. Also, what accompanies the pasta will affect the amount necessary. If, for example, sausage is part of the dish, less pasta is necessary than if peas are the only accompaniment.

How to Serve Pasta

In Italy, where a meal is more courses than the average American can sit through, pasta is a first course. But, American style, pasta is the main event. Salad is the traditional accompaniment and bread—which should be a hard, crusty white, French, Italian, or sourdough. Soft white bread is the wrong texture and strong-flavored loaves like rye are incompatible. Freshly grated cheese should be on the table to be passed, if the sauce allows. And a bottle of wine, red or white, should be standing by. The choice is personal, but should also be sensible. A strong red wine is not appropriate to a delicate sauce just as a demure white is too fainthearted for a robust sauce.

How to Eat Pasta—Pasta Manners

The correct way to eat pasta is a bit of a balancing act with a fork alone. There are etiquette books that allow for twirling strands with a fork against a spoon, and there are certainly no pasta police to prevent this. But the elegant, the sophisticated, and, alas, the *right* way is to take just a few strands and roll them around the fork with a little assist from the side of the dish. If the pasta is cooked *al dente*, some will hang down, so lifting it to your mouth needs to be done as quickly and suavely as possible. The spoon in the place setting is there to mix the sauce and pasta, add cheese, and help with especially juicy sauces.

To Cheese or Not

Seafood and cheese make poor bedfellows according to most Italian cooks and few will add cheese to a seafood pasta. In general, that can be considered a rule, and like most rules has been known to be broken. An exception is a sauce based on butter rather than oil. A bit of cheese may help to bind the sauce.

The Tomato: Preparing to Meet Pasta

Rich and red, tart and sweet, the tomato is the romance in many pasta recipes. It was the New World, not the Old that brought the tomato to pasta when it came to Europe via the conquistadors who explored South America. But it was the imaginative cooks of the pasta producing city of Naples that, between the seventeenth and eighteenth centuries, created the tomato sauce. Now fresh and canned tomatoes are indispensable to pasta preparation.

Decisions on which tomatoes to use depend on the length the sauce will be cooked and the texture of the tomato.

Egg-shaped plum tomatoes are the basis of many fine sauces. Packed in their own juices, at times with addition of basil, they have the sweetness of flavor and texture right for slow-cooking sauces. The combination of one can of plum tomatoes and one of tomato paste is the beginning of a good sauce.

Canned tomato purée is the base for long-simmering sauces. Canned crushed tomatoes work alone or in combination with purée, depending on the thickness of the sauce.

Tomato paste can be used for deepening a sauce's tomato taste. Most often, just a little is enough; use it sparingly. To keep the rest from spoiling in the can, pour olive oil over the top. To use a little at a time, try tomato paste in a tube.

Sun-dried tomatoes have a distinctly intense flavor. They are used on their own or added to enliven a sauce. Choose the ones found in jars packed in olive oil rather than those that are literally dry. The dry ones must be soaked before you use them, which leads to uneven results.

Fresh tomatoes are best for lightly cooked sauces and better, in terms of texture, without their skins. Peeling tomatoes is not an ordeal if you blanche them first. Begin by scoring each tomato with a large X across the bottom. Then drop the tomatoes into boiling water for about 30 seconds. Remove with a slotted spoon. Cool to handle. Peel off the skin with a paring knife. If a recipe calls for removing the seeds, halve the tomatoes cross-wise and squeeze them by hand over a strainer to collect the juice.

Pasta Prerequisites

Ingredients Defined from Anchovies to Pancetta

Here is a list of ingredients, and some clarification about their use, that are frequently found in pasta dishes.

Anchovy An anchovy is a little slip of a three-inch fish that some people love to hate, but others adore. Most recipes presume them to be canned, cured in oil. Anchovies are widely available. They add richness and complexity to a sauce, but their preparation

includes quite a bit of salt. When using them, you might want to taste the sauce before adding more salt.

Butter Substitutes for butter may be acceptable on toast, but not in a sauce. Sweet (unsalted) butter is the best.

Bread Crumbs Open a can of prepared bread crumbs, especially the "seasoned" kind and you are getting more than you want. For sauces, you want bread crumbs, fresh and unadorned. Often used in preparing pasta, they are not hard to have on hand. Crumbs can easily be made from stale, hard bread in a food processor or blender, or even with a grater. They keep well in a tightly closed jar in a dry place, not the refrigerator.

Garlic Many recipes call for a lot of garlic. The skin of garlic cloves seems to be maddeningly attached, but can usually be loosened by a good whack with the blunt side of a knife or the heel of your hand. The clove will then split so that the skin peels easily.

Herbs and Spices

Herbs are a case of fresher is better, but not stronger. In fact, dried herbs are more potent than fresh. The rule for recipes is that a half teaspoon of dried equals a tablespoon of fresh herbs. Dried herbs crushed between your fingers will have an even stronger flavor. Your palate is the most sensitive guide to choosing the herbs you use, but there are a few that regularly occur in pasta recipes.

Basil Inhale the bouquet of fresh basil and you will know why more Italian cooks include it in their sauces and soups than any other herb. It smells like good cooking. Leaves of fresh basil can be snipped right into a sauce. Although it is not the same, dried can be substituted for most recipes, except for pesto.

Bay Leaves Strong and aromatic, bay should be used sparingly. It is especially compatible with meat sauces and soups.

Fennel Fennel is a multitalented root vegetable. The bulb can be cut up and eaten on its own or in a sauce, and the seeds and leaves are used for seasoning. There is a hint of anise about fennel.

Marjoram Here is a Mediterranean herb that dries well, holds its own, and is well-suited to soups.

Nutmeg Nutmeg may seem more reminiscent of Christmas than pasta cooking, but it is indispensable to many noodle and stuffed pasta preparations. Whole nutmegs can be bought and grated for superior taste.

Oregano More American than Italian in cooking, oregano has a strong flavor that should be used judiciously.

Parsley Widely used and sometimes not granted proper respect, parsley is important in many pasta dishes. The flat-leafed variety, often called "Italian" parsley, is definitely preferable for flavor, while the curly version has mostly decorative value. It is best used chopped on the spot, but it also freezes well. Putting the

parsley in a food processor squishes the leaves and their taste. Pallid dried parsley is best left on the supermarket shelf.

Pepper There's more to pepper than the "add salt and pepper to taste" directive in recipes. It's colorful. Whole peppercorns are the berries of the pepper plant. Black pepper is a mature berry dried. White pepper is the milder kernel hiding inside the black peppercorn. Green peppercorns are immature berries dried or sold in brine. Red pepper, as in flakes, are pieces of dried whole red peppers, a pepper of a different sort. Previously ground pepper is a very poor cousin to freshly ground.

Rosemary Lovely rosemary loses little flavor when dried. Crushing in the hand before using brings out its perfumey flavor.

Saffron It is not far-fetched to think that you could have dinner at a restaurant for the same price as a bit of saffron. It is expensive, but then it takes the stigmas of 4,000 crocuses to produce one ounce. Check the ingredients of every vial or packet to make sure it's the real thing. It is often found in recipes with a Sardinian source.

Capers Capers and their piquant taste add a complexity to many sauces. The bud of the caper plant, they are sold in bottles, packed in brine. Size is the secret to their delicacy. The finest are small and tulip-shaped.

Mortadella Sausage made of pure pork (no scraps, no boloney), sweet and spicy

mortadella is often used for the fillings of many stuffed pastas like tortellini.

Porcini Mushrooms Most often found dried, these are wild mushrooms that bring the richness of the earth right into a meal. Soak them first for about half an hour in cool water, and rinse if they still seem dirty. They are then ready to be used.

Olive Oil Like butter, there is no substitute for olive oil. But unlike butter, there is a confusing number of choices. The flavors range from fruity to peppery and the colors range anywhere from pale golden to lemony green. "Virgin" olive oil is from the first pressing of the olives; "extra virgin" is from the first pressing of the best, young hand-picked olives. These two are greener in color and more intense in flavor. They are wonderful in most cooking, but too much in delicate dishes. Like all ingredients that are meant to blend with others, the olive taste should not overpower the other elements. There are regional variations in olive oils and the best way to choose is to indulge yourself—dip a piece of crusty bread into a bit of oil and decide what you like.

Olives Olives are not an afterthought in Mediterranean cooking, but a pungent, often bold ingredient. When specific olives like Nicoise or Gaeta (Italian) or Kalamata (Greek) are called for, they may substitute for one another, although the taste may be slightly different. However, don't substitute the "jumbo" black or green olives from a can or

jar. They are useless alternatives. Pick ones sold packed in brine, better if they are unpitted than pitted. Olives should have a clean, tangy flavor. The green, which are the unripe version, are sharper.

Pancetta *Pancetta* is bacon the Italian way, not smoked but salt-cured, spiced and rolled. There is no American version, but you can substitute smoked bacon if it is not available. If choosing bacon, blanch before using.

Prosciutto *Prosciutto,* Italian ham, can be bought *crudo* (raw) or *cotto* (cooked). The most famous is prosciutto di Parma, which has been imported into the United States since 1989.

Onions Onions, like garlic, are a common ingredient with pasta, and should be adjusted according to taste. Yellow are the strongest. The lingering aroma of both garlic and onions can be banished from hands and cutting board by rubbing with lemon juice. If onions make you cry, try to cut them when they are really cold.

Cheeses Italian cheeses, acidic and pungent, buttery and mild, are a subject in themselves, but only a few are meant for pasta. Freshly grated, the following two are the elusive perfect partners that people dream of for themselves, and pasta is fortunate to have. They are at their best aged at least two years.

Parmesan The Italian version is *parmigiano-reggiano,* and is made from cow's milk and aged for grating. Good *parmigiano* is golden and moist, never dry or crumbly. It should be bought in a chunk and kept tightly wrapped in the refrigerator to be grated when used. Once grated, it can also be frozen without too much loss of flavor. American grated Parmesan, which lacks the Italian's sweet, buttery flavor, is not at all comparable.

Pecorino is a sheep's milk cheese, which is sharper, saltier, and more pungent than *reggiano.* A hard cheese, aged for grating, it should also be kept in the refrigerator to be grated at the time of use. *Pecorino romano,* the most common version in America, is not interchangeable with *parmigiano,* and should be saved for more pungent sauces.

In addition, hard, golden *asiago,* a cow's milk cheese, is a good, less expensive substitute for *parmigiano.*

Ricotta is a fresh cottage cheese made from whey of other cheeses. It is used for stuffed pastas, most notably lasagne, and sweet pastry. It should be drained before using.

Mozzarella that is found in most American dairy cases tastes a little like bleached rubber. The real thing, creamy and slightly sweet, is made from whole cow's milk, fresh, and always salted. It should be bought swimming in brine and never dry.

CHAPTER 3

THE FRESHEST *PASTA FRESCA:*
MAKING PASTA AT HOME

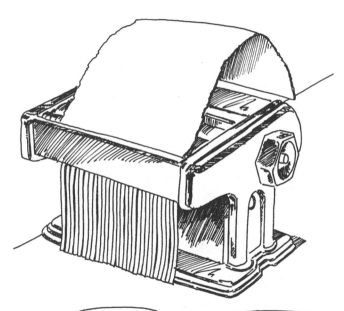

The beauty of *pasta fresca*, fresh pasta, is not just in the eating, but in the making. A pasta that is both light and chewy is so enticing that the project is hard to resist. But *pasta fatta a mano*, pasta made by hand, takes time and work space and, in the beginning, practice. So, first consider your own kitchen habits and how much help you want to enlist from machines. A pair of hands and a long rolling pin can do it all. Of course, there is nothing that will replace the tactile sensation of combining flour and eggs, kneading, rolling and, finally, stretching the dough. But a mixer with a dough hook or a food processor with a blade can also mix and knead the dough. A pasta machine can roll it beautifully, saves a great deal of time, and is very good for cutting. And the all-in-one electric wizards can take the process from beginning to end.

The pasta described here is *pasta all'uovo*, egg pasta, the most practical dough to work with by hand. (Pasta made with just flour and water is more difficult to roll.) The specialties of handmade pasta are the Italian ribbons like *fettuccine*, the stuffed shapes like ravioli, and the small hand turns like *orecchiette*.

Tools

There is nothing like having your tools at hand to make a project go smoothly, so the first step in successful pasta making is to bring out what you need. Here are the essentials:

- A surface, as large as possible, to roll out the dough. It should not be cold.
- A dough scraper to scrape up bits of dough stuck to the work surface.
- Cookie cutters, with straight or fluted sides, in whatever sizes you want to use.

- A fork to beat the eggs.
- Flat cotton kitchen towels for laying out the pasta. They will absorb excess moisture.
- A long knife to cut strands of pasta and sections of dough.
- A pastry wheel for cutting noodles and shapes with fluted edges.
- A rolling pin. The classic model is 1½ inches thick and 32 inches long, not an easy size to find. You can get by with one that is 2 inches thick and 24 inches long.
- A drying rack to hang strands that are going to be dried and/or stored.
- A pasta machine, if desired.
- A food processor, as a choice for mixing the dough.

Ingredients

All the pleasures of pasta begin with nature's most rudimentary gifts: Flour and eggs are all you need. The basic proportions are:

¾ cup of all-purpose unbleached flour and one extra large egg. The rest is arithmetic and you can simply increase accordingly: 1½ cups of flour to 2 extra large eggs; 2¼ cups of flour to 3 extra large eggs.

A "3 egg" recipe makes about a pound of pasta. There are some variables to these proportions that depend on unpredictable conditions. The humidity of the day always affects a dough, making it harder to roll. The eggs may have more or less liquid. So it is possible that a little warm water might be needed if the dough is too dry, or extra flour if it is too sticky. Starting with the eggs at room temperature helps the consistency, too. You will always need extra flour for dusting the work surface and the dough.

There are regions of Italy that vary from the strict flour and eggs tradition with the additions of salt and olive oil. The oil softens the dough and makes it easier to handle. For the basic 3 egg proportions, 2 teaspoons of extra-virgin olive oil and ½ teaspoon of salt are mixed in with the eggs.

Making the Dough

- Pour flour onto a clean, dry surface into a mound. Make a well in the center with your fingers or a knife. Be sure the sides are high enough to keep eggs in the center from running out.
- Break the eggs in the center of the well.
- Beat the eggs with a fork, using one hand to support the sides of the well. Beating in the same direction helps prevent air pockets.
- When the eggs are scrambled, use the fork to gradually incorporate the flour into the eggs, being careful not to let the eggs escape. Little by little the sides of the well should combine with the eggs.

- Then quickly use both hands to sweep the flour over the eggs and scoop everything together, bringing all the flour toward the center.
- Form the dough into a ball. Add loose flour if the dough is sticky. Include a few drops of water if the dough is too dry. When all the flour and eggs are mixed together, the dough should feel firm but pliable, soft but not wet, and moist but not sticky. Flour or water should be added a bit at a time until the dough is the right consistency.
- Sticky dough is impossible to work with, so never be afraid to dust with flour anywhere in the process if the dough clings and separates.

Kneading the Dough

- When the dough is the right consistency, wrap it in a damp kitchen towel or plastic wrap or under an inverted bowl and set aside. Whenever your hands are off the dough it must be protected from drying out. Quickly scrape the work surface clean and wash your hands. The dough should not be left to rest too long.
- Flatten the dough with the heel of your hand and begin kneading. Push down firmly in the middle of the disk

with the heel of your hand and then fold the dough over. Give the dough a quarter turn and repeat. Knead both sides. If the dough sticks to your hands, dust with flour. A 1 egg recipe is only kneaded for 5 minutes; a 2 egg requires 8 to 10 minutes of kneading; a 3 egg about 15 minutes.
- When you are finished kneading, the dough should feel smooth and silky, not hard. Wrap or cover the dough and let it rest for about 15 minutes.

Pasta Dough in the Food Processor

For a hands-off version of handmade dough, a food processor works very well. The dough will be slightly softer than hand-kneaded dough and should roll with ease.

- Begin with the flour and the eggs in the processor bowl. Use the steel blade. Run the machine for 30 seconds.
- The goal here is to form a clean, moist ball of dough. However, the amount of liquid in the eggs and the flour do not always cooperate. So after 30 seconds of processing make these observations and adjustments:
- If the mixture is too dry, the dough will look like grains. Add a *little* warm water though the feeding tube with the motor running.

- If the mixture is too wet, it will form a ball and leave sticky dough on the sides of the bowl. In that case, add a little flour to the bowl and process for 30 seconds more.

- When a ball has formed, with no dough sticking to the sides, success is yours. Remove the dough, dust it with flour, and knead it briefly by hand. The whirl of the processor's blade has already worked the dough sufficiently. The dough is *ready* to be rolled out by hand or pasta machine.

Rolling and Thinning

Here is the adventuresome part of pasta making. Expect at least some imperfections to begin with. The goal is simple enough: to quickly roll out a dough of even thinness (*thick* is not even part of pasta vocabulary) that is silky and flexible. The steps that go beyond rolling as you would a pie crust are all about stretching the dough, almost daring it to become more and more elastic and nearly transparent. Work as speedily as dexterity allows. Pasta dough dries out quickly, then its texture toughens and it becomes hard to roll. Be prepared to sacrifice a batch and then begin again undaunted. Your hands will teach you the proper *feel* of the dough, just like your teeth tell you when cooked pasta is *al dente*. Follow the directions, but let your body instruct you.

- Begin working at a counter or table that is big enough to roll a large circle. Make sure the surface is clean and then dust it with flour to keep the dough from sticking.

- Divide the dough. If you are making a large batch, the conventional rule is to divide by the number of eggs. Protect the pieces you are not working with by covering with an inverted bowl or a damp kitchen towel or wrapping tightly in plastic wrap.

- Place the dough on the floured work surface. Knead for a brief minute and flatten into a round disk with your hands.

- Begin by rolling away from you and stop just short of the edge. Do not press heavily. Push away, but not down onto the surface. With each roll, rotate the rolling pin a quarter turn so that you will form a circle with even thickness all around. If you have to, dust the surface with flour to prevent the dough from sticking. Continue rotating and rolling until the dough is as thin as you can handle it. One-eighth of an inch thick is okay. One-sixteenth is better.

- For the next step, you must have a long rolling pin. You are ready to stretch the dough. Center the rolling pin on the top edge of the circle and curl the dough onto it. Using quick

motions, roll the pin toward you, curling the dough onto the pin. Roll with the palms of your hands, moving them outward along the rolling pin and back inward quickly and evenly. This motion helps stretch the dough to the thinness you are aiming for.

- When the dough is rolled up, rotate one-quarter turn, unroll, and repeat until the dough is very, very thin, nearly transparent. Again, dust with flour, if necessary, but try not to use too much because the dough can become dry and hard to stretch.
- If a tear occurs in the dough, patch it with a small piece torn from the edge. If the piece refuses to adhere, smooth it with a bit of water. Dust with flour and roll out.

The next step is cutting. Dough that is to be used for stuffed pastas should be used quickly because drying out makes it difficult to shape. Dough that is to be cut for noodles can rest about 15 minutes before cutting.

There is a less traditional method of rolling that is a good way for beginners to start. The result is one or two rectangles of dough instead of one large circle, which can be difficult to handle. After kneading and letting the dough rest, place the dough on a floured surface and begin rolling. Press firmly

but not heavily, rolling away from your body and then back toward you. Direct the rolling pin to one side and then the other, creating the shape of an elongated rectangle. Dust the dough with flour if it sticks to the rolling pin. As the dough becomes thin, turn it over. Lightly flour the work surface, if necessary. If the rectangle becomes too long, cut it in half and work with one piece at a time. Be sure to cover the resting piece. Again, try to roll the dough until you can almost see through it.

Cutting by Hand

Of all the shapes from twists to little shells, only a fraction can be cut by hand or with a home pasta machine. These are the noodles like *fettuccine* and *lasagna* and the squares and circles that become stuffed pastas like *ravioli* and *tortellini*. The cutting calls for a long knife and a steady hand. The thin sheet of pasta is rolled to cut most of the noodles, or left flat to create squares, rectangles, and circles.

To cut noodles from a roll:

- Roll the pasta sheet into a log, being careful to keep the outside edges in line. Flatten it slightly with your hand. To begin cutting, start at one end, place one hand on the pasta roll, and use your fingers as a measurement guide. With the knife in

your other hand, cut across in the width you desire. *Fettuccine* is $\frac{1}{4}$", *tagliatelle*, $\frac{1}{3}$", *tagliarnini*, about $\frac{1}{16}$", and *capelli d'angelo* is angel hair thin, a cutting feat best left to professionals. Move your hand back from the edge at each cut. Make a clean cut, not a sawing motion. And again, work as quickly as possible.

- As soon as the noodles are cut, unravel them and place them on a lightly floured kitchen towel to dry. If they are not going to be used within an hour or so, follow directions for storing.
- Two other shapes, perfect for soups, are commonly cut from the roll, *quadrucci*, which are little squares, and *maltagliati*, irregular triangles.
- To make *quadrucci*, cut the roll in the width for *tagliatelle*, and then cut the ribbons crosswise to make small squares. Separate the pieces.
- *Maltagliati* means "bad cut," probably because the pieces are not geometrically aligned. To make these triangles, cut the corner off one side of the roll's end and then cut the corner from the other side. You should be left with a log with V-shaped ends. Slice the log across and you have a third triangle. Separate the pieces and proceed along the whole roll.

To cut noodles from a sheet:

- Some noodles like *pappardelle* are cut from a sheet, not from a roll. *Pappardelle* are about $\frac{3}{4}$" wide with a frilled edge. Simply start with a flat sheet of thin pasta and cut ribbons with a fluted pastry wheel. Use a ruler as guide.
- *Cannelloni* and *manicotti* are respectively the larger and largest of the squares. *Cannelloni* is about 3" x 4" and *manicotti*, 4" x 4". The easiest "stuffed" pastas, they are rolled around a filling.
- The fluted pastry wheel is also used to create *farfalle* or bow ties. These begin as $1\frac{1}{2}$ to 2-inch squares cut from a sheet on a flat surface. Pinch the middle of each square with two fingers and you have a bow-tie shape.
- Lasagna is truly a homemade noodle—made to fit *your* home. The longest noodle cut from a sheet, lasagna can be made to fit exactly the size of your own pan. Two or 3 inches wide and 9 to 10 inches long are customary sizes, but any dimensions that work for you are best. Either a fluted pastry wheel or a knife are appropriate for cutting.

Using a Pasta Machine

Purists will tell you that kneading, rolling, and cutting by hand produce a finer, more porous pasta that embraces every sauce like a new lover. But perfection is time-consuming. For those who adore fresh pasta but lack the time and devotion handmade requires, a pasta machine is the answer. All pasta machines, whether motorized or hand-cranked, have a set of rollers for kneading and thinning the dough and a set for cutting into ribbons. Most come with cutting heads that will turn out *fettuccine* and *tagliarini* noodles and have further attachments available for spaghetti, lasagna, and others. Circles and squares for stuffed pastas must be cut by hand from sheets made by the machine. Using a machine is fun, and the best way to keep it that way is to have a large surface to work on and everything you need at hand. Follow the directions and plan on very close to perfect pasta. Note: Never wash a pasta machine, just wipe it and clean the rollers with a dry pastry brush. Cover it when finished to keep out the dust.

- Begin by cutting your ball of dough into several pieces. If you follow the customary rule and cut a 3-egg dough into 3 pieces, the dough may still be unwieldy. Four to 6 pieces is even better. Cover or tightly wrap the pieces you are not using.

- Flatten the dough with your hands so that it can fit between the rollers. Dust it with flour.
- Set the machine at the widest setting and feed the dough through the rollers. Do not pull it or stretch it going into or coming out of the machine.
- As it emerges from the rollers, do not hold the dough in your palms. Rather, hold your hands perpendicular to the counter and drape the pasta across your fingers with your thumbs up.
- Fold the dough in thirds with the top third overlapping the bottom and middle thirds. Press down with your fingers so that there is no air between the layers. If the dough is sticky, dust one side with flour. You can flour the pasta by just barely dragging it across the floured work counter.
- Turn the dough so that an open edge faces the rollers and feed it into the machine. Repeat this routine of folding, pressing, flouring, and feeding at least six times or until the dough feels smooth and satiny. This process kneads the dough and shapes it into a workable rectangle.
- Repeat with all the pieces of dough. Place the resting pieces on a clean, lightly floured kitchen towel.

- The next step is to thin out the dough. Begin by decreasing the width of the rollers by one notch. Do not fold the dough. Run each rectangle through the machine.
- Decrease the space by another notch and repeat with all the pieces. With every repetition, the sheets will stretch and thin, moving closer and closer to the ideal texture. Progressing notch by notch may seem laborious, but this gradual thinning is essential to the dough's elasticity.
- If the strips become too long to handle, cut them in half crosswise.
- At every point, it is important to dust with flour on both sides, if the dough is sticky. A sticky dough is always in danger of tearing in the machine.
- Continue to decrease the width of the rollers until you have reached the thinnest or next to thinnest position. The thickness of the pasta depends to some degree on what shape you are making and on personal preference. The only way to know what is best is to experiment with your machine.
- Finish all the rolling and thinning before moving on to the cutting.

Cutting by Machine

The exact size and thickness of the noodles you cut with the machine is in the cutting head of each brand, so you will have to choose the setting that is best for the noodles you desire. *Fettuccine* will be wider than *tagliarini*, and *tonnarelli* will be thinner still.

- The trick to successful cutting is dough that is slightly dry. If you let the dough rest uncovered for about five minutes before cutting, it should be ready to cut.
- If the dough sticks to the cutting attachment and tears, simply fold it and pass it through the rollers again before cutting.
- If the edges of the strip become too dry, the dough will be brittle and break. Trim the dry edges with a knife and feed the dough through the rollers again.
- Work as quickly as you can. If the waiting strips seem to be drying, cover them with a damp cloth.
- Feed each strip through the cutting attachment and hold one hand to catch the noodles as they are formed.
- Place the noodles on a lightly floured kitchen towel or a rack to dry.

Cooking and Storing Fresh Pasta

Whether you are going to cook homemade pasta right away or store it, the object is to keep the strands in the best possible condition.

To Dry and Store

Pasta strands can be dried for long-term storage by hanging them on a drying rack, a towel rack, a floured towel, or any place you can improvise where they will remain separate and exposed to the air. They can also be twirled around your hand into nests, an excellent way to store them. After they have dried for about twenty-four hours, place them in a container with a tight fitting top or seal them in a plastic bag. Paper towels between layers will help to keep the strands from breaking. Homemade dry pasta will remain fresh for about a month.

To Refrigerate and Freeze

Fresh undried pasta is fine in the refrigerator for a week. First, lightly flour the pasta and let it dry for about fifteen minutes. Then coil the strands loosely into nests and place them in sealed containers or plastic bags. Follow the same procedure to freeze; it will keep well for about a month.

If you are going to store large noodles, such as those for *lasagna* or *cannelloni*, they will handle better if they have been just barely cooked first. Dry them for about fifteen minutes and then give them a 15-second immersion in boiling, salted water. Drain and plunge them into cold water. Drain again and seal them in containers or plastic bags for either refrigerator or freezer storage. When you are ready to use them, immerse them in boiling, salted water, stir, and they will separate. Watch them rise to the top, and drain.

To Cook

- Separate the strands of pasta. If it is going to be cooked within the hour, it can rest on a kitchen towel or rack to dry. It should dry for about fifteen minutes before cooking.
- When cooking fresh pasta, you must be on guard from the moment the pasta enters the boiling water. As soon as the water returns to a boil, check for doneness. Thirty seconds is an eternity in the lifetime of fresh pasta. The amount of time depends on the thickness, of course, but a minute and a half is more than enough time for most noodles. Start checking immediately, stir constantly, and check every few seconds. *Al dente* is really a term for dried pasta, so fresh pasta will have a different texture. It is soft to begin with and will be tender and springy when done.

• Frozen homemade pasta should not be thawed, but immersed frozen in boiling water. It will only take a few more seconds to cook than fresh.

Making Stuffed Pastas

The leap from cutting pasta strands to creating stuffed pastas is not a huge one. You do not have to have the manual dexterity of a safe-cracker. All you need is a couple of cookie cutters, pastry wheels with fluted or straight edges, and a knife. A teaspoon will usually do for placing the fillings, but a pastry bag is nice if you can handle one.

Dough Directions

• Wrestling with dough that has become too dry is the most common stumbling block in making stuffed pastas. To prevent this problem, roll out only the strip you are going to be working with and use it without delay. The remaining dough is set aside, covered, or tightly wrapped.

• It is possible to give the dough a little extra moisture by adding water or milk to the eggs during the mixing. As a guide for the added liquid, think of 2 tablespoons of water or milk to be included with the eggs. The result will be a softer dough that is better for rolling out by hand than in a machine.

• Another way to combat stiff dough is to incorporate a tablespoon of olive oil in the egg and flour mixture.

• The dough for stuffed pastas should be a little thicker than for strands. It has to stand up to more manipulation in filling and cooking and there are more possibilities for tearing and splitting.

• Finally, work with this dough as soon as it is rolled out and as quickly as possible. You want it to be soft and pliable in order to make shapes and seal edges.

Filling

• The more moist the filling, the more the danger of soggy pasta. Vegetables should be squeezed as dry as possible, sautéed ingredients should be strained, and, if ricotta is in the recipe, it should be drained.

• Fillings can be of meat, fish, vegetables, and cheese. They should be finely chopped or puréed so that they fit neatly in these pasta packages. Make sure the filling is totally prepared before working with the pasta.

• A stuffed pasta cannot sit too long before cooking or storing. If the

filling is very moist, it may begin to stick to the surface and refuse to give without tearing. Flouring the surface should help.

Shaping

Most stuffed pastas start with a square or a circle. Where you go from there depends on a flick of the wrist, a twirl of a finger, and the fun of folding, pinching, and twisting. Squares, the most familiar shape, are often generically called *ravioli*. Traditionally only those filled with ricotta cheese were properly named *ravioli* and any other filling transformed the same shape into *agnolotti*. But today, squares are filled with anything from lobster to pumpkin and still called *ravioli* and, yes, sometimes *agnolotti*. So the best approach is to be less concerned with the name than the technique and the taste.

Squares

Tortelli, which are also called *ravioli*, *agnolotti*, and *pansoti*, are all made from squares of about two inches. *Raviolini*, the diminutive in name, are sometimes smaller. There are several methods and gadgets that can be used to fill and cut the squares, but the traditional is the simplest and surprisingly easy. Once pasta dough is in hand, there is every reason to take the next step and stuff— you will be well rewarded.

The No Gadget Method

- Roll out two strips of dough the same size. Trim the strips to uniform rectangles. Cover or tightly wrap one.
- With a pastry bag or a spoon, make 2 rows of rounded teaspoon-sized dots of filling on one strip. Place the mounds at 2-inch intervals. Leave a 1-inch margin on the edges.
- Make an egg wash of one beaten egg white with a little cold water. With a pastry brush, apply the egg around the mounds of filling. This will help the two layers of pasta stick together and firm the edges for the ravioli.
- Place the second strip directly on top of the first.
- Press down with your fingers or the side of your hands all around the mounds. This presses out the air and helps the pasta layers stick together.
- With a fluted pastry wheel, cut between the rows of filling and along the four edges to shape the *ravioli*. A straight wheel or knife can also be used.
- As always, work as quickly as possible or the dough will dry out and keep the *ravioli* from sealing properly.

Variations in Method

- Roll out a double length of dough. Place the mounds of filling on one half the length of the rectangle. Brush with egg wash, and then fold the other half over. Press between the mounds and cut.
- If you have hand-rolled the dough into a large circle, use the circle to your advantage. Trim the circle into a rectangular shape. Plan to use half the circle for rows of filling and the other half to fold over. After folding, press carefully with your hands from the folded edge to the cut edge to squeeze out the air.

From *Ravioli* to Little Hats

Ravioli Form Method

In a mechanized, computerized world, a *ravioli* form, a kind of muffin tin for pasta, is hardly a high-tech tool. The form has two parts, like a mold, which creates the shape of the *ravioli* and the pockets for filling. To look at one is to guess how to use it, but these directions eliminate the guesswork.

- Start with two sheets of dough that are a bit longer and wider than the form. Flour one side of a sheet and carefully place it on the bottom of

the mold. Gently press the top of the form over the pasta sheet, creating the pockets for filling.
- Using a spoon, drop the filling into the pockets. Less filling is better than more because too much will breach the edges of the finished ravioli.
- Layer the second sheet over the filled pockets. Press all around with your fingers so that the sheet is flat. Then take a rolling pin and roll over the top until the cutting edges of each piece show through. Trim the extra dough on the sides.
- Turn the mold over and drop the ravioli onto a lightly floured cooking sheet.

Cannelloni and *Manicotti*

These are "stuffed" pastas the easy way, one piece of pasta wrapped around a filling. Their only difference is the size of the piece and the method of rolling or wrapping. Traditionally, *cannelloni* is filled with meat and *manicotti* with cheese, but like so many established rules, these have been overtaken by innovation. Now both size and filling are open to new possibilities.

- *Cannelloni* are large squares about 4 x 4 inches. *Manicotti* are rectangles about 4 x 6 inches. There is certainly room for personal preference in size

here. Cut the shape that fits your pan or appetite from a sheet of pasta with a knife. Place them on a lightly floured kitchen towel and allow them to rest for 15 minutes.

- Partially cook in boiling, salted water for just a minute or two. Do not drain into a colander where they will stick together, but bring the pot to the sink and add cold water until you can grab the pieces by hand and put them on a towel.
- *Cannelloni* are filled and rolled like a tube. Place a cylinder containing the filling in the center of the pasta, positioned so that you can roll it once with the seam side down. The filling should go from end to end. These are filled, topped with sauce, and baked according to recipe.
- *Manicotti* are filled the long way with a half inch to an inch of margin along the shorter sides. They are shaped like an envelope with the short sides tucked in and the long sides folded over seam side down. *Manicotti* are also filled, topped with sauce, and baked according to recipe.

Pansoti

Pansoti are squares that become triangles. Cut 2-inch squares from a sheet of pasta with a sharp knife. Fill each square with a

teaspoon of filling. With a pastry brush, apply a light coating of egg wash around the filling. Fold one corner of each square to the opposite corner to form a triangle. Press carefully with your fingers to seal the edges. Place on a floured surface until ready to use.

Circles

Get out the cookie cutter or use the rim of a glass and press. Working with circular shaped stuffed pastas is as simple as that. The cutter can be straight-edged or fluted. There are cutters designed for *ravioli* that help seal the edges, but nothing more sophisticated is required.

Round *Ravioli* or *Raviolini*

Ravioli is by definition two layers of pasta with a filling in between, so they can be round as well as square. Round *ravioli* are not quite as neat as square to prepare. When making square *ravioli*, the whole sheet of dough is cut and becomes part of the finished product. When making *raviolini*, the circles are cut out of the sheet and pieces of dough will be left over. These can be combined and rolled again to make more *ravioli*.

- To make round *ravioli*, follow the directions for square *ravioli*.

- Be sure to press between the mounds of filling with your fingers before cutting. Center the circular cutter over the filling and cut.

Mezzelune

Mezzelune, or half moons, and crescents are made by folding over circles. In this case, there is only one sheet of pasta to work with. The amount of filling must be reduced to accommodate the shape.

- Roll out a sheet of dough as you would for any stuffed pasta. Cut a 2-inch circle with a fluted or straight-edged cutter.
- Place a half teaspoon of filling in the center. Brush the edges with egg wash.
- Carefully, fold each circle in half and press the edges together with your fingers.
- For crescents, gently curve the straight edge to form a moderate "C" shape. Place on a floured surface until ready to use.

Navels and Hats

Tortellini and *cappelletti* are the glamour twins of stuffed pastas. The legendary origin of *tortellini* has romantic allure and *cappelletti* has a religious reference. As the story goes, *tortellini* was invented by an innkeeper whose good fortune brought the goddess Venus to his lodging. So enamored was he that he tried to spy on the beautiful deity, only to catch a glimpse of her navel. *Tortellini* is his pasta version of that vision. *Cappelletti*, which means "little hats," has a more subdued inspiration. The pointed peak is said to be reminiscent of a bishop's miter (hat). Both are folded shapes with a flourish, a final twist and pinch. They can be cooked or frozen as any stuffed pasta.

Tortellini

- Roll out a thin sheet of dough. With a cookie cutter or glass, cut 2- or 3-inch circles.
- Place a small amount, about a half teaspoon of filling in the center of each circle.
- Use warm water to moisten the edge with a pastry brush or your finger.
- Fold the circle in half, pressing carefully with your fingers to seal the edges.
- Grasp one corner of the semicircle in each hand between your thumb and forefinger, thumbs up. Pull the corners down and together, wrapping the corners around the tip of your index finger. Pinch the two ends together. Place on a floured surface until ready to use.

Cappelletti

- Roll out a thin sheet of dough. With a cookie cutter or glass, cut 2-inch squares.
- Place a small amount, about a half teaspoon of filling in the center of each circle.
- Use warm water to moisten the edge with a pastry brush or your finger.
- Fold the square into a diagonal so that the top corner does not quite meet the bottom corner. Press with your fingers to seal the edges.
- Grasp one corner of the triangle in each hand between your thumb and forefinger, thumbs up. Pull the corners down and together, wrapping them around the tip of your index finger. Pinch the two ends together. Place on a floured surface until ready to use.

Cooking and Storing Stuffed Pasta

All varieties of stuffed pasta can be used fresh or frozen, but obviously, never dried. The directions for freezing are designed to keep each piece an independent delicacy.

Stuffed pastas can remain in the refrigerator for two to three hours. Be sure to lay them out on a lightly floured tray or they will stick together. Never layer them.

To cook:

- Drop the pieces one at a time into boiling, salted water and stir to make sure that none sticks to the bottom of the pot.
- The length of cooking time depends on the size, shape, and stuffing, so testing for doneness must be a constant enterprise. It is also subjective.
- A minute or two after the pieces float to the top, retrieve one and cut off an edge with a fork. When done, it should cut off easily.
- Four or 5 minutes is probably the maximum cooking time.
- Do not drain, but lift cooked *ravioli* out of water with a slotted spoon and place directly on the plate. Dress with sauce and serve.

To freeze:

- Lightly flour a cookie sheet that will fit in your freezer. Place the completed pasta shapes on the sheet and allow to dry for 10 minutes. Turn each piece over and repeat.
- Place the sheet in the freezer uncovered for about two hours or until the pasta is completely frozen.
- Remove the pasta from the cookie sheet and seal in plastic bags to freeze. They can also be stored in a

container with aluminum foil or waxed paper between the layers.

- Stuffed pastas will remain fresh tasting after freezing for no more than six weeks.

Making Colored and Flavored Pastas

Some people think of them as colorful, others think of them as tasty, and a few try not to think of them at all. The green lent by spinach is the classic. Colors along the orange/red/pink spectrum are produced by tomato and beets. Exotic saffron pronounces itself in a finely flavored yellow pasta. Herbs added to the dough incorporate taste and variegated flecks. Chocolate and/or spice go a long way to making pasta a dessert. The possibilities are limited only by taste, a fact that troubles purists but encourages innovators.

The recipes here suggest additions for a 3-egg pasta dough. The amount of colorful ingredient should be adjusted for the amount of dough—and the degree of color. The hot pink of beets may not be your idea of pasta. Because of the moisture in some of these ingredients, additional flour may be needed to balance the dough.

Tomato Add 3 tablespoons of tomato paste to the beaten eggs and mix well.

Spinach Use about ½ box of frozen chopped spinach. Cook in salted water and chop finely. Squeeze as much of the water out of the spinach as possible. Add to the beaten eggs.

Carrot Add ½ cup of cooked, puréed carrots to the eggs.

Corn Substitute ½ cup cornmeal for ½ cup of the flour. Cook and purée ½ cup of frozen corn kernels. Squeeze the water from the corn and add to eggs.

Beet Boil 2 small beets in salted water, with their skins on, for about 40 minutes or until tender. Peel and purée. Add ½ cup to the eggs. (Less beets may be required.)

Herbed Finely chop a fresh herb or a combination of your choice: basil, parsley, thyme, sage, rosemary. Add ½ cup to the eggs.

Saffron Add a pinch of saffron to the flour and stir with a fork to incorporate.

Black Pepper Add one tablespoon of freshly ground black pepper to the eggs. For the right bite, the pepper should be fresh. The grind must be fine or it will tear the dough.

Parmesan Add ½ cup Parmesan cheese and 1 tablespoon oil to the eggs.

Buckwheat Substitute ½ the flour with buckwheat flour.

Orange or Lemon Add 3 tablespoons of juice and 2 tablespoons of grated zest to the eggs.

Spice The amount of spice is a personal preference. Experiment with up to 3 table-spoons. For savory, try curry or cumin. For sweet, vanilla or cinnamon.

Chocolate Add ¼ cup of cocoa to the flour. A ½ cup of confectioner's sugar can also be added to the flour.

Flavored Pastas à la Juice

There is a method for coloring and flavoring pastas that can be used with dried pastas as well as fresh, a boon when you are using all those shapes that are only available dry. Of course, there is some work involved, in this case, juice extraction. A juice extractor is the best tool for this method, but a food processor and strainer should work well enough to get the juice you need. Choose any vegetables, fruits, or herbs and follow these directions.

- Extract the juice.
- Cook the pasta in salted boiling water until *al dente*. Drain and place in a warm bowl.
- Immediately add extracted juice and toss until the desired color occurs, adding more juice for more color.
- Drain again, if necessary.
- Transfer to plates and sauce.

CHAPTER 4

BASIC SAUCES AND BEYOND

When we talk about classic sauces for pasta, we are speaking Italian. Certainly a more international approach to saucing pasta offers a larger scope, and some of those recipes appear in the Asian and ethnic sections of this book. But the basic Italian sauces that follow have entered into the Western lexicon of cooking and serve as points of departure for an untold number of more complex creations. This is not to imply that they are not complete and delicious in and of themselves. One of the glories of Italian cooking is its adaptability. It is seldom grouchily codified and generously makes room for improvisation. The following basic sauces will give you the vocabulary and facility you need to cook and enjoy pasta in an infinite number of ways.

The tomato came late to pasta, not until the seventeenth century, and was a contribution from the New World, not the Old, returning to Europe from South America with the conquistadors. Now the marriage of tomato sauce and pasta seems preordained, for no two food elements are more suited to one another.

Classic Tomato Sauce

For 16 ounces of pasta

*2 pounds fresh, vine-ripened tomatoes, or
    one 28-ounce can Italian plum
    tomatoes, with juice, chopped*
2 cloves garlic, minced
2 tablespoons olive oil
3 or 4 fresh basil leaves, torn
Salt and freshly ground pepper to taste

Peel, seed, and chop the fresh tomatoes.
Put the olive oil in a deep skillet over medium heat. Add the garlic and cook until it begins to soften and sizzle. Do not allow the garlic to brown. Immediately add the tomatoes. Cook the tomatoes for a few minutes, reduce the heat, and simmer, uncovered, for 15 to 20 minutes, until the sauce thickens. Stir occasionally to prevent scorching. The tomatoes will be watery at first, but the liquid will reduce in cooking. Add the basil leaves and

salt and pepper to taste. Stir and cook for 1 to 2 minutes.

Pour the hot sauce over drained cooked pasta. Serve with grated Parmesan.

Neapolitan Tomato Sauce

For 16 ounces of pasta

2 pounds fresh, vine-ripened tomatoes,
*   or one 28-ounce can Italian plum*
*   tomatoes, with juice, chopped*
2 tablespoons olive oil
1 medium onion, chopped
1 carrot, peeled and chopped
2 celery stalks, chopped
1/4 cup fresh basil leaves, torn
Salt and freshly ground pepper to taste

Peel, seed, and chop the fresh tomatoes.

Put the olive oil in a deep skillet over medium heat. Add the onion, carrot, celery, and basil and cook for about 10 minutes, or until the vegetables are soft and the onion is transparent. Add the tomatoes and simmer, uncovered. Stir occasionally to prevent scorching. Fresh tomatoes should take about 20 minutes; canned tomatoes, 30 minutes. Season with salt and pepper.

Pour the hot sauce over drained cooked pasta. Serve with grated Parmesan.

May'de good

Puttanesca Sauce

For 16 ounces of pasta

The tanginess of capers, the piquancy of olives, and the intense saltiness of anchovies make *puttanesca* sauce earthy and complex.

8 anchovy fillets, chopped
1/4 cup extra virgin olive oil
1 clove garlic, minced
One 28-ounce can Italian plum tomatoes,
*   with juice, chopped*
2 tablespoons capers
12 good-quality black cured olives,
*   pitted and sliced*
2 tablespoons minced flat-leaf parsley
1/2 teaspoon dried oregano

In a large saucepan cook the anchovies in the oil over low heat until they have nearly melted. Add the garlic and cook briefly, being careful not to brown it. Add the tomatoes and raise the heat to bring them to a boil. Simmer for about 30 minutes. The capers, olives, parsley, and oregano, which should be added close to serving time, should only be heated through. Adjust the seasonings and serve hot over drained cooked pasta.

Tomato Sauce Variation

For 16 ounces of pasta

1 cup medium-dry sherry
1 cup Kalamata olives (about 8 ounces),
*   pitted and coarsely chopped*
1¹/₂ tablespoons extra virgin olive oil
One 6-ounce can tomato paste
2 cloves garlic, minced
3 tablespoons dry red wine
1 tablespoon balsamic vinegar
1 teaspoon sugar
¹/₄ teaspoon anchovy paste
¹/₈ teaspoon dried hot red pepper flakes
Pinch each of dried oregano, tarragon,
*   and thyme or rosemary, crumbled*

In a saucepan combine ¹/₂ cup of the sherry with the remaining ingredients and salt and pepper to taste. Simmer the mixture over moderate heat, stirring occasionally, 10 minutes. Add the remaining ¹/₂ cup sherry and simmer 10 minutes more, until the sauce is very thick.

Serve hot over drained cooked pasta.

Making a Roux

A roux is one of the simplest and most basic elements in creamed sauces and soups—and it's one of the most important. A roux is a mixture of flour and fat, usually butter, that lays the groundwork for the consistency of a dish. It's the thickening agent that works behind the scenes so that the important flavors can dominate. To make a roux, follow the proportions of unsalted butter to flour in your recipe. Melt the butter over a low heat and then blend in the flour over a period of about 3 to 5 minutes. The recipe will indicate if the roux should be white or golden or brown, depending on its use. The longer the flour cooks, the more it will color. In order to make a roux work, it's important to keep the heat low and stir constantly. The idea is to eliminate the raw taste of the flour, distribute the heat evenly, and, above all, to keep the roux from burning. All that takes place in just a few minutes, requires very little technique other than stirring, and makes all the difference in sauces.

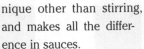

Béchamel Sauce

For 16 ounces of pasta

Béchamel, also called white sauce, is creamy in color and consistency and begins with a butter-flour paste called a *roux*, a thickening agent. Hot milk is added and once these elements have been combined, all that is necessary is steady stirring and a good eye for texture. If lumps form as the sauce cooks, do not despair: Strain the sauce through a fine sieve. Seasoned with herbs, with its consistency adjusted thick or thin, this sauce can be used in innumerable creamy guises.

> 3 tablespoons unsalted butter
> 2 tablespoons flour
> 2¼ cups hot milk
> Salt and freshly ground white pepper
>   to taste

In a saucepan melt the butter over medium heat. (Do not let it brown.) Using a wooden spoon or whisk, blend in the flour to make a *roux*, a smooth paste. Continue to stir until the *roux* bubbles for about 2 minutes. Remove from the heat.

Meanwhile, heat the milk almost to boiling.

When the *roux* stops bubbling, add all but ¼ cup of the hot milk. Return the pan to medium-high heat and whisk quickly to blend well. Then stir more slowly until the sauce begins to simmer. Continue to simmer for 5 minutes as the sauce thickens. Add the remaining milk, a little at a time, if a thinner consistency is desired. Add the salt and pepper to taste.

To keep, cover with plastic wrap pressed directly on the surface of the sauce or a skin will form. The sauce will keep for several days in the refrigerator. The safest way to reheat *béchamel* is in a double boiler. Small amounts of hot milk can be added if the sauce has thickened too much.

Serve hot over drained cooked pasta.

Sauce Bolognese

For 16 ounces of pasta.

This is the classic, hearty meat sauce from the Emilia-Romagna region of Italy. It requires the gentlest of cooking, so that all the flavors are imparted to the meat and, in return, the meat contributes a stout robustness. The milk and cream add a sweetness not found in other sauces. *Prosciutto* is included in this recipe, but sometimes *pancetta* and even chicken livers are added instead for depth of flavor. If all three types of ground meat are not available, very lean, well-ground beef will do.

> 4 tablespoons unsalted butter, in chunks
> 1 small onion, chopped
> 1 celery stalk, chopped

(continued)

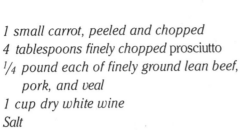

1 small carrot, peeled and chopped
4 tablespoons finely chopped prosciutto
1/4 pound each of finely ground lean beef,
    pork, and veal
1 cup dry white wine
Salt
Freshly ground pepper to taste
1/2 cup milk
1/4 teaspoon ground nutmeg
One 28-ounce can Italian plum tomatoes
    in purée, with juice, chopped
1/4 cup heavy cream

Combine the butter, onion, celery, and carrot in a large, deep saucepan and cook over medium heat until the vegetables are softened. Lower the heat, and add the *prosciutto* and ground meats, being careful not to brown them. Break up the meat with a spoon. It should remain pink and soft so that it can absorb surrounding flavors. Add the wine and salt and pepper, and simmer gently for a few minutes. Add the milk and nutmeg, stir, and cook over very low heat for 10 minutes.

Add the tomatoes, bring to a simmer, then lower the heat as much as possible. Cover and cook, stirring occasionally and making sure that the cooking is ever so gentle—just a bubble—for 3 hours. Stir in the cream just before serving the pasta.

Serve hot over drained cooked pasta.

Summer Tomato Sauce

For 16 ounces of pasta

The freshest possible sauce can be made with vine-ripened tomatoes, peeled, seeded, and chopped. Little else is needed to improve upon their garden taste but salt and pepper and a favorite herb. This recipe calls for garlic, basil, and parsley, but any fresh herb combination will do.

4 cloves garlic
1 cup basil leaves, lightly packed
1/2 cup flat-leaf parsley
2 pounds vine-ripened tomatoes, peeled
    and seeded
Salt and freshly ground pepper to taste
1/2 cup freshly grated Parmesan cheese
4 ounces mozzarella cheese cut in 1/4 inch
    cubes (optional)

Peel and seed the tomatoes, then drain them. In a food processor, finely process the garlic. Add basil and parsley and process coarsely. Add tomatoes and salt and pepper and process very briefly.

The sauce can stand at room temperature for up to 5 hours.

When ready to serve, fold in mozzarella.

Serve over drained cooked pasta. Sprinkle with Parmesan or pass the cheese at the table.

Red Wine Marinara Sauce

For 16 ounces of pasta

1 teaspoon olive oil
1½ cups onions, finely chopped
1 red bell pepper, finely chopped
½ cup thinly sliced mushrooms
3 cloves garlic, minced
1 tablespoon dried basil
1 teaspoon dried oregano
One 15-ounce can tomato sauce
One 6-ounce can tomato paste
1 tablespoon soy sauce
½ cup dry red wine

Heat the oil in a skillet over medium heat. Add the onions and cook, stirring, until transparent. Stir in the pepper, mushrooms, garlic, basil, and oregano. Continue to cook until the ingredients are soft.

Add the tomato sauce, tomato paste, soy sauce, and red wine and continue to cook over medium heat, stirring frequently, until the sauce just boils and then thickens.

Serve hot over drained cooked pasta.

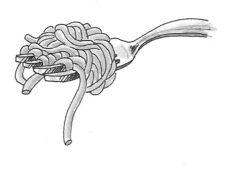

Arrabbiata Sauce

For 16 ounces of pasta

"Angry" is the name of this sauce and red pepper flakes are the reason. It's hot and can be hotter, depending on how much pepper is added—a personal decision. Either more or less than what is called for in this recipe can be used. It depends how angry you are! This famous sauce is traditionally served over *penne*.

¼ cup virgin olive oil
1 teaspoon garlic, minced
2 ounces pancetta, cut into very thin strips
One 28-ounce can Italian plum tomatoes, with juice, chopped
½ teaspoon dried hot red pepper flakes
¼ cup fresh basil leaves, torn into pieces
Pinch of salt
2 tablespoons freshly grated pecorino romano cheese

Heat the oil in a large saucepan. Add the garlic and cook until golden, not brown. Add the *pancetta* and cook through, but do not brown. Add the tomatoes and red pepper flakes. Taste and add salt, if desired. Lower the heat and simmer for about 30 minutes, or until the sauce has thickened. Stir frequently to prevent scorching. Set aside while pasta is cooking.

When the pasta is ready, return the sauce to the heat, add the basil, then toss the pasta in the sauce. Stir in the grated cheese.

Serve hot over drained cooked pasta.

Garlic and Olive Oil

For 16 ounces of pasta

Aglio e olio, Italian for garlic and oil, could not be simpler or better. This sauce, just garlic, olive, and parsley, sometimes includes red pepper flakes, an essential ingredient by some counts. If desired, add 1/4 teaspoon pepper flakes and see for yourself.

> *1/2 cup virgin olive oil*
> *1 tablespoon finely minced garlic*
> *2 tablespoons finely chopped flat-leaf parsley*
> *Salt to taste*

In a large saucepan gently cook the garlic and optional red pepper flakes in the olive oil until the garlic is soft and barely golden. Add the parsley and salt to taste and remove the pan from the heat.

Cook the pasta in the meantime and when *al dente*, toss in the pan with the sauce.

Genovese Basil Pesto

For 16 ounces of pasta

Pesto is the classic from the sweet basil leaf of the Italian Riviera. In its original form, pesto was made, pounded, in fact, in a mortar with a pestle, but hardly anyone can resist the lure of a blender or food processor when it comes to making pesto these days. Because it freezes well, pesto can be made several months in advance. It should be frozen in individual containers without the salt, butter, and cheese added. A layer of plastic wrap pressed directly on the surface of the sauce will keep the basil from blackening. Spaghetti, rather than an egg noodle, stands up best to the strength of this lovely, world-class sauce. This recipe is traditional, but not ironclad, for there are many variations, beginning with the simple substitution of walnuts for pine nuts.

> *2 cups packed fresh basil leaves*
> *1/2 cup virgin olive oil*
> *1/3 cup pine nuts*
> *1 clove garlic*
> *1/2 teaspoon salt*
> *1/2 cup freshly grated Parmesan*
> *2 tablespoons freshly grated pecorino romano*
> *3 tablespoons unsalted butter, softened to room temperature*

Put the basil leaves, olive oil, pine nuts, garlic, and salt in a blender or food processor and blend until completely chopped and combined. Remove the mixture to a bowl to fold in the grated cheeses and butter.

Serve hot over drained, cooked pasta.

Broccoli Pine Nut Pesto

For 16 ounces of pasta

8 cups broccoli florets (from about
    1³/₄ pounds broccoli)
¹/₄ cup pine nuts
4 large cloves garlic
3 tablespoons olive oil
1 tablespoon white wine vinegar
¹/₂ teaspoon dried hot red pepper flakes
Salt and freshly ground black pepper
    to taste

Bring a large pot of water to a boil. Add
1 tablespoon salt. Immerse the broccoli in the
water and cook until just tender, about
5 minutes.

Reserve ¹/₄ cup of the cooking liquid, then
transfer the broccoli to a colander and drain.

Combine the pine nuts and garlic in a
blender or food processor and chop fine.
Scrape down the sides of the machine, add
the broccoli, the reserved cooking liquid, the
oil, vinegar, and red pepper and process to a
coarse purée. Season with salt and freshly
ground pepper.

Serve hot over drained cooked pasta.

Spinach Pesto

For 16 ounces of pasta

4 cups fresh spinach, trimmed, well rinsed,
    and dried
4 cloves garlic
¹/₂ cup freshly grated Parmesan cheese
Salt and freshly ground pepper to taste
¹/₂ cup olive oil

Combine the spinach, garlic, and salt and
pepper to taste in a blender or food
processor and blend until evenly combined.
Gradually add the oil and blend. Add the
Parmesan and blend until the sauce is only
slightly thick.

Red Pesto

For 16 ounces of pasta

4 red bell peppers
¹/₃ cup almonds
¹/₃ cup pine nuts
5 plum tomatoes, peeled and seeded
³/₄ cup olive oil
3 cloves garlic
1 teaspoon salt
¹/₂ teaspoon dried oregano
¹/₈ teaspoon cayenne
¹/₂ cup freshly grated Parmesan cheese
Salt to taste

(continued)

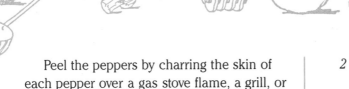

Peel the peppers by charring the skin of each pepper over a gas stove flame, a grill, or under the broiler, turning until blackened. Cool, remove the skin and seeds, and chop coarse.

Toast the almonds and pine nuts in a preheated 300° oven for about 5 minutes.

In a blender or food processor, blend the peppers, toasted nuts, tomatoes, olive oil, garlic, salt, oregano, and cayenne. Pour into a bowl, and stir in the cream and Parmesan. Add salt to taste.

Serve hot over drained cooked pasta.

Carbonara

For 16 ounces of pasta

The distinctive ingredient in *carbonara* sauce is egg, which when combined with freshly grated cheese, adheres to the pasta in a way that no other sauce can. The result is rich and sensuous.

> 2 tablespoons unsalted butter
> 2 tablespoons virgin olive oil
> 4 ounces pancetta or 6 slices unsmoked bacon, cut into thin strips
> 1/4 cup dry white wine
> 4 eggs
> 2 tablespoons freshly grated Parmesan cheese

> 2 tablespoons freshly grated pecorino cheese
> 1 tablespoon chopped flat-leaf parsley
> Freshly ground pepper to taste

Melt the butter with the olive oil in a small skillet over medium heat. Add the *pancetta* and sauté it until golden but not crisp. Add the white wine and simmer until the liquid is reduced by half. Remove from heat.

In a bowl large enough to hold the pasta, lightly beat the eggs, cheeses, parsley, and pepper to taste. Meanwhile, cook the pasta *less* than *al dente*, drain, and return to the pot.

Add the *pancetta* and egg mixtures to the pasta. Cook over *very low* heat, stirring constantly so that the eggs do not scramble. If necessary, remove the pot from the heat now and then. The pasta should be covered with a thin sauce. Serve immediately.

Primavera Sauce

good
muy oo

For 16 ounces of pasta

Pasta primavera comes in as many guises as there are vegetables and pastas, but the traditional choice is made with *fettuccine*. Certainly the seasons should be taken into account, for the fresher the vegetables, the better their flavor and the more successful the recipe.

1 cup asparagus pieces
(¹/₂-inch lengths)
3 tablespoons unsalted butter
¹/₄ cup minced shallots
¹/₂ cup diced carrots
¹/₂ cup diced zucchini
¹/₄ cup diced red bell pepper
Salt and freshly ground pepper to taste
1 cup heavy cream
¹/₄ cup freshly grated Parmesan cheese

[handwritten: dense veg exists]

Cook the asparagus pieces in salted boiling water until nearly tender. Drain and set aside.

Melt the butter in a large saucepan over medium-high heat. Add shallots and sauté until golden. Add the carrots and sauté, stirring for another 5 minutes. Add the zucchini and red pepper and sauté until the vegetables are tender, at least 10 minutes. This longer cooking enhances their flavor. Add the asparagus and salt and pepper to taste and heat through.

Pour the cream into the pan. When the cream bubbles slightly, continue to cook it until it has thickened and reduced by half, about 8 to 10 minutes. Remove from the heat.

Toss drained cooked pasta with the sauce, add the grated cheese, toss lightly, and serve.

Alfredo Sauce

For 16 ounces of pasta

This butter, cream, and cheese sauce was made so famous by a restaurateur named Alfredo in Rome in the 1920s when he served it with *fettuccine*. Hence the delicious, and ubiquitous, dished named *fettucine all'Alfredo*. Any fresh egg pasta will do, and spinach pasta is often used. In that case, Alfredo does not get the credit, but the butter, cream, and pasta do.

3 tablespoons unsalted butter
1 cup heavy cream
Salt and freshly ground black pepper
to taste
¹/₄ teaspoon ground nutmeg, preferably
grated fresh
²/₃ cup freshly grated Parmesan cheese

In a large skillet or the top of a double boiler, melt the butter over medium heat. Turn up the heat and add the cream, stirring to combine. Bring the mixture to a slow boil for several minutes to thicken and reduce slightly. Remove the pan from heat. Stir in a pinch of salt, a few grindings of fresh pepper, and the nutmeg.

Rewarm the sauce over medium heat. Add the drained cooked pasta and toss quickly with two forks to coat all the strands. Add the Parmesan and toss again. Turn into a heated bowl. Serve, with additional Parmesan on the side.

Alfredo Sauce with Bacon

For 16 ounces of pasta

> 3 tablespoons unsalted butter
> 3 cloves garlic, minced
> 2 tablespoons flour
> 2 cups half-and-half (or heavy whipping
>   cream for a richer sauce)
> 1/3 cup freshly grated Parmesan cheese
> 1/2 pound bacon, cooked, drained, and
>   cut into bite-size pieces
> 1/4 cup coarsely chopped parsley

Melt the butter in a medium saucepan over medium heat. Add garlic and cook just until softened but not brown. Add the flour and stir constantly until very well blended.

Add half-and-half and reduce the heat to medium-low. Do not let the sauce boil. Stir constantly so that it does not stick to the bottom of the pan. Cook about 20 minutes, or until thickened. The sauce should not be too heavy. A light cream sauce should pour from a spoon smoothly.

When the consistency seems right, add the cheese and stir until melted. Fold in the bacon and parsley.

Serve hot over drained cooked pasta.

Red Clam Sauce

For 16 ounces of pasta

> 4 dozen small littleneck clams, well
>   scrubbed and rinsed
> 1/4 cup olive oil plus 1 tablespoon for
>   the clams
> 1 teaspoon finely chopped garlic
> 1 tablespoon chopped flat-leaf parsley
> 1/3 cup dry white wine
> 2 cups canned whole tomatoes, with the
>   juice, or 1 pound fresh tomatoes,
>   peeled, seeded, and chopped
> 1 tablespoon tomato paste
> *Salt and freshly ground pepper to taste*

Place the scrubbed clams with the 1 tablespoon olive oil in a large pot over high heat. Cover and steam until the clams open, about 5 minutes. Remove from the heat and cool. Pour the liquid through a strainer lined with a paper towel to catch any sand. Reserve the cooking broth. The clams can remain in the shells or be removed and returned to the liquid at this point.

Cook the garlic in 1/4 cup olive oil in a large saucepan until softened. Stir in the parsley. Pour in the wine and cook until the liquid is reduced by half. Add the tomatoes and the paste. Stir well to combine, then add 1/2 cup of the clam liquid. Add salt and freshly ground pepper to taste. Simmer for 15 minutes, or until the sauce thickens. Add the

clams, heat through quickly, being careful not to overcook. Remove the pan from the heat.

Add drained cooked pasta to the pan and toss well.

Roasted Garlic

For some foods, the transformation from raw to roasted is dramatic. With garlic, the change is subtle, but still surprising. While there's no question that the roasted version is still garlic, the taste is rather sweet. All the harshness and bite of uncooked garlic mellows into fragrant nuttiness after about an hour in the oven. To roast garlic, leave the whole heads as they are. Only remove the papery outer layer. Place however many heads you wish to roast in a small baking dish. Dot them with butter and add enough chicken stock so that they are resting in a little liquid. Cover with foil and bake in a 350° over for 45 minutes to an hour. Uncover and bake about 10 minutes longer. The cloves should slip out of their skins easily. Any you don't use for a recipe is delicious spread on toast.

White Clam Sauce

For 16 ounces of pasta

4 dozen small littleneck clams, well scrubbed
¼ cup virgin olive oil plus a tablespoon for the clams
2 cloves garlic, finely chopped
¼ cup dry white wine
Salt and freshly ground pepper to taste
⅛ teaspoon dried hot red pepper flakes
¼ cup chopped flat-leaf parsley
2 tablespoons unsalted butter

Place the scrubbed clams with the 1 table-spoon olive oil in a large pot over high heat. Cover and steam until the clams open, about 5 minutes. Remove from the heat. Pour the liquid through a strainer lined with a paper towel to catch any sand. Reserve the clam broth. Note: The clams can remain in the shells or be removed and returned to the liquid at this point.

Heat the garlic in the ¼ cup olive oil in a large saucepan until softened. Pour in the white wine and cook about 1 minute, until the alcohol has evaporated. Add ¼ cup of the clam liquid and salt to taste. Simmer 2 minutes to blend. Add the clams, and sprinkle in the pepper flakes and parsley. Heat through quickly and remove from heat. Swirl in the butter.

Add drained cooked pasta to the pan and toss well.

(continued)

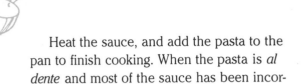

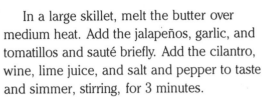

Heat the sauce, and add the pasta to the pan to finish cooking. When the pasta is *al dente* and most of the sauce has been incorporated, swirl in the butter.

In a large skillet, melt the butter over medium heat. Add the jalapeños, garlic, and tomatillos and sauté briefly. Add the cilantro, wine, lime juice, and salt and pepper to taste and simmer, stirring, for 3 minutes.

Serve hot over drained cooked pasta.

Beyond Basic Sauces

There is no line, fine or cleanly drawn, when it comes to defining basic sauces. The following are just a few that can be used on any kind of pasta, plus one that will feed twelve hungry people, which shouldn't be daunting but is a bit of extra work for the cook. It's also great for a party.

Herbed and Ricotta Sauce

For 16 ounces of pasta

One 15-ounce container ricotta cheese
2/3 cup milk
1/2 cup freshly grated Parmesan cheese
2 teaspoons olive oil
1 cup chopped onion
2 cloves garlic, chopped
1/2 cup chopped fresh basil
1/4 cup chopped scallions
1/4 cup chopped flat-leaf parsley
1/2 teaspoon salt
Freshly ground pepper to taste

Jalapeño Butter Sauce

For 16 ounces of pasta

6 tablespoons unsalted butter
1/4 cup diced jalapeño peppers
1/2 teaspoon minced garlic
1 1/2 cups peeled and diced tomatillos (available in most fresh produce sections of the supermarket)
2 tablespoons chopped fresh cilantro
1/2 cup dry white wine
3 tablespoons fresh lime juice
Salt and freshly ground black pepper to taste

In a blender or food processor with a metal blade, blend the ricotta, milk, and Parmesan until smooth.

Heat the oil in heavy large skillet over medium heat. Add the onion and sauté until softened. Stir in the ricotta mixture, basil, scallions, and parsley and cook until heated through. Season with salt and fresh pepper to taste.

Serve hot over drained cooked pasta.

Zucchini Sauce

For 16 ounces of pasta

2 tablespoons olive oil
1 clove garlic, crushed
3 to 4 zucchinis, cut into 2-inch-long strips
1 cup coarsely chopped walnuts
1 cup ricotta cheese
1/2 teaspoon dried hot red pepper flakes
1 large tomato, seeded and cut into cubes

Heat a large skillet. Add the olive oil and in it sauté the garlic until just golden. Add the zucchini and sauté until crisp tender. Add the walnuts, ricotta, and pepper flakes. Stir in the tomato and continue to cook until just heated.

Serve hot over drained cooked pasta.

Salsa Verde (Green Sauce)

For 16 ounces of pasta

1 cup lightly packed flat-leaf Italian
*   parsley, leaves only*
2 anchovy fillets
2 cloves garlic
1/2 teaspoon salt
Freshly ground black pepper
2 tablespoons lemon juice
1/2 cup olive oil
1 tablespoon softened green peppercorns

In a blender or food processor with a metal blade, blend the parsley leaves, anchovies, garlic, salt, pepper, and lemon juice. When puréed, gradually add the olive oil. Remove the sauce to a bowl and stir in the whole green peppercorns.

Serve hot over drained cooked pasta.

My Pasta Sauce for 12 Hungry People

Chef Louis Lindic
Treehouse Restaurant
Atlanta, Georgia

For 3 to 4 pounds of pasta

1/2 cup good-quality olive oil
4 cloves garlic
2 large onions, or 3 medium, chopped
2 green bell peppers, chopped
4 celery stalks, chopped
7 pounds fresh tomatoes, or canned
*   Italian tomatoes*
Two 6-ounce cans tomato paste
2 pounds beef marrow bones
1 pound pork neck bones
1 1/2 pounds ground chuck
1 pound sweet and/or hot Italian sausage
1 1/2 cups dry red wine
2 tablespoons dried parsley or 1/3 cup
*   chopped fresh*

(continued)

1 tablespoon dried basil or 20 fresh leaves

1½ tablespoons dried oregano or 1 tablespoon fresh

½ teaspoon dried tarragon or 1 tablespoon fresh

2 bay leaves

½ teaspoon dried rosemary or 2 tablespoons fresh

1 teaspoon fennel seed

12 ounces mushrooms, quartered

If using fresh tomatoes, remove the skins by dropping the tomatoes in boiling water for 15 seconds. Remove, run under cold water, and peel.

Place garlic, onions, and ¼ cup olive oil in large pot, and heat until simmering. Turn down the heat and simmer until onions are translucent, about 10 minutes.

Meanwhile, in a skillet, heat the remaining ¼ cup olive oil, and sauté the meats until they lose all pinkness. (First the ground chuck, then the mild sausage, then the hot.) Drain. Pour out excess grease from frying pan and deglaze pan with wine.

Add the green peppers and celery to the pot and sauté for 5 minutes. Then add the meat, sausages, tomatoes, tomato paste, marrow bones, neck bones, and wine and bring to a simmer.

Add all the herbs and mushrooms and simmer for 3 hours minimum, stirring occasionally. Before serving, remove the bones and bay leaves.

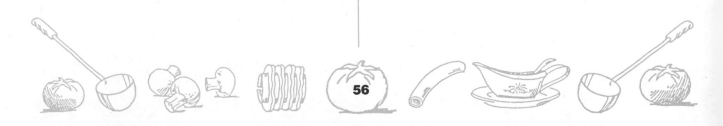

CHAPTER 5

GREAT BEGINNINGS:
APPETIZERS

I t could be said that pasta is an appetizer when you can pick it up with your fingers. But it is much more. Some of the recipes here are first course, sit-at-the-table starters, the better to enjoy in small amounts. Others are miniature packages or roll-ups with a pasta shell that are meant to be dipped in sauce, then devoured. Imagine the egg roll but with a chicken curry filling; or hot Vietnamese spring rolls cradled in crisp lettuce leaves with sprigs of mint; or triangular wontons filled with rich melted cheese. How easy it is to forget that these delicacies are even related to pasta. Multipurpose-purpose, versatile, and adaptable pasta makes them all possible.

Red Snapper and Spinach Lasagna

Chef Kaspar Donier
Kaspar's
Seattle, Washington

Serves 4 as an appetizer size

12 wonton skins, each 3 inches square
2 tablespoons olive oil
2 bunches spinach, cleaned and coarsely
     chopped
2 tablespoons chopped onion
1/2 teaspoon chopped garlic
Salt and freshly ground pepper to taste
Pinch of ground nutmeg
12 ounces skinless red snapper fillets
1/2 cup low-fat cottage cheese
1/4 cup freshly grated Parmesan cheese

1/4 teaspoon curry powder
Fresh herbs of choice for garnish

Preheat the oven to 375°. Cook the wonton skins in salted boiling water to cover for 1 minute. Remove with a slotted spoon and chill briefly in ice water; set on dry towel.

Brush 4 ovenproof soup bowls with olive oil. Put remaining olive oil in a large frying pan and sauté the spinach, onion, and garlic for 2 minutes, or until spinach is wilted. Season with salt, pepper, and nutmeg to taste. Remove from heat and cool.

Slice the snapper into 8 thin slices. Place 1 wonton skin in the bottom of each soup bowl. Spread 1/8 of spinach mixture evenly on top of each skin, then cover with 1 slice of the snapper. Repeat, making a complete second layer and ending with a wonton skin.

58

Mix together the cottage cheese, Parmesan, and curry. Sprinkle cottage cheese mixture on the top of each serving and bake for approximately 15 minutes. Garnish with fresh herbs immediately before serving.

Sun-Dried Tomato Pasta Wheels

Makes 24 pieces

Filling

1¹/₂ pounds whole-milk ricotta cheese
3 cloves garlic
4 ounces minced grated pecorino romano
    cheese
¹/₂ cup freshly grated Parmesan cheese
¹/₂ cup oil-packed sun-dried tomatoes,
    coarsely chopped
¹/₂ cup toasted and coarsely chopped
    walnuts
2 tablespoons finely chopped parsley
¹/₃ cup scallions, finely chopped
¹/₂ teaspoon dried hot red pepper flakes
¹/₄ teaspoon white ground pepper
Salt to taste

1 tablespoon salt
12 ruffle-edged lasagna noodles

Make the filling: In a large bowl, combine all the filling ingredients and mix very well, adjusting the salt to taste.

Meanwhile, in a large pot, bring at least 4 quarts of water to a rolling boil. Add the tablespoon salt. Add the lasagna noodles, stirring carefully. Cook until *al dente*. To drain, do not pour the noodles directly into a colander or they will stick together. Bring the pot to the sink and position over a colander. Run cold water into the pot as you pour out the noodles. Grab each one with your hand. Gently shake, and place on a paper towel or cloth to blot. Keep moist under a lightly dampened towel until ready to fill.

To fill: Take 1 lasagna noodle and spread with about ¹/₂ cup of the filling. Roll each noodle up lengthwise into a right roll. Cut each in half. Place, cut side down, on a lightly greased baking sheet.

When ready to serve, bake in a preheated 350° oven until warm, about 10 minutes. Do not overbake.

At Home With Duckling

Long Island is the presumed home of the domestic duck in America, but ducks are also raised in large numbers in Wisconsin, North Carolina, Virginia, and Indiana. The roasting pan is the place where you will meet this bird, however, and there are a few things to know about preparing it.

First, ducks are fatty and most of the fat is stored beneath the skin. To rid a bird of some of it, prick it all over with a pointed knife. Place the bird on a rack in a roasting pan, so the fat will drip off of it. Roast a 5-pound duck, uncovered, in a preheated 350° oven for about 1½ hours. Ducks are big- and heavy-boned, so only expect enough meat for four people from a single bird. Most ducks are bought frozen and should be defrosted in the refrigerator for a full day in advance.

Spicy Pasta with Roast Long Island Duck

Chef Michael Meehan
Tupelo Honey
Sea Cliff, New York

Serves 6 as an appetizer

3 ounces canola oil
2 tablespoons finely diced fresh ginger
12 ounces duck, roasted, skinned, and julienned
1 carrot
1 yellow squash julienned
1 zucchini
6 ounces sake
3 cups duck stock or chicken stock
3 to 4 ounces fresh pasta
1½ teaspoons ancho *or* chipotle *powder*
2 tablespoons unsalted butter
6 scallions greens chopped for garnish

Heat a wok or large skillet until hot. Add the canola oil and heat. Add the ginger, duck, and vegetables and sauté for 1 minute. Deglaze with sake. Ladle in the duck stock and simmer until reduced by one third.

While the stock is simmering, cook the pasta. Add the chili powder and butter to duck mixture. Add cooked pasta and toss. Season with salt and pepper. Place noodles in center of pasta bowl. Top with duck, vegetables, and sauce. Garnish with scallion greens.

Meatballs Wrapped in Noodles

Makes 36 meatballs

Dipping Sauce

1/2 cup fish sauce (or soy sauce to taste)
1/4 cup fresh lime juice
1 tablespoon minced garlic
3 teaspoons sugar
1/2 teaspoon minced fresh red chile
1/2 teaspoon hot chili oil
1 tablespoon Chinese chives or minced green part of scallions

Meatballs

1 pound minced pork
1 tablespoon minced fresh cilantro
1 teaspoon minced garlic
1 teaspoon salt
1 teaspoon freshly ground black pepper
1 egg
1 tablespoon flour
1/4 cup water chestnuts, finely chopped
1/4 cup bamboo shoots, finely chopped
1/2 cup mushrooms, finely chopped

1/2 pound fresh or dried thin egg noodles
Vegetable oil for deep frying
Lettuce leaves

To make the dipping sauce: In a bowl combine all ingredients, stirring to dissolve the sugar. Reserve.

Make the meatballs: In a medium bowl, combine the pork, cilantro, garlic, salt, pepper, egg, flour, water chestnuts, bamboo shoots, and mushrooms and blend thoroughly. Combine well with hands or fork: The mixture should be soft, almost a paste. Form meat mixture into 1-inch balls.

If using dried noodles, soak in warm water just long enough to soften; drain. Wrap each meatball in a few strands of noodle, enclosing it completely.

In a 5-quart saucepan or a deep fryer, heat 2 inches of oil to 370°. Fry the meatballs, a few at a time, until golden brown. Cut one open after frying to be sure the meat is thoroughly cooked; if not, reduce oil temperature and increase cooking time. Serve as is or wrap each meatball in a lettuce leaf, and serve with dipping sauce.

Calzoni

Makes 4 dozen

1/2 pound mozzarella cheese, shredded
1/2 pound ricotta cheese
1/4 pound pepperoni, chopped finely
1/4 cup freshly grated Parmesan cheese
1 egg, beaten
1/2 teaspoon cayenne
1/4 teaspoon salt

(continued)

*1 package fresh wonton skins (preferably
   cut in circles)*
Vegetable oil for deep frying

In a large bowl, combine all the ingredients except the wonton skins and oil and blend well.

To make *calzoni*: Lay out about 10 wonton skins on the work surface. Keep others covered with a towel. Place 1½ teaspoons of cheese mixture in the lower center of each wonton skin. Fold over and press edges firmly to seal. To ensure a tight seal, moisten the lower edge with water before pressing closed. Cover filled skins with a kitchen towel to prevent drying.

In a 5-quart saucepan or a deep fryer, heat 2 inches of oil to 370°. Fry *calzoni* 8 at a time, until golden brown on both sides. Remove and let drain on paper towels. Serve hot.

It is possible to refrigerate or even freeze cooked *calzoni*. Freeze them in a single layer on a cookie sheet. Then transfer to airtight plastic bags. To serve, reheat in a preheated 375° oven for 10 minutes, or until brown.

Pasta Soufflé

Serves 6 to 8

2 tablespoons unsalted butter for the dish
*2 tablespoons freshly grated Parmesan
   cheese for the dish*
5 tablespoons unsalted butter
10 scallions, finely chopped
¼ cup small dice green pepper
¼ cup small dice red bell pepper
2 tablespoons oil
1½ teaspoons salt
½ pound vermicelli
3 tablespoons all-purpose flour
1½ cups half-and-half
1 teaspoon Dijon-style mustard
*1½ teaspoons finely chopped fresh basil
   or ½ teaspoon dried*
Pinch of freshly ground white pepper
Pinch of ground nutmeg
1 cup freshly grated Parmesan cheese
3 egg yolks
5 egg whites

Preheat the oven to 350°. Butter a 1½-quart soufflé dish. Sprinkle the 2 tablespoons Parmesan cheese into dish and tap sides of dish to distribute cheese evenly over bottom and sides. Turn upside down and tap to remove excess cheese.

In a medium skillet, melt 2 tablespoons of the butter over medium heat. Add the scallions and peppers and sauté, stirring

occasionally, until they begin to soften, about 3 to 5 minutes. Set aside.

Add 1 tablespoon of the oil and 1 teaspoon of the salt to a medium pot of boiling water. Add the pasta and cook over high heat until *al dente*. Drain well. Pour cold water over the pasta and drain well again. Place in a medium bowl. Add 1 table-spoon oil to prevent sticking and toss. Reserve.

Melt 3 tablespoons of the butter over low heat in a medium saucepan. Add the flour and whisk for about 2 minutes. The mixture should start to bubble but not change color. Add the half-and-half and whisk until thick-ened. Add the mustard, basil, the remaining $1/2$ teaspoon salt, pepper, nutmeg, and $1/2$ cup plus 2 tablespoons Parmesan cheese. Allow mixture to cool and then whisk in the egg yolks, one at a time.

Beat the egg whites with a pinch of salt until stiff. Fold whites into the cooled cheese mixture.

Spoon the cooked pasta over the bottom of the prepared soufflé dish and sprinkle with 2 tablespoons Parmesan. Spread the sautéed vegetables over the pasta and sprinkle with 2 more tablespoons cheese. Pour the soufflé mixture over the vegetables and sprinkle with the remaining cheese. Bake for 35 to 40 minutes, or until puffed and brown. Serve immediately.

Spinach Wontons with Apricot Mustard Sauce

Lois Ringelheim
Professional Chef
Fairfield, Connecticut

Makes about 4 dozen

Filling
1 bunch scallions, chopped (dark green discarded)
1 tablespoon unsalted butter
8 ounces cream cheese, softened
1 large egg, beaten
10-ounce package frozen chopped spinach, cooked and squeezed of all excess moisture
$1/2$ cup freshly grated Parmesan cheese
3 tablespoons minced parsley
$1/4$ teaspoon salt
Pinch of ground nutmeg

Mustard Sauce
$3/4$ cup spicy mustard (Guldens)
$1/4$ cup Dijon-style mustard
$1/2$ cup apricot preserves
$1/3$ cup dark brown sugar
$1/3$ cup honey

1 package square wonton skins
1 egg white (or more), slightly beaten
Vegetable oil for deep frying

(continued)

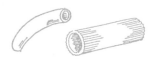

Make the filling: Sauté chopped scallions in the butter in a medium saucepan. Add cream cheese and spinach. Cook over very low heat until the cream cheese melts. Remove from heat. Add beaten egg, Parmesan, parsley, salt, and nutmeg. Combine well.

Make the sauce: Combine all the sauce ingredients in a small saucepan. Bring to a simmer over medium heat, stirring frequently, then simmer over very low heat about 5 minutes. Let cool before serving.

Makes about 1½ cups.

Lay out about 10 wontons at a time on work surface. Keep remainder covered with kitchen towel to prevent drying. Brush each wonton very lightly with the beaten egg white. In the center of each, place 1 teaspoon of filling. Fold to form a triangle. With the center point at the top, fold back the two other corners so that the right overlaps the other. Press ends together to seal. Use additional beaten egg to hold, if necessary. Place on baking sheet and cover with towel. Continue making wontons with remaining ingredients.

In a 5-quart saucepan or a deep fryer, heat 2 inches of oil to 370°. Fry wontons, a few at a time turning, if necessary, until golden brown. Total cooking time is about 5 minutes. Remove with slotted spoon and drain on paper towels. Serve warm, with apricot mustard sauce.

Shells Stuffed with Chicken and Fennel

Makes about 3 dozen

¾ pound jumbo shells
1 tablespoon salt

Filling

¾ pound ground chicken, white meat only
1 tablespoon ground fennel seeds
1 egg white
1¼ cups cold heavy cream plus
   1 teaspoon
1 teaspoon olive oil
2 dashes Tabasco

Sauce

2½ cups heavy cream
½ cup freshly grated Parmesan cheese
1 teaspoon salt
½ teaspoon pepper
2 tablespoons chopped scallions

Preheat the oven to 400°.

In a large pot, bring at least 4 quarts of water to a rolling boil. Add the tablespoon salt. Add the shells and stir to prevent sticking. Cook until *al dente.* Drain. Transfer to a bowl and toss lightly with olive oil.

Make the filling: Purée the chicken, fennel, and egg white in a food processor until smooth. Transfer to a bowl, then set in a

larger bowl containing ice water to chill. Add the cream, $1/4$ cup at a time, stirring after each addition. Stir in the teaspoon salt and Tabasco. When thoroughly chilled, fill shells with the filling, using a pastry bag with a plain tube tip or a spoon.

Make the sauce: Combine all the sauce ingredients in a saucepan and bring to a boil over low heat.

Place a single layer of filled shells in a baking dish, keeping them separated, and pour the sauce over them. Bake until the sauce is thick and bubbly, about 15 minutes. Arrange attractively on a warm serving tray and place a toothpick in each shell.

Capellini Frittata with Peas and Pancetta

Serves 10 to 12 as an appetizer

$1/4$ pound capellini, broken into $1/2$-inch pieces
1 tablespoon salt
4 eggs, beaten
1 cup shredded mozzarella
Salt and freshly ground black pepper to taste
Pinch dried hot red pepper flakes

6 thick slices pancetta, *cut into small pieces and cooked until crisp*
1 cup frozen tiny peas, thawed
$1/3$ cup freshly grated Parmesan cheese
2 tablespoons olive oil
3 cloves garlic, crushed

In a large pot, bring at least 3 quarts of water to a rolling boil. Add the salt. Add the capellini and stir to prevent sticking. Cook until *al dente*. Drain.

In a medium bowl, combine the eggs, cooked capellini, mozzarella, and salt and pepper to taste. Add red pepper flakes and mix well.

In another bowl, gently combine the cooked *pancetta*, peas, and Parmesan.

In a 10-inch nonstick skillet, heat the oil over medium heat. Add the garlic and sauté about 1 minute, until softened. Pour one half the egg and pasta mixture into the skillet and top with the *pancetta* mixture. Cover with the remaining pasta mixture. Cook 8 or 9 minutes, pressing down slightly. Invert the frittata onto a plate. Add more oil to the skillet, if necessary, and return the omelet to pan, uncooked side down. Cook until golden, about 5 more minutes.

Cut into small wedges and serve.

Nut-Filled Pesto Rolls

Makes 24 pieces

Filling
1 cup broken pecans, chopped
¹/₄ cup slivered almonds, chopped
1 clove garlic, minced
1 teaspoon dried basil
¹/₂ teaspoon dried thyme
3 tablespoons olive oil
1 cup ricotta cheese
¹/₄ cup freshly grated Parmesan cheese
1 tablespoon milk
¹/₄ teaspoon dried hot red pepper flakes
Salt
¹/₂ cup finely chopped parsley

12 ruffle-edged lasagna noodles
1 tablespoon salt

Preheat the oven to 350°.

Make the filling: Combine the pecans, almonds, garlic, basil, and thyme in a food processor or blender. Blend completely. Slowly add the olive oil and blend until smooth.

In a medium bowl, beat the ricotta until smooth. Add the nut mixture, Parmesan, milk, red pepper flakes, and salt to taste. Beat until smooth. Fold in the parsley. Reserve.

Meanwhile, in a large pot, bring at least 4 quarts of water to a rolling boil. Add the salt. Add the lasagna noodles, stirring carefully.

Cook until *al dente.* To drain, do not pour the noodles directly into a colander or they will stick together. Bring the pot to the sink and position over a colander. Run cold water into the pot as you pour out the noodles. Grab each one with your hand. Gently shake, and place on a paper towel or cloth to blot. Keep moist under lightly dampened towel until ready to fill.

To fill: Spread about 3 tablespoons of the nut mixture onto each noodle. Roll each noodle up lengthwise into a tight roll. Cut each in half.

Place, cut side down, in a buttered baking dish. Make rolls with the remaining ingredients in the same manner. Bake 20 minutes, or until heated through. Do not overbake.

Toasted Ravioli with Pesto Cream Dipping Sauce

Makes about 40 pieces

1-pound bag small cheese ravioli
1 tablespoon salt plus ¹/₂ teaspoon
¹/₂ cup heavy cream
1 tablespoon beaten egg
³/₄ cup dry plain bread crumbs
1 tablespoon fresh finely chopped parsley
¹/₂ teaspoon garlic powder

Vegetable oil for frying
5 tablespoons butter, melted
1/2 cup freshly grated Parmesan cheese

Pesto Cream Sauce
1/4 cup Genovese basic pesto (see Chapter 4)
1 cup heavy cream
1 tablespoon unsalted butter
1/3 cup freshly grated Parmesan cheese

In a large pot, bring at least 4 quarts of water to a rolling boil. Add the tablespoon salt. Add the ravioli and stir to prevent sticking. Cook until *al dente*. Drain, pat dry, and let cool.

In a shallow bowl, mix together cream and beaten egg.

In a medium bowl, combine bread crumbs, parsley, the 1/2 teaspoon salt, and garlic powder.

Dip each ravioli in the cream and egg mixture, then coat well with the bread crumb mixture. Set on a baking sheet lined with waxed paper.

In a large, heavy skillet, heat about 1/2 inch of oil until hot, about 375°. In small batches, fry the ravioli until golden, about 30 seconds. Place on paper towels to drain.

Before serving, arrange the *ravioli* in a baking dish. Drizzle with the melted butter and sprinkle with the Parmesan. Bake in a preheated 350° oven until hot and puffy, about 10 minutes.

Make the sauce: Combine the pesto, cream, and butter in a saucepan and bring to a simmer over low heat. Let simmer slowly for about 5 minutes. Before serving, slowly stir in the grated Parmesan. Place sauce in small attractive serving bowl.

To serve, place bowl of sauce in center of serving tray and surround with the toasted ravioli.

Chilies are Hot

They're also mild and sweet, pleasantly peppery, and everywhere in between. There are over a hundred different chilies, each with its own zip and zing. Indispensable in Asian and Latin American cooking, they now enliven many other cuisines with a subversive pungency that is not always easy to identify. Jalapeños are the most widely used and they are considered hot, but not nearly as strong as habaneros, which can be fifty times as fiery. Anchos (dried poblanos, which have an earthy flavor) are aromatic and sweet. Chipotles are dried, smoked jalapeños and are found mostly in sauces.

Vietnamese Spring Rolls

Makes about 24 pieces

Dipping Sauce

$\frac{1}{2}$ cup fish sauce (nuoc mam), or
   $\frac{1}{4}$ cup soy sauce
$\frac{1}{4}$ cup fresh lime juice
1 tablespoon minced garlic
1 tablespoon sugar
$\frac{1}{2}$ teaspoon minced fresh red chili
$\frac{1}{2}$ teaspoon hot chili oil
Note: Nuoc mam, *the Vietnamese sauce
   made from fermented fish, and hot
   chili oil are available at Asian markets
   and specialty food stores.*

Filling

2 ounces dried rice sticks
1 pound white chicken meat, ground
8 ounces crabmeat, flaked
$\frac{1}{2}$ cup minced scallions
$\frac{1}{4}$ cup minced celery
Salt and freshly ground black pepper
   to taste

1 pound wonton skins (if available,
   dried rice paper wrappers, 8 inches
   in diameter, are traditional)
Egg white for brushing skins
24 lettuce leaves
1 cup fresh mint leaves
Vegetable oil for deep-frying

Make the dipping sauce: In a small bowl, combine all the sauce ingredients, stirring to dissolve sugar.

Make the filling: Break up rice sticks and soak in hot water for 15 minutes. Drain. Squeeze dry and coarsely chop. In a large bowl, combine all the remaining filling ingredients. Add the rice sticks and combine well.

To make spring rolls: Work with a few wonton skins at a time. Cover others to keep from drying out. Spoon 1 tablespoon of filling diagonally across and just below the center of the wrapper. Fold the bottom point over the filling. Fold in the side corners and roll to form a cylinder. Place seam side down on an oiled platter.

In a 5-quart saucepan or a deep fryer, heat 2 inches of oil to 370°. Fry spring rolls, a few at a time, until golden brown on both sides. Remove with slotted spoon and drain on paper towels.

Serve with a platter of lettuce leaves, the mint, and dipping sauce. The roll is wrapped with mint in a lettuce leaf, then dipped in the sauce.

Shrimp Egg Rolls with Mustard Sauce

Makes 8 pieces

Filling

1 tablespoon peanut oil
1 clove garlic, minced
³/₄ pound shrimp, shelled and deveined
¹/₄ cup sliced scallions
¹/₄ cup finely chopped celery
¹/₄ cup finely chopped carrots
¹/₂ cup finely chopped mushrooms
1 egg, beaten
2 tablespoons soy sauce
¹/₂ teaspoon five spice powder

8 egg roll skins
Vegetable oil for deep frying

Mustard Sauce

¹/₂ cup dry mustard
¹/₂ cup boiling water
2 teaspoons horseradish
2 teaspoons Asian sesame oil

Make the sauce: Place the mustard in a small bowl. Pour in boiling water and mix well. Add the horse radish and sesame oil. Stir together until wellblended.

Make the filling: Heat the peanut oil in a large skillet over medium heat. Add the garlic and sauté until softened. Add the shrimp and cook 3 minutes on both sides until just pink. Remove with slotted spoon to paper towels to drain. Add the scallions, celery, carrots, egg, and mushrooms to the skillet and sauté 3 minutes. Stir in soy sauce and five spice powder.

Dice the cooked shrimp. Stir completely into filling. Remove filing to a bowl.

To make egg rolls: Spoon ¹/₃ cup of filling diagonally across and just below the center of the wrapper. Fold the bottom point over the filling. Fold in the side corners and roll to form a cylinder. Press corners to seal firmly. Moisten with water if necessary. Place, seam side down, on an oiled platter.

In a 5-quart saucepan or a deep fryer, heat 2 inches of oil to 370°. Fry egg rolls, a few at a time, until golden brown on both sides. Remove with slotted spoon and drain on paper towels. Keep warm in 200° oven while frying others.

Serve with the mustard sauce.

Pot Stickers

About 3 dozen piece

Filling

10 ounces ground pork
¹/₂ cup finely chopped onion
¹/₂ cup grated carrot
1 cup chopped Asian cabbage, bok choy
  or napa
2 teaspoons grated fresh ginger

(continued)

1 tablespoon oyster sauce
1 tablespoon soy sauce
Salt and freshly ground black pepper
    to taste

3 dozen fresh round gyoza or pot sticker
    skins or square wonton skins, cut into
    circles
Oil for frying
2 cups chicken broth

For Dipping
Hot chili oil
Rice vinegar
Soy sauce

In a large bowl, combine the pork, onion, carrot, cabbage, ginger, oyster sauce, soy sauce, and salt and pepper to taste. Mix well and reserve.

To make dumplings: Work with one wonton skin at a time. Cover others to prevent drying out. Place 2 teaspoons of filling just below center. Fold over dough to form a $1/2$ circle. Moisten edge with water, if necessary, and press to seal. Pot-sticker edges are traditionally "pleated." To pleat, start in one corner and form "pleats" by pressing down with your index finger and pulling over a bit of dough toward the center. Make 3 pleats from one side and 3 from the other.

Add enough oil to wok or deep skillet to cover bottom. Heat over high heat swirling pan. Reduce heat to medium and add pot

stickers smooth side down, lining them up. Increase heat to high and cook until the bottoms brown. Add chicken broth so that about one half of each dumpling is in liquid. Reduce heat. When the broth simmers, cover and cook until the broth is almost absorbed. Uncover and cook until the bottoms are crisp. Remove from pan to an oiled baking sheet. Keep warm in a 200° oven while cooking remaining dumplings. Serve with dipping accompaniments, each in a separate bowl.

Curried Chicken Egg Rolls with Yogurt Dipping Sauce

Makes 8 pieces

Yogurt Sauce
1 cup plain yogurt
3 tablespoons fresh lemon juice
$1/2$ teaspoon ground turmeric
$1/4$ teaspoon dried hot red pepper flakes
Pinch of ground nutmeg

Filling
$3/4$ pound skinless, boneless chicken breasts
1 tablespoon peanut oil
$1/4$ cup chopped onion
1 clove garlic, minced
1 egg, beaten

¹/₄ cup ground cashews
¹/₄ cup shredded coconut
2 tablespoons fruit chutney of your choice
¹/₂ teaspoon curry powder

3 egg roll skins
Vegetable oil for deep frying

Make the sauce: Combine all the sauce ingredients in a bowl and reserve.

Make the filling: Slice the chicken thin, then chop very fine.

In a large, deep skillet heat the oil over medium heat. Add the onion and garlic and sauté until softened. Add the chicken and stir-fry until cooked through. Cool.

In a medium bowl, combine the egg, nuts, coconut, chutney, and curry powder. Stir in the cooled chicken mixture.

To make egg rolls: Spoon 3 tablespoons of filling diagonally across and just below the center of the wrapper. Fold the bottom point over the filling. Fold in the side corners and roll to form a cylinder. Press corners to seal firmly. Moisten with water if necessary. Place seam side down on oiled platter.

In a 5-quart saucepan or a deep fryer, heat 2 inches of oil to 370°. Fry egg rolls, a few at a time, until golden brown on both sides. Remove with slotted spoon and let drain on paper towels. Keep warm in 200° oven while frying others.

Serve with yogurt dipping sauce.

Melted Cheese Triangles

Makes 20 to 30 pieces

¹/₄ pound mozzarella, Brie, Camembert,
*   or other melting cheese*
2 cups fresh dill, packed
20 to 30 wonton skins
1 egg, beaten
Vegetable oil for deep-frying

Slice the cheese into about 30 strips, each 1 inch long and ¹/₄ inch thick. Cut dill into 1-inch pieces.

Work with a few wonton skins at a time. Keep others covered with a damp cloth to prevent drying. Brush edges with beaten egg. Place 1 strip of cheese and 1 piece of dill in the middle and fold to form a triangle. Press edges firmly to seal. Place the triangles on a lightly oiled surface and cover with a kitchen towel to keep from drying out.

In a 5-quart saucepan or a deep fryer, heat 2 inches of oil to 370°. Fry the triangles, 5 at a time, until golden brown on both sides. Remove and drain on paper towels. Serve hot.

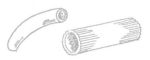

Fried Spaghetti

Serves 4

12 ounces spaghetti
4 tablespoons unsalted butter
3 eggs
1/3 cup milk
1/2 cup freshly grated Parmesan cheese,
    plus additional for serving
Salt and freshly ground black pepper
    to taste
2 tablespoons finely chopped fresh parsley
2 tablespoons finely chopped scallions

In a large pot, bring at least 4 quarts of water to a rolling boil. Add 1 tablespoon salt. Add the spaghetti and stir to separate strands. Cook until not quite *al dente*. Drain. Transfer to a warm bowl and toss with 1 tablespoon of the butter. Cool to room temperature.

Beat together the eggs and milk with an electric mixer. Beat in the Parmesan. Stir in the parsley and scallions. Add salt and fresh pepper to taste. Pour the egg mixture over the pasta and toss well.

Melt the remaining 3 tablespoons of butter in a large skillet. When the butter foams, turn spaghetti mixture into the skillet. Spread and flatten the pasta into a pancake and cook over low heat until a golden crust forms on the bottom. Invert onto a plate, flip over, and cook other side to form another crust.

Slide the pancake out onto a hot plate and sprinkle with additional grated cheese to taste. Cut into wedges and serve hot or warm.

CHAPTER 6

STOCK POT:
PASTA IN SOUPS

S oup, the most sustaining and comforting of all combinations, is a natural for pasta. After all, noodles come alive in liquid. Noodles are elegant in clear broths; rustic in rough-textured soups; and comforting, to say nothing of nourishing, in soups wispy with greens. The recipes here reflect the universal attraction of noodles and pasta to soups—pasta in soups with greens and beans, shrimp and crabmeat, meat and vegetables. It's hard to imagine a soup in which some pasta would not be an improvement. Good memories are made with noodles and soup. They begin in childhood, with pastina and alfabetini floating in a golden broth, and are rekindled every time we sit down to a steaming bowl of pasta-filled broth.

Pork and Escarole Soup with Ditalini

Serves 4

2 tablespoons olive oil
2 minced cloves garlic
1 1/2 cups sliced pork (cut in 1/2-inch pieces)
3 cups packed thinly sliced escarole
6 cups chicken broth
1 tablespoon chopped fresh oregano or 1 teaspoon dried
1/2 teaspoon dried thyme
1/2 cup freshly grated Parmesan cheese
Salt and freshly ground black pepper to taste
1/2 cup ditalini

In a deep soup pot, heat the olive oil over medium-low heat. Add the garlic and sauté until soft. Add the pork and brown quickly. Add the escarole and cook just until wilted. Add the broth, increase heat to high, and bring to a boil. Add the oregano, thyme, and 3 tablespoons of the Parmesan and simmer 5 minutes. Add salt and fresh pepper to taste.

Meanwhile, in a saucepan, bring at least 2 quarts of water to a boil. Add 1 teaspoon salt. Add the ditalini and stir to prevent sticking. Cook until *al dente*. Drain and stir it into the soup. Ladle into warm soup bowls and sprinkle with the remaining Parmesan.

Sweet Potato Ravioli in Wild Mushroom Broth

Chef Roger M. Jamison
Painted Plates
St. Louis, Missouri

Serves 4

Filling

1 large sweet potato
2 ounces chèvre *(goat cheese)*
2 tablespoons unsalted butter
1 tablespoon brown sugar
1/4 teaspoon sugar
1 tablespoon chopped shallots
Pinch of salt and white pepper
1 ounce dried currants
1/2 cups port wine
32 round ravioli sheets or wonton
*   wrappers (yield 16 raviolis)*
1 egg, beaten

Wild Mushroom Broth

1/4 pound portobello mushrooms, sliced
1/4 pound crimini mushrooms, sliced
1/4 pound shiitake mushrooms, sliced
1/4 pound oyster mushrooms, sliced
1 teaspoon chopped fresh rosemary
1/2 teaspoon chopped fresh thyme
2 cups water
1/2 teaspoon salt
1/4 teaspoon black pepper
8 ounces unsalted butter
1/4 cup fresh minced parsley for garnish

Make the filling: Preheat the oven to 350°. Bake the sweet potato for 40 minutes, or until the potato is soft to the touch. Let cool. Skin and press through a fine sieve to remove fibers.

Steep the currants in the port wine until plump. Drain.

Caramelize the shallots. Melt 1 tablespoon of the unsalted butter in a small skillet over low heat. Add the shallots plus 1/4 teaspoon of sugar. Cook, stirring constantly, until the shallots turn very brown.

Melt the other tablespoon of unsalted butter in a small saucepan over low heat. Add the sweet potato, goat cheese, currants, and shallots and mix well. Remove from the heat. Transfer to a bowl and mash into a fine paste.

Make the broth: Place a small saucepan over high heat. Add all the mushrooms and cover with a lid. When hot, turn the heat to medium and let the mushrooms sweat in their own natural juices. Add rosemary and thyme. Steam for 1 minute. Add water and reduce by a quarter. Add salt and pepper. Add butter, 1 piece at a time, and whisk briefly until incorporated into mushroom broth. Remove from stove.

Make the ravioli: Place one ravioli round on the work surface. Then spoon a teaspoon of paste in the center of the pasta. Brush the edges with egg wash and top with a second round. Press the edges firmly so they do not separate. You may also crimp with a fork.

(continued)

Bring at least 4 quarts of water to a rolling boil. Add 1 tablespoon of salt. Add the ravioli a few at a time. Stir to separate. Test for doneness by removing one piece with a slotted spoon and cutting an edge with a fork. If the edge comes off easily, they are done.

To assemble: Spoon mushroom broth into bowls. With a slotted spoon, place ravioli in broth. Sprinkle with parsley and serve.

Zuppa Maritata

Owner Joey Vallone
Tony's * Anthony's * Grotto *
La Griglia
Houston, Texas

Serves 4

Meatballs
One 8-ounce skinless, boneless uncooked
* chicken breast*
1 cup bread, soaked in water and drained
1 tablespoon chopped garlic
1 cup freshly grated Parmesan cheese
Salt and freshly ground pepper to taste
1 tablespoon chopped fresh parsley

Soup
1 quart homemade chicken stock
1 cup chopped celery
2 cups ditalini
16 chicken meatballs
1 cup peeled, seeded, and chopped plum
* tomatoes*
1 cup chopped spinach
4 slices toasted Italian bread

Make the meatballs: Place all ingredients in a food processor and pulse. When chopped and well mixed, shape meatballs, each 1 inch in diameter.

Make the soup: Heat stock in a medium saucepan. Add the celery and ditalini and bring to a simmer. Add the chicken meatballs and simmer for 10 minutes. Add the tomatoes and spinach, ladle into soup bowls, and serve with the toasted bread.

Chicken and Tortellini Soup

Serves 4

1 tablespoon olive oil
1/2 cup diced green bell pepper
1/2 cup chopped onion

1 large chopped clove garlic
1 tablespoon dried basil
2 teaspoons fennel seeds
1/2 teaspoon dried hot red pepper flakes
6 cups chicken stock
1 cup sliced celery
1 carrot, diced
One 9-ounce package fresh "mini" cheese
    tortellini
1 1/2 cups diced uncooked chicken
Salt and freshly ground black pepper to
    taste
Freshly grated Parmesan cheese
    for serving

Heat the oil in large, deep soup pot over medium heat. Add the bell pepper and onion and sauté until softened. Add broth, basil, fennel seeds, and crushed red pepper. Cover pot and simmer 10 minutes. Add celery and carrot. Cover and simmer until carrot is tender, about 5 minutes. Increase heat to high and bring soup to boil. Add chicken and cook just until heated through, about 3 minutes. Season soup with salt and pepper to taste.

Meanwhile, in a medium saucepan, bring at least 3 quarts of water to a boil. Add 1 teaspoon salt. Add tortellini and stir to prevent sticking. Cook until *al dente*. Drain and stir into soup. Heat through.

Chickpea and Pasta Soup

Serves 4 to 6

3 tablespoons olive oil
3 cloves garlic, crushed
4 plum tomatoes, peeled, seeded, and
    roughly chopped
1 teaspoon dried rosemary, or
    2 teaspoons fresh
2 cups canned chickpeas, drained and rinsed
Salt and freshly ground pepper to taste
4 cups beef stock
1/2 cup quadretti
1/4 cup freshly grated Parmesan cheese

In a large, deep soup pot, heat the oil over medium heat. Add the garlic and cook until browned. Discard. Stir in the tomatoes and rosemary. Reduce heat to medium-low and cook until the tomatoes have reduced, about 15 minutes. Add the chickpeas and salt and pepper and heat through. Pour in the stock, cover, and cook another 15 minutes. With a strainer or slotted spoon, remove about 1/2 cup of the chickpeas. Mash them with a fork or purée them in a blender; and return to the soup.

Meanwhile, in a medium saucepan, bring at least 2 quarts of water to a boil. Add 1 teaspoon salt. Add the quadretti, stir to separate, and cook until *al dente*. Drain, stir into soup, and heat through. Remove soup from heat, stir in Parmesan, and serve in warmed soup bowls.

Chicken Soup
The Real Thing

It is probably ironic that most of us who crave homemade chicken soup reach for a can of stock to make our own "homemade" soups. Today, the quality of canned stock *is* excellent, but let us not fool ourselves—canned is also quicker and that counts.

•But in the interest of integrity in the kitchen, here is a recipe for real chicken stock, beginning as it must, not with a can opener, but with a chicken.

1 chicken, about 4 pounds
3 quarts water
1 large onion, cut into quarters
5 stalks of celery, with leaves, cut in half
3 large carrots, cut in half
2 parsnips, cut in half
1 bay leaf
6 sprigs parsley
Salt and freshly ground pepper to taste

Rinse the chicken, cut into quarters, and trim off as much fat as possible. Place in a large pot and add water to cover. Bring to a boil, skimming off the residue as it rises. Add the onion, celery, carrots, parsnips, bay leaf, and parsley. Reduce the heat, cover, and simmer until the chicken is tender, about 2 hours. Using a large slotted spoon or tongs, remove the chicken and vegetables. Strain the stock through a fine-mesh sieve lined with cheesecloth. Season with salt and pepper. Makes about 8 cups stock.

Macaroni, Sausage, and Bean Soup

Serves 6

2 tablespoons olive oil
1 pound Italian sausage, casings removed
1 cup chopped onion
1 cup diced carrot
1 celery stalk with leaves, chopped
1 tablespoon minced garlic
1 teaspoon dried basil
1 teaspoon dried rosemary
1/4 teaspoon dried hot red pepper flakes, crushed
1/4 teaspoon dried sage
5 cups chicken broth
One 16-ounce can chopped tomatoes
One 16-ounce can kidney beans, drained
1 cup elbow macaroni
Salt and freshly ground pepper to taste

In a large heavy soup pot, heat the oil over medium-high heat. Add the sausage and sauté until it begins to brown, breaking it up with a wooden spoon, about 5 minutes. Add the onion, carrot, celery, garlic, basil, rosemary, red pepper, and sage. Sauté until the vegetables begin to soften, about 10 minutes. Add the broth, tomatoes with their juices, and beans. Bring the soup to boil, reduce the heat, and simmer until the vegetables are tender and flavors blend, about 20 minutes.

Meanwhile, in a medium saucepan, bring at least 2 quarts of water to a boil. Add 1 teaspoon salt. Add the macaroni, stir to separate, and cook until *al dente*. Drain, stir into soup, and heat through. Remove the soup from the heat, season to taste with salt and pepper, and serve.

Chinese Noodle Soup

Serves 4

6 cups chicken stock
2 tablespoons dry sherry
1 cup sliced mushrooms
1/2 cup sliced carrots (cut thin on diagonal)
1/2 cup snow peas, halved
1/2 cup thinly sliced water chestnuts
1/2 cup thinly sliced scallions
2 tablespoons soy sauce
1 teaspoon grated fresh ginger
1 teaspoon grated lemon zest
2 cups fresh spinach, leaves shredded
6 ounces thin Chinese egg noodles
Salt and freshly ground pepper to taste

In deep soup pot, combine the chicken stock, water, sherry, mushrooms, carrots, snow peas, water chestnuts, and scallions.

(continued)

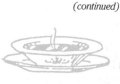

Bring to a boil and simmer for about 10 minutes, until the vegetables soften. Add the soy sauce, ginger, and lemon peel. Cook 5 minutes more. Add the spinach and cook briefly, just until it wilts.

Meanwhile, in a medium saucepan, bring at least 3 quarts of water to a boil. Add 1 teaspoon salt. Add the noodles and stir to separate, and cook until *al dente*. Drain and stir into the soup, and heat through. Remove the soup from the heat, season with salt and pepper to taste, and serve.

Escarole Soup

Serves 8

> 2 large cloves garlic, minced
> 2 tablespoons olive oil
> 1 cup chopped onion
> 2 1/2 quarts chicken stock
> 1/2 teaspoon dried oregano
> 1 pound escarole, cut into 1/2-inch-wide
>   strips
> Salt and freshly ground pepper to taste
> 1/2 cup pastina
> 1 cup freshly grated Parmesan cheese

In a large soup pot, cook the garlic in the oil over low heat, stirring, until golden. Add the onion, and cook, stirring, until softened.

Add the stock and oregano, bring to a boil, and simmer the soup for 5 minutes. Add the escarole and salt and pepper to taste, and simmer the soup for 5 minutes more.

Meanwhile, in a medium saucepan, bring at least 2 quarts of water to a boil. Add 1 teaspoon salt. Add the pastina, stir to separate, and cook until *al dente*. Drain and stir into soup. Heat through. Ladle the soup into warmed soup bowls and sprinkle each serving with Parmesan.

Tomato Soup with Meatballs and Anellini

Serves 4 to 6

Meatballs
> 1 slice white bread, torn into pieces
> 1/4 cup milk
> 1 tablespoon unsalted butter
> 1/2 cup minced onion
> 1/2 pound ground veal
> 1/2 teaspoon dried tarragon
> 1 egg yolk
> Salt and freshly ground pepper to taste

Soup
> 2 tablespoons unsalted butter
> 1/2 cup minced onion
> 1/2 cup grated carrot

1 1/2 pounds plum tomatoes, peeled,
   seeded, and chopped
5 cups beef stock
1 cup dry white wine
1 tablespoon tomato paste
1/2 cup anellini

Make the meatballs: Place the bread in a
small bowl and cover with the milk. Soak for
5 minutes, then squeeze the liquid from the
bread.

Melt the butter in a small pan and sauté
the onion until soft.

In a medium bowl, mix the veal, onion,
bread, tarragon, egg yolk, and salt and pepper
to taste. Form small meatballs, about the size of
a grape, with the mixture. Chill for 15 minutes.

Make the soup: In a large pot, melt the
butter over medium heat and sauté the onion
until softened. Add the carrot and tomatoes,
and cook until the tomatoes are reduced,
about 10 to 15 minutes. Reduce the heat, add
the beef broth, wine, and tomato paste, and
simmer 15 minutes.

Force the soup through a sieve into a
clean pot and bring to a boil. Add the meatballs, reduce the heat, and simmer
15 minutes.

Meanwhile, in a medium saucepan, bring
at least 2 quarts of water to a boil. Add
1 teaspoon salt. Add the anellini and stir to
prevent sticking. Cook until *al dente*. Drain,
stir into the soup, and heat through. Serve in
heated soup bowls.

Alfabetini and Zucchini Soup

Serves 4 to 6

2 tablespoons unsalted butter
3/4 cup chopped onion
1/2 cup grated carrot
1/3 cup chopped celery
3 cups chopped zucchini
6 cups chicken stock
1/4 cup chopped flat-leaf parsley
Salt and freshly ground pepper to taste
1 egg
2 teaspoons fresh lemon juice
2 tablespoons freshly grated Gruyère
   cheese
1/2 cup alfabetini

In a large soup pot, heat the butter over
medium heat. Add the onion, carrot, and
celery and cook until softened. Add the
zucchini and cook 3 minutes. Add the stock,
and bring to a boil. Reduce the heat, add the
parsley and salt and pepper to taste, and
simmer, covered, 10 minutes.

In a small bowl, beat together the egg,
lemon juice, and cheese. Add 1/2 cup of the
hot soup to the egg mixture. Then stir it into
the soup and bring to a simmer.

Meanwhile, in a medium saucepan, bring at
least 2 quarts of water to a boil. Add
1 teaspoon salt. Add the alfabetini, stir to separate, and cook until *al dente*. Drain, stir into the
soup, and heat through. Serve in heated bowls.

Soup with Tubetti and Greens

Serves 4

3 tablespoons olive oil
1/2 cup finely chopped onion
3 tablespoons diced pancetta
1/2 cup finely chopped carrot
1/2 cup finely chopped celery
2 cups finely shredded green cabbage
1 1/2 cups roughly chopped chicory
1 1/2 cups roughly chopped kale
1 teaspoon finely chopped fresh basil, or
    1/2 teaspoon dried
1 teaspoon finely chopped fresh or dried
    parsley
5 cups beef stock
1/2 cup tubetti
1/3 cup freshly grated Parmesan cheese

In large soup pot, heat the oil over medium heat. Add the onion and sauté until softened. Add the *pancetta* and cook until lightly browned. Add the carrot and celery and cook until the vegetables are slightly softened. Add all the greens and sauté until wilted. Add the stock, basil, and parsley and bring to a boil. Cover and simmer for 30 minutes.

Meanwhile, in a medium saucepan, bring at least 2 quarts of water to a boil. Add 1 teaspoon salt. Add the tubetti, stir to separate, and cook until *al dente*. Drain, stir into the soup, and heat through. Serve the soup sprinkled with Parmesan in warmed bowls.

Tagliolini Soup with Yogurt

Serves 4

2 tablespoons unsalted butter
1/2 cup chopped onion
5 cups chicken stock
2 tablespoons chopped parsley
1 tablespoon grated lemon zest
1 teaspoon dried mint
1 cup plain yogurt
1 egg yolk, beaten
Salt and freshly ground pepper to taste
1 cup tagliolini, broken into pieces

In a deep soup pot, melt the butter over medium heat. Add the onion and cook until softened. Add the chicken stock, parsley, and lemon zest. Bring to a boil and simmer 10 minutes. Turn off the heat.

In a small bowl, combine the yogurt and egg yolk and mix well. Remove about 1/2 cup of the hot soup, and very gradually add to the yogurt mixture, stirring to warm it. Gradually add to the soup, stirring constantly. Add salt and fresh pepper to taste.

Meanwhile, in a medium saucepan, bring at least 2 quarts of water to a boil. Add 1 teaspoon salt. Add the tagliolini, stir to separate, and cook until *al dente*. Drain and stir into the soup. Do not let the soup boil. Heat through gently and serve.

Soup of Shrimp and Shells

Serves 4

2 tablespoons unsalted butter
3/4 cup finely chopped onion
1/2 cup chopped carrot
1/2 cup chopped celery
1/2 teaspoon dried thyme
1 small bay leaf, crumbled
1/2 pound medium shrimp, peeled and
    deveined
4 cups chicken stock
1/2 cup dry white wine
1/2 cup shells
1/4 cup half-and-half
Salt and freshly ground pepper to taste
2 tablespoons chopped parsley

In a large soup pot, heat the butter over medium heat. Add the onion, carrot, celery, thyme, and bay leaf and sauté until softened. Add the shrimp and sauté quickly until just pink. Add the chicken stock, bring to a boil, and simmer 20 minutes. Add the wine, bring to a boil, reduce heat, and simmer 10 minutes.

Meanwhile, in a medium saucepan, bring at least 2 quarts of water to a boil. Add 1 teaspoon salt. Add the shells and stir to prevent sticking. Cook until *al dente*. Drain and stir into the soup.

Remove the soup from the heat. Stir in the half-and-half, add salt and fresh pepper to taste, and return the pan to the heat to rewarm. Do not let boil. When heated through, sprinkle with the parsley and serve.

Avgolemono with Orzo

Serves 6 to 8

8 cups chicken stock
4 eggs
Juice of 2 lemons
3/4 cup orzo
Salt and freshly ground pepper to taste

In a large soup pot, bring the stock to a boil. Remove from the heat.

Beat the eggs with a beater until frothy. Gradually beat in the lemon juice. Remove 2 cups of broth from the pot and little by little add it to the egg and lemon mixture, stirring constantly until well combined. Return egg and broth mixture to soup pot. Stir to combine well.

Meanwhile, in a medium saucepan, bring at least 2 quarts of water to a boil. Add 1 teaspoon salt. Add the orzo, stir to separate, and cook until *al dente*. Drain and stir into the soup. Heat the soup through, and add salt and pepper to taste. Do not let soup boil or it will curdle. Serve at once.

Curried Soup with Angel Hair Pasta

Serves 4 to 6

2 tablespoons peanut oil
1/2 cup chopped onion
1/2 tart apple, grated
1 teaspoon curry powder
1 tablespoon ground coriander
1 small bay leaf, crumbled
1/4 teaspoon cayenne
6 cups chicken stock
Salt and freshly ground pepper to taste
1/4 pound angel hair pasta, broken into
   4-inch-long pieces
Chopped fresh cilantro for garnish

In a large stock pot, heat the oil over medium heat. Add the onion and sauté until softened. Add the apple, curry powder, coriander, and cayenne and cook over low heat, stirring, for about 3 minutes. Add the stock and bay leaf and bring to a boil. Simmer 5 minutes to blend flavors. Add salt and pepper to taste.

Meanwhile, in a saucepan, bring at least 2 quarts of water to a boil. Add 1 teaspoon salt. Add the pasta, stir to separate, and cook until *al dente*. Drain and stir into soup. Heat the soup through, garnish with the cilantro, and serve.

Dilled Tomato Soup with Farfallini

Serves 6

2 tablespoons olive oil
1/2 cup chopped onion
1 clove minced garlic
6 plum tomatoes, peeled, seeded, and
   chopped or one 16-ounce can, drained
   and chopped
2 sprigs fresh dill, snipped with scissors
1 tablespoon tomato paste
5 cups chicken stock
2 cups shredded escarole
1/2 cup farfallini

In a large soup pot, heat the oil over medium heat. Add onion and garlic and sauté until the onion is softened. Stir in the tomatoes and dill and simmer until the tomatoes cook down, about 15 minutes. Blend in the tomato paste. Add the stock and escarole, bring to a boil, and simmer for 10 minutes.

Meanwhile, in a medium saucepan, bring at least 2 quarts of water to a boil. Add 1 teaspoon salt. Add the farfallini and stir to prevent sticking. Cook until *al dente*. Drain, stir into soup, and heat through. Serve.

Crabmeat and Conchigliette Soup

Serves 6 to 8

> 3 tablespoons unsalted butter
> 1 cup chopped onion
> 3 tablespoons all-purpose flour
> One 28-ounce can plum tomatoes, with
>   juice
> 2 cups crabmeat, separated into pieces
> 1 small bay leaf
> 6 cups chicken stock
> 1/2 teaspoon dried basil
> 1/2 teaspoon dried oregano
> 1/2 teaspoon dried rosemary
> Salt and freshly ground pepper to taste
> 3/4 cup conchigliette

In a large soup pot, heat the butter over medium heat. Add the onion and sauté until softened. Stir in the flour and cook until brown. Add the tomatoes, crabmeat, and bay leaf. Cover and simmer for 10 minutes. Add the chicken stock, basil, oregano, and rosemary, bring to a boil, and simmer, covered, for 20 minutes. Add salt and pepper to taste.

Meanwhile, in a medium saucepan, bring at least 2 quarts of water to a boil. Add 1 teaspoon salt. Add the conchigliette, stir to separate, and cook until *al dente*. Drain, stir into soup, and heat through. Serve in heated soup bowls.

Lentil Soup with Semi Di Melone

Serves 6

> 2 tablespoons olive oil
> 1/2 cup chopped onion
> 1 clove garlic, minced
> 1/2 cup chopped celery
> 1/2 cup chopped carrots
> 8 cups chicken stock
> 1 smoked pork hock
> 1 cup lentils
> One 16-ounce can Italian plum tomatoes,
>   with juice, chopped
> 1 teaspoon Worcestershire sauce
> 2 teaspoons fresh lemon juice
> 1/4 teaspoon cayenne
> 1 tablespoon fresh parsley
> 3/4 cup semi di melone (*melon
>   seed-shaped pasta*)
> Salt and freshly ground pepper to taste

In a large soup pot, heat the oil over medium heat. Add onion, garlic, carrots, and celery, and sauté until softened. Add the chicken stock, pork hock, lentils, and plum tomatoes. Bring to a boil and simmer, covered, for 30 minutes. Remove the pork hock. Add the Worcestershire sauce, lemon juice, and cayenne and simmer, partially covered, for 15 minutes.

Meanwhile, in a medium saucepan, bring at least 3 quarts of water to a boil. Add 1 teaspoon salt. Add the *semi di melone* and

(continued)

stir to prevent sticking. Cook until *al dente*. Drain, stir into the soup, and add salt and fresh pepper to taste. Heat through and serve in heated soup bowls.

Pasta and Bean Soup

Serves 6

1/4 cup olive oil
1/4 cup finely chopped onion
1 clove garlic, minced
1/4 cup finely chopped carrot
1/4 cup finely chopped celery
4 pork ribs
1 cup canned whole tomatoes, with juice,
   chopped
4 cups beef stock
3 cups canned kidney beans, rinsed
1/2 pound tubetti
Salt and freshly ground pepper to taste
1/4 cup freshly grated Parmesan cheese

In a large soup pot, heat the olive oil over medium heat. Add the onion and garlic and sauté until the garlic is golden. Add the celery and carrot and cook briefly. Add the pork ribs and cook, stirring, about 10 minutes. Add the tomatoes and cook until reduced, about 20 minutes.

Add the stock and beans, cover the pot, and cook until heated through. Remove about 1/3 of the beans with a slotted spoon and mash with a spoon or purée in a food processor. Return the mashed beans to the pot.

Meanwhile, in a medium saucepan, bring at least 3 quarts of water to a boil. Add 1 teaspoon salt. Add the tubetti, stir to separate, and cook until *al dente*. Drain before serving, stir into the soup, and add salt and fresh pepper to taste. Heat the soup through. Stir in the freshly grated Parmesan before serving.

Color By Lentil

The stick-to-your-ribs texture and earthy flavor of lentils makes them perfect for soups. The lentils that stand up best to the simmering are green, but these are more expensive and not as common as the brown variety. Although brown lentils may lose their shape, they are certainly acceptable and, indeed, seep heft into the body of a soup. Red lentils, which are available in gourmet shops, are rather shockingly orange, and lack the taste that adds sturdiness to a soup. They are better suited to soaking up the vinaigrette flavors in salads.

CHAPTER 7

ADDING GREENS TO PASTA: VEGETABLES

In the seventeenth century, tomatoes were the first vegetables to share a plate with pasta. With the advent of *pasta primavera*, all vegetables seem to have gotten into the act together. It's no wonder. The combination is naturally complementary. Noodles with their uniformity and consistent taste make an agreeable background to the colorful flamboyance of vegetables. The green of zucchini, broccoli, and asparagus, the red of bell peppers and tomatoes, the darker shades of eggplant and olives are all beautifully set off by the limpid paleness of pasta dough. And so are the flavors—sweet versus tart, earthy versus pungent. The recipes that follow demonstrate that delicious variety and contrast.

Penne with Arugula and Tomatoes

Serves 4

1 tablespoon unsalted butter
6 ounces arugula (about 6 bunches), tough
    stems trimmed, leaves coarsely chopped
3/4 cup freshly grated pecorino romano *cheese*
1 pound penne
2 tablespoons olive oil
1/2 cup chopped onion
2 cloves garlic, minced
3 1/2 pounds tomatoes, peeled, seeded, and
    chopped, or 3 cups canned tomatoes,
    diced, with juice
1 teaspoon dried oregano
1 teaspoon dried thyme
1 teaspoon dried basil
1/2 teaspoon sugar
Salt and freshly ground pepper to taste

Heat the oil in a large saucepan over medium heat. Add the onion and sauté until translucent. Add the garlic and sauté 1 minute. Add the tomatoes, herbs, and sugar. Reduce the heat and simmer until the sauce thickens, stirring frequently, about 20 minutes. Season with salt and pepper to taste.

Meanwhile, in a large pot, bring at least 4 quarts of water to a rolling boil. Add 1 tablespoon salt. Add the penne and stir to separate. Test frequently for doneness and cook until barely *al dente*. Drain, transfer to a warm bowl, and add the butter. Toss and add half the cheese. Toss again.

Add the arugula to the sauce and stir briefly. Add the penne and heat just long enough, a few minutes, for the pasta to take on the flavor of the sauce. Transfer the pasta to a platter or individual bowls and sprinkle with the remaining cheese.

Spaghettini con Broccoli Siciliano

Chef Giovanni "Jackie" Galati
Dominic's Restaurant
St. Louis, Missouri

Serves 4

> 1 small onion, chopped
> 1/4 cup virgin olive oil
> 2 large tomatoes, peeled and diced
> 3 cloves garlic, finely chopped
> 4 large mushrooms, sliced
> 1/2 cup dry white wine
> 1 pound spaghettini
> 1 pound broccoli, coarsely chopped
> 1/2 cup freshly grated pecorino
> Salt and freshly ground pepper to taste

In a large skillet, sauté the onion in the olive oil until golden brown. Add the tomatoes and garlic and cook for 7 minutes. Add the mushrooms and cook 3 minutes. Add the wine and cook for 5 minutes more. Set aside.

Bring a medium pot of lightly salted water to boil. Add broccoli and cook just until bright green, about 3 minutes. Drain well and add to the sauce.

Bring a large pot of salted water to boil. Add the spaghettini, stir to separate, and cook for about 7 minutes, or until *al dente*. Drain and combine with tomato sauce. Serve with the *pecorino* cheese.

Asparagus Ascending

Asparagus has been around for over two millennia, and sometimes the ones you buy seem to be that old. Select asparagus with tips that don't look dried out, and the greener the stalk the better.

Or the whiter. Asparagus comes in three colors, green, white, and violet. The white ones are actually grown beneath mounds of earth to keep them from the sun, which stimulates the production of chlorophyll, the greening of the plant. The freshest, of course, are those that have just sprouted and are promptly picked. This is something only the home gardener can do, and it has to be done quickly. Asparagus plants are perennial, that is, once a bed is planted, the vegetable comes up every year. But they come up rapidly, with a stalk growing as much as 10 inches a day. So only gardeners who are vigilant about picking are rewarded with true fresh asparagus.

Rigatoni with Asparagus

Serves 4

> 1 pound thin fresh asparagus, trimmed
>   and cut into 2-inch pieces
> 1/4 cup virgin olive oil
> 2 large cloves garlic, well crushed
> 1 1/2 pounds tomatoes, peeled, seeded,
>   and chopped
> 16 ounces rigatoni
> 1 cup freshly grated pecorino cheese,
>   plus additional for serving
> 2 large eggs, lightly beaten
> Salt and freshly ground pepper to taste

Blanch the asparagus in boiling salted water for 5 minutes. Drain and reserve.

Heat the oil in a large saucepan over medium heat. Add garlic and cook until golden but not brown. Add the tomatoes, stir well, and bring to just below a simmer. Cook for 8 minutes. Reserve off the heat.

In a large pot, bring at least 4 quarts of water to a rolling boil. Add 1 tablespoon salt. Add the rigatoni, stir to separate, and cook until *al dente*. Drain. Immediately transfer the rigatoni to a warm deep bowl and add the asparagus. Toss gently. Add the cheese and combine well. Add the eggs and mix thoroughly. When the pasta and asparagus are completely coated with eggs and cheese, add the tomato sauce and toss until thoroughly combined. Add salt and pepper to taste. Divide the pasta among heated plates, and pass the additional cheese separately.

Ribbon Pasta with Rapini, Roasted Bell Peppers, Ripe Olives, and Goat Cheese

Chef Chris Freeman
Wauwinet Inn
Nantucket, MA

Serves 4

> 1 pound ribbon pasta
> 3 tablespoons extra virgin olive oil
> 2 red bell peppers
> 1 bunch rapini (broccoli rabe)
> 1 teaspoon chopped garlic
> 2 tablespoons chopped shallots
> 1 cup pitted ripe olives
> 1 teaspoon chopped flat-leaf parsley
> 1 teaspoon chopped oregano
> 1 cup chicken stock
> 1 cup crumbled goat cheese

Cook the ribbon pasta in boiling salted water until *al dente*. Drain and toss with 1 tablespoon of the olive oil. Place in bowl and cover with damp towel until ready to use.

Roast the bell peppers under broiler, turning often, until skin is black. Place in a bowl, cover with plastic wrap, and let steam. When peppers are cool, peel, skin, remove seeds, and julienne. Remove the florets and leaves from the stems of *rapini*. Wash to remove any sand.

In a large sauté pan, heat the remaining olive oil, and add the garlic, shallots, and *rapini*. Sauté until the *rapini* has wilted. Add the roasted peppers, olives, and fresh herbs. Add the chicken stock and heat, letting the flavors marry, for 1 minute.

Add the pasta, toss, and heat through. Crumble in the goat cheese and toss well. Season with salt and fresh pepper and serve at once.

Penne with Tomato and Fresh Basil

Chef Michael N. Schlow
Café Louis
Boston, Massachusetts

**Makes 1 hearty serving or
    2 tasting plates**

> *2 handfuls of dried penne*
> *6 tablespoons extra virgin olive oil*
> *12 fluid ounces milled whole fresh tomato*
> *6 basil leaves, cleaned*
> *2 pinches salt, Kosher*
> *1 small pinch freshly ground black pepper*
> *1 small pinch crushed red pepper*
> *Freshly grated Parmesan cheese*

Boil pasta in salted water until *al dente*. Be careful to stir frequently so pasta does not stick together.

Meanwhile, in a medium-sized skillet, heat basil leaves in olive oil over high heat. Cook until basil starts to sizzle. Add all spices to hot oil, then add tomato. Cook over high heat for approximately 5 minutes so that the sauce reduces.

Drain pasta in colander, then toss in skillet with sauce. Sprinkle Parmesan over pasta and stir, cooking briefly over high heat until sauce completely adheres to the pasta. Serve immediately.

Angel Hair Pasta with Grilled Vegetables

Chef Waldy Malouf
The Rainbow Room
New York, New York

Serves 4

> *Olive Oil*
> *2 zucchini, sliced on the diagonal*
>   *¹/₄ inch thick*
> *2 yellow squash, sliced on the diagonal*
>   *¹/₄ inch thick*
> *2 tomatoes, sliced ¹/₄ inch thick*
> *2 onions, halved and sliced into*
>   *¹/₄-inch half-circles*

(continued)

Sauce

*1 red bell pepper, roasted, peeled, seeded,
    and rough-chopped*
*4 large ripe tomatoes, peeled, seeded, and
    rough-chopped*
1 fresh hot chili pepper, finely chopped
1 shallot, chopped
1/3 cup olive oil

Crisp Fried Shallots

Vegetable oil for deep-frying
All-purpose flour for dredging
1 cup sliced large shallots (1/8 inch thick)

1/2 pound angel hair pasta

Brush 2 or 3 cookie sheets lightly with
olive oil. Lay the sliced vegetables on the
sheets, brush on a little more oil, and set the
oven rack 6 inches from the element. Broil
the vegetables; as soon as the first side is
lightly browned, turn the vegetables, using
tongs or a spatula, and cook until the second
side is lightly browned. Cooking time varies
widely depending on your broiler. The only
way to grill vegetables properly is to watch
them closely. Let the vegetables cool on the
sheets, then arrange them decoratively around
the edge of a large round platter.

Make the sauce: Put all the sauce ingredients in a large pot, cover, and cook over high
heat, stirring from time to time, until all the
vegetables are soft. Strain the sauce and
return it to the pot.

Make the fried shallots. Heat about
1½ inches vegetable oil in a saucepan. Put
the flour on a plate and toss the shallots in it,
breaking the slices into rings. Each ring
should be thoroughly coated with flour. Put
the shallots in a sieve and shake out any
excess flour. When a pinch of flour sizzles
and browns in the hot oil, put in the shallots
and fry them over high heat until they are
crisp and brown, 3 or 4 minutes. Drain on
paper towels.

Boil the pasta in plenty of salted water for
2 or 3 minutes, until *al dente*. Drain and toss
it with the sauce. Taste for seasoning. Put the
pasta in the center of the ring of grilled
vegetables, garnish with the fried shallots, and
serve immediately.

Spaghetti with Saffroned Onions, Sun-Dried Tomatoes, and Escarole

Serves 4

1/3 cup olive oil
2½ cups sliced onions
*1/4 teaspoon crushed saffron dissolved in
    1/4 cup chicken stock*
1 cup thinly sliced fennel
2 teaspoons minced garlic
1 tablespoon finely minced anchovies

*¹/₂ to ²/₃ cup finely julienned sun-dried
   tomatoes*
5 cups coarsely chopped escarole
1 pound spaghetti

In a large skillet, heat the olive oil over medium heat. Add the onions and cook until translucent. Add the dissolved saffron and cook 1 minute. Add the fennel, garlic, anchovies, and sun-dried tomatoes and cook until the fennel has softened, 3 to 4 minutes. Add the escarole and cook briefly, stirring, until wilted.

Meanwhile, in a large pot, bring at least 4 quarts of water to a rolling boil. Add 1 tablespoon of salt. Add the pasta, stir to separate, and cook until *al dente*. Drain.

Add the pasta to the skillet and toss with the sauce. Transfer to a heated serving platter.

Asparagus and
Pappardelle Pasta

Owner Joey Vallone
Tony's * Anthony's * Grotto *
   La Griglia
Houston, Texas

Serves 4

1 pound pencil-thin asparagus (32 stalks)
1 cup dry white wine

¹/₄ cup unsalted butter, in pieces
1 cup heavy cream
1 pound fresh pappardelle or fettucine
2 tablespoons extra virgin olive oil
Juice of 6 lemons
Freshly ground black pepper to taste
Dried hot red pepper flakes
Freshly grated Parmesan cheese

Break off by hand the tough ends of the asparagus and discard. Cutting on the diagonal, slice the stalks into 3 or 4 even pieces. Blanch the cut asparagus in boiling lightly salted water for 2 minutes, or until just tender. Remove from the water, reserving the water. Plunge the asparagus into cold water to chill, then drain.

In a saucepan reduce the wine by half over medium heat. Whisk in the butter, a piece at a time. Add the cream and bring the mixture to a low simmer.

Meanwhile, cook the pasta in boiling salted water until *al dente*. Drain well.

While the pasta is boiling, heat the oil in a large skillet and add the asparagus. Add the hot cream sauce and stir in the lemon juice. Season with black pepper to taste.

Add the drained pasta to the sauce, toss well, and divide among 4 pasta bowls. Serve with the Parmesan cheese and pepper flakes.

Colorful Avocado Spirals

Serves 4

2 tablespoons unsalted butter
1/4 chopped scallions, white and green
    parts
1 teaspoon grated orange peel
1 teaspoon grated lemon peel
1/2 teaspoon coriander
3/4 cup light cream
1/4 cup plain yogurt
Salt and freshly ground pepper to taste
2 to 3 avocados, cut into 1-inch cubes
1 pound of tricolor spirals

Melt butter in a large skillet over low heat. Add scallions and sauté 1 minute. Add orange and lemon peels and coriander. Stir and remove from heat.

In a bowl, combine the cream and yogurt, and salt and pepper to taste. Stir well.

Pour the cream mixture into the skillet, carefully add the cut-up avocado, and heat through on a low heat. Do not boil or the sauce will curdle and the avocado will become mushy.

Meanwhile, bring at least 4 quarts of water to a rolling boil. Add 1 tablespoon of salt. Add pasta and stir to separate. Drain. Transfer to a warm serving bowl. Pour sauce over pasta and toss carefully. Serve.

Fettucine with Potatoes and Tomatoes .

Serves 4

1 1/2 pounds small new potatoes
2/3 cup olive oil
Salt and freshly ground pepper to taste
2 cups diced tomatoes (fresh or canned)
1 cup tomato sauce (see Classic Tomato
    Sauce, Chapter 4)
2 teaspoons minced garlic
1 tablespoon finely shopped fresh sage,
    plus 1 teaspoon
1/2 teaspoon dried thyme
Salt and freshly ground pepper to taste
1 pound fresh fettucine
Freshly grated Parmesan cheese to taste

Preheat the oven to 400°. Wash the potatoes, pat dry, and rub with a few tablespoons of olive oil. Place them in a shallow baking pan. Sprinkle with salt and pepper and bake until cooked through, 20 to 35 minutes, depending on the size of the potatoes. Cut into 3/4-inch chunks.

In a large skillet, heat the remaining olive oil over high heat and sauté the potatoes until browned. Add the tomatoes, tomato sauce, garlic, sage, and thyme and cook until heated through. Add salt and fresh pepper to taste.

Meanwhile, in a large pot, bring at least 4 quarts of water to a rolling boil. Add 1

tablespoon of salt. Add the pasta, stir to separate, and cook until *al dente*. Drain and transfer to a warm bowl. Add the sauce and toss quickly to combine. Sprinkle with Parmesan cheese to taste and serve at once.

Fettuccine with Zucchini, Pearl Onions, and Cardamom

Chef Christophe Vessaire
The Grapevine Café
Atlanta, Georgia

Serves 4

7 ounces white pearl onions
1/4 cup olive oil
1 teaspoon cardamom seeds
3 bay leaves
Salt and freshly ground pepper to taste
1/2 dried chili pepper
1 1/4 pounds small firm zucchini
1/4 pound dried figs
1 teaspoon tomato paste
2 juicy lemons
2 tablespoons fresh mint leaves
2 tablespoons fresh cilantro leaves
1 1/2 pounds fresh fettuccine

Peel the pearl onions, and put them into a large, heavy saucepan with 2 tablespoons of the olive oil, the cardamom, and bay leaves. Add water to cover, salt, and pepper, and the chili pepper. Cook over high heat, covered, for 10 minutes.

Meanwhile, trim the ends of the zucchini, and cut them into 2-inch lengths, cut each piece in half lengthwise, or into quarters if the zucchini is on the large size. Cut the figs into small dice, put them in a sieve, and rinse under warm running water for a few minutes. Drain.

Add the zucchini, figs, and the tomato paste to the onions. Make sure that there is enough liquid; if not, add a little water. Cover the saucepan and return to high heat for 5 minutes.

Meanwhile, remove the peel and white pits from the lemons and cut the flesh into small dice, being careful to discard the membranes and the seeds. Chop the mint and cilantro.

Uncover the saucepan, add the lemon and remaining 2 tablespoons of olive oil, and let it boil fiercely to emulsify the oil and cooking juices.

Cook the fettuccine in a pan of boiling salted water for 5 minutes. Before serving, remove the bay leaves and chili pepper from the sauce and stir in the chopped mint and cilantro.

Capellini with Snow Peas

Serves 4

1 pound dried capellini
3 tablespoons olive oil
1 red bell pepper, seeded, and julienned
$^{1}/_{2}$ pound fresh mushrooms, julienned
$^{1}/_{2}$ pound snow peas, julienned
4 large tomatoes (about 2 pounds),
    peeled, seeded, and finely chopped
$^{3}/_{4}$ cup heavy cream
$^{1}/_{2}$ cup chicken stock
1 teaspoon tomato paste
3 tablespoons finely chopped basil
1 teaspoon salt
Pinch of hot red pepper flakes
1 cup freshly grated Parmesan cheese

Heat 2 tablespoons of the olive oil in a large skillet over medium-high heat. Add the bell pepper, mushrooms, and snow peas and sauté, stirring, for 3 to 4 minutes. The vegetables should be crisp. Remove from skillet and drain off any leftover oil.

In the skillet heat the remaining tablespoon of oil over medium heat. Add the tomatoes and sauté briefly, until softened. Add the cream, chicken stock, tomato paste, basil, salt, and pepper flakes. Bring to a simmer and cook until slightly thickened. Add the reserved vegetables to the sauce and cook over low heat until the vegetables are heated through.

Meanwhile, in a large pot, bring at least 4 quarts of water to a rolling boil. Add 1 tablespoon of salt. Add the pasta, stir to separate, and cook until *al dente*. Drain and transfer to a warm bowl. Add the sauce and toss quickly to combine, distributing the vegetables evenly. Sprinkle with the Parmesan cheese and serve.

Cleaning Baby Artichokes

An artichoke can be a daunting food, but despite its prickly exterior, it is the easiest of vegetables to prepare. To clean a small artichoke to be included in a recipe is not the same as the labor of love involved in eating a large artichoke, leaf by delicious leaf. First cut off the stems. Then slice off the tops, removing the triangular peak of the globe. Snap off the tough outer leaves. And cut the artichoke into quarters. After ten minutes of sautéing in a little olive oil, baby artichokes are done.

Cavatelli Primavera

Chef William Crego
Milford, Connecticut

Serves 4

$^1/_4$ cup unsalted butter
12 medium fresh mushrooms, sliced
8 canned artichoke hearts, quartered
6 scallions, cut $^1/_8$-inch thick
$^1/_2$ cup diced fresh roasted or jarred red
    peppers, diced in $^1/_4$-inch pieces
6 asparagus spears, cut on diagonal into
    $^1/_2$-inch-long pieces
2 cloves garlic, minced
1 tablespoon minced parsley
1 tablespoon minced fresh basil
1 teaspoon minced fresh sage
$^1/_2$ teaspoon minced fresh thyme
$^1/_2$ teaspoon minced fresh rosemary
4 cups (1 quart) heavy cream
Salt and pepper to taste
$1^1/_2$ pounds cavatelli
1 cup crumbled Stilton cheese or blue
    cheese

In a large sauté pan or saucepan, melt the butter over medium heat. Add the mushrooms, artichoke hearts, scallions, roasted red peppers, fresh asparagus, garlic, and all fresh herbs and sauté for 3 to 4 minutes. Add the heavy cream and bring to a boil. Lower the heat and simmer for 15 minutes, or until the sauce thickens. Season with salt and pepper.

Meanwhile, in a large pot, bring at least 4 quarts of water to boil. Add 1 tablespoon of salt. Add cavatelli, stir to separate, and cook until *al dente*.

Drain the cavatelli and toss with the sauce. Serve the pasta on dinner plates and top each serving with crumbled Stilton or blue cheese.

Spinach Linguine with Ratatouille-Stuffed Tomatoes

Serves 4

Ratatouille
$^2/_3$ cup olive oil
2 red onions, cut into medium dice
4 cloves garlic, chopped
1 tablespoon each dried oregano, basil,
    and thyme
1 teaspoon dried hot red pepper flakes
1 large eggplant, cut into small dice
$^1/_4$ cup balsamic vinegar
$^1/_3$ cup dry red wine
One 28-ounce can Italian plum tomatoes,
    with juice, diced
1 medium zucchini, cut into small dice
1 red bell pepper, cut into medium dice
1 green bell pepper, cut into medium dice
$^1/_2$ pound mushrooms, chopped fine
2 tablespoons unsalted butter
Salt and freshly ground pepper to taste
4 large firm tomatoes

(continued)

Pasta

1 pound fresh or dried spinach linguine
2 large onions, cut into 1-inch wedges
2 tablespoons unsalted butter
2 tablespoons olive oil
1/3 cup dry white wine
1/2 cup oil-cured olives, pitted and coarsely chopped
1/2 cup pine nuts, toasted
1/3 pound freshly grated Parmesan cheese
Salt and freshly ground pepper to taste

Make the ratatouille: In a large saucepan, heat the olive oil over medium heat. Add the red onions, garlic, herbs, and red pepper flakes and cook until the onions are soft. Add the eggplant, and cook briefly over high heat, stirring constantly. Add balsamic vinegar and red wine, stir, reduce heat, and simmer until the eggplant is tender but not soft. Add the tomatoes, zucchini, peppers, and mushrooms and simmer over low heat until the vegetables are tender, about 10 minutes. Swirl in the butter. Add salt and pepper to taste. The mixture should be fairly thick. Set aside and cool slightly. Up to this point the recipe may be done a day in advance.

Peel each tomato. Cut a 1/2-inch slice off the top of each. Remove the seeds and pulp, creating a shell. Turn upside down to drain.

Preheat the oven to 350°. When the tomatoes have drained, blot up any additional moisture from the inside, with a paper towel. Fill each shell with the ratatouille. (There will be some left over for another use.) Bake on a baking sheet for 30 minutes, or until the filling is hot.

While the tomatoes bake, prepare the pasta and sauce: In a large skillet, cook the onions in the butter and oil for 5 minutes, stirring constantly. Add the wine and continue cooking until the alcohol evaporates. Reduce the heat to low and cook until the onions are a deep golden brown, about 20 to 30 minutes. Add the olives and pine nuts and turn off the heat.

Meanwhile, in a large pot, bring at least 4 quarts of water to a rolling boil. Add 1 tablespoon salt. Add the pasta, and stir to separate. Fresh pasta will cook very quickly, so test for doneness immediately. Dried will take longer. When barely *al dente*, drain. Transfer the pasta to a warm bowl and toss with the cheese. Add to the onion mixture and combine well.

When the tomatoes are done, reheat the pasta quickly, stirring constantly. To serve, divide pasta among plates and position one tomato in the center of each serving.

Fettucine alla Genovese

Chef Massimo Saltino
VIVO
Chicago, Illinois

Serves 6

Pesto
The leaves of 5 small bunches fresh basil
3 cloves garlic
3 to 4 tablespoons each of pecorino
and Parmesan cheese
1 tablespoon pine nuts, toasted
Pinch of coarse salt
1⅓ cups olive oil

4 medium potatoes, peeled and diced
½ pound string beans, cut into
1-inch lengths
1½ pounds fresh or dried fettucine
Freshly grated pecorino *or Parmesan*
cheese for serving

Blend all the pesto ingredients in a
blender for 1 to 2 minutes, or until smooth
paste forms. Set aside.

Meanwhile, put the diced potatoes in a
large pan of 3 quarts salted water. Bring to a
boil, then add the string beans and the pasta.
Stir well and cook until tender but *al dente*,
3 to 4 minutes for fresh pasta, 8 to 10 minutes
for dried. Drain the pasta and the
potatoes/beans, reserving some of the cooking
water to dilute the pesto, if desired. Toss the

pasta and vegetables with the pesto, sprinkle
with more cheese, and serve at once.

Pasta Provençale

Serves 4

1 tablespoon olive oil
3 yellow onions, sliced
3 green bell peppers, seeded and sliced
1 clove garlic, crushed
3 zucchini, cut into medium dice
3 yellow summer squash, cut into medium
dice
4 tomatoes, cut into large pieces
¼ cup fresh basil leaves, torn
Salt and freshly ground pepper to taste
1 tablespoon all-purpose flour
1 cup heavy cream
⅓ cup chicken stock
1 pound rotini or other twist shape pasta

In a large, deep skillet, heat the oil over
medium heat. Add the onions, bell peppers,
and garlic, and sauté 3 minutes. Add the
zucchini and yellow squash and sauté
1 minute. Add the tomatoes and basil and
cook briefly, just until the tomatoes soften.
Season with salt and pepper to taste.

Drain the vegetables in a colander set over
a bowl to catch the juices. Let the juices cool
and add the flour. Stir well so that there are

(continued)

no lumps and the mixture is smooth. Add the heavy cream and stock, stirring constantly. Stir the cream mixture into the vegetables. Bring to a simmer over low heat and cook 2 to 3 minutes. Do not boil.

Meanwhile, in a large pot, bring at least 4 quarts of water to a rolling boil. Add 1 tablespoon salt. Add the pasta, stir to separate, and cook until *al dente*. Drain. Transfer the hot pasta to a serving platter or to individual plates and spoon the vegetable mixture over the top.

Linguine alla Cherrysela

Chef Wilton Olivera
Oscar's Villa Capri
Dunwoody, Georgia

Serves 4

> 1 cup virgin olive oil
> 10 cloves garlic, sliced
> 12 hot cherry peppers, cut in half and
>   seeded
> 12 fresh basil leaves
> 1/2 cup fresh chopped parsley
> 2 tablespoons capers, drained
> Salt and freshly ground pepper to taste
> 1 pound linguine
> 1/2 cup chicken stock
> Freshly grated romano cheese for serving

In a large skillet, heat the olive oil over medium heat. Add the garlic and cherry peppers and cook until the garlic is golden but not brown and the peppers are soft. Add the basil, capers, parsley, and salt and fresh pepper to taste and heat through.

Meanwhile, in a large pot, bring at least 4 quarts of water to a rolling boil. Add 1 tablespoon of salt. Add the pasta, stir to separate, and cook until *al dente*. Drain. Add the linguine to the sauce and combine thoroughly. Add the chicken stock and heat over high heat, tossing, until the liquid is absorbed. Transfer to a serving platter and sprinkle with Romano cheese.

Egg Bow Ties and Wild Mushrooms in Herbed Broth

Chef J. M. Matos
Deco's
Adams Mark Hotel
Houston, Texas

Serves 8

> 2 pounds fresh bow ties
> 1/2 cup olive oil
> 1/2 cup chopped garlic
> 1/2 cup chopped shallots
> 1 bunch fresh thyme

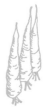

1 bunch fresh basil
1 bunch fresh marjoram
*1 pound fresh medium mushrooms,
    quartered*
*1 pound fresh cremino mushrooms,
    quartered*
1 pound fresh oyster mushrooms, chopped
$\frac{1}{2}$ cup dry white wine
4 cups chicken stock
$\frac{1}{2}$ cup freshly grated Parmesan cheese
Salt and freshly ground pepper to taste

Cook the bow ties in a large quantity of boiling salted water until *al dente* and drain.

In a large skillet, combine the olive oil, the garlic, shallots, and fresh herbs and sauté for 2 to 3 minutes. Add all the mushrooms and sauté for 2 to 3 minutes, or until soft. Deglaze the pan with the wine and reduce by half over high heat. Add the chicken stock and bow ties and cook for 4 to 5 minutes longer. Serve with the grated Parmesan.

Fettucine and Portabello Mushrooms with Balsamic Butter Sauce

Serves 4 to 6

*very
good
Oct. 00*

1 pound fettucine
2 tablespoons extra virgin olive oil
$\frac{1}{2}$ cup thinly sliced onion
1 clove garlic, minced
*$1\frac{1}{2}$ cups fresh sliced portabello
    mushrooms*
*1 cup fresh tomatoes, peeled, seeded,
    and diced*
$\frac{1}{3}$ teaspoon lemon pepper seasoning
1 teaspoon grated lemon zest
$\frac{3}{4}$ cup chicken stock
$2\frac{1}{2}$ tablespoons balsamic vinegar
3 tablespoons unsalted butter, softened
Salt and freshly ground pepper to taste
$\frac{1}{2}$ cup freshly grated Parmesan cheese
2 tablespoons minced scallions

Peel, seed, and dice the tomatoes.

In a large, deep skillet, heat the oil over medium heat. Add the onion and garlic and cook, stirring, for 2 minutes. Add the mushrooms, tomatoes, and lemon pepper and zest. Combine well and cook for 6 minutes. Pour in the chicken stock, balsamic vinegar, and butter. Simmer, stirring for 2 minutes. Add salt and fresh pepper to taste.

In a large pot, bring at least 4 quarts of water to a rolling boil. Add 1 tablespoon salt.

(continued)

Add the fettuccine, stir to separate, and cook until not quite *al dente*. Drain.

Add the fettuccine to the sauce and toss to coat the pasta. Transfer to a warm platter, sprinkle with Parmesan and scallions, and serve.

Vegetable Vermicelli

Serves 4

5 tablespoons unsalted butter
1 pound white mushrooms, finely sliced
2 cloves garlic, minced
1 bunch scallions, white and light green
    part only, thinly sliced
1 large turnip, peeled and sliced into fine
    julienne strips
1 large red bell pepper, peeled, seeded,
    finely julienned
1 zucchini, sliced into fine julienne strips
$^1\!/_4$ pound snow peas, sliced into fine
    julienne strips
1 large tomato, peeled, seeded,
    and diced
$1^1\!/_2$ cups tomato juice
1 tablespoon fresh lemon juice
1 cup water
Salt and freshly ground pepper to taste
2 cups freshly grated Parmesan cheese,
    plus additional for garnish
1 pound vermicelli

To peel pepper: Roast under broiling, turning until skin is black. Place in a bowl, cover with plastic wrap, and let steam. When cool, peel skin, remove seeds, and julienne.

In a large skillet, melt 3 tablespoons of the butter over medium-high heat. Add the mushrooms and cook until slightly colored. Add the garlic, cook briefly, and reduce the heat to medium. Add scallions, turnip, red pepper, zucchini, and snow peas. Cook until the vegetables soften, about 3 minutes.

Add the tomato, tomato juice, lemon juice, and water. Bring to a boil and whisk in the remaining 2 tablespoons butter. Remove the pan from the heat, add salt and pepper to taste, and stir in the cheese.

Meanwhile, in a large pot, bring at least 4 quarts of water to a rolling boil. Add 1 tablespoon of salt. Add the pasta, stir to separate, and cook until *al dente*. Drain, add to vegetable mixture, and toss to combine. Serve in warm bowls, sprinkle with additional Parmesan, and serve.

Linguine with Sun-Dried Tomatoes

Serves 6

1 pound linguine
3 tablespoons unsalted butter
$1/3$ cup olive oil
1 cup thinly sliced mushrooms
$1/2$ cup minced scallions
$3/4$ cup sun-dried tomatoes, coarsely
    chopped
1 tablespoon fresh lemon juice
$1/2$ teaspoon dried thyme
Salt and freshly ground pepper to taste
2 cups spinach leaves, chopped
$1/2$ cup freshly grated Parmesan cheese

In a large pot, bring at least 4 quarts of water to a rolling boil. Add 1 tablespoon salt. Add the linguine, stir to separate, and cook until not quite *al dente*. Reserve 1 cup of the pasta cooking water. Drain. Transfer the pasta to a warm bowl and toss with 1 tablespoon of the butter while making the sauce.

In a large, deep skillet, heat the oil over medium heat. Sauté the mushrooms and scallions for 4 minutes. Add the sun-dried tomatoes, pasta water, lemon juice, and thyme, and season with salt and pepper to taste. Simmer briefly. Swirl in the remaining butter. Add the spinach and toss just to coat. Add the linguine, toss again, and transfer to a warm bowl. Sprinkle with Parmesan cheese and serve.

Spinach and Pasta Frittata

Serves 4

$1/2$ pound spaghetti, cooked and drained
$1/2$ cup finely diced Fontina cheese
$1/2$ cup freshly grated Parmesan cheese
One 10-ounce package frozen chopped
    spinach, thawed and squeezed of all
    moisture
2 tablespoons chopped parsley
3 eggs, lightly beaten
Salt and freshly ground pepper to taste
1 tablespoon unsalted butter

Mix together all the ingredients except the butter. In a large nonstick skillet melt the butter. Add the pasta mixture, and spread evenly over the pan. Cook until the bottom is set. Invert the omelet onto a large plate, then slip it back into the skillet and cook until completely set. Cut into wedges to serve.

Lemon Pepper Pasta

Serves 4

Sauce
$1/3$ cup dry white wine
3 tablespoons fresh lemon juice
$1^1/2$ teaspoons lemon pepper seasoning
$1^1/2$ teaspoons Dijon-style mustard
1 clove garlic, crushed

(continued)

103

¹/₂ cup olive oil
Salt to taste

3 tomatoes, coarsely chopped
2 green bell peppers, seeded and julienned
¹/₂ cup thinly sliced scallions (include green part)
1 cup fresh or frozen tiny peas, thawed
1 cup green beans, uncooked or blanched
1 cup sliced mushrooms
1 cup pitted oil-cured olives
1 pound spaghetti
¹/₂ cup freshly grated Parmesan cheese
¹/₂ cup chopped flat-leaf parsley
Freshly ground pepper to taste

Make the sauce: Combine the first 5 ingredients in a small bowl. Gradually whisk in the oil until the dressing is thick and well blended.

Place all the vegetables in a bowl and combine with one third of the sauce. Let marinate 15 minutes.

Meanwhile, in a large pot, bring at least 4 quarts of water to a rolling boil. Add 1 tablespoon of salt. Add the spaghetti, stirring to separate the strands. Cook until *al dente*. Drain, rinse under cold water, and transfer to a large bowl. Toss the spaghetti a small amount of the sauce. Add the sauced vegetables and toss again. Season with more dressing as desired. Add olives, Parmesan, and parsley, tossing lightly. Sprinkle with freshly ground pepper. Serve at room temperature.

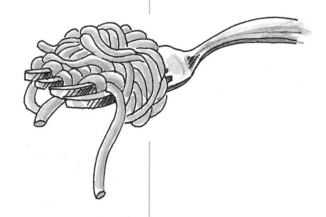

CHAPTER 8

WHITE MEAT:
PASTA AND POULTRY

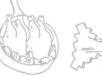

One of the beauties of pasta is that it absorbs and reflects back the flavors that surround it. And when paired with poultry, there is yet another dimension. These two foods, so essentially different, both have the capacity to share the limelight. In dishes whose main ingredients must complement, not contrast with one another, poultry and pasta make remarkably good partners. pasta in dishes where the main ingredients need to complement, not contrast with, one another. The recipes that follow make the most of this advantage in assertive sauces, salsas and fruity accompaniments, peppery combinations, and creamy dressings. Still, the texture and taste of the noodles and poultry remain distinct. They are never lost in the sauce.

Bella Luna's Chicken Penne Pasta with Tomatoes

Chef Horst Pfeifer
Bella Luna
New Orleans, Louisiana

Serves 6

½ pound haricots verts *(French green beans)*
2 tablespoons olive oil
1 pound boneless, skinless chicken breast, cut into bite-size strips
1 red onion, diced
1 tablespoon chopped garlic
⅔ cup mixed mushrooms, sliced
3 ounces sun-dried tomatoes, oil packed
¾ pound penne, cooked

½ cup chicken stock
2 tablespoons basil
6 tablespoons freshly grated Parmesan cheese
¼ cup shaved Asiago cheese
Salt and freshly ground pepper for taste

Trim the beans, blanch in boiling water for 1 minute, drain, then plunge into ice water to set color. Heat the olive oil in a large sauté pan, add the chicken, and sauté until golden. Add the onion, garlic, mushrooms, and tomatoes. Add the beans, drained, the cooked penne, chicken stock, and cook, tossing, until hot. Add the basil and 4 tablespoons of the Parmesan. Mix well. Season with salt and fresh pepper. Serve in heated bowls and garnish each with a whole basil sprig, truffle shavings, and the remaining cheese.

Spicy Duck with Avocado

Chef Robert Boone
Stephens
An American Café

Serves 4

Duck

1/2 teaspoon coarse salt
1/8 teaspoon ground sage
1/8 teaspoon ground rosemary
1/4 teaspoon freshly ground white pepper

four 4- to 6-ounce duck breasts
1 teaspoon minced garlic
1/4 pound fresh oyster mushrooms, sliced
1 large tomato, diced
2 jalapeño chili peppers roasted, peeled, seeded, and diced
3/4 cup dry white wine
1/4 cup unsalted butter, cubed
1 1/2 pounds linguine, cooked
2 avocados, pitted, peeled, and halved, and the halves cut into fans
2 oranges, peeled and separated into supremes*
2 tablespoons finely chopped fresh cilantro
2 tablespoons finely chopped red cabbage

Prepare the duck: Combine the salt, sage, rosemary, and pepper and set aside.

Cut cross slits into the duck skin but don't cut the meat (about 1 inch apart). Sauté the duck in a hot skillet over medium to high heat for about 10 minutes, or until the skin is crisp, seasoning it with the mixed spices as it cooks. Turn and cook for about 3 minutes longer, or until it is cooked medium-rare. Remove from pan and set aside.

Drain all but 3 tablespoons of fat. Sauté in the pan the garlic, mushrooms, tomato, and jalapenos until the mushrooms begin to cook down and the garlic is lightly browned. Deglaze the pan with the wine, remove from the heat, and whisk in the butter.

Toss the pasta in the sauce. Portion pasta on 4 plates. Slice and arrange duck around the outer edge of each plate. Place avocado on top center of dish. Arrange orange supremes around the avocado and sprinkle cilantro and red cabbage like confetti over the dish.

*Orange supremes are the orange segments without any rind or membrane attached. Remove the peel with a knife, then use a sharp paring knife to cut the flesh from the membranes.

Ziti with Dijon Chicken and Broccoli

Serves 4

8oz — *1 pound boneless, skinless chicken breasts,*
cut into 1-inch pieces
½ teaspoon salt
¼ teaspoon freshly ground pepper
3 cloves garlic, minced
2 teaspoons vegetable oil
3 cups broccoli florets
1 large red bell pepper, seeded and cut
into short narrow strips
½ cup chicken stock
One 12-ounce can evaporated skim milk
1 tablespoon cornstarch
3 tablespoons Dijon-style mustard
1 pound ziti or penne
1 tablespoon dried tarragon (opt.)

In a medium bowl, combine the chicken, salt, pepper, and garlic. In a large, deep skillet, heat the oil over medium heat. Add the chicken mixture and sauté until the chicken is tender. Return to the bowl.

Add the broccoli, red pepper, and chicken stock to the skillet. Cover and simmer over medium heat for 5 minutes, or until the vegetables are tender-crisp. Transfer to the bowl with the chicken.

In a small bowl, combine ¼ cup of the milk with the cornstarch, mixing until smooth. Add the mixture to the skillet with the remaining milk, and bring to a boil, stirring

constantly. Reduce the heat, and stir in the mustard with the reserved chicken mixture.

Meanwhile, in a large pot, bring at least 4 quarts of water to a rolling boil. Add 1 tablespoon salt. Add the ziti, stir to separate, and cook until *al dente*. Drain.

Transfer the ziti to a large serving bowl. Add the chicken mixture, toss, sprinkle on the tarragon, and serve.

Spinach Linguine with Chicken, Pesto, and Pine Nuts

Chef John Dubrick
Bravissimo
Chicago, Illinois

Serves 4

¼ cup olive oil
½ pound boneless, skinless chicken breast,
cut into medium dice
2 green apples (Granny Smith), cut into
large dice
½ cup pesto (see Genovese Basil Pesto,
Chapter 4)
Salt and freshly ground pepper
Additional olive oil (optional)
¼ cup pine nuts, toasted
Chopped fresh parsley for garnish
1 pound spinach linguine

Apply salt and pepper to taste to chicken. Heat the olive oil over medium heat in a large sauté pan, add the chicken, and brown lightly. Add the apples and pesto and cook until chicken is cooked.

In a large pot, bring at least 4 quarts of water to a rolling boil. Add 1 tablespoon of salt. Add pasta and stir to separate. Cook until al dente. Drain well.

Transfer the pasta to the skillet and toss with the apple-pesto mixture. If the pesto needs to be lightened, add olive oil a little at a time, stirring constantly. Add salt and pepper to taste. Heat through.

Garnish with toasted pine nuts and fresh parsley and serve.

Fedelini with Pacific Rim Chicken

Serves 4

good wt brown rice

1/4 cup soy sauce
2 tablespoons honey
2 tablespoons fresh lime juice
1 tablespoon whole-grain mustard
1 clove garlic, minced
1 pound boneless, skinless chicken breasts, cut into 1/2-inch cubes
2 tablespoons Asian sesame oil

2 small red bell peppers, seeded and cut into short, narrow slices
1/2 cup snow peas, slivered on the diagonal
1/2 cup thinly sliced scallions
Freshly ground pepper to taste
1/2 cup chicken stock
1/2 cup sliced water chestnuts
3/4 pound fedelini
1/4 cup chopped fresh cilantro

Combine the soy sauce, honey, lime juice, mustard, and garlic in a small bowl and stir until the honey dissolves. Add the chicken pieces and toss until coated with the marinade. Refrigerate for 30 minutes to 1 hour.

In a small skillet, heat 1 tablespoon of the sesame oil over medium heat. Add the red peppers, snow peas, and scallions and stir-fry until tender-crisp. Remove from the heat and reserve.

In a large, deep skillet, heat 1 tablespoon sesame oil over medium heat. Add the chicken and marinade and cook over medium heat until the chicken is cooked through, about 4 minutes. Remove from the heat and pour in the chicken stock. Stir in the reserved red pepper mixture and water chestnuts. Add fresh pepper to taste.

Meanwhile, in a large pot, bring at least 4 quarts of water to a rolling boil. Add 1 tablespoon salt. Add the fedelini, stir to separate, and cook until al dente. Drain.

(continued)

Bring the chicken mixture to a simmer. Add the pasta to the skillet, toss well, and heat through. Place the pasta in a large bowl, sprinkle with the cilantro, and serve.

A Chicken in Every Freezer

Chicken breasts are such a natural partner for pasta and so versatile in absorbing flavors, that they should be kept on hand in the freezer the way pasta is stocked for ready use in the pantry. Buy breasts in quantity when they are least expensive, wrap each *half* breast individually, and freeze. That way they'll be available for large or small meals. Chicken breasts defrost quickly, and if they are going to be used in small pieces, as in a stir-fry, they will cut more evenly if they are partially frozen. Defrosting chicken breasts in the microwave is an option, but it must be done carefully, because the chicken might cook and then toughen. A good way to precook breasts and keep them moist and tender is to poach them briefly in stock.

Smoked Chicken and Pasta

Co-owner, Chef Bert P. Cutino
Sardine Factory Restaurant
Monterey, California

Serves 4

2 tablespoons finely chopped red onion
1½ teaspoons finely chopped shallots
½ teaspoon finely chopped garlic
½ cup white wine vinegar
½ cup dry white wine
1 cup heavy cream or half-and-half
½ pound smoked skinless, boneless chicken breasts, cut into strips
3 fresh sage leaves, finely chopped
4 tablespoons unsalted butter
Freshly ground coarse pepper to taste
1 pound pasta, cooked
½ cup fresh diced tomatoes, marinated in olive oil with salt and pepper

In a large skillet over medium heat, sauté the onion, shallots, and garlic until the onions are translucent. Stir in the vinegar and add the wine. Cook over medium-high heat and reduce to syrup consistency. Add the cream, lower heat to a simmer, and reduce further. Add the chicken and sage and continue simmering until the chicken is cooked. Reduce heat. Whisk butter into sauce, then add cracked pepper to taste.

Meanwhile, bring at least 4 quarts of water to a rolling boil. Add 1 tablespoon of salt. Add pasta. Cook until *al dente*. Drain.

Transfer to a warm serving bowl. Pour sauce over pasta, toss well, and serve.

Capellini with Chicken and Roasted Pepper Salsa

okay

Serves 4

Roasted Pepper Salsa
1 red bell pepper
1 yellow bell pepper
1/4 cup chopped fresh basil
1 teaspoon balsamic vinegar
2 cloves garlic, minced
1/4 teaspoon salt, or to taste
Freshly ground pepper to taste

1 tablespoon olive or vegetable oil.
8 ounces boneless, skinless chicken breasts, cut into small cubes — *I used 1 lb.*
1/2 cup chicken stock
1 pound capellini — *too much pasta for amt. of sauce*

Make the salsa. To roast and peel the peppers: Place the peppers directly over a gas flame (or under a preheated broiler), turning them often with a pair of tongs, until blackened on all sides. Transfer them to a bowl and cover tightly with plastic wrap. Let them stand until cool. Cut the peppers in half lengthwise and remove the stems and seeds. Scrape off the blackened skin of the pepper. Cut the peppers into 1/4-inch dice.

In a small bowl, combine the diced roasted peppers with the basil, balsamic vinegar, garlic, salt, and pepper.

In a large, deep skillet, heat the oil over medium heat. Add the chicken and sauté it until cooked through, but tender. Add the roasted pepper salsa and stir-fry 30 seconds. Add the chicken stock, and cook 1 minute, scraping the bottom of the pan. Remove from the heat.

Meanwhile, in a large pot, bring at least 4 quarts of water to a rolling boil. Add 1 tablespoon of salt. Add the pasta, stir to separate, and cook until not quite *al dente*. Reserve 1/4 cup of the pasta cooking water. Drain.

Add the cooking water to the skillet and heat the sauce over high heat. Add the pasta, toss, and continue to cook until the sauce is boiling and reduced enough to coat the pasta lightly. Adjust the seasonings and serve hot.

Crescent City Pasta

Chef William Liebhart
The Bayou
Bellmore, New York

Serves 4 to 6

1 cup sliced sun-dried tomatoes
1½ cups dry white wine
1½ cups water
3 tablespoons olive oil
12 large shrimp, peeled and deveined
1 cup flour
4 ounces each of unsalted butter and flour
   (for roux)
2 cups chopped onion
1 cup chopped celery
1 cup chopped green bell pepper
2 tablespoons minced garlic
1 teaspoon each of chili powder, paprika,
   black pepper, dried basil, and dried
   oregano
½ teaspoon dried thyme
½ teaspoon salt
1 pound smoked chicken breast, skin
   removed and thinly sliced
4 cups chicken stock
2 cups heavy cream
1 bunch of spinach, rinsed and chopped
Pinch of cayenne pepper
1 pound pasta of choice, cooked until al
   dente, drained, and kept warm

In a saucepan, combine the sun-dried tomatoes, wine, and water, bring to a boil, and reserve.

In a large sauté pan, heat the olive oil. Lightly flour the shrimp, shaking off the excess. Sauté the shrimp in the oil until golden brown, and remove from the heat. Set aside and discard the oil.

In a large saucepan make a blond *roux*. Add the onion, celery, and green bell pepper and cook until onion turns translucent. Add the garlic and cook 5 minutes. Stir in the sun-dried tomatoes with soaking liquid. Add spices and herbs and cook 5 minutes. Add the smoked chicken and chicken stock and bring to a boil. Reduce the heat, add the cream, and simmer 7 minutes. Add the shrimp. Reduce the sauce over medium-high heat for 5 minutes. Add the spinach and remove the pan from the heat. If the sauce is too thick, add a little more chicken stock to reach the desired consistency.

Meanwhile, in a large pot, bring at least 4 quarts of water to a rolling boil. Add 1 tablespoon of salt. Add pasta, stir to separate, and cook until *al dente*. Drain.

Transfer the hot cooked pasta to a large serving platter, ladle the sauce over it, and serve.

Chicken Lasagna

Serves 10

12 lasagna noodles, uncooked
2 tablespoons olive oil, plus additional,
*   if necessary*
1 pound boneless, skinless chicken breasts,
*   diced*
3 cups sliced fresh mushrooms
1 cup thinly sliced carrots
½ cup sliced onions
1 cup frozen green peas, thawed and well
*   drained*
1 teaspoon thyme
½ cup unsalted butter
½ cup flour
3½ cups milk
½ cup dry sherry
½ teaspoon salt
¼ teaspoon cayenne pepper
One 12-ounce container low-fat ricotta cheese
2 cups grated part-skim mozzarella cheese

Preheat the oven to 350°.

In a large, deep skillet, heat the oil over medium heat, add the chicken, and sauté until cooked through. Remove with a slotted spoon, drain on paper towels, and reserve.

Add a bit more oil to the skillet, if necessary. Add the mushrooms and cook briefly. Add the onion and mushrooms and sauté until softened. Set aside.

In a large saucepan, melt the butter over medium heat. Blend in the flour with a wooden spoon to make a loose paste. Cook over low heat until light golden color.

Gradually add the milk, stirring with a wire whisk until blended. Stir in the sherry, bring to a boil over medium heat, and cook for 5 minutes, or until thickened, stirring constantly. Stir in the salt and cayenne. Reserve 1 cup of the sauce, set aside.

In a bowl, combine the ricotta and 1 cup of the mozzarella.

Bring at least 4 quarts of water to a rolling boil. Add 1 tablespoon of salt. Add noodles and stir to separate. Cook only until flexible, not until done. Drain by pouring off hot water and adding cold. As the cool noodles slide into the colander, remove them to a kitchen towel to drain.

Spread 1 cup sauce over the bottom of a 13-by-9-by-2-inch baking dish. Arrange 4 lasagna noodles (3 lengthwise, 1 crosswise) over the sauce. Top with half of the ricotta mixture, half of the chicken mixture, and half of the remaining sauce. Repeat the layer. Top with 4 remaining lasagna noodles. Spread the 1 cup sauce over the last complete layer of lasagna, being sure to cover the lasagna completely.

Cover the dish with foil and bake for 1 hour. Remove the pan from the oven, uncover, and sprinkle with the remaining cup of mozzarella. Bake 5 minutes, uncovered. Remove from oven, cover, and allow to rest for 15 minutes before cutting into squares for serving.

Santa Fe Fusilli

Chef Horst Pfeifer
Bella Luna
New Orleans, Louisiana

Serves 4 to 6

2 tablespoons vegetable oil
2 ears of corn kernels, cut from cob
1/2 cup julienned sun-dried tomatoes, rehydrated
1/2 medium onion, cut in strips
3 whole chicken boneless, skinless breasts, cut into strips and rubbed with jerk seasoning (see below)
1/2 cup chicken stock or canned broth
1 bunch scallions, chopped

Jerk Seasoning
1 teaspoon sugar
1 teaspoon salt
1/4 teaspoon ground cloves
1/2 teaspoon garlic, minced
1/4 teaspoon ground allspice
1/2 teaspoon onion powder
1/4 teaspoon cayenne pepper
2 tablespoons chopped cilantro
1/2 cup freshly grated hard cheddar cheese

Pasta
3/4 pound fusilli, cooked
1/2 teaspoon ground cumin
1/2 teaspoon salt
1/4 teaspoon ground allspice

Place the sun-dried tomatoes in a small bowl and cover with boiling water until softened.

Heat the oil in large pan over medium heat. Add the corn and sauté. Add the tomatoes, onion, chicken, and scallions. Cook, stirring, for about 5 minutes, or until the chicken is golden and cooked through.

In a large pot, bring at least 4 quarts of water to a rolling boil. Add the cumin, salt and allspice. Add the pasta and stir to separate. Cook until *al dente.* Drain.

Place in a warm bowl. Toss with sauce. Transfer to a serving platter. Sprinkle with cheese. Garnish with cilantro.

Linguine with Turkey, Tomatoes, and Olives

Serves 4 to 6

2 teaspoons olive oil
1 cup finely diced onion
3 large cloves garlic, finely chopped
1 pound turkey breast, skin removed and cut into bite-sized pieces
1 tablespoon chopped fresh basil
1/2 teaspoon dried thyme
1/2 teaspoon dried rosemary
12 to 16 Kalamata or other oil-cured olives, pitted and coarsely chopped
1 1/2 tablespoons capers, drained

2 ripe tomatoes, coarsely chopped
2 cups chicken stock
1 pound linguine
1 cup freshly grated pecorino romano
  cheese

In a large, deep skillet, heat the oil over medium heat. Add the onion and garlic and cook until the onion is translucent. Add the turkey, basil, thyme, and rosemary and sauté until the turkey is lightly browned. Stir in the olives, capers, and tomatoes and cook briefly, until the tomatoes begin to give off liquid. Remove the turkey from the skillet. Add the chicken stock, bring to a boil, and simmer over medium heat until the broth is reduced by half. Return turkey to sauce and stir well.

Meanwhile, in a large pot, bring at least 4 quarts of water to a rolling boil. Add 1 tablespoon salt. Add the linguine, stir to separate, and cook until *al dente*. Drain.

Transfer the linguine to the skillet and toss with the sauce until the sauce is evenly distributed. Transfer to a warm serving dish, top with the cheese, and serve.

Smoked Chicken Penne

Chef Paul Bleuer
Dakota's
Dallas, Texas

Serves 1 to 2

1 ounce olive oil
1/2 teaspoon chopped garlic
6 ounces smoked chicken, julienned
1/8 cup dry white wine
1 teaspoon chopped fresh basil
1/4 cup roasted red pepper, julienned
1/4 cup unsalted butter
8 ounces penne, cooked
Salt and freshly ground pepper to taste
1/8 cup pine nuts, toasted

In a sauté pan, heat the olive oil until hot. Add the garlic and sauté 10 seconds. Add the chicken and sauté 1 minute. Add the wine, basil, and peppers and cook 1 minute. Add the butter and heat until melted. Add the pasta and season with salt and pepper. When hot, transfer to a bowl and sprinkle with the pine nuts on top.

Turkey and Broccoli with Fusilli in Cream Sauce

Serves 4

> 5 cups broccoli florets (from about
>   1 large head)
> ³/₄ pound fusilli
> ¹/₄ cup olive oil
> 2 tablespoons chopped garlic
> 1 pound turkey breast, skin removed and
>   cut into ¹/₂-inch-thick strips
> 1 cup dry white wine
> 1 cup chicken stock
> 1 cup heavy cream
> ¹/₂ cup freshly grated Parmesan cheese

In a large pot, bring at least 4 quarts of water to a rolling boil. Add 1 tablespoon salt. Add the broccoli and blanch it for about 3 minutes. Remove with slotted spoon to a bowl of cold water. Let stand briefly, drain, and return to bowl.

Add the fusilli to the boiling water in the pot and stir to prevent sticking. Cook until just not quite *al dente*. Drain, place in warm bowl, and toss with a bit of the olive oil.

In a large, deep skillet, heat the oil over medium heat. Add the garlic and turkey and sauté until the turkey is just cooked through and tender. Using a slotted spoon, transfer the turkey to the bowl with the broccoli.

Add the wine, stock, and cream to the skillet, bring to a boil, and cook until thickened slightly, about 8 minutes. Add the pasta,

broccoli and turkey, and cheese to the sauce and toss until heated through and evenly coated.

Fedelini Inverno

Owner Jeff Vallone
Tony's * Anthony's * Grotto * La Griglia
Houston, Texas

Serves 4

> 2 tablespoons extra virgin olive oil
> 2 tablespoons minced garlic
> 1 red bell pepper, seeded
> 1 green bell pepper, seeded and cut into
>   medium dice
> 2 cups dry white wine
> 2 tablespoons white vinegar
> 2 tablespoons fresh lemon juice
> 2 tablespoons curry powder
> 2 Roma tomatoes, peeled and cut in
>   medium dice
>
> 1 cup heavy cream
> 8 ounces unsalted butter, softened, cut into
>   pieces
> ¹/₂ teaspoon salt
> ¹/₄ teaspoon ground white pepper
> Salt and freshly ground pepper to taste
> 4 tablespoons finely chopped Italian flat-
>   leaf parsley

Chicken

1 tablespoon olive oil
1 pound boneless, skinless chicken breasts
¹/₂ teaspoon salt
¹/₄ teaspoon ground white pepper
1 pound fedelini

¹/₄ cup slivered almonds, toasted golden
*   brown in 325° oven for about*
*   15 minutes*
2 tablespoons chopped flat-leaf parsley
¹/₄ teaspoon dried hot red pepper flakes

In a saucepan heat the olive oil over medium heat and add the garlic, and sauté lightly until fragrant. Add the peppers and stir to combine. Season with salt and pepper. Add the white wine, vinegar, and lemon juice. Simmer 12 minutes until the peppers are tender. Remove the peppers and reserve.

To the liquid remaining in the pan, stir in curry powder, return the pan to the heat, and whisk in the heavy cream. Bring the mixture just to a simmer and add the butter, a few pieces at a time, stirring until melted. Reduce the heat to low and reserve the sauce.

Prepare the chicken: In a sauté pan, add the olive oil over medium heat, add the chicken, and sauté 3 to 4 minutes per side. Season with the salt and pepper. Remove the chicken from the pan, let cool, and slice into strips.

Bring the curry sauce to a simmer. Add the reserved peppers, the tomatoes, and the

parsley. Stir in the chicken strips, bring the sauce just to a boil, and remove from the heat. Keep warm, covered.

Meanwhile, in a large pot, bring at least 4 quarts of water to a rolling boil. Add 1 tablespoon salt. Add the pasta, stir to separate, and cook until *al dente*. Drain, return to pot, and pour about 1 cup of the curry sauce over it. Stir to coat.

Divide the pasta among 4 pasta bowls, and spoon over the remaining curry sauce, dividing it evenly. Garnish each serving with toasted almonds, parsley, and red pepper flakes.

Farfalle with Turkey and Sausage

Serves 4

12 ounces farfalle
1 tablespoon olive oil
1 cup coarsely chopped onion
1 clove garlic, minced
1 green bell pepper, seeded and julienned
12 ounces boneless, skinless chicken
*   breasts, cut into ¹/₂-inch-wide pieces*
¹/₂ pound sweet or hot Italian sausages,
*   cut crosswise into ¹/₂-inch-thick pieces*
One 16-ounce can Italian plum tomatoes,
*   with juice, chopped*
¹/₄ cup dry red wine

(continued)

¹/₂ teaspoon dried oregano
¹/₄ teaspoon dried basil
1 teaspoon sugar
¹/₄ cup heavy cream
Salt and freshly ground pepper to taste

In a large, deep skillet, heat the oil over medium heat. Add the onion, garlic, and bell pepper and sauté until just softened. Add the turkey and sausage and sauté until slightly browned. Add the tomatoes with the juice, the wine, oregano, basil, and sugar. Bring to a boil, lower the heat, and simmer gently, stirring occasionally, for 10 minutes, or until the tomatoes cook down and thicken slightly.

Meanwhile, in a large pot, bring at least 4 quarts of water to a rolling boil. Add 1 tablespoon of salt. Add the farfalle and stir to prevent sticking. Cook until *al dente*. Transfer to a warm serving bowl.

Add the cream and salt and pepper to taste to the tomato sauce and simmer for 3 minutes, or until it thickens slightly. Pour the hot sauce over the farfalle, toss well, and serve.

Poached Chicken Breasts with Ratatouille Orzo Ragout

Chef David Burke
Park Avenue Café
New York, New York
Serves 4

1¹/₂ cups light chicken stock
1¹/₂ cups tomato sauce (see classic tomato sauce, Chapter 4)
4 boneless, skinless chicken breasts, about 6 ounces each
Coarse or kosher salt to taste
Freshly ground pepper to taste
1 red bell pepper, seeded and diced
1 yellow bell pepper, seeded and diced
1 zucchini, diced
1 yellow squash, diced
1 small eggplant, unpeeled, outer 1¹/₂ inches only diced (not seeded part)
¹/₂ small onion, diced
3 gloves garlic, minced
1 cup fresh whole basil leaves, chopped, or 2 tablespoons dried
2 cups orzo, cooked
¹/₂ cup mascarpone cheese or freshly grated Parmesan cheese
4 fresh basil leaves or parsley sprigs for garnish

Combine the light chicken stock and tomato sauce in a soup pot and bring to a simmer.

Season the chicken with salt and pepper and add to the pot. Cover and simmer for 5 to 10 minutes, or until cooked. Add all remaining ingredients, except for the cheese and basil leaves or parsley, stir to combine, and simmer for an additional 2 minutes.

Remove the chicken breasts and keep warm. Cook vegetable-pasta mixture until the vegetables are tender and the orzo is hot. Correct the seasoning.

Spoon the ratatouille orzo ragout into 4 large bowls. Cut each chicken breast horizontally into 2 pieces and place over ragout. Top with a tablespoon of *mascarpone* cheese or Parmesan cheese and garnish with a basil leaf or parsley sprig.

Chicken Cacciatore with Rotelle

Serves 6

¹⁄₄ cup vegetable oil
One 3¹⁄₂ -pound chicken, cut into serving
*   pieces*
1 cup finely chopped onions
¹⁄₂ pound fresh mushrooms, thinly sliced

1 clove garlic, minced
One 28-ounce can Italian plum tomatoes,
*   with juice*
¹⁄₂ cup dry red wine
1 teaspoon dried oregano
1 bay leaf, crumbled
1 pound rotelle
¹⁄₂ cup chopped parsley

In a large, deep skillet, heat the oil over moderately high heat. Pat the chicken dry and brown it in batches. Do not crowd the pan. Transfer to a bowl.

Pour off all but about 3 tablespoons of oil. Add the onions and mushrooms and sauté until the onions are golden. Add the garlic and cook 1 minute. Add the tomatoes with juice, wine, chicken, and any juices that have accumulated in the bowl, oregano and bay leaf, and simmer, covered, stirring occasionally and breaking up the tomatoes, for 30 to 35 minutes, or until the chicken is tender.

Meanwhile, in a large pot, bring at least 4 quarts of water to a rolling boil. Add 1 tablespoon of salt. Add the rotelle and stir to prevent sticking. Cook until *al dente*. Drain.

Transfer the pasta to the skillet and toss with the sauce to coat. Remove the mixture to a large warm serving platter and sprinkle with the parsley.

Chicken in Aromatic Tomato Sauce with Perciatelli

Serves 6

1 pound perciatelli
1/4 cup olive oil
One 3-pound chicken, cut into 8 pieces
1 1/2 cups chopped red onions
1 teaspoon ground allspice
1 teaspoon ground cinnamon
1 teaspoon ground cumin
1 teaspoon paprika
1/2 teaspoon ground nutmeg
1/2 teaspoon ground cloves
Pinch of cayenne pepper
One 28-ounce can Italian plum tomatoes,
    with juices, chopped
1 cup water
2 tablespoons red wine vinegar, or more
2 tablespoons tomato paste
1 teaspoon sugar
Salt and freshly ground pepper to taste
3 tablespoons freshly grated Parmesan
    cheese

Heat the oil in a large, deep skillet over medium-high heat. Add the chicken in batches and cook until brown on all sides, about 8 minutes per batch. Place chicken on platter. Add the onions to the skillet and sauté until tender about 5 minutes. Add the spices and stir until fragrant, about 1 minute. Stir in the tomatoes and their juices and

water. Return the chicken to the skillet, and cover; simmer over medium-low heat until the chicken is very tender, about 35 minutes. Transfer the chicken to platter. Cover loosely with foil.

Add the vinegar, tomato paste, and sugar to the skillet. Simmer until thickened to sauce consistency, stirring occasionally, about 10 minutes. Season with salt and pepper to taste. Add more vinegar, if desired. Add the chicken, remove from heat, and cover to keep warm.

Meanwhile, in a large pot, bring at least 4 quarts of water to a rolling boil. Add 1 tablespoon salt. Add the pasta, stir to separate, and cook until *al dente*. Drain.

Transfer the pasta to a warm platter, top with the chicken and sauce, and toss gently. Sprinkle with the Parmesan and serve.

Garlic and Sun-Dried Tomatoes with Chicken and Penne

Serves 6

2 tablespoons virgin olive oil
6 cloves garlic, chopped
3 large boneless, skinless chicken breasts,
    about 6 ounces each
3 cups chicken stock
1/2 cup oil-packed sun-dried tomatoes, diced

$^1/_4$ cup chopped parsley
8 scallions, white and half of green tops,
    chopped
Salt and freshly ground pepper to taste
$^1/_4$ cup unsalted butter, softened
1 pound penne

In a large, deep skillet, heat the oil over
medium heat. Add the garlic and sauté until
golden. Do not allow to burn. Add the
chicken and sauté for 2 minutes on each
side, or until cooked through. Remove the
chicken from pan, cut it into 1-inch cubes,
and reserve.

Pour the chicken stock into a saucepan
and add the tomatoes, parsley, and scallions.
Add salt and pepper to taste. Bring to a boil
and reduce over high heat 5 to 10 minutes.
Add the chicken to the pan and whisk in the
butter, a bit at a time, to thicken sauce.
Remove from the heat and keep warm.

Meanwhile, in a large pot, bring at least
4 quarts of water to a rolling boil. Add
1 tablespoon salt. Add the penne, stir to
prevent sticking. Cook until *al dente*. Drain.

In a bowl toss the penne in the sauce,
transfer to a warm platter, and serve.

Cavatappi with Chicken, Tomato, and Leek Sauce

Serves 4

3 cups chicken broth
1 pound boneless, skinless chicken breasts
$^1/_3$ pound thinly sliced pancetta
4 small leeks, cleaned and cut lengthwise
    into 1-inch strips
3 cups red wine marinara sauce
    (see Chapter 4)
$^1/_4$ cup heavy cream
1 teaspoon dried thyme leaves
Pinch of dried hot red pepper flakes
$^1/_2$ teaspoon salt
1 pound cavatappi
$^1/_2$ cup freshly grated Parmesan cheese

In a large skillet, bring the chicken broth
to a boil. Add the chicken breast, reduce to a
simmer, and poach until tender, about
10 minutes, depending on size. Drain, pat dry,
and cut into $^1/_2$-inch slices. Reserve.

In another large skillet cook the *pancetta*
over medium-low heat until crisp and lightly
brown. Remove from the pan with a slotted
spoon and drain on paper towels. Crumble
and reserve.

Discard all but 2 tablespoons of the drippings. Add the leeks and sauté over medium
heat, stirring occasionally, until soft but not
brown. Add the marinara sauce, cream,
thyme, red pepper, and salt. Increase the heat
to high and simmer for 3 to 5 minutes to
thicken. Just before serving, add the *pancetta*

(continued)

and sliced chicken to the sauce and heat briefly. Taste for seasoning.

Meanwhile, in a large pot, bring at least 4 quarts of water to a rolling boil. Add 1 tablespoon of salt. Add the *cavatappi* and stir to prevent sticking. Cook until *al dente*. Drain.

Transfer the pasta to a large, warm serving bowl. Pour the sauce over the pasta and toss. Serve immediately, and pass Parmesan separately.

Radiatore and Chicken in Tricolor Pepper Sauce

Serves 4 to 6

good Jan 2000

not very sauce-y

3 cups chicken stock
1 pound boneless, skinless chicken breast
3 tablespoons unsalted butter
1 tablespoon vegetable oil
1 cup coarsely chopped onion
1 cup diced green bell pepper
   ($^1\!/_2$-inch cubes)
1 cup diced red bell pepper
   ($^1\!/_2$-inch cubes)
1 cup diced yellow bell pepper
   ($^1\!/_2$-inch cubes)
$^2\!/_3$ cup heavy cream
Salt and freshly ground pepper to taste
1 pound radiatore
2 tablespoons chopped parsley
$^1\!/_2$ cup freshly grated Parmesan cheese

In a large skillet, bring the chicken stock to a boil. Add the chicken breast and reduce the heat to a simmer. Poach the chicken, depending on the size, until tender, about 10 minutes. Drain, pat dry, and slice into thin strips.

In a large, deep skillet, heat the butter and oil over medium heat. Add the onion and sauté until golden. Add all the diced peppers, increase the heat to medium-high, and cook until tender, turning occasionally. Add the cream, increase the heat to high, and cook until the cream is reduced by half. Season with salt and pepper. Add the chicken to the sauce and warm through.

Meanwhile, in a large pot, bring at least 4 quarts of water to a rolling boil. Add 1 tablespoon salt. Add the pasta, stir to separate, and cook until *al dente*. Drain.

Add the pasta to the skillet and toss with the chicken and sauce. Sprinkle with the parsley and grated cheese, toss again, and serve at once.

The Goods on Garlic

Garlic, sublime or maligned, is an ingredient found in so many pasta recipes that it seems indispensable. Of course, garlic is famous for its smell, but place your nose to the bulb, or head, with its papery-covered cloves, and you will smell . . . nothing. The odor (or aroma, depending on who is doing the smelling) begins as soon as a clove is penetrated. The more you chop, mince, or crush, the more the scent increases. Thus whole cloves of garlic, roasted or added to a dish while it's cooking and then removed, are the most subtle ways to introduce the flavor.

The best way to remove the stubborn outer skin is to place a clove on a cutting board and give it a good whack with the flat plane of a knife blade. The skin will split and simply fall away. A light hit with a mallet will also do.

Garlic is purported to be a health food in the extreme, beneficial for everything from asthma to lowering cholesterol, and there are some medical justifications for these claims. At the very least, giving garlic a solid smack on the counter is good for the disposition.

Fettuccine with Chicken, Herbed Onions, and Nuts in Cream Sauce

Serves 4 to 6

> 1/3 cup olive oil
> 2 cloves garlic, minced
> 2 cups diced onions
> Salt and freshly ground pepper
>   to taste
> 1 teaspoon ground coriander
> 1/4 teaspoon cayenne pepper
> 1 pound boneless, skinless chicken breasts,
>   cut into short, narrow strips
> 3/4 cup coarsely chopped pecans, toasted
> 1/2 cup chopped slivered almonds, toasted
> 1 1/2 cups heavy cream
> 1 1/2 cups chicken stock
> 1 pound fresh fettuccine
> 1/4 cup chopped fresh dill
> 1/4 cup chopped parsley

In a large, deep skillet, heat 3 tablespoons of the olive oil over medium heat. Add the garlic and onions and cook until the onions are translucent, about 7 minutes. Add 1 teaspoon salt and 1/4 teaspoon pepper and cook 3 minutes longer. Add the coriander and cayenne and cook 3 minutes. Set aside. (There should be about 1 cup onions.)

In another large, deep skillet, heat 2 tablespoons of the olive oil over medium

(continued)

heat. Add the chicken and sauté, turning frequently, until golden brown. Season with salt, pepper, and cayenne, if desired.

Add the herbed onions to skillet along with the nuts, cream, and broth and simmer 5 or 6 minutes to reduce. The sauce should be creamy, but no too thick. The nuts and fresh pasta will absorb some of the cream.

Meanwhile, in a large pot, bring at least 4 quarts of water to a rolling boil. Add 1 tablespoon of salt. Add pasta and stir to prevent sticking. Fresh pasta will cook in just 1 or 2 minutes, so check for doneness immediately. Cook until *al dente*. Drain.

Stir the parsley and dill into the sauce. Add the fettuccine and toss completely. Transfer to a warm bowl and serve.

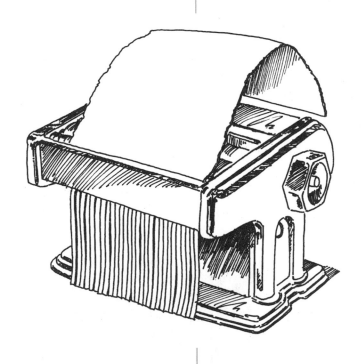

CHAPTER 9

A FULL PLATE:
PASTA AND MEAT

Together, the heartiness of meat and the tenderness of pasta make a nearly perfect dish. Beef, pork, veal, lamb, sausage, and the lovely Italian exports, *prosciutto* and *pancetta*, all deepen and enrich the flavor of pasta without overwhelming it. Ground meat, especially, marries well with pasta, nestling into the curves and holes of twist and tubular shapes. The result is a heady contrast in textures and a medley of flavors—spicy, smoky, and full-bodied. In the pasta recipes that follow, meat is a player is an ensemble production. It is not the star; but without meat, the show could not go on.

Lumache with Leek and Sausage Sauce

Serves 4

> 2 large leeks, coarse outer layers and
>   tough green part removed
> 2 tablespoons olive oil
> 1 clove garlic, minced
> The meat of 2 sweet Italian sausages
>   (casings removed)
> 1 cup chicken stock
> One 10-ounce package frozen tiny peas,
>   thawed
> Salt and freshly ground pepper to taste
> 1 pound lumache
> 1/2 cup freshly grated Parmesan cheese

Rinse the leeks well. Cut into 1/2-inch rounds and rinse again until all dirt is washed away.

In a large, deep skillet, heat the oil over medium heat. Add the leeks, garlic, and sausage and cook until the leeks soften and sausage browns. Add the chicken stock and simmer 3 minutes. Stir in the peas, add salt and pepper to taste, and cook 2 minutes.

Meanwhile, in a large pot, bring at least 4 quarts of water to a rolling boil. Add 1 tablespoon salt. Add the pasta, stir to separate, and cook until just *al dente*. Drain.

Add the pasta to the skillet. Sprinkle with the Parmesan and toss to coat well. Transfer the pasta to a warm platter and serve.

Rigatoni Alla Grappa

Chef Cary Wolfson
Caffe Angelica
Garden City Park, New York
Serves 4

> 2 tablespoons unsalted butter
> 1 tablespoon chopped garlic
> 1 tablespoon chopped shallots
> 1 tablespoon chopped fresh sage
> 1/2 teaspoon dried hot red pepper flakes
> 1/2 cup sliced fresh cremino mushrooms
> 1/2 cup diced prosciutto
> 1/4 cup grappa (a liqueur)
> 1 cup heavy cream
> 2 cups tomato sauce
> 1/2 cup green peas
> 1/4 cup freshly grated Romano cheese
> 1 pound rigatoni, cooked, drained, and
>   still warm

Place the butter in a large saucepan over medium heat and cook until it starts to brown. Add the garlic, shallots, sage, and red pepper flakes. Sauté, stirring occasionally, until the garlic slightly browns. Add the mushrooms and *prosciutto*, sauté briefly, and add the *grappa*. Raise the heat and reduce the liquid until almost dry. Add the heavy cream and simmer until reduced by half. Add the tomato sauce, bring to a boil, and reduce the heat. Add the green peas, and simmer, stirring occasionally, until the sauce has a thick, creamy consistency.

Bring at least 4 quarts of water to boil. Add 1 tablespoon of salt. Add rigatoni and stir to separate. Cook until *al dente*. Drain.

Transfer to a warm bowl. Toss with the sauce and Romano cheese. Serve on heated plates.

Paglia and Fieno (Straw and Hay)

Chef Massimo Saltino
VIVO
Chicago, Illinois

Serves 6

> 4 tablespoons unsalted butter
> 1 clove garlic, minced
> 1/2 onion, finely chopped
> 1/2 pound sliced prosciutto, diced
> 2 fresh sage leaves
> 1 1/2 cups heavy cream
> 1 pound fresh or dried fettuccine or
>   linguine
> 1 pound fresh or dried spinach fettuccine
> 3/4 cup freshly grated Parmesan cheese
> 1 sprig flat-leaf parsley, finely chopped

Heat the butter in a deep skillet. Add the garlic, and cook until golden. Add the onions and cook until transparent. Add the *prosciutto* with the sage leaves and cook for 30 to 40

(continued)

seconds. Add the cream and simmer for 1 to 2 minutes.

Meanwhile, bring a large pot of salted water to a boil and cook both pastas until tender. if the pasta is fresh, it will be ready almost as soon as the water comes back to a boil. Drain.

In a large heated bowl toss the pasta with the cream sauce, sprinkle with the Parmesan and parsley, and serve.

Shells with Prosciutto, Peas, and Mushrooms

Serves 4

ok/
very brothy —

> 1 pound shells
> 2 tablespoons olive oil
> Two ¹/₄-inch-thick slices prosciutto, fat removed, cut into ¹/₄-inch dice
> ¹/₂ cup chopped onion
> 2 cups sliced fresh mushrooms
> 1¹/₂ cups blanched young peas or frozen, thawed
> 1 teaspoon unsalted butter
> 2 cups chicken stock
> ¹/₂ cup freshly grated Parmesan cheese
> Salt and freshly ground pepper to taste

In a large, deep skillet, heat the oil over medium heat. Add the *prosciutto* and onion and cook, stirring, until the onion is wilted.

Add the mushrooms and continue to cook until they lose all moisture, about 5 minutes. Add the peas, butter, stock, and chicken. ? Simmer until the liquid is reduced by half, about 10 minutes. Season with salt and pepper to taste.

Meanwhile, in a large pot, bring at least 4 quarts of water to a rolling boil. Add 1 tablespoon salt. Add the pasta, stir to separate, and cook until not quite *al dente*. Drain.

Transfer the pasta to the skillet and combine with the hot sauce. Cook briefly to heat through. Remove to a large warm bowl, toss with the Parmesan, and serve at once.

Rigatoni with Sausage and Porcini

Chef Massimo Saltino
VIVO
Chicago, Illinois

Serves 4

> 1 ounce dried porcini, soaked in warm water for 10 minutes; or fresh when in season
> 2 tablespoons olive oil
> 1 tablespoon unsalted butter
> ¹/₃ cup chopped onion

128

½ pound mild Italian sausage, casing
    removed
½ cup Chianti or Merlot
3 cups crushed tomatoes
Salt and freshly ground pepper to taste
1 pound rigatoni
⅓ cup freshly grated Parmesan cheese
1 sprig flat-leaf parsley, chopped

Drain the porcini, reserving the liquid. Heat the oil and butter in a medium saucepan. Add the onion and cook until lightly golden. Add the sausage and mix well. When the sausage is lightly colored, add the porcini and stir for a minute or two. Add the wine and cook until it evaporates. Add the liquid from the mushrooms and the crushed tomatoes. Season with salt and pepper. Bring the sauce to a boil, then reduce the heat to low and simmer for 25 to 30 minutes.

Meanwhile, cook the pasta in boiling water until *al dente*. Drain.

Transfer the pasta to a large bowl, add the sauce, and toss. Sprinkle with cheese and chopped parsley, and serve.

Rotelle with Kielbasa and Rapini

Serves 4

1 large bunch rapini (broccoli rabe)
1 pound kielbasa, halved lengthwise and
    cut into ½-inch-thick pieces
4 cloves garlic, minced
1 cup water
Salt and freshly ground pepper to taste
1 pound rotelle
3 tablespoons olive oil, or to taste

In a large, heavy skillet, sauté the kielbasa over moderate heat until brown. Transfer with a slotted spoon to paper towels to drain.

Pour off all but 1 tablespoon of fat from the pan. Add the garlic and cook over medium-low heat until golden. Add the *rapini*, and cook, stirring, for 1 minute, or until wilted. Add the water and simmer, stirring occasionally, for about 5 minutes, or until the *rapini* is tender. Stir in the kielbasa. Add salt and fresh pepper to taste.

Meanwhile, in a large pot, bring at least 4 quarts of water to a rolling boil. Add 1 tablespoon salt. Add the pasta, stir to separate, and cook until *al dente*. Drain.

Transfer the pasta to a large, warm bowl and toss with the olive oil. Add the *rapini* and kielbasa mixture, toss well, and serve in heated bowls.

Penne with Tasso, Olives, Sun-Dried Tomatoes, and Porcini

Stephen Cavagnaro
Cavey's Restaurant
Manchester, Connecticut

Serves 4

> *¹/₄ cup canola oil*
> *¹/₂ cup dried porcini*
> *¹/₂ cup sun-dried tomatoes, rehydrated*
> *¹/₂ pound tasso*
> *¹/₄ cup kalamata olives*
> *1 pound penne, cooked until* al dente,
> *   drained well, and kept warm*
> *4 tablespoons unsalted butter, melted*
> *¹/₂ cup freshly grated Parmesan*

Soak the porcini in 1 cup hot water, covered for at least 3 hours until tender and the liquid is potent. Soak the sun-dried tomatoes in just enough hot water to cover, until softened, drain, and cut into julienne strips before using.

In an ovenproof sauté pan, sauté the tasso in the canola oil until it just begins to crisp. Add the porcini and the sun-dried tomatoes and mix well. When combined, deglaze the pan with reserved mushroom soaking liquid. Simmer very slowly for 10 minutes to allow flavors to blend.

Add the penne and toss until it is coated with the sauce mixture. Put in a 300° oven for 10 minutes, stirring every 3 or 4 minutes. Toss with grated Parmesan and butter.

Cappelletti Carbonara

Serves 4 to 6

> *¹/₄ pound bacon, cut into 1-inch pieces*
> *2 medium onions, chopped*
> *3 tablespoons olive oil*
> *5 tablespoons chopped parsley*
> *2 tablespoons chopped fresh basil*
> *¹/₂ cup chopped* prosciutto
> *¹/₂ pound freshly grated Fontina cheese*
> *Salt and freshly ground pepper to taste*
> *1 pound cappelletti*
> *4 eggs, beaten*
> *Freshly grated Parmesan cheese*

Sauté the bacon in a large, deep skillet until crisp. Drain well and pour off the fat. In the skillet, sauté the onions in the olive oil until softened. Add the parsley, basil, *prosciutto*, and cheese with salt and pepper to taste. Cover and simmer over low heat, stirring often, 5 to 10 minutes.

Meanwhile, in a large pot, bring at least 4 quarts of water to a rolling boil. Add 1 tablespoon salt. Add the pasta, stir to separate, and cook until *al dente*. Drain.

Place the pasta in a warm serving bowl. Add the eggs and toss well. Transfer to the

skillet and heat and stir well to heat through. Sprinkle with Parmesan and serve at once.

Penne with Ham in a Spicy Mixed Pepper Cream Sauce

Chef Louis Lindic
Treehouse Restaurant
Atlanta, Georgia

Serves 4

*1/4 pound smoked ham, cut into
    1/4-inch cubes
1 tablespoon olive oil
1 small red bell pepper, seeded and
    chopped
1 small yellow pepper, seeded and
    chopped
2 fresh jalapeño or ancho chili peppers,
    seeded and minced
Salt and freshly ground pepper to taste
1/4 cup dry white wine
2 cups chicken stock
1 1/2 cups heavy cream
1 pound penne, cooked and still hot
Freshly grated Parmesan cheese*

Sauté the ham in the olive oil over medium heat until slightly golden, but do not brown. Remove the ham from the pan, add the red and yellow peppers, and sauté for a minute. Add the spicy peppers and salt and pepper and sauté until the peppers are softened, about 2 to 3 minutes. Remove the peppers and deglaze the pan with the wine. Add the chicken stock and reduce to 1/3 cup over high heat. Add the heavy cream and reduce over high heat until desired sauce consistency. Taste for salt and pepper, add the ham, then the peppers and reheat.

Meanwhile, in a large pot, bring at least 4 quarts of water to a rolling boil. Add 1 tablespoon salt. Add pasta, stir to separate, and cook until just *al dente*. Drain.

Place the hot pasta in a large bowl and pour the sauce over it. Toss well, sprinkle with the Parmesan cheese, and serve at once.

Spaghetti Pie

Serves 4 to 6

*1 pound lean ground beef or sweet Italian
    sausage
1/2 cup chopped onion
1/4 cup chopped green bell pepper
One 8-ounce can tomatoes, with juice,
    chopped
One 6-ounce can tomato paste
1 large clove garlic, minced
1 teaspoon sugar
1 teaspoon dried oregano*

(continued)

¹/₂ teaspoon dried basil
¹/₄ teaspoon salt
6 ounces spaghetti
2 tablespoons unsalted butter or margarine
¹/₃ cup freshly grated Parmesan cheese
2 eggs, beaten
1 cup large curd cottage cheese, drained
¹/₂ cup shredded mozzarella cheese

Combine the ground beef, onion, and bell pepper in a large skillet and cook over medium heat, stirring, until the beef is browned and the vegetables are tender. Drain off excess fat. Stir in the tomatoes, tomato paste, garlic, sugar, oregano, and salt. Cook until heated through and fragrant. Set aside.

In a large pot, bring at least 3 quarts of water to a rolling boil. Add 2 teaspoons salt. Add the spaghetti, stir to separate, and cook until *al dente*. Drain.

Transfer the spaghetti to a large bowl. Add the butter. Stir in the Parmesan cheese and eggs until well combined. Press the spaghetti mixture into a buttered 10-inch pie plate to form a crust.

Spread the cottage cheese over the spaghetti. Top with the tomato meat sauce. Chill, cover with aluminum foil, at least 2 hours or overnight.

Bake, covered, in a preheated 350° oven for 1 hour. Sprinkle with the mozzarella and bake 5 minutes longer, or until the cheese melts.

Savory Sausage

There was a time when Americans ate sausage for breakfast while the world was enjoying sausage as an appetizer, in main courses, in casseroles, and, yes, with pasta. This is no longer the case, of course. Every supermarket carries "sweet" and "spicy" Italian sausages, and these are only the beginning. Sweet and spicy *mortadella* is a favorite from Italy, as is the garlic sausage called *cotechino*. *Andouille,* the Spanish sausage, is found on many restaurant menus. The possibilities for flavor combinations are endless. An adventurous recipe here that calls for ostrich sausage—and offers as a substitute turkey and apple sausage—is an indication of the enormous variety that sausages have to offer. Because sausages so fully intermingle the flavors of meat and spices, they impart their combined flavors to pasta dishes in a way no single ingredient can.

Penne in Oven-Roasted Tomato Broth with Sun-Dried Cherry Pork Loin Meatballs Topped with Hot Pepper Coppa

Chef Roger M. Jamison
Painted Plates
St. Louis, Missouri

Serves 6

Meatballs

2 cups Cabernet Sauvignon
1/2 cup sun-dried cherries
1 pound ground pork loin
1 tablespoon chopped shallot, cooked
 until brown
1 teaspoon chopped garlic
1 teaspoon salt
1/3 teaspoon cayenne pepper
2 eggs

Preheat the oven to 350°.

In an enameled saucepan, bring the Cabernet Sauvignon to a boil, add the cherries, simmer until plump and 2/3 of the wine has evaporated. Remove from heat, cool, and dice. Discard the wine.

Add the cherries to pork, garlic, salt, pepper, eggs. Add browned shallots to the mixture. Mix ingredients thoroughly. Shape into 1/2-inch meatballs. Place on a baking sheet and bake in a preheated 350° oven from 15 to 20 minutes. Remove from oven and reserve.

Sauce

8 large tomatoes, cored
1/2 teaspoon salt
1/4 teaspoon fresh black pepper
2 tablespoons tomato paste
2 ounces unsalted butter
1/4 pound diced hot pepper coppa
 (sautéed) (Italian pork sausage)
1/4 pound freshly grated Asiago cheese
2 tablespoons chopped fresh parsley
1 pound penne

Preheat the oven to 350°.

Make the sauce: Place the tomatoes in a roasting pan and roast for about 30 minutes, or until the skins begin to turn black. Remove from the oven, let cool, and peel. Press the tomatoes through a mesh sieve to remove the seeds. Put the juice and tomatoes in a saucepan, along with the juices remaining in the roasting pan, add salt and pepper, bring to a boil. Add tomato paste, whisking to incorporate it into the sauce. Reduce the heat to a simmer and reduce by one quarter. If too thin, add a touch of cornstarch and water to thicken. Whisk in the butter until smooth.

On 4 plates ladle a little of the sauce. Combine the remaining sauce with the pasta. Put 8 meatballs on each plate, encircling the pasta. Top with 1 ounce of the sautéed coppa. Garnish with the grated Asiago cheese and chopped parsley.

Orange Pasta with Pork Chops

Serves 4

Orange Pasta

1 cup all-purpose white flour
1 cup durum wheat (or substitute white or whole-wheat flour)
1 egg
2 teaspoons orange extract
4 tablespoons orange juice
1 to 3 tablespoons water

Make the orange pasta: Combine the dry ingredients and place on counter. Make a well in the center and fill with egg, orange extract, and juice. Mix together with hands until a dough forms. Add water, 1 tablespoon at a time, as needed, if the dough is too dry. Add flour if sticky. Let dough rest at least 15 minutes or up to 1 hour, wrapped in plastic or in a covered bowl. (See Chapter 3 for detailed directions.)

Roll out and cut into strips or use a pasta machine (setting #5) and cut into strips.

Pork

1 tablespoon balsamic vinegar
1 tablespoon olive oil
¹/₂ teaspoon dried thyme
¹/₂ teaspoon dried basil
Four boneless loin pork chops

Mix all ingredients in a shallow baking dish, add the chops, and marinate for 30 minutes to 1 hour at room temperature.

Orange Sauce

1 tablespoon butter
4 teaspoons all-purpose flour
³/₄ cup orange juice
³/₄ teaspoon dried thyme
³/₄ teaspoon dried rosemary
2 teaspoons stoneground or Dijon-style mustard
¹/₂ cup freshly grated Parmesan

In a small saucepan, melt the butter over low heat. Stir in the flour until well combined. Add the remaining ingredients and continue cooking over heat, stirring occasionally, until sauce has thickened.

In a large skillet, cook the pork chops with the marinade, covered, for about 5 minutes on each side.

Meanwhile, in a large pot, bring at least 4 quarts of water to a rolling boil. Add 1 tablespoon of salt. Add the pasta and stir to separate the strands. It will cook very quickly, so check for doneness promptly. Cook until *al dente*. Drain.

Transfer the pasta to a heated platter. Arrange the pork on top. Pour the sauce over the chops, toss gently, top with freshly grated Parmesan and a grinding of fresh pepper, and serve.

Beep Beep "Roadrunner" Pasta

Corporate Chef Alan Kaplan
Prestige Caterers
Queens Village, New York

Serves 6

> 1 pound spinach radiatori
> 1 pound ostrich sausage (or chicken and
>   apple sausage)
> 1 teaspoon vegetable oil
> 5 cloves garlic, chopped
> ¼ cup extra virgin cold-pressed olive oil
> 4 cups fresh tomatoes, peeled, seeded,
>   and chopped or one 28-ounce can
>   plum tomatoes chopped
> Pinch of dried oregano
> One 15-ounce can white cannellini beans
> ½ cup tiny peas
> 1 head broccoli florets, blanched
> 8 red radishes, blanched and quartered
> ¼ cup hand-shredded Romano cheese
> Salt and fresh ground pepper to taste

Cook the pasta in boiling salted water until *al dente*, drain, and reserve.

In a large skillet heat the vegetable oil and brown the sausage on all sides. Then remove to paper towels to drain. Pour off any fat. In the same skillet, sauté the garlic in the olive oil until golden, add the tomatoes and oregano, and cook over low heat 15 minutes. Add the beans, peas, broccoli, and radishes and combine well. Slice the sausage and add it to the sauce. Heat and stir thoroughly. Pour the sauce over the pasta, toss, and garnish with the cheese. Serve at once.

Pork Partner

Pasta and pork do not exactly come to mind in the kitchen like peanut butter and jelly, apple pie and ice cream, or even ham and cheese, but they often complement each other. The Italians have several varieties of pork that are practically requirements in their pasta pantry. Pancetta, Italian bacon, and prosciutto, Italian ham, are so infused with taste and mythology that they can never be duplicated in another country. But since cooking is nothing if not the art of compromise and improvisation, feel free to substitute bacon and ham from the local deli when necessary. Pork loin is well worth using in a stir-fry. It long ago outgrew its fatty ancestry—today a three-ounce serving contains only six grams of fat—and it contributes a wonderful flavor.

Capellini with Basil, Tomatoes, and Sliced Grilled Steak

Serves 6

Marinade
1 pound ripe tomatoes, peeled, seeded, and chopped
3 large cloves garlic, mashed to a paste
2 cups chopped fresh basil
1/2 teaspoon salt
1/2 teaspoon freshly ground pepper
Pinch of dried hot red pepper flakes
2 tablespoons olive oil
1/2 tablespoon red wine vinegar
1/2 pound New York strip steak, cut 1-inch thick

1 teaspoon olive oil
1 1/2 pounds capellini, broken into 4-inch pieces
2 tablespoons fresh basil leaves, shredded

Make the marinade: In a large baking dish, combine the tomatoes, garlic, basil, salt, pepper flakes, olive oil, and vinegar. Add the steak, cover, and marinate for at least 10 minutes or up to 2 hours at room temperature.

In a large, deep skillet, heat the olive oil over medium heat. Remove the steak from the marinade, reserving the mixture, and sear on both sides over high heat, then cook about 4 minutes on each side, until medium-rare. Transfer to a platter and let stand 5 minutes before slicing thin.

Meanwhile, in a large pot, bring at least 4 quarts of water to a rolling boil. Add 1 tablespoon salt. Add the pasta, stir to separate, and cook until *al dente*. Drain.

Transfer the pasta to a large warm serving bowl, and toss well with the reserved marinade. Arrange the steak slices on top, garnish with the basil, and serve at room temperature.

Creole Belle Pasta

Chef J.P. Gelinas
Big Daddy's Restaurant
Massapequa, New York

Serves 4

Dry Seasoning Mix
1 teaspoon freshly ground black pepper
1/2 teaspoon Old Bay Seasoning
1/2 teaspoon kosher salt
1/2 teaspoon cayenne pepper
1/2 teaspoon dried thyme
1/2 teaspoon dried tarragon
1/4 teaspoon ground white pepper
1/4 teaspoon dried hot red pepper flakes

12 ounces freshly grated Romano cheese
1 tablespoon unsalted butter
1 tablespoon virgin olive oil

1 bunch scallions, coarsely chopped
¼ pound tasso, finely chopped
*1 New Mexican chili pepper, coarsely
    chopped*
1 tablespoon Chablis wine
¼ pound peeled crawfish tails, finely diced
¼ cup peeled finely diced eggplant
¼ cup finely chopped fresh basil
1 tablespoon finely chopped fresh cilantro
1 cup heavy cream
1 pound tomato fettuccine, cooked until al
    dente, *drained well, and kept warm*

Make the dry seasoning mix: In a bowl,
combine all the dry seasoning mix ingredients. Add the Romano and combine well, and
set aside.

In a large skillet, melt the butter with the
oil over high heat. Add the scallions, tasso,
and New Mexican pepper. Sauté for 4
minutes, stirring occasionally. Deglaze the
skillet with the wine. Reduce the heat to
medium and add the crawfish tails, eggplant,
basil, and cilantro. Cook for 3 minutes, stirring well. Add the heavy cream and bring the
mixture just to a low boil. Gradually whisk in
the seasoned Romano mixture. Cook for
2 minutes, stirring frequently.

Add the fettuccine to the skillet and, using
a pair of tongs, toss the pasta until it is
completely blended with the sauce. Reduce
the heat to low, cook for 3 minutes more,
and toss again. Serve steaming portions in
individual bowls.

Spaghettini with Veal

Serves 4 to 6

1 pound veal steak, cubed
¼ cup all-purpose flour
1 teaspoon salt
½ teaspoon dried tarragon
Freshly ground pepper
2 tablespoons olive oil
2 tablespoons unsalted butter
1 cup chopped onion
1 cup chicken stock
Juice of ½ lemon
¼ cup freshly grated Parmesan cheese
1 pound spaghettini

Preheat the oven to 400°.
Dredge the veal cubes in the flour and
season with the salt, tarragon, and pepper.

In a large, deep skillet, heat the oil and
butter over medium heat. Add the onions and
cook until soft. Add veal cubes and brown on
all sides. Stir in the chicken stock and
simmer, uncovered, for 10 minutes. Remove
from the heat and stir in the lemon juice.
Place the mixture in a baking dish, sprinkle
with a little of the cheese, and cover. Bake
for 20 minutes, or until the sauce is thickened
and the veal is fork-tender.

Meanwhile, in a large pot, bring at least
4 quarts of water to a rolling boil. Add
1 tablespoon salt. Add the pasta, stir to
separate, and cook until *al dente*. Drain.

(continued)

Transfer the pasta to a large warm bowl. Toss with the remaining cheese. Add the veal and toss gently. Serve in warm bowls.

Fusilli All'Arturo

Chefs Vincent and Joseph Gismondi
Arturo's Ristorante
Boca Raton, Florida

Serves 4

> 1 pound fusilli
> 2 tablespoons chopped onion
> 3 tablespoons vegetable oil
> 4 strips bacon
> 1/3 cup coarsely chopped ham
> 1/3 cup Cognac
> 1 cup plain tomato sauce
> 4 tablespoons unsalted butter, in pieces
> 1 tablespoon minced parsley
> 4 dashes Tabasco sauce
> 1/3 cup heavy cream
> Freshly grated Parmesan cheese for serving
>   (optional)

Cook the fusilli in boiling salted water until *al dente*, or still firm. Drain well, set aside, and keep warm. While the pasta is cooking prepare the sauce: In a large skillet, sauté the onion in the oil with the bacon for 2 minutes. Add the ham and cook for 2 minutes longer.

Remove the bacon. Add the cognac and ignite.

When the flames die down, add tomato sauce, butter, parsley, and Tabasco and stir gently to combine. Add the drained pasta and toss well. Stir in the cream, toss again, and cook over low heat for 3 minutes. Serve until heated through. Serve with grated Parmesan on the side, if desired.

Ziti with Hearty Lamb Sauce

Serves 4 to 6

> 1 tablespoon olive or vegetable oil
> 3/4 pound lean ground lamb
> 2 cloves garlic, finely chopped
> 1 onion, finely chopped
> 1/2 teaspoon dried rosemary
> 1 cup canned crushed tomatoes
> 1 1/2 cups dry red wine
> 1 pinch of ground nutmeg
> 1 pinch of ground cloves
> Salt and freshly ground pepper to taste
> 1 pound ziti
> 1/3 cup freshly grated Parmesan cheese

In a large, deep skillet, heat the oil in a medium saucepan over medium-high heat. Add the lamb, breaking it up with a wooden spoon, and garlic and cook until the meat

begins to brown, about 3 minutes. Add the onion and rosemary and cook briefly. Add the crushed tomatoes, wine, nutmeg, and cloves. Bring to a boil and reduce to simmer. Add salt and pepper to taste. Cook, uncovered, until the lamb is tender, about 20 minutes. Check the lamb occasionally to make sure there is enough liquid to cover it. If not, add a small amount of water.

Meanwhile, in a large pot, bring at least 4 quarts of water to a rolling boil. Add 1 tablespoon salt. Add the pasta, stir to separate, and cook until *al dente*. Drain.

Stir half the Parmesan into the lamb sauce. Add the pasta, toss well, and heat through over low heat. Transfer to a warm platter, sprinkle with the remaining cheese, and serve.

Fettuccine Romanissimo

Owner Tony Vallone
Tony's * Anthony's * Grotto * La Griglia
Houston, Texas

Serves 4

8 ounces pancetta, *diced*
$^1/_4$ pound foie gras, *diced*
2 shallots, diced
3 cloves garlic, thinly sliced
1 cup fresh shiitake mushrooms, sliced
1 cup tomatoes, peeled, seeded, and diced

1 cup dry white wine
$^1/_2$ cup heavy cream
Salt and freshly ground pepper to taste
1 pound fettuccine, cooked until al dente, drained well, and kept warm
$^1/_4$ cup freshly grated Parmesan cheese
Dried hot red pepper flakes

In a large sauté pan, brown the *pancetta*. Add the *foie gras* and sauté until golden brown. Remove the *pancetta* and *foie gras* and reserve.

Add the shallots and sliced garlic to the pan and sauté for 2 minutes. Add the mushrooms, tomatoes, and wine and reduce the liquid by half over high heat.

Add the cream with the salt and pepper to taste. Add the fettuccine with the reserved *pancetta* and *foie gras* and toss gently. Portion into pasta bowls. Sprinkle with the Parmesan cheese and pepper flakes.

Beef Bourguignon with Pappardelle

Serves 4 to 6

2 tablespoons unsalted butter
$^1/_4$ cup all-purpose flour
$^1/_2$ teaspoon salt
$^1/_2$ teaspoon freshly ground pepper

(continued)

*1 pound beef tenderloin, cut into
 $^1/_2$-inch pieces
2 teaspoons minced garlic
One $10^1/_2$-ounce can double-strength beef
 broth, undiluted
One 10-ounce bag frozen pearl onions,
 thawed
$^1/_2$ cup dry red wine
$1^1/_2$ teaspoons dried thyme leaves
1 bay leaf
1 pound pappardelle
1 pound baby carrots
Chopped flat-leaf parsley for garnish*

In a large, deep skillet, melt a tablespoon of the butter over medium-high heat.

Combine the flour, salt, and pepper in a plastic bag. Add half the beef to the bag and shake to coat. Add to the skillet and quickly brown, turning once, about 2 minutes. Transfer to a plate and set aside. Repeat with the remaining butter and meat.

Add the garlic to the drippings in the skillet and cook for 2 minutes, stirring occasionally. Add any remaining seasoned flour; mix well. Add the beef broth, thawed pearl onions, wine, thyme, and bay leaf and bring to a boil. Stir in the reserved beef. Simmer, uncovered, for about 4 minutes, or until the beef is pink in the center and the sauce has thickened slightly. Remove the bay leaf.

Meanwhile, in a large pot, bring at least 4 quarts of water to a rolling boil. Add 1 tablespoon salt. Add the pasta, stir to separate. Add carrots for the last 5 minutes of cooking time. Cook the pasta until *al dente*. Drain the pasta and carrots.

Add the pasta and carrots to the skillet with the meat, toss, and heat through. Transfer the mixture to a warm bowl, garnish with the parsley, and serve.

Black Pepper Fettuccine with Venison Sausage, Sun-Dried Tomatoes, Spinach, and a Venison Parmesan Herb Sauce

**Chef Christopher Pyun
The Green Room
Dallas, Texas**

Serves 4

*1 ounce olive oil
1 shallot, minced
$^1/_2$ pound venison sausage, sliced
$^1/_4$ pound spinach, cooked, roughly
 chopped
$^1/_4$ pound sun-dried tomatoes, julienned
$^1/_2$ cup heavy cream
$^1/_2$ cup finely grated Parmesan
Select fresh herbs such as: parsley, chives,
 basil, 1 to 2 tablespoons, chopped
Salt and freshly ground pepper to taste
1 pound fresh black pepper fettuccine*

Bring a large pot of salted water to a boil. Add the fresh fettuccine and cook only until *al dente*. Drain, return to pot, and keep warm while making sauce.

In a large sauté pan, heat the olive oil until hot. Add the shallot and cook for 30 seconds. Add the venison sausage and cook 1 minute. Add spinach, tomatoes, cream, and Parmesan and simmer for 1 minute and add salt and pepper to taste. Add the hot fettuccine to the sauce, top with the fresh herbs, toss, and serve.

Pasta Jambalaya

Chef J.P. Gelinas
Big Daddy's Restaurant
Massapequa, New York

Serves 4

1 pound linguine, cooked until al dente, *drained well, and kept warm*

Dry Seasoning Mix
1 teaspoon dried basil
1 teaspoon dried thyme
¹/₂ teaspoon cayenne pepper
¹/₂ teaspoon freshly ground black pepper
¹/₄ teaspoon kosher salt
¹/₄ teaspoon ground white pepper

2 egg yolks
1 cup heavy cream
¹/₄ cup unsalted butter
¹/₄ cup chopped celery
¹/₄ cup chopped onion
¹/₄ pound tasso, coarsely chopped
¹/₄ pound andouille *sausage, coarsely chopped*
6 jumbo shrimp, peeled, deveined, and coarsely chopped
3 tablespoons Madeira wine
¹/₄ cup freshly grated Romano cheese
Coarsely chopped fresh basil

Make the dry seasoning mix: In a bowl, combine all the dry seasoning mix ingredients and set aside.

Place the egg yolks in a medium bowl, add the cream, and whisk until frothy. Set aside.

In a large skillet, melt the butter over high heat. Add the celery, onion, tasso, and *andouille* and cook until the onion turns translucent, scraping the bottom of the skillet from time to time. Add the shrimp and dry seasoning mix, stirring well. Deglaze pan with the wine. Cook for 2 minutes. With the heat still on high, add the egg/cream mixture and heat through for a minute or so before adding the cheese. Stir well and cook for 1 minute.

Add the linguine, tossing it and scraping the bottom of the skillet thoroughly. Reduce the heat to low and simmer the pasta for 2 minutes. Serve in heated bowls, garnished with basil, with hunks of cornbread, if desired.

Farfalle with Turkey, Beef, and Mushroom Meatballs

Serves 6

Tomato Sauce

1 teaspoon olive oil
1 onion, chopped
2 cloves garlic, chopped
Two 28-ounce cans Italian plum tomatoes
One 6-ounce can tomato paste
$1/2$ teaspoon dried basil
$1/2$ teaspoon dried oregano
$1/2$ teaspoon dried thyme
2 bay leaves
Salt and freshly ground pepper to taste

Meatballs

1 teaspoon butter
$1/2$ pound fresh mushrooms, chopped
$1/2$ pound ground turkey
$1/2$ pound extra-lean ground beef
1 cup fresh whole-wheat bread crumbs
   (about 2 slices)
2 large egg whites
$1/4$ cup freshly grated Asiago cheese
1 teaspoon dried oregano
1 teaspoon dried basil
$1/2$ teaspoon salt
$1/4$ teaspoon freshly grated pepper
1 teaspoon olive oil

1 pound farfalle

Make the sauce: In a food processor or blender, purée the tomatoes.

In a large, deep skillet, heat the oil over medium heat. Add the onion and garlic and cook until soft. Add the tomatoes and tomato paste and bring to a simmer over medium-high heat. Stir in the basil, oregano, thyme, and bay leaves. Add salt and pepper to taste. Reduce the heat to very low and let the sauce simmer slowly for 30 minutes, stirring often to prevent burning on the bottom.

While sauce is simmering, make the meatballs: In a small saucepan, melt 1 teaspoon butter over medium heat. Add the mushrooms and sauté until soft. Drain and chop fine.

In a medium bowl, combine the mushrooms, ground turkey, ground beef, bread crumbs, egg whites, Asiago cheese, oregano, basil, salt, and pepper. Mix well with hands. Form into about thirty 1-inch balls.

In a large, deep skillet, heat the olive oil over medium heat. Add half the meatballs and brown on all sides. Spoon into tomato sauce. Repeat with the remaining meatballs and add to sauce.

Meanwhile, in a large pot, bring at least 4 quarts of water to a rolling boil. Add 1 tablespoon of salt. Add the farfalle, stirring to prevent sticking. Cook until *al dente*. Drain.

Transfer the pasta to a large warm serving bowl. Remove the bay leaves from the sauce. Pour the sauce over the pasta, toss, and serve.

CHAPTER 10

OCEAN ABUNDANCE: PASTA AND SEAFOOD

Linguine with white clam sauce (see Chapter 4) is a wonderful dish, blending the perfume of the sea with the earthy fragrance of garlic. But it is only the beginning. Virtually any type of seafood can share a recipe with pasta. Oriental cultures have been doing it for centuries. Italians use the *frutti di mare*, fruits from the sea, with nearly all of the famous sauces—garlic and oil, tomato, béchamel, and pesto. Beyond the basic sauces, seafood appears here with eggplant and wild mushrooms, cabbage and spinach, goat cheese, and even pistachios. Salmon, tuna, shrimp, crawfish, calamari, clams, mussels, and even caviar nestle in raviolis, cling among the curls of fusilli, and rest on strands of vermicelli.

Smoked Salmon and Dill in Cream Sauce with Angel Hair Pasta

Serves 4

2 cups heavy cream
1 cup milk
2 tablespoons chopped fresh dill
1/2 cup chopped scallions
2 teaspoons grated lemon zest
3 tablespoons capers, drained
Salt and freshly ground pepper to taste
1 pound angel hair pasta
6 ounces thinly sliced smoked salmon,
    cut into thin strips

Combine the cream, milk, dill, scallions, and lemon zest in heavy-bottomed saucepan. Bring to a boil over medium-high heat. Reduce to a simmer and cook briefly until thickened. Stir in the capers. Season with salt and pepper.

Meanwhile, in a large pot, bring at least 4 quarts of water to a rolling boil. Add 1 tablespoon salt. Add the pasta, stir to separate, and cook until *al dente*. Drain. Transfer the pasta to a large, warm bowl. Pour the sauce over it and toss to coat. Add the smoked salmon and toss again to combine. Serve.

Linguine Saporiti

Chef Ricardo Tognozzi
Ristorante La Bussola
Coral Gables, Florida

Serves 8

3 tablespoons olive oil
5 cloves garlic, chopped
2 shallots, chopped

10 anchovy fillets
1 pound shrimp, peeled, deveined, and
    cut into big pieces
1 bunch fresh basil, chopped
1 bunch parsley, chopped
Pinch of peperoncino or dried hot red
    pepper flakes
6 red bell peppers, seeded and sliced
2 tablespoons capers, drained
2 tablespoons pitted black olives
    (preferably Greek Kalamata)
$^{1}/_{2}$ cup white wine
6 tomatoes, peeled, seeded, and finely
    chopped
Salt and freshly ground pepper to taste
2 pounds fresh linguine

In a large saucepan combine the olive oil, garlic, shallots, and anchovies over medium heat. Sauté until the garlic starts to brown, then add the shrimp, basil, parsley, peperoncino, bell peppers, capers, and olives. Sauté for 5 minutes, then add the white wine and cook until it evaporates. Add the tomatoes and cook until heated through. Season with salt and pepper.

Meanwhile, in a large pot, bring at least 4 quarters of water to a rolling boil. Add 1 tablespoon salt. Add the linguine, stirring to separate, and cook until *al dente*. Drain.

Transfer the pasta to a large bowl. Pour the sauce over the pasta and toss well.

Prawns Sambuca

Co-owner, Chef Bert P. Cutino
Sardine Factory Restaurant
Monterey, California

Serves 4

$^{3}/_{4}$ pound angel hair pasta
$^{1}/_{2}$ cup olive oil
1 tablespoon chopped garlic
1 tablespoon chopped shallot
16 fresh large prawns, peeled and deveined
6 tablespoons dry white wine
$^{1}/_{4}$ cup Sambuca liqueur
$^{1}/_{4}$ cup tomato, peeled, seeded, and diced
1 tablespoon finely chopped fresh tarragon,
    plus whole leaves for garnish
2 teaspoons salt
Freshly ground pepper to taste
$^{1}/_{2}$ cup unsalted butter, cut into pieces

Meanwhile, in a sauté pan, heat the olive oil, add the garlic, shallots, and prawns. Cook over medium heat until fragrant, 1 to 2 minutes. Add the wine and Sambuca and ignite with a match to flambé.

When the flame dies, add the tomato, tarragon, salt and pepper and cook for 2 more minutes. Add the butter and reduce until the sauce is slightly thickened.

In a large pot, bring at least 4 quarts of water to a rolling boil. Add 1 tablespoon salt. Add pasta, stir to separate, and cook until *al dente*.

(continued)

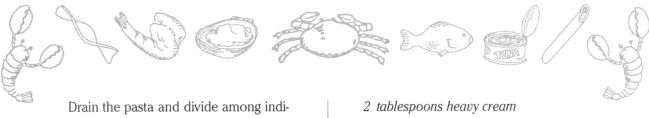

Drain the pasta and divide among individual plates. Spoon on equal amount of the sauce over each serving. Garnish with tarragon leaf.

Ravioli of Salmon with Cabbage and Caviar

Chef David Waltuck
Chanterelle
New York, New York

Serves 4

> 1 pound pasta dough (see Chapter 3 for making dough, and shaping and cooking ravioli)

Sauce
1 cup smoked salmon stock or fish stock
Squirt of fresh lemon juice
1 cup heavy cream
$\frac{1}{2}$ head savoy cabbage, finely shredded
1 tablespoon mixed chopped fresh dill and chives
2 ounces black caviar (American or osetra)

Filling
1 pound salmon filet, skinned
1 tablespoon chopped shallots
Squirt of fresh lemon juice

2 tablespoons heavy cream
2 tablespoons fine dried bread crumbs
Salt and freshly ground pepper to taste

Make the filling: Mash the salmon into a fine texture and place it in a bowl. Add the shallots, lemon, cream, salt and pepper, and bread crumbs and mix well. Taste and adjust seasonings.

Make the sauce: In a saucepan, bring the stock to a boil over high heat. Lower the heat to simmer and cook until reduced by half. Add the lemon juice and cream. Continue to simmer until lightly thickened. Add the cabbage and cook until it is wilted, about 1 minute. Add the herbs.

Make the ravioli: Roll out the pasta dough and shape ravioli as described in Chapter 3.

Cook the ravioli: Bring a large pot of water to a rolling boil. Add 1 tablespoon of salt. Drop the pieces in one at a time and stir to separate. Do not cook too many at one time. Two minutes after the ravioli float to the top, test for doneness. Remove one with a slotted spoon and cut off an edge with a fork. When done, it will cut off easily. The total cooking time should be about 5 minutes.

Lift the ravioli out of the water with a slotted spoon and place on individual plates, dividing equally. Pout the sauce over and around each portion. Garnish with black caviar.

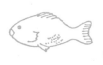

A Craving for Crawfish

The crayfish, or crawfish as it is known in the United States, tends to be a southern regional specialty in America, but a popular favorite throughout the world. Species and subspecies of these little lobsterlike creatures swim in fresh waters all over the globe. They have been a source of food in Europe for centuries, and are the *pièce de résistance* of the *krebfests* of Sweden, where heaping platters of hot crayfish are devoured like so much finger food. In America, they are most beloved in Louisiana, where Creole or Cajun cooking works down-home miracles with the shellfish. Their size varies, but, generally, ten crawfish in the shell weigh about one pound, which yields about three-quarters of a pound of meat. Produced by the ton and raised in Louisiana, Mississippi, California, and Wisconsin, crawfish may still be hard to find in your local fish market. Small shrimp can be used as a substitute.

Soft-Shell Crabs Over Angel Hair Pasta

Chef William Liebhart
The Bayou
Bellmore, New York

Serves 2

> 4 soft-shell-crabs
> 1 cup all-purpose flour
> ½ cup clarified butter
> 1 tablespoon minced garlic
> 1 teaspoon minced jalapeño chili pepper
> 1 bunch scallions, white parts chopped and green tops reserved
> 6 plum tomatoes, peeled, seeded, and chopped
> ½ teaspoon salt
> ½ teaspoon freshly ground pepper
> ½ teaspoon dried basil
> ½ teaspoon dried oregano
> ½ teaspoon dried tarragon
> Pinch of dried thyme
> 1 pound frozen crawfish tails, thawed
> 2 cups seafood stock or bottled clam juice
> ¾ cups white wine
> 2 tablespoons chopped fresh parsley
> 1 pound angel hair pasta

First, clean the crabs: Rinse the crabs with cold water to remove the sand. With scissors, snip off the feathery fronds from under both sides and snip off the facial area and tail apron. (Alternatively, ask your fishmonger to

(continued)

clean the crabs for you.) Pat the crabs dry and dust lightly with the flour, tapping off the excess.

To clarify the butter, melt the butter over low heat. Remove from the heat and let stand 5 minutes. Skim off the white butterfat that rises to the top. Pour off the clear liquid, which is the clarified butter.

In a large sauté pan, heat the clarified butter over medium heat. Add the crabs and cook until golden brown on the first side. Turn over and cook for 1 minute. Then add garlic, jalapeño, and white parts of scallions. Swirl the pan to mix the ingredients and cook down for 2 minutes. Add the tomatoes and all the seasonings, except parsley, and continue to swirl the pan, cooking for 2 minutes longer. Add the white wine and stir to deglaze the pan. Add the crawfish and cook down for 2 minutes. Add the seafood stock and cook over low heat until the sauce reduces slightly. Chop the reserved scallion tops and add to pan along with the parsley.

Meanwhile, in a large pot, bring at least 4 quarts of water to a rolling boil. Add 1 tablespoon salt. Add the pasta, stir to separate, and cook until *al dente.* Drain.

Divide the pasta among 2 plates. Place 1 crab onto each mound of pasta and spoon the sauce evenly over the top. Soft shell crabs are usually served 2 per entree. You will need less pasta for 2 servings.

Tomato Linguine with Jumbo Shrimp, Scallops, Diced Leeks, Feta Cheese, and Saffron Cream

Chef J.M. Matos
Adams Mark Hotels
Houston, Texas

Serves 8

2 pounds tomato linguine
½ cup extra virgin olive oil
32 medium shrimp, peeled and deveined
32 sea scallops
4 leeks, cleaned and diced
2 tablespoons chopped garlic
2 tablespoons chopped shallots
2 tablespoons saffron
½ cup dry white wine
¾ pound feta cheese, crumbled
4 cups (1 quart) heavy cream
Salt and freshly ground pepper to taste

In a large pot, bring at least 4 quarts of water to a rolling boil. Add 1 tablespoon salt. Add the pasta, stir to separate, and cook until not quite *al dente*. Drain and set aside.

In a large sauté pan heat the oil over medium heat until it is hot. Add the shrimp, scallops, leeks, garlic, shallots, and saffron and sauté for 3 to 4 minutes. With a slotted spoon, remove the seafood and set aside. Add the wine and deglaze the pan, stirring to scrape up the browned bits and slightly

reduce the sauce. Add the feta cheese, reserved pasta, and cream and return the seafood to the pan. Toss all ingredients for about 2 minutes more, then season with salt and pepper. Serve immediately.

Spaghetti with Clams, Asparagus, and Pancetta

Chef Tony Mantuano
Tuttaposto
Chicago, Illinois

Serves 4

1 pound spaghetti
¼ cup olive oil
2 ounces pancetta, *diced*
2 tablespoons sliced garlic
2 cups trimmed and chopped asparagus
16 Manila clams, well scrubbed
1 teaspoon red pepper flakes
¾ cup shrimp or chicken stock
1 teaspoon dried oregano
¼ cup chopped flat-leaf parsley, plus 4
*   sprigs for garnish*
6 tablespoons dry white wine
Salt and freshly ground pepper to taste

In a large pot, bring at least 4 quarts of water to a rolling boil. Add 1 tablespoon salt. Add the pasta, stir to separate, and cook until not quite *al dente*.

Meanwhile, in saucepan large enough to accommodate all the ingredients, heat the olive oil over medium heat. Add the *pancetta* and cook for 1 minute. Add the garlic and asparagus, and sauté for 2 minutes, being careful not to burn. Add the clams and red pepper flakes and sauté over medium heat for 1 minute. Add the stock, oregano, chopped parsley, wine, salt, and pepper. Cover and raise the heat to high. Cook until the clams open, 3 to 4 minutes. Using a slotted spoon, remove the clams from the sauce and cover to keep warm; discard any that did not open.

Drain the pasta and add the sauce in the pan. Simmer together for 1 to 2 minutes. Divide the pasta and sauce among 4 individual plates. Garnish with the reserved clams and the parsley sprigs.

Spaghetti with Calamari in a Garlic, Pepper, and Spicy Olive Oil Sauce

Chef Louis Lindic
Treehouse Restaurant
Atlanta, Georgia

Serves 4

½ cup quality olive oil
3 cloves garlic, minced
½ red onion, sliced crosswise

(continued)

Salt
2 hot banana peppers, sliced into rings
¼ cup pepper olive oil
1 pound spaghetti or spaghettini
1¼ pounds calamari (squid), bodies cut into ½-inch-wide rings and tentacles left whole
¼ cup flat-leaf parsley, finely chopped
Juice of 1 lemon
Freshly ground pepper to taste

In a skillet, heat ¼ cup of the olive oil over low heat. Add the garlic and onion, salt lightly, and cook until softened, about 5 minutes. Add the banana peppers and cook for another 2 minutes. Set the pan aside.

In a large pot, bring at least 4 quarts of water to a rolling boil. Add 1 tablespoon salt.

Meanwhile, place the pepper oil and the remaining ¼ cup olive oil in a pan large enough to accommodate all the ingredients, including the pasta. Heat the oils over medium heat. At the same time, add the pasta to the boiling water, stir to separate, and cook until *al dente*. While the pasta is cooking, add the calamari to the oil and fry quickly for 1 minute. Add the garlic mixture to the calamari and turn off the heat. (There will be enough heat remaining to heat the ingredients and finish cooking the calamari.

As soon as the pasta is ready, drain quickly and thoroughly and add to the pan holding the calamari.) Mix gently. Transfer to a warm platter and sprinkle with the lemon juice and parsley.

Lemon Linguine with Rock Shrimp, Bay Scallops, Snap Peas, Plum Tomatoes with Goat Cheese and Peppered Vodka Sauce

Chef John Dubrick
Bravissimo
Chicago, Illinois

Serves 4 to 6

1 pound lemon linguine
¼ cup rock shrimp
¼ cup bay scallops
¼ cup plum tomato, peeled, seeded, and chopped
1 tablespoon fresh parsley, chopped
1 tablespoon garlic, minced
¼ cup snap peas
⅓ cup goat cheese, crumbled
⅓ cup peppered vodka
1 tablespoon fresh basil, chopped
Salt and freshly ground pepper to taste

In a large pot, bring at least 4 quarts of water to a rolling boil. Add 1 tablespoon salt. Add the pasta, stir to separate, and cook until *al dente*. Drain.

Meanwhile, in a skillet, heat the olive oil over medium heat. Add the garlic and sauté until lightly browned, about 3 minutes. Add the shrimp, scallops, tomato, parsley, and basil. Cook for 1 minute. Add the snap peas,

goat cheese, and vodka. Be careful, as the vodka may flame up.

Add the cooked pasta to the sauce. Toss to coat and serve.

Lobster with Spinach Fettuccine

Chef Horst Pfeifer
Bella Luna
New Orleans, Louisiana

Serves 1

1 lobster (steamed and broken from shell)
1/4 cup chicken stock
2 teaspoons chopped fresh basil
1 teaspoon chives
3 tablespoons peeled and diced tomato
3 ounces spinach fettuccine
2 teaspoons freshly grated Parmesan
  cheese
2 teaspoons freshly grated Asiago cheese

Place a colander or rack in the bottom of a large, deep kettle. Put 1½" of water in the bottom. Cover tightly. Bring the water to a boil over high heat. Place the lobster on the rack. Reduce heat to simmer water and produce steam. Steam for 15 minutes. Remove lobster, cool, break shell, and remove the meat.

In a saucepan, combine the chicken stock, lobster pieces, 1 teaspoon of the basil, chives,

and tomato over medium heat. Bring to a gentle boil. Make sure it doesn't boil hard, or the lobster will get tough. Cook for 2 minutes, just to combine.

In a pot, bring at least 2 quarts of water to a boil. Add 1½ teaspoons salt. Add the pasta, stir to separate, and cook until *al dente*.

Drain the pasta and add to the saucepan holding the lobster. Add 1 teaspoon of each of the cheeses and mix together. Transfer the entire mixture to a bowl and garnish with the remaining cheese and teaspoon of basil.

Ink Fettuccine with Calamari and Porcini Mushrooms Baked in Parchment Paper

Chef Fabrice Beaudoin
Picasso
The Lodge at Cordillera
Edwards, Colorado

Serves 4

1/2 pound calamari (squid) bodies and
  tentacles
3 cups chicken stock
1 cup white wine
1/4 pound dried ink fettuccine
1/4 cup virgin olive oil

(continued)

2 shallots, chopped

3 cloves garlic, chopped

*¹/₄ pound fresh porcini or chanterelle
mushrooms, sliced*

Salt and freshly ground pepper to taste

*8 plum tomatoes, peeled, seeded, and cut
in half*

¹/₄ cup flat-leaf parsley leaves

2 tablespoons white truffle oil

Preheat the oven to 380°.

Rinse the calamari under cool running
water. Separate the tubes from the tentacles
and remove the beak from the head. Rinse
the tubes thoroughly. Dry with paper towels.
Slice the calamari into rings.

Combine the stock and wine in the
saucepan and bring to a boil. Add the calamari and cook for 2 minutes. Using a slotted
spoon, remove the calamari from the broth
and set aside to cool. Bring the calamari
broth to a boil, add the pasta, and cook until
al dente. Drain and set aside.

In a large sauté pan, heat the olive oil
over medium heat. Add the shallots, garlic,
and mushrooms and sauté for 1 minute. Add
the calamari and cook for 2 minutes. Add the
salt, pepper, tomatoes, and parsley. Stir well
and place in a large bowl. Add the pasta and
the white truffle oil. Mix together.

Cut out 4 parchment-paper hearts, each
16 by 14 inches. Place an equal amount of
the pasta mixture on one-half of each heart.
Fold over other half and crimp together along
the edges to seal securely. Place on a baking
sheet and bake until the paper is light brown,
about 12 minutes. Serve immediately on hot
plates. Let your guests open the packets.

Pasta Quills with Beluga Caviar and Chives

Chef Theo Schoenegger
SANDOMENICO
New York, New York

Serves 4

1 pound pasta dough (see Chapter 3)

1 cup extra virgin olive oil

2 shallots, finely minced

1 medium potato, peeled and diced

2 cups chicken stock

Salt and freshly ground pepper to taste

¹/₄ cup fresh chives

2 ounces Beluga caviar

Roll out the pasta dough very thinly and
cut into 1-inch squares. Starting in a corner,
roll up each square to form a quill (see
Chapter 3).

In a large pot, bring at least 4 quarts
water to a rolling boil. Add 1 tablespoon of
salt. Add the pasta, stir to separate, and cook
for 1 minute. Drain.

Meanwhile, in a saucepan, heat the olive
oil over medium heat. Add the shallots and
potato and simmer until the shallots are

translucent, about 3 minutes. Add the chicken stock and season with salt and pepper. Cook for 10 minutes. In a blender or food processor, blend the sauce well. Return to the pan.

Add the well-drained pasta to the sauce. Cook the pasta in the sauce for 1 minute, stirring frequently.

Transfer to a warmed serving bowl and sprinkle with the chives. Garnish with the caviar.

Orecchiette Alla Rosa

Chef William Crego
Milford, Connecticut

Serves 4

1 pound orecchiette pasta
¹/₄ cup pine nuts
2 tablespoons unsalted butter
¹/₂ pound smoked salmon, cut into
    ¹/₄-inch-wide strips
5 plum tomatoes, cut into ¹/₄-inch chunks
3 shallots, finely chopped
2 cloves garlic, finely chopped
1 tablespoon finely chopped parsley
2¹/₄ cups tomato sauce
2 cups heavy cream
Salt and freshly ground pepper to taste
1 pound spinach, cleaned and stems
    removed
¹/₄ cup chopped fresh basil

Preheat the oven to 400°. Toast the pine nuts in the oven until lightly browned, watch them (do not burn them) about 3 minutes. In a large sauté pan or saucepan, melt the butter over medium heat. Add the pine nuts, smoked salmon, tomatoes, shallots, garlic, and parsley. Sauté for 2 minutes. Add the tomato sauce and heavy cream, stir together, and bring to a boil. Reduce the heat to low and simmer until the sauce thickens, about 15 minutes. Season with salt and pepper.

Meanwhile, in a large pot, bring at least 4 quarts of water to a rolling boil. Add 1 tablespoon salt. Add the pasta, stir to separate, and cook until *al dente*. Drain.

Transfer the pasta to a warm bowl. Add the sauce and toss well. Divide the spinach among 4 individual plates and spoon the pasta atop it. Garnish with the basil.

Linguine alla Pescatore

Owner Tony Vallone
Tony's • Anthony's • Grotto • La Griglia
Houston, Texas

Serves 4

¹/₄ cup olive oil
4 teaspoons chopped garlic
8 clams, well scrubbed
¹/₂ cup dry white wine

(continued)

8 jumbo shrimp, peeled and deveined
1 cup sliced calamari or squid with tentacles
8 mussels in shell, well scrubbed and debearded
1 cup crab claws
Salt and freshly ground pepper to taste
1 teaspoon oregano
1 teaspoon dried hot red pepper flakes
2 cups marinara sauce (see red wine marinara sauce, Chapter 4)
1 pound linguine
1 tablespoon chopped flat-leaf parsley

In a large skillet, heat the oil over medium heat. Add the garlic, clams, and wine, cover, and steam until the clams open, 3 to 5 minutes. Discard any that do not open. Add the remaining seafood, the salt, pepper, oregano, and red pepper flakes and sauté for 2 to 3 minutes. Add the marinara sauce and cook for another 3 minutes, or until the shrimp is opaque and the mussels open.

Meanwhile, in a large pot, bring at least 4 quarts water to a rolling boil. Add 1 tablespoon salt. Add the pasta, stir to separate, and cook until *al dente*.

Stir the parsley into the sauce. Drain the pasta, place in a warm serving bowl, and pour the sauce over the top.

Cannelloni with Salmon and Tomato Cream Sauce

Serves 6

10-ounce package frozen, chopped spinach, thawed and drained
One 16-ounce container ricotta cheese
1 1/2 pounds salmon fillet
1 cup dry white wine
1/2 cup chicken stock
2 cloves garlic, sliced
Salt and ground pepper to taste
4 tablespoons unsalted butter
2 medium tomatoes peeled, seeded, and chopped
2 cups medium cream
2 tablespoons tomato paste
1 pound fresh pasta sheets or 1 package cannelloni (12 pieces)
1 egg, lightly beaten
1/4 cup freshly grated Parmesan cheese
Note: pasta sheets can be bought in stores where fresh pasta is sold. (Or see Chapter 3 for detailed directions.)

Place the salmon in a large skillet. Pour the wine and chicken stock over the over the fish and add the garlic slices. Bring liquid to a boil over high heat. Reduce heat to a simmer and cover. Poach the salmon until pale pink and just cooked through. Cool. Break up the salmon into flakes. There should be about 2 cups.

To make the filling: In a large bowl, combine the spinach, ricotta, and salmon. Salt and pepper to taste. Set aside.

To make the sauce: Melt the butter over medium heat. Add the tomato and sauté 1 minute. Add the cream and tomato paste, stir, and bring to a boil. Reduce the heat and simmer until the liquid is reduced by one-third. Set aside.

To make the cannelloni: Preheat the oven to 350°. Lightly grease a baking dish. Cut the pasta sheets into twelve 5 x 6-inch rectangles. Brush with egg. Place fish filling on the longer edge. Roll and overlap the edges, placing seam side down on the baking dish. Pour tomato sauce over and sprinkle with Parmesan.

Note: If using dried cannelloni, cook them in boiling, salted water until less than *al dente*. Drain and fill.

Bake 20 to 30 minutes until the sauce is bubbling and the cheese golden. Serve.

Spirals with Shrimp and Artichokes

Serves 4

2 packages frozen artichoke hearts
48 large shrimp peeled and deveined
2 egg yolks
1 cup extra virgin olive oil
1/2 cup peanut oil

1/2 cup wine vinegar
4 tablespoons Dijon mustard
1/4 cup chopped fresh parsley
1/4 cup scallions, sliced, including green parts
2 tablespoons minced shallots
Salt and freshly ground black pepper to taste
3/4 pound shells

Cook the artichokes according to package directions. Drain well.

Bring 4 quarts of water to boil. Add 1 tablespoon of salt. Add shrimp all at once. When the water returns to a boil, cook only until shrimp turn pink, less than 5 minutes, depending on size of shrimp. Drain.

Place olive and peanut oils, vinegar, and mustard in a mixing bowl. Beat with a wisk to blend. Stir in parsley, scallions, and shallots. Add salt and pepper to taste.

Place shrimp and artichokes in a large bowl. Pour sauce over to cover. Reserve some sauce. Refrigerate to marinate for at least 2 hours or overnight.

When ready to serve, bring at least 4 quarts of water to a rolling boil. Add 1 tablespoon of salt. Cook pasta until *al dente*. Drain.

Transfer to a large serving bowl. Pour shrimp and artichoke mixture over pasta. Add reserved sauce and toss. Serve cold or at room temperature. The shrimp and artichoke mixture can be added to the pasta ahead of time, but the reserved sauce should be added only just before serving.

Crabmeat Fettuccine Primavera

Chef Julia Richardson
Great Beginnings
Monroe, Michigan

Serves 4 to 6

½ cup thinly sliced carrot
1 cup unsalted butter
½ cup diced celery
½ cup diced onion
1 cup chopped broccoli florets
1 cup sliced fresh mushrooms
1 pound dried fettuccine
Two 8-ounce packages imitation crabmeat
Salt and freshly ground pepper to taste

Sauce
1 cup unsalted butter
1 cup all-purpose flour
3 cups chicken stock
1 cup freshly grated Parmesan cheese
½ teaspoon salt (optional)

In a saucepan, combine the carrots with water to cover. Bring to a boil and cook until the carrots are tender-crisp, about 10 minutes. Drain and set aside. In a large skillet, melt ½ cup of the butter over medium heat. Add the celery and onion and sauté until the vegetables are tender, about 5 minutes. Add the drained carrots to the skillet holding the sautéed vegetables, and

add the remaining ½ cup butter. When the butter is melted, add the broccoli florets and mushrooms and sauté for 3 minutes. Toss in the imitation crabmeat and sauté for 2 minutes more, or until heated through.

At the same time, make the sauce: In a saucepan, melt the butter. Whisk in the flour, stirring constantly until well blended. Slowly whisk in the chicken stock, and cook until thickened. Stir in the Parmesan cheese and salt.

Meanwhile, in a large pot, bring at least 4 quarts of water to a rolling boil. Add 1 teaspoon salt. Add the pasta, stir to separate the strands, and cook until *al dente*.

Drain the pasta and place in a warm bowl. Add the crabmeat mixture and toss to mix. Spoon the sauce over the top, then sprinkle with the Parmesan cheese, if desired.

Lobster and Vegetable Stew

Chef Bradley Ogden
The Lark Creek Inn
Larkspur, California

Serves 6

3 live lobsters, about 1¼ pounds each
2 tablespoons kosher salt, plus salt to taste
5 cups lobster stock (see below)
¼ cup olive oil
1 cup diced fennel

1 cup diced onion

1 cup peeled and diced tomato

Freshly ground pepper to taste

*Basic pasta dough, rolled and cut into
    ¹/₂-inch-wide noodles (see Chapter 3)*

*1 bunch spinach, rinsed, stems removed,
    and coarsely chopped*

2 tablespoons unsalted butter, softened

1 tablespoon chopped fresh tarragon

1 tablespoon chopped flat-leaf parsley

Stock

¹/₈ teaspoon saffron threads

¹/₂ cup dry white wine

Reserved lobster shells

1 onion chopped

2 carrots, chopped

2 celery stalks, chopped

1 bay leaf

5 cups water

To kill the lobsters, insert the tip of a heavy sharp knife into the head of each lobster, between the eyes. Pull off the claws by twisting where they are attached to the body. Twist off the tails where they join the body. Lift the back shells from the bodies and reach into the head cavity to remove the small sand sack (stomach). Rinse the back shells and the bodies to remove the tomalley and reserve the shells for the stock.

Bring a large pot with 2 gallons water to a rolling boil. Add the 2 tablespoons salt and the lobster tails and claws. Cover the pot and start timing after the water returns to the boil. After 6 minutes, remove the claws and plunge them into a large bowl of ice water. After 3 more minutes, remove the tails and add them to the claws in the ice water. When the claws and tails are cool, remove and drain.

Crack the tails and claws and remove the meat. Wrap the meat in plastic wrap and refrigerate.

Prepare the stock using the reserved body shells and the shells from the tails and claws. Add all the vegetables and the bay leaf to 5 cups of water. Bring to a boil. Cover and simmer for 15 minutes.

In a small bowl, soak the saffron threads in the wine for several minutes. Add the saffron and wine to the stock, stir, and boil briefly. Set aside.

Make the noodles according to instructions in Chapter 3. Cover with damp kitchen towel until ready to use.

In a large sauté pan, heat the olive oil over medium heat. Add the fennel and onion and cook until the onion is translucent, about 5 minutes. Add the lobster stock and tomato and simmer until the vegetables are tender, about 5 minutes. Be careful not to overcook the vegetables. Season with salt and pepper and set aside or refrigerate.

Bring 4 quarts of water to a rolling boil. Add 1 tablespoon of salt. Add noodles and cook *very* briefly until less than *al dente*. Fresh noodles will cook in 1 or 2 minutes. Drain.

(continued)

When ready to serve, reheat the lobster-vegetable broth to a simmer. Add the spinach and simmer for 2 minutes. Slice the lobster tails and coarsely chop the claws and knuckles. Add the meat to the broth. Swirl in the butter and the tarragon and parsley. Add the cooked noodles and simmer for 2 minutes to heat the noodles and lobster meat. Serve immediately in warm bowls.

Shrimp Orecchiette Genovese

Chef John Jones
Difiore Ristorante
Hartford, Connecticut

Serves 1

6 medium shrimp, peeled and deveined
1/4 cup flour
2 tablespoons extra virgin olive oil
1 large shallot, minced
1/2 hot frying pepper, julienned
1 tablespoon garlic, minced
1/2 cup dry white wine
1 tablespoon mascarpone cheese
1/4 cup freshly grated Romano cheese
1 tablespoon unsalted butter
1 tablespoon pesto (see Genovese basil pesto, Chapter 4)
1/4 cup heavy cream
6 ounces orecchiette

Dust the shrimp with the flour. In a sauté pan, heat the olive oil over medium heat. Add the shallot, hot peppers, and shrimp and sauté until shrimp is pink, about 3 to 5 minutes. Add the chili pepper, garlic, and wine and let simmer for 2 to 3 minutes. Stir in the mascarpone cheese, Romano cheese, butter, pesto, and heavy cream.

Meanwhile, in a large pot, bring at least 4 quarts of water to a rolling boil. Add 1 tablespoon salt. Add the pasta, stir to separate, and cook until *al dente*.

Drain the pasta. Bring the sauce to a gentle boil and add the pasta. Toss to mix, then transfer to a bowl to serve.

Spicy Sun-Dried Tomato Pesto with Shrimp and Scallops

Chef Robert Boone
Stephens
An American Café
Albuquerque, New Mexico

Serves 4

1/2 cup sun-dried tomatoes, chopped coarsley
2 chipotle chili peppers
3 cloves garlic
2 tablespoons chopped fresh basil

1/4 cup pine nuts
6 tablespoons olive oil
12 large shrimp, peeled and deveined
12 sea scallops
1/2 pound fresh mushrooms, sliced
1 yellow bell pepper, seeded
    and julienned
1/2 cup heavy cream
1 1/4 pounds fettuccine
1 bunch scallions, sliced on the diagonal
1/2 cup freshly grated Parmesan cheese

In a food processor, combine the sun-dried tomatoes, *chipotle* pepper, garlic, basil, pine nuts, and 4 tablespoons of the olive oil. Process until smooth to make a pesto; set aside.

In a sauté pan, heat the remaining 2 tablespoons olive oil over medium heat. Add the shrimp, scallops, mushrooms, and bell pepper. Cook until the shrimp are bright pink and the scallops begin to split apart, about 5 minutes. Add the pesto and cream and bring just to a boil. Reduce the heat and simmer for 1 to 2 minutes.

Meanwhile, in a large pot, bring at least 4 quarts of water to a rolling boil. Add 1 tablespoon salt. Add the pasta, stir to separate, and cook until *al dente*.

Drain the pasta and divide among 4 individual plates. Spoon the seafood-pesto mixture over the pasta and top with the scallions and Parmesan cheese.

Auntie Sugar's Rock Shrimp and Langostino Marinara

Thomas Ingalls C.E.C.
Director, Research and Development
    Department
Statler Commissary, State University
    of New York at Buffalo
Buffalo, New York

Serves 4

Tom's Basil Marinara
1/4 cup extra virgin olive oil
4 large onions, finely diced
5 cloves garlic, minced
Red wine, to taste
1 cup rich chicken stock (optional),
    base or bouillion can be substituted
3 quarts crushed fresh tomatoes
20 fresh basil leaves, chopped or
    1/4 cup dried basil
Pinch of brown sugar
2 cups tomato paste

Seafood
1 tablespoon butter
3 tablespoons olive oil
2 cloves garlic, minced
8 fresh basil leaves, chopped
1 tablespoon fresh parsley, chopped
1/2 cup white wine
2 tablespoons fresh lime juice

(continued)

Freshly ground pepper to taste
1 cup rock shrimp
1 cup langostino meat (Chilean mini
lobster tails)
1 pound dried capellini or vermicelli

First, make the marinara: In a skillet, heat the olive oil over medium heat. Add the onions and sauté for 3 minutes. Add the garlic and wine and continue to cook for 5 minutes. Add the stock, if desired, the tomatoes, basil, and sugar. Simmer over low heat for 1 hour. Leftover sauce is excellent to freeze.

In a large sauté pan, heat the olive oil and butter over medium heat. Add the garlic, basil, parsley, wine, lime juice, and pepper and sauté for 3 minutes to develop the flavors. Add the shrimp and langostinos and cook until light pink, about 3 to 5 minutes. Add 5 cups of the marinara sauce. Heat through so that the flavors can blossom.

Meanwhile, in a large pot, bring at least 4 quarts water to a rolling boil. Add 1 table-spoon salt. Add the pasta, stir to separate, and cook until *al dente*. Drain.

Drain the pasta and place in a warm bowl. Add the sauce and toss well.

Shrimp and Shiitake Dijonaise

Chef Robert Boone
Stephens
An American Café
Albuquerque, New Mexico

Serves 4

½ cup finely shredded spinach
1½ pounds tortiglioni
2 cups freshly grated Parmesan cheese
¼ cup clarified butter (see Clarified Butter)
20 large shrimp, peeled and deveined
1 cup fresh shiitake mushrooms, sliced
2 tablespoons minced shallot
1½ tablespoons minced garlic
¼ cup dry white wine
2 tablespoons Dijon-style mustard
1 cup heavy cream
Salt and freshly ground pepper to taste

In a sauté pan, melt the butter over medium heat. Add the shrimp, mushrooms, shallot, and garlic and sauté until the shrimp are bright pink, about 3 minutes. Add the wine and deglaze the pan, stirring to scrape up any browned bits. Add the mustard and cream and reduce the cream by one-half. Season with salt and pepper.

In a large pot, bring at least 4 quarts water to a rolling boil. Add 1 tablespoon salt. Add the pasta, stir to separate, and cook until *al dente*.

Drain the pasta and divide among 4 bowls. Arrange the shrimp mixture over the pasta. Top with the Parmesan and the spinach.

Note: The shrimp will not be cooked all the way through after sautéing, but will finish while the cream reduced. If using smaller shrimp, remove them from the sauté pan while reducing the cream. They don't need to cook as long as larger ones.

Clarified Butter

Clarifying butter is much the same as clarifying a conversation. Just as you can eliminate words that obscure your point, in clarifying butter, you get rid of the milky residue that causes butter to burn and speckle. Cut the butter into small pieces and melt them in a saucepan. Bring it to a slow boil over a low heat. The butter should bubble, but watch it carefully so that it does not brown or burn. When the white part separates from the clear butter, remove the pan from the heat and strain through a fine mesh strainer. This clarified butter is perfect for the most delicate tasks and elegant flavors.

Crawfish Pasta Renaldo

Chef J.P. Gelinas
Big Daddy's Restaurant
Massapequa, New York

Serves 4

Dry Seasoning Mix

1 tablespoon dried basil
$1/2$ teaspoon dried thyme
$1/2$ teaspoon dried cilantro
$1/4$ teaspoon kosher salt

Jalapeño Pecan Pesto

1 pound penne
1 cup coarsely chopped fresh basil
$1/4$ cup coarsely chopped parsley
1 teaspoon sugar
$1/2$ cup coarsely chopped pecan
$1/4$ cup roasted garlic (See "The Goods on Garlic," Chapter 8)
$1/4$ cup diced canned green chilies
2 large jalapeño chili peppers, coarsely chopped
$1/4$ cup Madeira wine
2 cups freshly grated Romano cheese
1 cup virgin olive oil
$1/2$ cup unsalted butter
$1/4$ cup celery, coarsely chopped
$1/4$ cup onion, coarsely chopped
1 pound crawfish tails, peeled

Combine the ingredients for the seasoning mix, stir well, and set aside.

(continued)

Make the pesto: Place the basil, parsley, sugar, pecans, garlic, green chilies, jalapeño peppers, and wine in a food processor. Process for 30 seconds. Add the Romano cheese and, with the processor running, add the olive oil in a thin, steady stream. Continue processing for 1 minute more. Set aside.

In a large pot, bring at least 4 quarts water to a rolling boil. Add 1 tablespoon salt. Add the pasta, stir to separate, and cook until *al dente.* Drain.

Meanwhile, in a large skillet, melt the butter over high heat. Add the celery and onion and sauté until the onion begins to turn clear, about 3 minutes. Add the crawfish tails, reduce the heat to medium, and cook for 2 minutes. Add the seasoning mix, stir well, and cook for 1 minute more. Reduce the heat to low and add the pesto. Cook for 2 minutes. Drain the pasta and add to the skillet. Stir well, making sure all the pasta is integrated with the pesto. Raise the heat to medium and cook for 2 minutes more, stir-ring occasionally. Serve in bowls.

"Badly Cut" Pasta with Eggplant and Tuna

Chef Salvatore Anzalone
Caffe Bondí
New York, New York

Serves 4

Pasta
4 eggs
1 tablespoon salt
2 tablespoons olive oil
1 cup semolina flour

Sauce
¼ cup pine nuts
1 pound small eggplants, cut into 1-inch cubes
¼ cup fresh lemon juice
½ cup extra virgin olive oil
1 onion, chopped
1 teaspoon chopped garlic
¼ cup drained chopped capers
1 teaspoon dried oregano
½ pound tuna fillet
2 tablespoons Malvasia or other Italian dessert wine

Make the pasta: Mix eggs, salt, oil and flour into an elastic dough. Roll pasta on pasta machine and cut into assorted shapes. (See Chapter 3 for detailed directions for making pasta.)

Preheat the oven to 300°. Toast the pine nuts in the oven until lightly golden, about 5 minutes. Reserve.

Sprinkle the eggplant cubes with half of the lemon juice. In a large sauté pan, heat the olive oil over medium heat. Add the eggplant cubes and fry until tender but not mushy. With a slotted spoon, transfer to paper towels to drain. Add the onion and garlic to the same pan and sauté until translucent, about 3 minutes. Add the pine nuts, capers, oregano, and tuna and continue cooking until tuna is half-cooked. Return the eggplant to the pan and add the remaining 2 tablespoons lemon juice and the Malvasia. Cook until the tuna is opaque throughout and the flavors blend.

Meanwhile, in a large pot, bring at least 4 quarts of water to a rolling boil. Add 1 tablespoon of salt. Add pasta and cook *very briefly*. Check for doneness almost immediately. Cook until *al dente* and drain.

Remove pasta to large heated bowl, dress with sauce, and serve.

Commander's Shrimp

Chef James P. Shannon
Commander's Palace
New Orleans, Louisiana

Serves 4

1/4 cup unsalted butter
1 teaspoon shallot, minced
1 teaspoon minced garlic
24 medium shrimp, peeled and deveined
2 tablespoons seafood seasoning (found at fish, and supermarkets)
1/4 cup brandy
3/4 cup heavy cream
1 pound vermicelli
4 teaspoons fresh chopped chives

In a skillet, melt the butter over medium heat. Add the shallot and garlic and sauté for 2 minutes. Add the shrimp and seafood seasonings and sauté until shrimp is pink, about 3 to 5 minutes. Add the brandy and cream and reduce slightly.

Meanwhile, bring at least 4 quarts of water to a rolling boil. Add 1 tablespoon of salt. Add pasta and stir to separate. Cook until *al dente*. Drain well.

Take 4 plates, use one-quarter of the pasta for each. Swirl the vermicelli in a circle, making a "pasta nest" on the plate. Spoon shrimp mixture, dividing equally, into the centers. Garnish with chives and serve.

New Orleans' Crawfish Pasta

Harry Gilbert
River's End
Savannah, Georgia

Serves 1

2 tablespoons vegetable oil
¹/₄ cup red bell peppers,
  ¹/₄-inch dice
¹/₄ cup green bell peppers,
  ¹/₄-inch dice
2 tablespoons white onion,
  ¹/₄-inch dice
¹/₄ pound crawfish tails, peeled
¹/₂ cup heavy cream
1 teaspoon cayenne pepper
Salt and freshly ground pepper to taste
5 ounces rotelle

In a large pot, bring at least 4 quarts water to a rolling boil. Add 1 tablespoon salt. Add the pasta, stir to separate, and cook until *al dente*. Drain.

Meanwhile, in a large sauté pan, heat the oil over medium heat. Add the bell peppers and onions and sauté until the onion is translucent, about 3 minutes. Add the crawfish and cook for 2 minutes. Add the cream and cook, stirring, until it coats the crawfish.

Add the pasta to the sauté pan along with the cayenne. Heat until well combined, then season with salt and pepper. Serve immediately

Grilled Swordfish Medallions and Shrimp in a Roasted Yellow Tomato Sauce with Asparagus and Red Pepper over Penne Rigate

Owners & Chefs Gary, Martin, and
  Laurie Butera
Butera's
Massapequa Park, New York

Serves 4 to 6

Roasted Yellow Tomato Sauce
1¹/₂ pounds yellow tomatoes, seeded and
  cut into 2-inch chunks
¹/₄ cup white wine
4 or 5 cloves garlic
5 fresh basil leaves
Salt and freshly ground pepper to taste

¹/₂ pound swordfish fillet, cut into
  medallions or strips
Olive oil for brushing
¹/₂ cup olive oil
1 onion, diced
6 cloves garlic
2 tablespoons chopped garlic
1 bunch asparagus, cut in 1-inch pieces
1 large red bell pepper, ¹/₄-inch dice
¹/₂ cup dry white wine
¹/₂ cup chicken, vegetable or fish stock
1 pound penne rigate

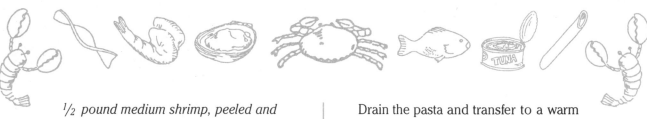

*1/2 pound medium shrimp, peeled and
    deveined*
*1/4 cup basil pesto (optional)
    (see Genovese basil pesto, Chapter 4)*

First, make the sauce: Preheat oven to
450°. Place the tomatoes in a roasting pan
and coat with the olive oil. Place in the oven
and, once the tomatoes start to brown, add
the wine, garlic cloves, basil leaves, salt, and
pepper. Continue to roast until tomatoes break
down into a chunky sauce, 30 to 40 minutes.
Remove from the oven and set aside.

Meanwhile, prepare a fire in a charcoal
grill or preheat a gas grill. Brush the swordfish
with oil and place on the grill. Cook, turning
once, until cooked through, a few minutes on
each side. Set aside. (This step may be
omitted, and swordfish could be pan-sautéed.)
Keep warm.

Fill a large pot with at least 4 quarts water
and bring to a rolling boil.

Meanwhile, in a large sauté pan, heat the
olive oil over medium heat. Add the onion
and chopped garlic and sauté until the garlic
is lightly browned. Add the asparagus and red
bell pepper and sauté briefly. Add the tomato
sauce, wine, and stock and bring to a boil.

Drop the pasta into boiling water, stir well,
and cook until *al dente.*

When the sauce reaches a boil, reduce
the heat to a simmer, and add the shrimp.
Cook until shrimp are done, 3 to 5 minutes.

Drain the pasta and transfer to a warm
bowl. Pour on the sauce, toss well, and divide
among individual plates. Place the grilled
swordfish on top and garnish with the basil
pesto, if desired.

Spinach Fettuccine with Smoked Salmon, Goat Cheese, Leeks, and Zucchini

Serves 4 to 6

1/4 cup olive oil
*4 medium leeks (white and light green
    parts), cleaned, halved lengthwise,
    and sliced*
*4 scallions (white and part of green),
    thinly sliced*
2 zucchini, cut into julienne strips
2 tablespoons finely chopped parsley
1 cup half-and-half
*5 ounces fresh goat cheese such as
    Montrachet, crumbled*
*Salt and freshly ground black pepper to
    taste*
1 pound spinach fettuccine
1/4 pound smoked salmon, chopped

In a large, deep skillet, heat the olive oil
over medium-high heat. Add the leeks and

(continued)

scallions and sauté until golden and tender, about 10 minutes. Add the zucchini and sauté until beginning to soften. Add the parsley, half-and-half, and goat cheese and stir until the cheese melts. Remove the sauce from the heat. Add salt and a generous amount of pepper.

Meanwhile, in a large pot, bring at least 4 quarts water to a rolling boil. Add 1 table-spoon salt. Add the pasta, stir to separate, and cook until *al dente*. Drain.

Return the pasta to the pot. Add the sauce and toss until thoroughly coated. Transfer the pasta to a large warm serving bowl and top with the smoked salmon.

Herb Linguine with Salmon, Cream, and Pistachios

Serves 4

2 tablespoons chopped pistachio nuts
$1/4$ cup unsalted butter
$1/4$ red bell pepper, seeded and diced
$1/2$ teaspoon minced garlic
$3/4$ pound salmon fillet, diced
$1^1/2$ cups heavy cream
2 teaspoons grated lemon zest
$3/4$ pound fresh herb linguine
Salt and freshly ground white pepper
    to taste
$1/4$ cup freshly grated Parmesan cheese

Preheat the oven to 300°. Toast the pista-chios until lightly browned, about 5 minutes. Reserve.

In a large, deep skillet, melt the butter over medium-low heat. Add the bell pepper and garlic, raise the heat to medium, and sauté for 1 minute. Add the salmon and sauté for 1 minute. Add cream and lemon zest and cook until reduced and thickened.

Meanwhile, in a large pot, bring at least 4 quarts water to a rolling boil. Add 1 table-spoon salt. Add the pasta, stir to separate, and cook until *al dente*. Drain.

Transfer the linguine to a large, warm bowl, add the sauce, and toss well. Sprinkle with the pistachios and Parmesan cheese.

CHAPTER 11

INSIDE/OUTSIDE:
PASTA STUFFED AND LAYERED

I n this chapter, lasagna is paired with lobster, ravioli meets wild mushrooms and truffles, cannelloni encircles crawfish, and pasta strips roll up with red pepper coulis. Although the excellence of a basic lasagna or of cheese-filled ravioli is irreplaceable, new ingredients add interest to the stuffed and layered pasta forms. When pasta is used as a wrap or casing both the fillings and the noodles are enhanced, each imparting its flavor and texture to the other until the two become inseparable and the recipe becomes far more than the sum of its parts.

Herb Ravioli with Basil Oil and Tomato Coulis

Chef Daniel Boulud
Restaurant Daniel
New York, New York
From *Cooking with Daniel Boulud*

Serves 4 to 6

Pasta Dough
1 pound all-purpose flour
¼ pound semolina flour
5 medium eggs
½ teaspoon salt
1 egg beaten with 1 tablespoon water

Filling
1½ teaspoons olive oil
½ cup finely chopped onions
1 sprig fresh rosemary, leaves only, finely chopped

1 sprig fresh thyme, leaves only, finely chopped
Pinch of freshly grated nutmeg
1 clove garlic, finely chopped
1½ teaspoons salt
½ pound Swiss chard, leaves only
⅓ pound arugula, leaves only
½ pound spinach, leaves only
2 ounces watercress, leaves only
3 tablespoons coarsely chopped chives
2 ounces chervil, leaves only
3 sprigs fresh dill, leaves only, chopped
3 sprigs fresh tarragon, leaves only, chopped
5 sprigs fresh cilantro, leaves only, chopped
3 tablespoons mascarpone cheese
2 tablespoons ricotta cheese, or more if needed
1 tablespoon freshly grated Parmesan cheese
Salt and freshly ground pepper to taste

Tomato Coulis

1 tablespoon olive oil
¼ cup finely chopped onion
3 cloves garlic, finely chopped
1 bay leaf
1 sprig fresh thyme
One 16-ounce can imported plum tomatoes,
*   drained and squeezed to remove any*
*   excess water*
3 pounds ripe tomatoes, seeded and finely
*   chopped*
1 stalk celery, cut into 4-inch-long pieces
*   and tied together with kitchen string*
Pinch of sugar
Salt and freshly ground pepper to taste

Basil Oil

¼ cup olive oil
6 sprigs fresh basil, leaves only
Salt and freshly ground pepper to taste

Make the dough: Combine both flours, the eggs, and the salt in a bowl or in a food processor. Mix by hand with a wooden spoon or process for 2 minutes until a dough forms. Transfer to a floured work surface and knead the dough by hand until well combined, 5 to 8 minutes. Wrap in plastic wrap and refrigerate until needed.

Make the filling: In a small pan, heat the olive oil over medium heat. Add the onion, rosemary, thyme, nutmeg, and garlic and sweat for 8 to 10 minutes without coloring the onion (add a few tablespoons water if needed

to keep moist while cooking). Remove from the heat and set aside to cool.

In a large pot, bring 3 quarts water to a boil and add 1½ tablespoons salt. Add the Swiss chard and boil for 2 minutes. Add the arugula and boil for 2 minutes more. Add the spinach and watercress and boil for another 3 to 4 minutes. Drain and chill the greens under cold running water, drain again, and press inside a colander very firmly with your hands to remove any excess water.

Transfer the cooked greens to a blender or food processor and add the cooked onion, ¾ each of the chives, chervil, dill, tarragon, and cilantro, along with all of the mascarpone, ricotta, Parmesan cheese, and salt and pepper to taste. Purée until smooth, 3 to 4 minutes. From time to time, scrape down the sides of the blender or food processor to avoid lumps. If the herb mixture is too dry, add 1 more tablespoon ricotta cheese (the mixture should be very green and smooth). Taste for seasoning before putting in a lock-top bag. Press any air out of the bag, seal, and refrigerate until needed.

To make the ravioli, remove the ravioli dough from the refrigerator and unwrap. Sprinkle the counter and rolling pin with flour. Divide the dough into 4 equal pieces. Flatten each piece into a 3-inch square with the rolling pin. Roll the pieces of dough through a pasta machine until about 12 inches by 5 inches and thin enough to see your hand through. (If using a ravioli tray, make sure the

(continued)

4 sheets of dough are slightly larger and longer than your ravioli tray.) Cut a $^1/_2$-inch tip off one of the bottom corners of the plastic bag containing the herb mixture and use it as a piping bag.

Here are two ways to make the ravioli: Place a layer of dough over a ravioli tray (2-inch-square size with 12 shallow bowls). Push lightly with your finger into each hole to line the hole with the dough. Brush a little of the egg wash along the ridges of each hole. Pipe 1 teaspoon of the herb mixture into each hole. Cover the top of the filled ravioli tray with a second sheet of pasta. Apply even pressure with your fingers over the top layer of pasta to seal each ravioli and roll a rolling pin over the ridging to sever each ravioli. Line a flat baking sheet the size of the ravioli tray with a piece of parchment paper sprinkled with flour. Flip the ravioli tray onto the baking sheet and gently shake the tray to release the ravioli onto the parchment paper. Repeat the same process with the rest of the dough and filling. Cover with a dry towel and refrigerate until ready to cook.

Alternatively, place a layer of dough on a flat surface. Brush it with the egg wash. Pipe 1 teaspoon of the herb mixture evenly every 2 inches along the length in 2 to 3 rows to make at least 12 ravioli. Cover with the second sheet of dough. Press well with your fingers all around each ravioli. Cut them out with a fluted rolling cutter or knife for square-shaped ones, or use a small round cookie cutter for round ravioli. Repeat the same process with the rest of the dough and filling. Place the ravioli on a baking sheet lined with parchment paper sprinkled with flour, cover with a dry towel, and refrigerator until ready to cook.

Make the coulis: In an enameled cast-iron pan heat the olive oil over medium heat. Add the onion, garlic, bay leaf, and thyme and sweat until soft and translucent, 5 to 7 minutes. Add both the canned and fresh tomatoes, celery, sugar, salt, and pepper. Mix well, reduce the heat to low, and cook until soft, 30 to 40 minutes. Remove from the heat, discard the thyme, bay leaf, and celery. Transfer the tomato mixture to a blender or food processor and purée until smooth. Return to the pan and keep warm until needed.

Make the basil oil: Combine the olive oil and basil leaves in a blender or food processor and process until smooth. Season with salt and pepper and strain through a sieve lined with cheesecloth or cotton towel into a small bowl. Cover and refrigerate until needed.

To cook the ravioli: In a large pot, bring at least 4 quarts of water to a rolling boil. Add 1 tablespoon salt. Plunge the ravioli into the boiling water and cook about 3 minutes. Delicately remove the ravioli with a mesh strainer and toss them gently in a pan with the basil oil over medium heat for a few minutes. Taste for seasoning.

Spoon the warm tomato coulis onto the bottom of warm individual plates or a platter. Divide the ravioli evenly among the serving plates over the tomato coulis or place on the platter. Sprinkle the remaining chives, chervil, dill, tarragon, and cilantro leaves on top of the ravioli. Serve with grated Parmesan cheese on the side.

Lasagna Frutti di Mare "Lasagna with Fruits from the Sea"

Chef Dwight Collins
Sanderlings at Seascape Resort
Aptos, California

Serves 8

Seafood Béchamel
1/2 cup unsalted butter
1/2 cup all-purpose flour
1 cup clam broth
1/2 cup Marsala wine
Dash Worcestershire sauce
2 1/2 cups half-and-half or heavy cream
Dash Tabasco sauce
Salt and white pepper to taste

2 tablespoons unsalted butter
2 tablespoons olive oil
1/2 pound mushrooms, sliced

1 teaspoon minced garlic
1/4 cup dry white wine
1 pound scallops
1/2 pound Dungeness crabmeat, cooked
1 pound large bay shrimp, peeled, deveined, and cooked
1/4 pound lobster meat, cooked (optional)
Salt and white pepper to taste
1/2 pound Monterey Jack cheese, shredded
1 cup freshly grated Parmesan cheese
3 sheets fresh pasta, each about 10 by 12 inches (or cut to fit pan with similar volume) (see Chapter 3)

Make the béchamel sauce: In a saucepan, melt the butter over low heat. Whisk in the flour and cook for 3 to 5 minutes, stirring constantly. Whisk in the clam broth, wine, Worcestershire sauce, half-and-half or cream, and Tabasco sauce. Bring to a boil, stirring constantly. Cook until the sauce is quite thick. Season with salt and pepper and remove from the heat. Let cool.

In a skillet, melt the butter with the olive oil over medium heat. Add the mushrooms and garlic and sauté until fragrant, about 3 minutes. Add the wine and continue cooking until the liquid evaporates. Add the scallops and cook until they just begin to firm. Toss in the crabmeat, shrimp, and the lobster meat, if using. Season with salt and white pepper.

Preheat the oven to 350°.

Place 1 pasta sheet in a 10-by-12-inch lasagna pan. Top with half of the seafood

(continued)

mixture. Sprinkle with one-third of the Jack and Parmesan cheeses. Cover with another pasta sheet, and top with the remaining seafood mixture and one-third of the cheeses. Add the third pasta sheet, and top with the remaining béchamel and cheeses. Bake until set with the top lightly browned and bubbling, about 40 minutes. Remove from the oven and let cool for 15 minutes before serving.

Beet and Spinach Pasta Rolls with Saffron Cream Sauce

Serves 6

8 small to medium beets
1 tablespoon olive oil
2 bunches spinach, cleaned and cut into
*   1-inch pieces*
1/2 cup unsalted butter
2 large onions, finely diced
4 cloves garlic, minced
Salt and freshly ground pepper to taste
2 tablespoons balsamic vinegar
1/2 teaspoon ground nutmeg
1/4 pound Parmesan cheese, grated
1/4 pound Italian Fontina cheese, shredded
11/2 pounds ricotta cheese
1 pound dried ruffle-edged lasagna noodles
*   (12 pieces)*

Olive oil for brushing
Pinch each of ground allspice, nutmeg,
*   and cinnamon*

Sauce
3 cups heavy cream
3 cloves garlic, minced
Pinch of powdered saffron or a few
*   threads*
Pinch each of nutmeg and cayenne
Salt and freshly ground pepper to taste

Prepare the beets: Preheat the oven to 350°. Trim the stems of the beets, leaving 1/2 inch intact; do not peel. Wash and place in a roasting pan and cover loosely with aluminum foil. Bake until tender, about 1 hour. Remove from the oven, let cool, peel, and cut up. Place in a food processor or blender and process until smooth. Set aside in a bowl.

In a saucepan, heat the olive oil over medium heat. Add the spinach and cook briefly, just until it wilts. Drain and let cool. Place in paper towels and squeeze out the excess liquid. Set aside in a separate bowl.

Rinse and dry the saucepan, add the butter, and place over medium heat. Add the onions and garlic and cook until softened, about 3 minutes. Place half of the onions and garlic in the bowl with the beets and the other half in the bowl with the spinach.

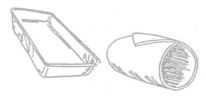

To the red beets, add the vinegar, and the pinch each of allspice, nutmeg, and cinnamon. Mix well and season with salt and pepper.

To the spinach, add the Parmesan, Fontina, ricotta, 1/2 teaspoon nutmeg, salt, and pepper. Mix well and season with salt and pepper.

In a large pot, bring at least 4 quarts of water to a rolling boil. Add 1 tablespoon salt. Add the lasagna noodles, stirring carefully until they are flexible. Cook until just barely *al dente*. Drain and rinse carefully with cool water. Immediately lay out the noodles on a towel, lightly brush both sides of each noodle with a little olive oil, and cover with a damp cloth.

Preheat the oven to 350°.

Spread some filling on each noodle, making 6 of each kind. Roll up and place seam side down in a greased shallow baking dish. Bake for 15 minutes, just to warm through. Allow to cook slightly before slicing.

Make the sauce: In a large, deep saucepan, heat together the cream, garlic, saffron, nutmeg, and cayenne over medium heat. Cook, stirring occasionally, until thick enough to coat the back of a spoon, about 5 minutes. Add salt and pepper and keep warm.

To serve, spoon some sauce on each plate, place one kind of each pasta wheel on top of the sauce.

Grilled Scallops–Eggplant Ravioli

Chef Hans Bergmann
Cacharel Restaurant
Arlington, Texas

Serves 4

Filling

1 pound eggplant, roughly sliced
Salt and freshly ground black pepper
*   to taste*
Cayenne pepper to taste
2 tablespoons olive oil
4 shallots, diced
2 cloves garlic, diced
1/2 pound tomatoes, peeled, seeded, and
*   diced*
8 fresh basil leaves, chopped
1/2 cup freshly grated Parmesan cheese

Make the filling: Preheat the oven to 300°. Season the eggplant slices with salt and pepper and place them on a baking sheet. Bake until tender, about 30 minutes.

Remove the eggplant from the oven and, when cool enough to handle, peel and freshly chop the slices. In a skillet, heat the olive oil over medium heat. Add the shallots and garlic and sauté until fragrant, about 2 minutes. Add the tomatoes and cook slowly for 15 minutes. Add the chopped eggplant and cook to a thick paste. Add the basil and

(continued)

Parmesan and season with salt and black and cayenne pepper. Set aside.

Red Bell Pepper Sauce

1/4 cup olive oil
2 red bell peppers, seeded and diced
1/2 onion, cubed
2 cloves garlic, minced
1 fresh sprig thyme
1 bay leaf
2 cups chicken stock
1/4 cup sun-dried dry packed tomatoes, cut into strips
Salt and freshly ground black pepper to taste
Cayenne to taste

16 jumbo sea scallops
4 baby eggplants (optional)
fresh chervil (optional)

Make the sauce: Heat a sauté pan, pour in olive oil, and heat for 1 minute. Add the peppers, onion, and garlic cloves and sauté for another 3 minutes over medium heat, stirring occasionally. Add the thyme, bay leaf, and stock, and deglaze the pan by scraping up any browned bits. Simmer for 10 minutes.

Remove the bay leaf and thyme and discard. Pour the sauce into a blender or food processor and process until smooth.

Pass the sauce through a fine-mesh sieve into a clean pan. Add the sun-dried tomatoes and simmer over medium heat for 5 more minutes. Season with salt, black pepper, and cayenne.

Pasta Dough

1 1/2 cups flour
2 eggs
1 tablespoon olive oil
1/2 teaspoon salt

Make the ravioli: Knead a smooth dough with flour, eggs, oil and a little salt. Form into a ball and put in a cool place for 1-2 hours. Roll out the dough into two thin sheets and put regularly spaced teaspoonfuls of the eggplant filling on one sheet. (See Chapter 3 for detailed directions.)

Using a pastry brush dipped in cold water, paint around each little heap of stuffing and lay the second sheet of dough on top of the first. Seal around each teaspoon of filling with your thumb and cut into rounds with a 1 1/2 inch cookie cutter. Should make 16 pieces.

Place ravioli on lightly floured baking sheet and cover with damp kitchen towel until ready to cook.

Grill the scallops: Under the broiler or on a grill until firm.

Cook the ravioli: Bring at least 4 quarts of water to a rolling boil. Add 1 tablespoon of salt. Add ravioli a few at a time. Test for doneness by removing 1 piece with a slotted spoon. Cut an edge with a fork. If it comes off easily the ravioli are done. They should take less than 5 minutes. Remove with a slotted spoon.

To assemble: Warm the sauce. Ladle into large soup bowls. Arrange 4 ravioli

and 4 scallops in a circle in each bowl. If available, garnish with baby eggplant slices and fresh chervil.

Spinach Cannelloni

Makes 10 cannelloni

10 spinach lasagna noodles
1 pound spinach, cleaned and stems
*   removed, or two 10-ounce packages*
*   frozen chopped spinach, thawed and*
*   squeezed of excess moisture*
1¹/₄ cups unsalted butter
1 pound boneless chicken breasts, finely
*   diced*
¹/₂ pound freshly grated Parmesan cheese
About ¹/₄ cup half-and-half
¹/₈ teaspoon ground nutmeg
Salt and freshly ground pepper to taste
Red wine marinara sauce (see Chapter 4)

In a large pot, bring at least 4 quarts of water to a rolling boil. Add 1 tablespoon salt. Add the lasagna noodles, stirring carefully, until they are flexible. Cook until just barely *al dente*. Drain and rinse carefully with cool water. Place on paper towels to drain. Cover with a damp kitchen towel.

Preheat the oven to 375°.

In a large, deep skillet, melt ¹/₄ cup of the butter over medium heat and add the

spinach. Cook until tender. Transfer to a large bowl.

Add another ¹/₄ cup butter to the skillet over medium heat. Add the chicken and sauté until cooked through, about 5 minutes. Add the chicken to the spinach in the bowl.

Melt the remaining ³/₄ cup butter in a small saucepan over moderately low heat. Stir in the Parmesan cheese, then gradually add enough half-and-half to form a smooth, creamlike sauce. Add the nutmeg and season with salt and pepper.

Pour the cream sauce over the chicken and spinach and stir until blended. Spread some of the chicken mixture on each lasagna noodle and roll up. Arrange in a 13-by-9-inch baking pan. Spoon the marinara sauce over the rolls. Bake until hot and bubbly, 20 to 30 minutes.

Black and White Ravioli with Sage Butter

Chef Faz Poursohi
Faz Restaurant & Catering
San Francisco, California

Serves 6 to 8

Filling for White Pasta
2 bunches Swiss chard, trimmed
1 pound (2 cups) ricotta cheese

(continued)

1 egg
2 teaspoons ground nutmeg
¹/₂ cup freshly grated Parmesan cheese
¹/₂ cup freshly grated Romano cheese
¹/₈ teaspoon chopped garlic
Pinch of salt and freshly ground pepper

Filling for Black Pasta

Follow the same recipe as above but substitute red chard in place of Swiss chard.

Black Pasta Dough

1 cup black beans
1 teaspoon ground cumin
¹/₄ teaspoon salt
¹/₄ teaspoon freshly ground pepper
3 cups veal stock
1¹/₂ cups semolina flour
1¹/₂ cups all-purpose flour
4 eggs
¹/₄ cup olive oil

White Pasta Dough

1¹/₂ cups semolina flour
1¹/₂ cups all-purpose flour
4 eggs
¹/₄ cup olive oil
¹/₂ teaspoon salt
1 egg beaten with 1 tablespoon water

Make the filling for white pasta: Cook the chard in boiling water until tender. Drain in a colander and let cool. Squeeze out any excess water until the chard is dry, then mince finely. Add the ricotta, egg, and nutmeg. Gradually add Parmesan and Romano cheese until mixture is a workable consistency for spooning onto the pasta. Cover and refrigerate until needed.

Make the filling for the black pasta using red chard instead of Swiss chard as in the filling for the white pasta. Cover and refrigerate until needed.

Make the white pasta: Combine all the ingredients in the bowl of a stand mixer fitted with a dough hook. Mix on slow speed with the standard attachment until the dough comes together. Knead with the dough hook until smooth, adding 2 to 4 tablespoons of water if necessary. The dough will be quite stiff. Wrap in plastic wrap and refrigerate until ready to use. (See Chapter 3 for detailed directions.)

To roll out the dough on a pasta machine, divide the dough into 4 pieces. Dust the table with flour or semolina. Set the machine's rollers on the highest number. Pass the dough through the rollers. Continue to pass the dough through the rollers, turning down the number by one increment each time, until you get to number 1. The dough will then be a rectangle about ¹/₁₆ inch thick and 6 inches wide. Cut the ends of the dough to make a straight edge. With a pastry brush, paint some of the egg wash onto the pastry sheet.

With a tablespoon, place small balls of filling lengthwise onto the bottom half of the dough, leaving about 1 inch between the balls

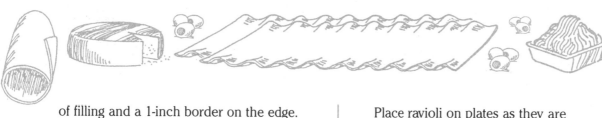

of filling and a 1-inch border on the edge. Fold the dough over the filling and press the edges down to seal. Using a pastry wheel, cut into individual squares.

Place a baking sheet lined with waxed paper and dusted with semolina.

Make the black pasta: Cook beans on low heat with cumin, salt, pepper, and veal stock until tender (approximately 2 hours); drain off excess liquid. Purée beans. Follow the same recipe as for white pasta, adding black bean mixture to ingredients. Note: Add the cup of very well-drained beans gradually to the dough to make sure that the dough is of a workable consistency.

Sauce
$3/4$ cup unsalted butter
5 or 6 sprigs fresh sage
$1/2$ cup freshly grated Parmesan cheese
$1/2$ cup freshly grated Romano cheese

Make the sauce: Melt the butter in a small sauté pan over medium heat. Add the sage and cook slightly.

To cook ravioli: Bring at least 4 quarts of water to boil in a large pot. Add 1 tablespoon of salt. Add ravioli a few at a time. Check for doneness as soon as they rise to the top, in 2 or 3 minutes. Remove 1 ravioli with a slotted spoon. Cut off an edge with a fork. If it comes off easily, the ravioli are done. Remove with slotted spoon.

Place ravioli on plates as they are removed from water and dress with sauce. Sprinkle with cheeses.

Chicken-Prosciutto Ravioli with Rosemary Oil

Serves 6

Filling
About $1^3/4$ pounds chicken thighs
Salt and freshly ground black pepper
   to taste
$1^1/2$ tablespoons fresh rosemary
2 large cloves garlic, minced
6 ounces thinly sliced prosciutto ham,
   fat removed and minced

Rosemary Oil
6 tablespoons extra virgin olive oil
6 small sprigs rosemary
3 cloves garlic

Freshly grated Parmesan cheese

One 3-egg pasta recipe. (See Chapter 3 for detailed directions.)

Make the pasta, wrap it, and set it aside to rest.

Make the filling: Sprinkle the chicken thighs with salt and pepper and place them,

(continued)

skin side down, in a large, deep skillet. Sprinkle the chicken with 1 tablespoon of the rosemary. Cook over low heat for 20 minutes or until the skin is very brown and crisp. Turn the chicken over and cook for another 20 minutes until brown and crisp on the second side. Transfer the thighs to a plate to cool. Pour off nearly all the fat in the pan.

While the pan is still hot, add the minced garlic and brown lightly over low heat. With a wooden spoon or spatula, loosen the bits of chicken adhering to the bottom. Add the prosciutto and the remaining 1/2 tablespoon rosemary. Cook for 2 minutes and transfer to a bowl.

When the chicken is cool, remove the skin. Working over the bowl containing the prosciutto, pull the chicken meat from the bones and let any juices fall into the bowl. Add any juices that have collected on the plate to the bowl. On a cutting board, finely chop the prosciutto and chicken meat. Season with salt and pepper.

To make ravioli: (See Chapter 3 for detailed directions.) Set them aside on a heated plate.

To make the rosemary oil: In a small saucepan, warm together the olive oil, rosemary, and garlic cloves over moderately low heat. Cook gently for 2 minutes and turn off the heat. Remove the garlic. Set the oil aside.

In a large pot, bring at least 4 quarts of water to a rolling boil. Add 1 tablespoon of salt. Add the ravioli, in batches, if necessary,

so they have adequate room to cook. Stir constantly and check for doneness after about 4 minutes. When they are done, they will float and the edges will be tender. Drain. Transfer to warm plates, allowing 5 per serving. Dress with the rosemary oil and sprinkle with Parmesan cheese.

Lobster Ravioli

Chef Milos Cihelka
Formerly of The Golden Mushroom
Southfield, Michigan

Serves 6

Filling
2 live lobsters, 1 1/2 pounds each
1/2 cup heavy cream
Salt and freshly ground pepper to taste

Pasta Dough
3 eggs
1 1/4 cups semolina flour
1 cup all-purpose flour
2 teaspoons milk

To make the filling: In a large pot, bring at least 4 quarts of water to a boil. Drop the lobsters into the water for 2 minutes, lift them out, and cool them in cold water. Using a large knife, split them lengthwise. Remove the

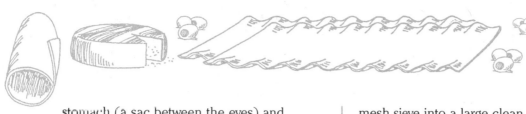

stomach (a sac between the eyes) and discard. Scoop out the liver (dark green, soft) and reserve. Remove all meat and save the shells.

In a food processor, purée the lobster meat. Add the cream, mix well, and season with salt and pepper. Transfer to a container, cover, and refrigerate until needed.

To make the dough: See Chapter 3 for detailed directions for how to make ravioli.

Roll out the dough. Place teaspoonfuls of filling 1 inch apart and 1 inch from the edge. Cover them with another sheet of dough. With a rolling cutter, cut into squares and press each around the edges to seal.

Sauce
Reserved lobster shells
1/4 cup unsalted butter
2 tablespoons Cognac
1/4 cup chopped onion
2 cups light cream
Reserved lobster liver
Salt to taste
Cayenne pepper to taste

Chop up the reserved lobster shells. In a heavy, stainless steel saucepan, melt the butter over medium heat. Add the shells and sauté, stirring, until a bronze tint develops. Pour in the Cognac and ignite. Let it burn out, add the onion, and stir for 15 seconds. Add the cream and cook over low heat until thickened, about 15 minutes. Strain through a fine-mesh sieve into a large clean saucepan. Whip in the lobster liver and return to a boil. Season with salt and cayenne.

Drop the ravioli into boiling, salted water and cook 3 minutes.

Test for doneness when they float to the top. Remove ravioli with a slotted spoon or a flat, long, handled strainer. Place them in the pan with the sauce. Gently reheat. Divide among plates and serve.

Chicken-Portabello Ravioli with Porcini and Sun-Dried Tomato Sauce

Chef Alfonso D'Onofrio
Spazzi
Fairfield, Connecticut

Serves 4

Filling
2 whole boneless, skinless chicken breasts
3 large cap portobello mushrooms, stems discarded
1 pound (2 cups) ricotta cheese
1/2 cup shredded mozzarella cheese
2 tablespoons extra virgin olive oil
1 tablespoon chopped garlic
1 pinch each of finely chopped fresh rosemary, thyme, oregano, and sage
Salt and freshly ground pepper to taste

(continued)

Porcini and Sun-Dried Tomato Sauce

1 tablespoon extra virgin olive oil
1 large Spanish onion, sliced
1 tablespoon chopped garlic
2 tablespoons dried porcini
1 cup sun-dried tomatoes (oil packed),
  cut in strips
2 cups heavy cream
1/2 cup unsalted butter, cut into pieces
Salt and freshly ground pepper

Fennel and Tomato Chutney

1 tablespoon extra virgin olive oil
1 fennel bulb
4 large portobello mushrooms, julienned
1 tablespoon chopped garlic
8 plum tomatoes, seeded and diced
Salt and freshly ground pepper to taste
1 fresh sprig each rosemary, thyme,
  oregano, and sage, very finely chopped

Additional 2 tablespoons unsalted butter

Make the filling: In a medium bowl, combine the olive oil with the herbs, chopped garlic, and salt and pepper. Marinate the chicken breasts and mushroom caps in the oil and herb mixture for 1 hour.

Grill chicken breasts and mushrooms or cook under broiler. Cool.

In a food processor, chop the chicken and mushrooms to a fine consistency. Transfer to a bowl and add ricotta and mozzarella cheeses. Combine well and season

with salt and pepper to taste. Filling may be stored in the refrigerator for up to 2 days.

Make the pasta dough and ravioli. Follow the directions for one pound of pasta and ravioli in Chapter 3. To make the ravioli, place teaspoonfuls of filling 1 inch apart, 1 inch from the edge of a sheet of dough. Cover with another sheet of dough. Cut into squares with pastry cutter. Press edges with fingers to seal.

Make the sauce: In a saucepan, heat the olive oil over medium heat. Add the onion and garlic and cook until the onion is translucent. Add the porcini and sun-dried tomatoes and cook for 2 minutes. Add the cream and cook over low heat until reduced by half. Whisk in the butter a little at a time and cool, stirring, until it coats the back of a spoon. Season with salt and pepper.

Make the chutney: Blanch the fennel bulb in boiling water for 5 minutes. Drain and cut into julienne. In a sauté pan, heat olive oil over medium heat. Add the portobello and garlic and sauté for 2 to 3 minutes. Add the tomatoes and cook for 1 minute. Season with salt and pepper and herbs.

To cook the ravioli: Bring a large pot water to a rolling boil. Add 1 tablespoon of salt. Add ravioli a few at a time, stirring to separate. When ravioli float to the top, about 3 minutes, check for doneness. Remove one with a slotted spoon. Cut an edge with a fork. If it cuts easily, the ravioli are done. Remove with slotted spoon to large bowl with additional 2 tablespoons of

unsalted butter. Carefully swirl with butter and cover to keep warm.

To assemble: Gently reheat the sauce and chutney. Cover the bottom of each plate with sauce. Arrange ravioli on top and place chutney in the center.

Ham and Chicken Lasagna

Chef Jean-Pierre Breahier
The Left Bank Restaurant
Fort Lauderdale, Florida

Serves 4

Béchamel Sauce
1 tablespoon sunflower oil
1/4 cup all-purpose flour
3 cups low-fat milk
1/2 teaspoon ground nutmeg
Salt and freshly ground pepper to taste

Turkey Bolognese Sauce
1 tablespoon extra virgin olive oil
1 cup diced onion
1 pound ground turkey
2 tablespoons chopped garlic
1/4 pound fresh button mushrooms, quartered
5 cups tomato concassée (tomatoes peeled, seeded, and chopped)

2 tablespoons tomato paste
1 teaspoon fresh thyme leaves, chopped
1 teaspoon fresh oregano leaves, chopped
Chicken stock, if necessary
Salt and freshly ground pepper to taste

15 dried lasagna noodles
2 whole boneless, skinless chicken breasts, 1/2 pound each, sautéed on all sides in olive oil and sliced into 1/4-inch-thick slices
10 thin slices of lean baked ham, cut into 1-inch squares
3/4 cup freshly grated Parmesan cheese
3/4 cup freshly grated provolone cheese

Make the béchamel sauce: In a saucepan, heat the oil over low heat. Add the flour and cook, mixing continuously with a wooden spoon, until the flour turns a very light brown. It should take no more than 3 minutes and remain a very light hazelnut brown.

Meanwhile, in a separate pan, scald the milk. Add 1 1/2 cups of the milk to the flour mixture and whisk continuously until the sauce starts to bubble and thicken. Simmer for 2 to 3 minutes, stirring continuously. Thin out the sauce as necessary with the remaining milk. The sauce should be thick enough to coat the back of a spoon. Season with the nutmeg, salt, and pepper. If there are lumps, strain through a fine sieve. Set aside. You should have 2 cups.

(continued)

Make the Bolognese sauce: In a large, heavy pot, heat the olive oil over medium heat. Add the onion and sauté for 2 minutes. Add the turkey, breaking it up with a fork or spoon, and cook until nice and golden brown. Add the garlic and mushrooms and sauté for 2 minutes. When the garlic becomes fragrant, add the tomato concassé, tomato paste, thyme, and oregano. Simmer slowly for 30 minutes, adding a little chicken stock if the sauce becomes too thick. Season with salt and pepper.

Preheat the oven to 375°. Coat a 13-by-9-inch baking dish with a nonstick olive oil cooking spray.

In a large pot, bring at least 4 quarts of water to a boil. Add the noodles and boil until barely cooked and beginning to soften. It should take less than 3 minutes. Drain and spread the noodles on a kitchen towel to absorb the moisture.

In a bowl, mix together the Parmesan and provolone cheese. Cover the bottom of the prepared baking dish with a layer of the lasagna noodles and spread half of the béchamel sauce over the pasta. Arrange half of the chicken and ham slices and one-fourth of the cheese mixture over the sauce and top with a second layer of pasta. Spread half of the Bolognese sauce and one-third of the remaining cheese mixture. Top with half of the remaining pasta, again in a single layer. Spread the remaining béchamel sauce and chicken and ham on top. Sprinkle on half of

the remaining cheese mixture and cover with the last layer of the pasta. Spread on the remaining Bolognese sauce and top with the last of the cheese mixture.

Cover and bake until set and top is golden brown and bubbling, about 1 hour. Let rest for 10 minutes before serving.

Crawfish Cannelloni with Basil and Ricotta in Creole Tomato Sauce

Chef Horst Pfeifer
Bella Luna
New Orleans, Louisiana

Serves 6

Creole Tomato Sauce
1/4 cup olive oil
3 pounds tomatoes
4 cups chopped onion
2 tablespoons garlic
1 cup chopped fresh basil, oregano, and
*   rosemary*
Salt and freshly ground black pepper
*   to taste*
Dried hot red pepper flakes to taste

2 tablespoons olive oil
1/2 pound crawfish, peeled
1/2 pound crabmeat
1/2 cup onion

1 teaspoon garlic
2 tablespoons basil
2 teaspoons parsley
1¹/₂ cup (³/₄ pound) ricotta cheese
12 pasta sheets, each 5 by 6 inches
*Note: Pasta sheets can be bought where
fresh pasta is sold. Or make pasta
according to directions in Chapter 3.*

Make the filling: In a sauté pan, heat the oil over medium heat. Add the onion and garlic and sauté until the onions are translucent. Add the crawfish and sauté until cooked. Add the basil, parsley, and crab, stir well, and remove from the heat. Let cool, then mix in the ricotta and season with salt and pepper.

In a 2-quart saucepan, heat the olive oil over medium heat. Add the onion and garlic and sauté until golden. Add the tomatoes, herbs, salt, black pepper, and pepper flakes and simmer over low heat until the sauce thickens, for 30 minutes.

Meanwhile, in a large pot, bring at least 4 quarts water to a rolling boil. Add 1 tablespoon salt. Add the pasta, stir to separate, and cook until *al dente*. Drain.

Preheat the oven to 350°. Divide the crawfish mixture evenly among the pasta sheets, positioning it near the long edge of each sheet. Roll up the sheets to form tubes and place seam side down in a lightly greased baking pan.

Pour tomato sauce evenly over the cannelloni. Bake for 30 to 40 minutes.

Ravioli alla Vodka

Owner Joey Vallone
Tony's * Anthony's * Grotto * La Griglia
Houston, Texas

Serves 4

Pasta Dough
2 eggs
3 cups all-purpose flour
1 teaspoon olive oil
¹/₂ teaspoon salt
*Note: Pasta sheets can be bought where
fresh pasta is sold. Or make pasta
according to directions in Chapter 3.*

*1 pound fresh pasta sheets**

Filling
¹/₂ pound ricotta cheese
¹/₂ pound mozzarella, grated
¹/₄ pound Parmesan cheese, grated
¹/₂ cup chopped fresh basil
Freshly ground pepper to taste

Mix eggs together with olive oil, salt, and flour until a smooth, elastic dough forms. Roll out the dough ¹/₁₆-inch thick. (See Chapter 3 for detailed directions.)

Make the filling: In a bowl, combine all the cheeses, basil, and pepper and mix well. Cover and refrigerate until needed. Place pasta sheet down on a work surface and place teaspoons full of the filling in rows on

(continued)

the sheet, spacing the mounds 1¹/₂ inches apart. Place another pasta sheet over the top and press down around the cheese. With a fluted pasta cutter, cut out the ravioli.

Sauce
¹/₂ cup chopped plum tomatoes
1 cup heavy cream
¹/₂ cup vodka
1 cup marinara sauce
Salt and freshly ground pepper to taste
1 teaspoon dried hot red pepper flakes
¹/₄ cup chopped fresh basil

1 tablespoon chopped, toasted pistachios

Make the sauce: In a large skillet, combine the tomatoes, cream, vodka, and marinara. Place over low heat and cook until reduced and thickened. Add the salt, pepper, crushed red pepper, and basil.

In a large pot, bring plenty of salted water to a boil. Add the ravioli and boil for 1 to 2 minutes. Drain and place in a warm serving bowl. Add the sauce, toss gently, and garnish with the pistachios.

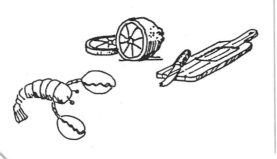

Citrus Lobster Lasagna

Chef Gert Dehnen
Citrus of Boca
Boca Raton, Florida

Serves 4

Dough
1¹/₄ cups all-purpose flour
3 eggs
1 tablespoon olive oil

Lobster
2 lobsters, 1¹/₂ pounds each

Bring a large pot of salted water to boil, at least 6 or 7 quarts. Plunge lobsters head first into water. Boil for 5 minutes, remove, and plunge into cold water. Cut in halves. Remove all meat and reserve the 4 head halves for presentation and the shells for the sauce.

Sauce
Reserved lobster shells, broken into pieces
¹/₄ cup olive oil
1 small carrot
2 leeks, white and some green part,
*   cleaned*
Onion, with skin on
2 celery stalks
1 bulb fennel, coarsely chopped
2 tablespoons tomato paste
2 bay leaves
6 peppercorns

2 tablespoons anisette liquor
1 cup white wine
4 cups fish or chicken stock
1/4 cup heavy cream
Salt and freshly ground pepper to taste

Make the dough: Knead to consistency and add a few splashes of water, if necessary. Let rest for 1 hour. Roll out and cut twelve 4, inch round sheets. Boil for 2 minutes in salted water and drain. Place on a lightly floured cookie sheet and cover with damp kitchen towel until ready to use.

Make the sauce: Crush the lobster shells and place in a saucepan with the oil. Sauté 3 minutes. Add the carrot, leeks, onion, celery, fennel, tomato paste, bay leaves, peppercorns, anisette, and wine and sauté for 2 minutes. Add the stock and simmer covered for 1½ hours. Strain and discard the solids. Add the cream and reduce over moderately low heat to 4 cups. Season with salt and pepper.

To make 4 individual lasagnas: Preheat the oven to 350°. In 4 ovenproof bowls spoon some sauce. Top each with a pasta round and then some lobster. Repeat layers. Add 1 more layer of sauce and another pasta round. There should be 3 layers of pasta and sauce and 2 layers of lobster. Bake until set, 7 to 9 minutes.

Remove from the oven and slip each portion onto a warm individual plate. Spoon more sauce over each portion and garnish with a fresh chive sprig and a lobster head.

Spinach and Three-Cheese Ravioli with Roasted Tomato, Olive, and Basil Essence Sauce

Chef Phillipe Chin
Chanterelles
Philadelphia, Pennsylvania

Serves 4

Filling
1 pound spinach, cleaned and stems
    removed
1/4 cup olive oil
2 cloves garlic, chopped
2 shallots, chopped
1/3 cup Parmesan cheese, grated
3 ounces smoked mozzarella
1/3 cup ricotta cheese
Salt and freshly ground pepper
4 sheets pasta dough
Note: Pasta sheets can be bought where
    fresh pasta is sold. Or make pasta
    according to directions in Chapter 3.

1 egg yolk mixed with 2 tablespoons water

Sauce
6 tomatoes, peeled and seeded
1/2 cup extra virgin olive oil
1 cup chicken stock
1/2 bunch fresh basil, chopped
Salt and freshly ground pepper to taste

Fresh basil leaves
Olive oil

(continued)

185

Make the filling: Cook the spinach in boiling salted water until tender. Drain and press out any excess moisture. Chop finely. In a skillet, heat the oil over medium heat. Add the garlic and shallots and sauté until golden brown, 3 minutes. Add the spinach and transfer to a large bowl. Add all the cheeses, mix well, and let it cool. Season with salt and pepper.

To assemble the ravioli: Lay a sheet of pasta dough on a work surface. Brush with egg yolk and water. Form 24 mounds of the cooled filling on the sheet, spacing 3/4 inch apart. Cover carefully with the second pasta sheet and press around the edges of each mound to seal. Cut into 1¹/₂-inch squares.

Make the sauce: In a food processor, purée the tomato. Place tomato in a saucepan over medium heat. Slowly add the olive oil and chicken stock. Bring to a boil, reduce the heat, and simmer until thickened. Add the basil and season with salt and pepper. Simmer 3 minutes. Strain.

Pour some of the sauce over each portion. Garnish with basil leaves and drizzle with olive oil.

Bring at least 4 quarts of water to boil. Add 1 tablespoon of salt. Add ravioli a few at a time. Cook about 6 minutes or until they rise to the top. Remove with slotted spoon and divide among warm soup plates.

Lobster-Stuffed Cappelletti in a Sherry Coral Sauce

Owner Tony Vallone
Tony's * Anthony's * Grotto * La Griglia
Houston, Texas

Serves 4 to 6

Pasta Dough
3 eggs
2¹/₄ cups all-purpose flour

Make the dough: Pour the flour onto a wooden or other smooth work surface and make a well in the center with your fingers. Break the eggs one by one into the well. Lightly beat the eggs with a fork until the yolks and white are evenly mixed together. Using the fork, gradually incorporate the flour into the eggs until fully combined. Knead the dough until a ball forms and then let rest for at least 20 minutes. Roll out the dough ¹/₄ inch thick. Cut 2-inch squares from the dough. Place about 1 teaspoon of filling in the center of each square. Fold the square in half, then pull the two corners together, wrapping them around the tips of your finger. Pinch the ends together to seal. (See Chapter 3 for detailed directions.)

Filling

1/4 cup finely chopped onion
3 tablespoons extra virgin olive oil
1 teaspoon finely chopped garlic
*1 tablespoon finely chopped flat-leaf
    parsley*
*1/2 pound cooked lobster meat, cut into
    1/4-inch pieces*
Salt and freshly ground pepper to taste
3 tablespoons unsalted butter, softened

Make the filling: In a skillet, heat the olive oil over medium heat. Add the onion and cook until it softens and turns golden brown. Add the garlic and parsley and cook for about 1 minute. Add the lobster meat and season with salt and pepper. Bring the mixture to a simmer and stir in the butter. Remove from the heat, cover, and chill well.

Sherry Coral Sauce

2 tablespoons olive oil
5 shallots, finely chopped
2 cloves garlic, minced
1 cup dry sherry
3 tablespoons brandy
1/4 cup tomato purée
1 cup good-quality fish or lobster stock
6 tablespoons unsalted butter

Dried red pepper flakes
Fresh parsley, chopped

Make the sauce: In a saucepan, heat the olive oil over medium heat. Add the shallots and garlic and sauté until golden. Add the sherry, white wine, and brandy. Simmer 3 minutes and add the tomato purée and lobster stock. Cook over moderately low heat until the sauce is reduced by two-thirds. Whisk in the butter and reduce to sauce consistency.

Cook the stuffed pasta in plenty of salted boiling water 3 to 4 minutes. Drain and add to the sherry coral sauce. Toss gently to coat. Place the pasta with the sauce in a pasta bowl and garnish with crushed red pepper and chopped parsley and serve.

Seafood Cannelloni with Tomato and Lemon Parmesan Cream Sauce

Chef Anita Hinojosa
Graham's
New Orleans, Louisiana

Serves 6

Cannelloni

1 large onion, diced
3 cloves garlic, minced
3 tablespoons vegetable oil
1 ounce fresh basil, finely shredded
1/2 ounce fresh oregano, chopped

(continued)

1 teaspoon dried hot red pepper flakes
2 cups (1 pound) ricotta cheese
1 cup shredded provolone
$^1\!/_2$ cup shredded Parmesan cheese
$^1\!/_2$ pound peeled crawfish tails, chopped
$^1\!/_2$ pound medium shrimp, peeled,
    deveined, and chopped
$^1\!/_2$ pound lump crabmeat
1 egg, lightly beaten
6 fresh pasta sheets, each 4 by 12 inches
    (see Chapter 3 for detailed instructions)
Shredded Parmesan cheese for garnish

Make the filling: Sauté onion and garlic
in 1 tablespoon of vegetable oil until onion
is translucent. Add basil, oregano, and
crushed red pepper at the last minute. Set
onion and garlic mixture aside to cool. In a
large bowl, combine the cheese and crabmeat. Lightly sauté shrimp and crawfish in
2 tablespoons of oil. Set aside to cool.
When cooled, add shrimp, crawfish, and
onion/garlic mixture to the cheese and crabmeat mixture. Season to taste with salt and
pepper and mix well.

Preheat the oven to 350°.

Cut each pasta sheet in half to form
pieces 4 by 6 inches. Brush each sheet with
beaten egg. Place a 1-inch-wide log of filling
along a short edge of a pasta sheet and roll.
Place in a baking pan, seam side down.
Repeat with remaining pasta and filling. Cover
with the tomato sauce. Bake until set, 20 to
25 minutes.

Portion out 2 cannelloni per plate and top
with the lemon sauce. Sprinkle with grated
Parmesan cheese.

Tomato Sauce

2 tablespoons olive oil
6 cloves, garlic, chopped
1 onion, diced
10 fresh tomatoes, peeled, seeded, and
    chopped
One 28-ounce can whole, peeled tomatoes
$^1\!/_4$ cup fresh thyme, chopped
$^1\!/_2$ cup fresh basil, chopped
$^1\!/_2$ fresh oregano, chopped
Pinch of dried hot red pepper flakes
10 black peppercorns
1 bay leaf
Salt to taste
$^1\!/_2$ cup sugar
$^3\!/_4$ cup red wine vinegar
1 cup heavy cream
Freshly ground black pepper to taste

In a heavy pan, heat the olive oil over
medium heat. Add the onion and garlic and
sauté until translucent. Add the fresh and
canned tomatoes. Add all the herbs, red
pepper flakes, black peppercorns, bay leaf,
and salt and simmer over low heat until
reduced by one-third, about 1 hour. Cool.
Purée in a food processor and strain through
a fine mesh sieve. Add the cream and return
to the heat. Bring just to a boil and season
with salt and pepper.

In a small sauté pan, melt the sugar. Do not let it burn. When light golden brown, slowly add the vinegar and heat until the sugar is dissolved. Use this mixture to adjust the sweetness of tomato sauce to your personal taste. You will probably not use all of it.

Lemon Parmesan Cream Sauce

3 lemons
2 tablespoons unsalted butter
3 shallots, chopped
1 bay leaf
Freshly ground pepper to taste
¹/₄ cup dry white wine
4 cups (1 quart) heavy cream
1 cup freshly grated Parmesan cheese
Salt and white pepper to taste

Peel the lemons, removing all the membranes. In a heavy saucepan, melt the butter over medium heat. Add the shallots and sauté until translucent. Add the bay leaf, pepper, lemons, and white wine. Simmer and watch carefully. Do not let it boil over. Cook until reduced by three-fourths. Add the cream and bring just to a boil. Reduce the heat to a simmer and reduce the sauce by half. Strain through a fine mesh sieve. While still very hot, whisk in the Parmesan cheese and season with salt and white pepper.

Ravioli with Swiss Chard and Ham Hocks

Chef Bradley Ogden
The Lark Creek Inn
Larkspur, California

Serves 8

Filling

¹/₂ cup ricotta cheese
1 cup blanched and chopped red Swiss chard
¹/₄ cup crème fraîche
2 teaspoons minced garlic
1 tablespoon chopped fresh basil
¹/₂ teaspoon kosher salt
¹/₄ teaspoon freshly ground pepper

Olive oil
¹/₄ pound aged Jack cheese, cut into shavings

Make the filling: In a bowl, combine the ricotta, chard, *crème fraîche*, garlic, basil, salt, and pepper. Mix well. Refrigerate until use.

Pasta Dough

(see Chapter 3 for detailed directions)
3 large eggs
1 tablespoon olive oil
3 cups all-purpose flour

Place the egg and the olive oil into a small well in the flour. Stir with a fork, gradually

(continued)

incorporating the flour, until a stiff dough forms. Knead 2 or 3 more minutes until smooth. Let the dough rest 1 hour, then roll it between the rollers of a pasta machine, starting with the widest setting. Continue rolling with successively smaller settings, folding the dough in thirds the first few times through the machine. If the dough sticks, flour lightly. When rolled, let it dry for a minute or two before cutting.

Roll out the pasta dough to the second thinnest setting on a pasta machine. Cut out twenty-four 3-inch circles and place a heaping tablespoon of filling in the center of each. Cut out 24 slightly larger circles ($3^3/4$ inches) for the tops. Paint the edges of the bottom circles with water and press on the tops, pressing out as much air as possible. Crimp the edges with a fork to seal. Place on lightly floured baking sheet and cover with damp kitchen towel until use.

Braised Ham Hocks

8 cloves garlic, crushed
1 large yellow onion, sliced
2 tablespoons olive oil
6 large tomatoes, or one 28-ounce can Italian plum tomatoes
$1/4$ cup balsamic vinegar
2 Anaheim chili peppers
$1/4$ cup chopped parsley
$1/4$ cup chopped fresh basil
4 cups chicken stock
3 large ham hocks

Make the ham hocks: Preheat the oven to 350°. In a skillet, heat the olive oil. Add the garlic and onion and sauté until softened, about 5 minutes. Transfer to a roasting pan and add all the remaining ingredients. Place in the oven and roast, basting frequently, until the meat is very tender, $1^1/2$ hours.

Remove from the oven and remove the hocks from the pan. When cool enough to handle, strip the meat from the bones. Strain the cooking liquid. Set the meat and liquid aside separately. Keep warm.

Roasted Mushroom Ragout

4 cups mixed fresh flavorful mushrooms such as shiitake (trimmed and quartered), chanterelle (trimmed but left whole), portobello or porcino (trimmed but left whole, quartered if large)
6 to 8 garlic cloves, slivered
5 shallots, thinly sliced
2 or 3 sprigs each fresh rosemary and thyme, or $1/4$ teaspoon each dried
3 tablespoons olive oil
$1/4$ cup balsamic vinegar
Kosher salt
Freshly cracked pepper
1 cup Zinfandel wine
$1^1/2$ cups chicken stock
3 tablespoons unsalted butter
$1/4$ cup coarsely chopped parsley

Make the ragout: Preheat the oven to 425°. In a bowl, combine mushrooms, garlic, shallots, rosemary, and thyme. Toss with the olive oil and balsamic vinegar. Season with salt and pepper. Arrange the mushrooms evenly in one layer in a heavy roasting pan. Roast until tender and lightly browned, stirring occasionally, about 15 minutes. Remove from the pan and keep warm. Place the pan on the stovetop over medium heat. Add the Zinfandel and deglaze the pan, scraping up any browned bits. Reduce the wine by half and add the chicken stock. Cook to reduce the sauce slightly. Add the butter, parsley, and mushrooms, and simmer for 5 minutes. Keep warm.

Add the ravioli to a large pot with plenty of boiling, lightly salted water. Boil slowly until tender, about 5 or 6 minutes. When the ravioli are cooked, drain well and toss lightly with olive oil. Meanwhile, reheat the strained hock cooking liquid and the ragout. Place 3 ravioli on each plate and top with the meat from the ham hocks and their broth and the ragout. Serve with the shaved Jack cheese.

Pumpkin Ravioli

Chef Nicola Civetta
Ristorante Primavera
New York, New York

Serves 4

Filling:
1 pound peeled pumpkin, sliced
2 tablespoons olive oil
1/4 cup unsalted butter
1 onion, finely chopped
1/4 pound Parmesan cheese, grated
1/2 cup mascarpone cheese
2 tablespoons fine dried bread crumbs
Salt and freshly ground pepper to taste
Pinch of grated nutmeg

Pasta Dough
2 cups flour
2 egg yolks plus 1 whole egg
Pinch of salt
Water as needed for mixing dough

Sauce
1/2 cup unsalted butter
8 fresh sage leaves

Make the filling: Place the pumpkin pieces in a saucepan with water to cover, bring to a boil, and cook until tender. Drain and pass through a sieve to purée. In a skillet, heat the oil and butter over medium heat. Add the onion and sauté until golden brown. Remove

(continued)

from the heat and let cool slightly. Add all the remaining ingredients and mix thoroughly.

Make the dough: (See Chapter 3 for detailed directions.) In a bowl, place the flour, eggs, and salt. Gradually add the water and mix until the dough forms a soft ball. Roll out the dough on a lightly floured surface until very thin. Cut the dough into 3" x 3" squares. Put 1 teaspoon of pumpkin filling on each square and fold into a ravioli.

Boil the ravioli in salted water for 3-5 minutes, stirring gently, and drain.

Make the sauce: In a large skillet, melt the butter over medium heat. Add the sage leaves and sauté until golden. Add the ravioli and mix gently for 1 minute. Serve immediately.

Lobster Lasagna

Chef Albert Lunalover
Luna Si
Atlanta, Georgia

Serves 2

Vegetable Stock
½ onion, chopped
1 carrot, chopped
1 celery stalk, chopped
1 bay leaf
3 sprigs fresh thyme
3 cloves garlic
3 cups water

1 lobster, about 1½ pounds
2 shallots, diced
1 fennel bulb, sliced against the grain
1 cup heavy cream
Salt and freshly ground pepper to taste
4 pieces lasagna pasta

Make the stock: Cut all the vegetables into cubes and place in a saucepan. Add the bay leaf, thyme, garlic, and water and bring to a boil.

Meanwhile, split the lobster. Add the lobster to the boiling stock and cook for about 6 minutes until the shells are bright red. Remove from the stock and, when cool enough to handle, remove the lobster meat from the shells. Strain the stock and set aside.

In a saucepan, combine the shallots and fennel. Add the cream and enough of the stock to form a good sauce consistency. Place over medium heat and cook until the vegetables are tender. At the last minute, add the lobster, salt, and pepper.

Meanwhile, bring at least 3 quarts of water to boil. Add 1 tablespoon of salt. Add noodles, stir to separate, and cook until *al dente*. Drain.

In a 7 x 12-inch baking dish, layer lasagna and half the lobster, put another layer of lasagna, and top with the rest of the lobster and the fennel.

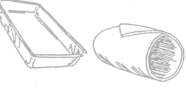

Versatile *Lasagna*

Stuffed and layered pastas can be filled with almost anything, and therein lies their beauty. Lasagna, especially, is amazingly versatile. Between those lovely, flat noodles can be layers of seafood, vegetables, or meat, and the sauce that enmeshes the dish can carry the flavors of cuisines as different as the north and south poles of the culinary world—from the Middle East to the American Southwest.

But lasagna, which offers such varied possibilities, is too often presented in a run-of-the-mill rectangular dish. For a change, make it in a round dish. Just overlap the noodles in a circular fashion and trim the edges to fit. If you use homemade dough, simply cut circles instead of strips. You can even make individual lasagnas in ramekins by cutting the noodles to fit a single portion.

Pasta Roulade with Red Pepper Coulis

Chef Stefan Kappes
Stefini Restaurant
Irvington, New York

Serves 4

1 sheet green (spinach) pasta
Pasta sheets are available in many stores that sell fresh pasta. Buy more than one to perfect the technique.
One 11-ounce log fresh goat cheese
1/2 cup heavy cream
Freshly ground pepper to taste
2 cups fresh basil leaves
2 tablespoons olive oil
1/2 pound prosciutto or cooked ham, very thinly sliced

Sauce
3 red bell peppers, roasted, peeled, and chopped
2 tablespoons olive oil
2 ounces shallots, minced
1/2 cup dry white wine
1/4 cup dry vermouth
3/4 cup heavy cream
Salt and freshly ground pepper to taste

Fresh basil sprigs

(continued)

In a large pot, bring 4 quarts of water to a rolling boil. Add 1 tablespoon salt. Place a large rectangular roasting pan on top of the stove over high heat, and transfer the boiling water to the roasting pan. Very carefully lower the pasta sheet into the water, reduce the heat, and cook for about 3 minutes until *al dente*. Remove the pasta and plunge it into ice water to cool.

Remove the pasta sheet to a flat, smooth work surface. In a food processor, combine the goat cheese and the heavy cream and process into a smooth spread. Using a spatula or large spoon, spread the surface of the pasta with the cheese mixture and sprinkle with the pepper. In the food processor, combine the basil leaves and olive oil and process until well blended. Cover the sheet with the thinly sliced prosciutto. Using a spatula or large spoon, spread the basil mixture over the prosciutto. Starting at the top, slowly and carefully roll up the sheet jelly-roll style. Wrap in plastic wrap and refrigerate overnight.

Make the sauce: In a large saucepan, heat the oil over medium heat. Add the shallots and sauté until translucent. Add the peppers and heat through. Raise the heat, add the wine and vermouth, and boil 1 minute. Lower the flame, add the cream, and cook on low heat until the sauce thickens to coat the back of a spoon. Add salt and pepper to taste. Puree in a food processor until smooth.

When ready to serve, unwrap the roll and slice carefully with a sharp knife. For each serving place a pool of the sauce on the bottom of a large dinner plate and place 2 slices of the roulade on top. Garnish with a sprig of fresh basil.

Sun-Dried Tomato Ravioli with a Wild Mushroom Filling

Chef Scott A. Vadney
The Rensselaerville Institute &
   Conference Center
Rensselaerville, New York

Makes 20 raviolis

Sauce
2 red bell peppers
2 yellow bell peppers
Vegetable stock as needed
Salt and freshly ground pepper to taste
Finely chopped fresh chives

Filling
1/2 pound fresh shiitake mushrooms
1/2 pound fresh portobello mushrooms
1/4 cup brandy
1 teaspoon brown mustard
1/4 cup seasoned fine dried bread crumbs

Splash of balsamic vinegar
Salt and freshly ground pepper to taste

Dough
2 ounces dry-packed sun-dried tomatoes
1 cup semolina flour
¹/₂ cup all-purpose flour
Tomato juice or water as needed
Dash salt

Make the sauce: Roast the peppers until charred on all sides, either under a broiler or over a gas burner. Place in a lock-top plastic bag to steam for 10 minutes. Peel under cool running water, discarding stems and seeds. Set aside, keeping the colors separate. Purée the colors separately in blender, adding stock as needed to make a smooth sauce. Season with salt and pepper. Set aside. (The sauce may be made 1 day ahead and stored in the refrigerator.)

Make the filling: Clean the mushrooms, discarding the stems. Dice the caps into small uniform cubes. Heat a nonstick skillet over moderate heat and add mushrooms. Carefully add the brandy (it may flare up, especially on a gas stove). As the mushrooms begin to sweat, add the mustard and half of the bread crumbs. Sauté, adding the vinegar and moving the pan constantly, until the mushrooms are nearly cooked through. Remove from the heat. When nearly cool, add the remaining bread crumbs and season with salt and pepper. Let cool and reserve.

Make the dough: Place the sun-dried tomatoes in hot water to cover and set aside for 30 minutes. Meanwhile, in a bowl, sift together the flours and salt. Drain the tomatoes and purée in a blender, adding water or tomato juice as needed to obtain a smooth sauce that is not too thin. Add this tomato sauce to the flour mixture, stirring to combine to make a firm pasta dough. Add additional water as needed to achieve correct consistency. Add salt and pepper as needed. Gather into a ball and cover with an inverted bowl. Let stand for 15 minutes.

Using a pasta machine, roll out the dough to the fifth level. The dough may be stiff and difficult to work with at first, but patience will prevail. Place dough in ravioli mold, and fill with approximately 2 teaspoons of mushroom filling. Seal, using water along the seams to "glue" dough together.

In a large pot, bring plenty of salted water to a boil. The water should be "smiling," not at all fierce and angrily boiling. Add the ravioli and cook until pasta is *al dente*, 3 to 5 minutes. Drain and rinse the cooked ravioli briefly in hot water. Place on a serving plate. Spoon some of each color pepper coulis along each ravioli, and serve the remainder on the side.

Note: See Chapter 3 for detailed directions and method for making ravioli without a mold.

Lasagna with Lobster and Watercress

Chef Pierre Pollin
Le Titi de Paris
Arlington Heights, Illinois

Serves 6

12 fresh pasta sheets flavored with
*   watercress and saffron, if available*
6 Maine lobsters, approximately
*   1¹/₂ pounds each*
Note: Pasta sheets are available in many
*   stores that sell fresh pasta. Buy enough*
*   sheets to make 2 pieces sized to fit the*
*   pasta bowls used for each serving.*

Sauce

1 tablespoon plus ¹/₄ cup unsalted butter
2 tablespoons chopped shallots
3 tablespoons sherry vinegar
1 cup dry white wine
1 cup fish stock
¹/₃ cup heavy cream
1 pound watercress, stems removed and
*   reserved, leaves blanched and puréed*
1 teaspoon minced fresh tarragon
Salt and freshly ground pepper to taste

Make the sauce: In a skillet, melt the 1 tablespoon butter over medium heat. Add the shallots and sauté until translucent, 3 to 5 minutes. Add the vinegar and reduce until about ¹/₂ teaspoon liquid remains. Add the wine, fish stock, and watercress stems. Reduce until 1 tablespoon liquid remains. Add the cream, bring to boil. Whisk in the ¹/₄ cup butter, cut into pieces; strain. Return to the pan and add tarragon and puréed watercress. Season with salt and pepper.

Plunge lobsters into boiling water, cook approximately 7 minutes. Remove and plunge into cold water. Remove lobster meat from shell. (Boil 2 lobsters at a time in 6 quarts of water.)

To cook the pasta sheets: Cut pasta to size to be used. Bring 4 quarts of water to a rolling boil. Add 1 tablespoon of salt. Add as many pasta pieces as will cook without crowding. When *al dente*, drain by pouring off water and slipping pieces into a roasting pan of cold water. Then, by hand, remove them to a kitchen towel to drain.

To serve, spoon the sauce into bowls. Place one pasta sheet, cut to fit, on the sauce. Garnish with the lobster meat and another layer of lasagna. Drizzle with the sauce.

CHAPTER 12

ANCIENT NOODLES: ASIAN PASTAS

The noodles of Asia have been in the Western marketplace for a long time, and now their popularity has increased along with the popularity of Asian-inspired cuisines. Western diners are ready to try the many variations the Asian noodle repertoire offers. Noodles made with eggs or without, from wheat, rice, or beans, remain the dietary staples of the Asian common man and, at the same time, are enthusiastically sought after by sophisticated diners all over the world. The recipes here can be made in a kitchen with no more exotic equipment than a pot for boiling water and a skillet. Supermarkets carry most of the necessary ingredients, which means that the pungent flavors of Asia are making home-cooked pasta more interesting than ever.

Chinese Noodles

Mein is the Chinese term for both wheat noodles and egg noodles, the most widely used noodles in many parts of Asia. Golden egg noodles vary from thin threads to wider, flatter strands like linguine. Slim or fat, they are sold in tightly wrapped bundles and are available fresh, dried, or even frozen.

Cooking: Asian egg noodles can be prepared in the same way as their Western counterparts. An alternative Japanese method is described with the recipe for fresh *udon* noodles. As always, avoid overcooking, especially with fresh noodles that must be watched mindfully; thin fresh noodles should be tested after just 30 seconds. The cooking time depends upon the thickness of the noodle. Any noodles that are not going to be used immediately can be tossed with a bit of Asian sesame oil to keep them from sticking. Noodles cooked for later use in soups or stir-fries should be, at the least, *al dente*, and, even better, undercooked. To reheat the noodles, douse them with boiling water.

Japanese Noodles

The West has a single premier hard, durum-wheat noodle, but the Japanese capitalize on the grain's possibilities for variation.

Somen are thin, white stick noodles made of wheat flour, water, and oil, and are almost always eaten cold. They are commonly sold in packages of single servings bound by a ribbon.

Udon are square-edged, thick whole-wheat noodles usually served in soups and hot pots. When they are sold fresh, they are called *nama udon.*

Soba are beige stick noodles of buckwheat, excellent both hot and cold. They can generally be substituted in recipes calling for *udon*.

Ramen are fine, white wheat noodles, a pasta that cooks quickly in water or broth. They have become the ultimate fast food, sold all over the world in packages with soup flavoring.

Cooking: All these noodles in their dried form can be cooked like any pasta in boiling water. Very thin noodles, to be served in broth, can be quickly cooked. *Somen* take only 3 to 4 minutes; *soba,* 6 to 7 minutes; and the thickest, *udon,* 15 minutes or more. Of course, these times can vary according to the noodle, so always check for doneness after the first few minutes.

Rice Noodles

Found throughout Southeast Asia and southern China, rice noodles are a staple consumed on the street and eaten in fine restaurants. Cooking is minimal because rice noodles have, in fact, been cooked in the manufacturing process.

Since the swelling of rice noodles is different from that of wheat pastas, amounts need to be adjusted. Plan on 8 ounces of *fresh* rice noodles for a single serving for a main dish, and 3 ounces for a side dish or soup. Plan on 3 ounces of *dried* rice noodles for a single serving for a main dish, and half that for a side dish or first course.

Dried rice noodles come in a variety of sizes. Those that are called "sticks" are sold in a wiry bundle. If they must be separated, find a place that will catch the broken pieces. Brittle and truly sticklike, they come alive after soaking and are usually deep-fried.

Cooking: First soak the noodles in cold water for about 15 minutes or until they are soft and pliable. Then rinse to remove the starches that leave a milky residue in soups and sauces. Very thin noodles will be ready for use in soups. Thicker noodles should be boiled for about 5 minutes or more after soaking. As always, check for doneness; aiming for *al dente* is the goal.

Rice vermicelli (*mi-fen* or *mai-fun*) are cream-colored noodles that turn white when they are cooked. The thinnest versions are ideal for soups, stir-frying, and deep-frying. Without soaking, they need 2 or 3 minutes boiling time.

Fresh rice noodles are sold chilled and need to stay that way. They will keep a week in the refrigerator and can be frozen. The noodles will be stiff if they have been refrigerated and will need softening. Begin by pouring hot water over them to remove the oil used in making them. Then steam them, but carefully, or they will turn to mush. Like dried rice noodles, they must be soaked before cooking.

Vegetable or Bean Starch Noodles

Vegetable noodles is the generic catch all term for the lovely transparent noodles of China and Southeast Asia called bean threads, cellophane noodles, shining noodles, or silver noodles. Most are made from mung beans. The Japanese variation, shirataki, is made exclusively from a plant called "devil's tongue plant" that is similar to a yam. Shirataki soak up the juices of sukiyaki. All these noodles have a spongy quality that is easily permeated, making them excellent flavor messengers.

Cooking: Soak in hot water to cover for about 20 minutes. Then drain and cook briefly, about 3 minutes.

Wontons

Wonton wrappers in the supermarket are a sign that Asian cooking has gone mainstream. Sold fresh, they freeze well. They can be stuffed, then boiled or deep-fried.

Making Fresh Asian Noodles

Asian egg noodles are not that different from their Italian counterparts. For the finer points of technique, refer to Chapter 3, on making fresh pasta. Rice noodles are a new challenge and involve steaming rather than rolling, a novel enterprise for Western cooks. These recipes make about 1 pound of noodles.

Egg Dough for Chinese Noodles, Wonton Wrappers, or Egg Roll Wrappers

These directions are essentially the same as those for Italian egg dough. Refer to those instructions for details. (See Chapter 3.)

2 cups all-purpose flour
1^1/$_4$ teaspoons salt
1 egg, beaten
^{1}/$_4$ cup water
^{1}/$_4$ teaspoon vegetable oil

In a bowl, sift together the flour and salt. In another bowl, combine the egg and water. Turn the dry ingredients onto a work surface and hollow out a well in the center with your fingers or fist. Incorporate the flour into the egg with your fingers until a dough forms. Knead the dough until it is smooth and firm, about 5 minutes. If the dough is too dry, add a little more water; if it is too sticky, add a little flour. Oil the dough, cover with an inverted bowl, or tightly wrap and allow it to rest for an hour. Roll and cut noodles as described for Italian pasta.

For wonton wrappers, roll out the dough paper-thin and cut into 3-inch squares for wontons or 7-inch squares for egg rolls. Alternatively, cut circles with a 3-inch round cookie cutter or glass for wontons. Let the pieces dry for about 10 minutes, and then dust them with cornstarch. They can be

stacked and refrigerated this way. To fill and roll, moisten the edges with a bit of water or egg wash to help the seal.

Rice Noodles

Two ingredients, tapioca starch and wheat starch, are found in Asian markets.

1¹/₂ cups regular rice flour
¹/₂ cup tapioca starch
5 tablespoons wheat starch
1¹/₂ teaspoons salt
3 cups water
2 tablespoons vegetable oil, plus additional oil for pans

In a bowl, combine the rice flour, tapioca and wheat starches, salt, and water. Stir well with a wooden spoon until velvety. Strain through a sieve into a bowl. Add the tablespoons oil and mix well. Let rest for 3 minutes.

Oil 2 shallow pans each 8 or 9 inches square. Bring about ¹/₂ inch water to a boil in a steamer pan with the rack in place. Stir the dough. Pour about ¹/₂ cup into an oiled pan, just enough to coat the bottom. Place on the rack, cover the batter with a kitchen towel, and place the lid on the steamer. Steam for 5 minutes until set. Remove the pan from the steamer and place it in a

larger pan with ¹/₂ inch cold water. When completely cool, loosen the noodle and transfer it to an oiled baking sheet. Lightly oil the top.

This sheet is complete. Repeat the process until all the batter is steamed. Then wrap tightly in plastic wrap and refrigerate for 2 hours before cutting. The sheet can be cut into any size noodles or any shape.

Remember that the noodles must be soaked before cooking. Very fine noodles need only to be doused in hot or boiling water.

Japanese *Udon* Noodles

Expect these noodles to be chewy with a pleasant nuttiness to the flavor. Substituting ¹/₄ cup gluten flour for an equal amount of the white flour can enhance these qualities. Gluten flour is sometimes found in natural-food stores. Kneading is important to the success of these noodles, so the number of minutes matters. The instructions for making the *udon* is the same as for Italian noodles; refer to Chapter 3, on fresh pasta, for details. The cooking, as described below, however, is definitely Japanese.

2 teaspoons salt
¹/₂ cup water
2 cups unbleached all-purpose flour.

(continued)

In a bowl, combine the salt and water. Place the flour on the work surface and make a well in the center. Pour the water and salt into the well. Incorporate the flour into the water with your fingers until the dough forms a ball. If the dough is too sticky, add a little flour; if it is too dry, add a little water. Be frugal with the water, however, because too much will spoil the preferred density of the dough. Knead for about 10 minutes. Place the dough in a bowl, cover tightly, and let stand for 3 hours. To roll out the dough, divide it in half and follow the directions for fresh pasta in Chapter 3. *Udon* noodles should be 1/8 to 1/4 inch thick.

The Japanese have a way of cooking *udon* and other fresh noodles that cooks them more evenly. This *sashimizu*, or "add water," method is worth trying not only for fresh *udon* and other Japanese noodles, but for any type of pasta. Bring a large amount of water to boil, enough for the pasta to have plenty of room. Add the noodles slowly so as not to break any. Stir to separate and keep any from sticking to the bottom. When the water comes to a full rolling boil, add 1 cup of cold water. When the water boils again, add another cup of cold water. How often you repeat this sequence depends on when the noodles reach *al dente*; bite to test often. When the noodles are done, drain and rinse with cold water to remove the starch. They can be reheated for serving by pouring boiling water over them. (Note: *Somen* should

not be doused with cold water, but served immediately after draining.)

Asian-English Food Dictionary: Common Asian Ingredients

Much of the feistiness or subtlety of Asian cooking is dependent on homegrown ingredients that were once unfamiliar in Western kitchens. But no longer. The basics, which are described here, are available in specialty stores and many supermarkets, and are, for the most part, simple to use.

Annatto seeds Reddish-orange seeds from the annatto tree used to impart their color to sauces. Found in Latin American and East Indian markets as well as Chinese markets, Annatto water and annatto paste are convenient forms that are also sold.

Asian chili peppers The chilies most commonly used in the West are mild compared to Asian dried red chilies. Found in Asian markets, they are also sold whole, crushed, and powdered. Whatever the form, they will be fiery. Substitute milder Western chilies if they are unavailable or you prefer less bite.

Bean curd, pressed Sold plain or seasoned and ready to cut into strips for stir-fry.

Chili oil Also known as hot chili oil. These are oils infused with the flavors of hot Asian chilies.

Chinese chives Bunches of yellow or green Chinese chives look like grass but taste more like garlic. "Yellow" chives are actually a type of leek.

Coriander, fresh Also called cilantro, this lacy-leaved herb is used in Southeast Asian cooking. Coriander *seeds* are often used in curries.

Curry powder A mixture of spices that varies with the brand. Look for the best in specialty stores.

Daikon A Japanese white radish that is over 1 foot long and 2 inches thick. Mild in flavor, it is used in soups and sauces because it absorbs their dominant flavors.

Dashi Japanese stock, made from bonito flakes and seaweed. The instant form is commonly sold in tea-bag-like satchels.

Fish sauce A sauce made from fermented fish that is indispensable to much of Southeast Asian cooking. Called *nam pla* in Thailand and *nuoc mam* in Vietnam, its addition to any dish enhances all the flavors in the recipe.

Five-spice powder A blend of spices—star anise, cloves, cinnamon, peppercorns, fennel—used in Chinese cooking.

Galangal Like ginger, galangal is sold both fresh and dried, but the flavor is much different in each of these forms. If unavailable, half as much ginger with a bit of cinnamon can be substituted.

Gyoza skins Round dumpling wrappers from Japan usually thinner than Chinese wonton wrappers.

Hoisin sauce Ground beans, garlic, sugar, vinegar, and sesame oil are combined to make a sweet, spicy sauce popular as a Chinese table condiment and sometimes used in cooking.

Jicama A crispy, white-fleshed, brown-skinned root vegetable with a slightly sweet taste. It can be eaten raw or briefly cooked and can be used as a substitute for water chestnuts.

Lemon grass This is citronella and it tastes like its name. Lemon grass can be bought fresh, dried, or frozen. The zest of 1 lemon can be used as a substitute.

Mirin A sweet rice wine from Japan that is used in cooking and is never drunk. Found not in liquor stores, but in markets with Asian condiments.

Miso An elementary Japanese seasoning, *miso* is found in both red and white forms. A paste of soybeans and grains, it should be stored in the refrigerator.

Enoke mushrooms Thin, tiny-capped Japanese mushrooms.

Oyster mushrooms Beige-gray mushrooms with a meaty texture that are excellent raw in salads or cooked quickly in stir-fry dishes.

Shiitake mushrooms Meaty, dark brown mushrooms most frequently sold dried, but sometimes fresh. Called *shiitake* in Japanese

cooking or black mushrooms in Chinese cooking. Soaked dried mushrooms in warm water to soften before using.

Tree ears or cloud ears Commonly sold dried, with the smaller black variety preferred. Best used in slices.

Nori A seaweed sold in sheets, roasted or unroasted. Although it most commonly known as a wrapper for rolled sushi, it is also crumbled over noodle and rice dishes.

Asian sesame oil Made from roasted sesame seeds, the oil is dark in color and should not be confused with the clear sesame oil made from unroasted seeds sold in natural-food stores. The Asian oil has a strong flavor and is used as a seasoning rather than for cooking.

Oyster sauce A sweet-salty sauce made from oysters. Used in Chinese cooking, the taste depends on the brand.

Rice flour There are two types of rice flour, sweet and regular. Sweet is used for making sweet food while regular rice flour is used for noodles.

Rice vinegar White rice vinegars are sold seasoned and unseasoned. The seasoned, although delicious on salads, is not to be used if a recipe calls for rice vinegar.

Chinese rice vinegar Also called Chinese black vinegar, this dark vinegar is made from fermented rice. Although sweeter, balsamic vinegar can be substituted with a reduction of other sugars in a recipe.

Rice wine Chinese rice wine, sometimes called Shaoxing wine, is used for drinking and cooking; dry sherry can be substituted. Japanese rice wine, or sake, is used for drinking and cooking. See also *mirin*.

Sesame paste Asian sesame paste is thick and brown and is made from roasted seeds. Tahini, the Middle Eastern version, is a product of unroasted sesame seeds.

Shrimp, dried Although not appealing on their own, dried shrimp, sometimes pounded or ground, are a flavorful addition to many Southeast Asian dishes.

Shrimp paste Sold fresh or dried, this pungent flavoring is essential to Southeast Asian cuisine.

Tahini Sesame paste made from unroasted sesame seeds. Used in Middle Eastern dishes.

Tamarind Fruit of the tamarind tree, sold in pods, paste, and concentrate. Its sour taste complements Southeast Asian sauces and soups. Available in Asian and some Latin American markets.

Tapioca powder or starch A thickening agent similar to cornstarch.

Turmeric A spice usually found in curries. Now also sold fresh, it is a rhizome like ginger and can be peeled, grated, or sliced.

Wasabi powder A root most commonly available as a dried powder. It is brought back to life with just enough water to make a paste. The resulting pale green, very hot, horseradish-like condiment is commonly served with sushi.

Sesame-Seared Scallops with Baby Bok Choy and Glass Noodle Salad

Chef Graham Duncan
Food Fetish Catering
Atlanta, Georgia

Serves 6

Vinaigrette

1 pound arugula, tough stems removed
1 teaspoon chopped shallot
1 tablespoon minced fresh ginger
1/3 cup rice vinegar
1 cup olive oil
2 tablespoons Asian sesame oil
Chicken stock as needed
Soy sauce to taste
Fresh lime juice to taste

Salad

Four 1/8-ounce packages bean thread noodles
3 heads baby bok choy, julienned
1 red bell pepper, seeded and julienned
1 yellow bell pepper, seeded and julienned
1 tablespoon unseasoned rice vinegar
1/4 cup olive oil

Scallops

12 sea scallops
1/4 cup Asian sesame oil
1/2 cup mixed black and white sesame seeds

Coarse sea salt
3 tablespoons olive oil
1-inch chive sticks pickled ginger for garnish
Asian sesame oil for garnish

Make the vinaigrette: Immerse the arugula in boiling water for 1 minute, drain, squeeze dry, and chop finely. Place in a blender along with the shallot, ginger, and vinegar. Purée, adding chicken stock as needed to liquefy. With the motor running slowly add both oils blending until emulsified. Season with soy sauce and lime juice.

Make the salad: Place the noodles in a bowl and add scalding hot tap water. Let stand until soft, about 10 minutes. Drain the noodles and place in a bowl. Add the bok choy and bell pepper and toss. Stir together the vinegar and olive oil in a small bowl and pour over the noodles and vegetables. Toss to mix well. Season with sea salt and cracked pepper.

Prepare the scallops: Preheat the oven to 350°. Remove the tough muscle on the side of each scallop. Place the sesame oil and sesame seeds in separate bowls. Dip each scallop into the sesame oil, and then into the sesame seeds, coating evenly. Sprinkle each with sea salt.

In a sauté pan, heat the olive oil to the smoking point. Add the scallops and cook for 30 seconds on each side. Transfer to a baking dish and place in the oven until cooked through 1 to 2 minutes. Do not overcook.

(continued)

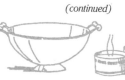

To assemble: Spoon vinaigrette in a pool over bottom of each plate. Cover with noodles and vegetables. Top with 2 sea scallops per plate.

Japanese Shrimp and Pineapple with Cold Noodles

Serves 6

Sauce
¼ cup fish sauce (nampla)
1 cup coconut cream
Juice of 1 lime
2 tablespoons sugar
2 tablespoons vegetable oil
10-ounce package Japanese thick somen noodles
½ fresh pineapple, peeled and coarsely chopped or crushed
¾ pound medium shrimp, peeled, deveined, and butterflied

Garnishes
2 scallions, including green tops, thinly sliced
1 tablespoon chopped fresh cilantro
1 tablespoon finely chopped fresh ginger

Make the sauce: In a saucepan, boil the coconut cream and let cool. Add the lime juice, sugar, and oil and mix completely.

In a large pot, bring 4 quarts of water to a rolling boil. Add 1 tablespoon salt. Add the noodles, stir to separate, and cook until *al dente*, about 3 minutes. Drain and immerse in cold water. Drain thoroughly. Transfer the noodles to a large bowl. Distribute the pineapple over the noodles.

Again, bring 4 quarts of water to a boil. Add the shrimp and cook until they turn pink and curl slightly, about 1 minute. Drain and let cool. Scatter the shrimp over the pineapple.

Pour the sauce over the noodles. Top with the scallions, cilantro, and ginger.

Chilled Soba Noodles with Caviar and Oba

Chef Hidemasa Yamamoto
The Ritz-Carlton
Washington, D.C.

Serves 4 as a first course

Sauce
¼ cup water
2 tablespoons soy sauce
3 tablespoons mirin
2 tablespoons dried bonita flakes

1/2 pound soba *noodles, dried*
1 bunch oba, *diced (Perilla leaves or*
    Aojiso, available in Japanese markets)
1/3 *bunch fresh chives, chopped*
1 *tablespoon extra virgin olive oil*
1 *ounce sevruga caviar*

Make the sauce: In a saucepan, combine the water, soy sauce, and *mirin*. Bring to a boil and add the bonita. Remove from the heat and let steep for 30 seconds. Pour through a fine-mesh sieve into a clean bowl.

In a large pot, bring at least 4 quarts of water to a rolling boil. Do not add salt. Add the noodles, stir to separate, and cook until soft (not *al dente*). Drain and rinse with cold water, then drain again.

In a bowl, combine the noodles, sauce, *oba*, chives, olive oil, and 1/2 ounce of the caviar. Toss well. Using a fork, roll the noodles into 4 equal portions, and place each in the center of a chilled dish. Garnish with remaining caviar.

Chinese Noodles with Asian Pesto

Serves 4

1 *cup vegetable oil*
1/2 *cup peanuts*
1 *small green chile pepper, seeded*
2 *teaspoons ginger, chopped*
3 *cloves garlic*
1 1/2 *cups fresh basil leaves*
1/4 *cup fresh mint leaves*
1/4 *cup fresh cilantro leaves*
3 *tablespoons lemon juice*
1 *teaspoon salt*
1 *teaspoon sugar*
1 *pound egg noodles, Chinese or*
    fettuccine

Heat the oil in a small skillet over high heat. Remove from heat and add the peanuts. Stir the nuts in the hot oil until they are lightly browned. Remove with a slotted spoon and drain on paper towels. Reserve the oil.

In a food processor or blender, blend the peanuts to a rough paste. Add the chile, ginger, and garlic and blend. Add the basil, mint, and cilantro and 1/4 cup of the reserved oil. Blend. Add the salt, sugar, and lemon juice and blend until the herbs are finely minced. Stir in the remaining oil a little at a time until the desired consistency is reached.

Bring at least 4 quarts of water to a rolling boil. Add 1 tablespoon of salt. Add pasta and cook until *al dente*. Drain.

Transfer pasta to a serving bowl, dress with pesto, and toss well. This may be served hot or at room temperature.

Pad Thai

Serves 3 or 4

1/2 pound dried flat rice noodles
1 teaspoon rice vinegar
3 tablespoons fish sauce
1 teaspoon sugar
1 tablespoon tomato paste
1/4 cup oil
1 tablespoon minced garlic
1/2 pound shrimp, peeled and deveined
1/3 pound ground pork
2 eggs, lightly beaten
1 cup bean sprouts

Garnishes

3 tablespoons unsalted peanuts, toasted and chopped
1 fresh red chile pepper, sliced
2 scallions, thinly sliced, white and green parts

Place the noodles in a bowl and add warm water to cover; let stand until soft, about 15 minutes. In a small bowl, combine the vinegar, fish sauce, sugar, and tomato paste and stir until the sugar is dissolved.

Drain the noodles and set aside. In a wok or deep skillet, heat 3 tablespoons oil over medium-high heat. Add the garlic and stir-fry until golden, about 1 minute. Add the shrimp and pork and stir-fry briefly, until they lose their raw color. Add the tomato paste mixture and bring to a boil. Add the noodles and cook, stirring, until the noodles have absorbed the sauce.

Push the noodles from the center of the pan. Add the remaining 1 tablespoon oil to the center of the pan and heat briefly. Add the eggs, allow to cook for 10 to 15 seconds, and then cover with the noodles. Fold the eggs into the noodles until the eggs are set. Stir in the bean sprouts.

Transfer to a warm serving plate and top with the peanuts, chile, and scallions, in that order.

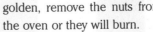

Toasting Nuts

When cooking with nuts, it's always good to have more than the recipe calls for on hand. Some are bound to be eaten during the preparation. Delicious in their natural state, nuts are irresistible when toasted. Their flavors are enhanced and deepened with just a few minutes under the heat. To toast nuts, spread them on a baking sheet in a single layer and place them in a 350° oven for about 3 to 5 minutes. How quickly they toast will depend on the nut. Check them after 3 minutes and enjoy the aroma. Shake the pan, and see if they are beginning to change color. As soon as they turn golden, remove the nuts from the oven or they will burn.

Thai Noodle Salad

The Moosewood Collective
Moosewood Restaurant
Ithaca, New York
From *Sundays at Moosewood*
Restaurant

Serves 6

1 pound angel hair pasta

Sauce
3 tablespoons minced fresh basil
1/4 cup minced fresh spearmint
1 cup coconut milk
2 tablespoons Asian sesame oil
1 tablespoon grated fresh ginger
1 tablespoon minced garlic
3/4 teaspoon salt
2 tablespoons fresh lime or lemon juice
1/8 teaspoon cayenne pepper, or to taste
2 tablespoons minced scallions

Vegetables
Choose any of the following to equal
   4 cups:
Small carrots, julienned 1 inch long
Asparagus spears, cut into 1 1/2-inch lengths
Red bell peppers, seeded and cut into
   2-inch strips
Snow peas, cut in half
Green peas or snap peas
Bean sprouts, blanched and chilled
Scallions, cut on the diagonal into 1-inch
   pieces
Sliced water chestnuts

Garnish
Lime wedges
Roughly chopped roasted peanuts
Minced fresh cilantro (optional)

Cook the linguine in plenty of boiling salted water, drain, and then cool completely. Make the sauce: In a bowl, combine all of the sauce ingredients and mix well. Set aside.

Any combination of vegetables is fine. Let color and contrasting textures be your guide. Prepare the vegetables as follows and set aside together in a bowl. Drop the carrots into boiling water and cook until barely tender. Do the same with asparagus. Blanch the peppers, peas, and bean spouts in boiling water, then plunge immediately into cold water and drain. Add the scallions and water chestnuts to the other vegetables and set the bowl aside to cool.

Combine the noodles, vegetables, and sauce. Mix well and refrigerate until cool, then serve at once. If you must refrigerate the salad longer, keep in mind that noodles absorb flavor like crazy and so you'll need to readjust the seasonings before serving. The salad will keep for about 2 days.

Each diner should have a wedge or two of lime to squeeze on top just before eating. Pass the chopped peanuts and, if you like, some fresh cilantro.

Spareribs with Noodles

Serves 6

Chili Sauce
$1/2$ cup rice vinegar
2 teaspoons sugar
1 tablespoon fish sauce
1 teaspoon chopped mixed fresh red and
    green chili peppers, or to taste

1 pound spareribs, cut into $1^1/2$-inch pieces
$1/4$ cup fish sauce
$1/2$ teaspoon dried hot red pepper flakes
$1/2$ cup sliced celery
2 cloves garlic, minced
$1/4$ cup chopped onion
3 thin slices fresh ginger
6 ounces rice vermicelli
Boiling water, to cover

Garnish
3 tablespoons chopped fresh cilantro
$1/4$ cup thinly sliced scallions, including
    green tops

Make the sauce: In a bowl, mix together the vinegar, sugar, fish sauce, and pepper flakes. Allow the flavors to blend for 1 hour.

Place the spareribs in a large pot with 2 quarts of water. Add the fish sauce, red pepper flakes, celery, garlic, onion, and ginger. Bring to a boil, reduce the heat, and simmer for 1 hour, or until the spareribs are tender.

Place the rice vermicelli in a bowl. Add boiling water to cover and let soak for 10 minutes.

Remove the spareribs from the pot. Allow them to remain as they are or remove the heat from the bones. Strain the broth through a fine-mesh sieve lined with cheesecloth into a saucepan. Heat and adjust the seasoning.

Drain the noodles and divide among individual bowls. Place the meat on top and pour the broth over the noodles and meat. Garnish with cilantro and scallions. Pour the sauce into small bowls for each diner to use for dipping.

Spicy Orange Beef with Glass Noodles

Serves 2

Marinade
2 tablespoons soy sauce
2 tablespoons Chinese rice wine or dry
    sherry
1 teaspoon cornstarch
$1/2$ teaspoon finely chopped garlic
$1/2$ teaspoon grated orange zest
$1/2$ teaspoon Asian sesame oil

$3/4$ pound ground beef round

Sauce

1 tablespoon minced garlic
1 teaspoon minced fresh ginger
*½ cup thinly sliced scallions, white and
    green parts*
2 teaspoons Chinese chili sauce
2 to 3 teaspoons grated orange zest
¼ cup chicken stock
2 tablespoons orange juice
1 tablespoon soy sauce
1 teaspoon sugar
1 tablespoon unseasoned rice vinegar

One small package bean thread noodles
2 tablespoons peanut oil
2 tablespoons chopped fresh cilantro

Make the marinade: In a large bowl, whisk
together all the marinade ingredients. Add the
meat, stirring to break it up slightly, cover,
and marinate for at least 2 hours at room
temperature or overnight in the refrigerator.
(Return to room temperature before cooking.)

Make the sauce: In a small bowl, combine
the garlic, ginger, scallions, chili sauce, and
orange zest. Cover until ready to use. In
another small bowl, mix together the
remaining sauce ingredients. Cover until ready
to use.

Place the noodle bundle, strings still
binding, in a bowl and add hot water to
cover. Soak until translucent and flexible,
about 3 minutes. Remove the strings and cut
the noodles into 4-inch lengths. Immerse in
cold water and drain completely. (The
noodles and the sauce may be prepared a
day ahead and refrigerated. Return them to
room temperature before cooking.)

Place the oil in a wok or large skillet over
high heat. When the oil is hot, reduce the
heat to medium and add the bowl containing
the garlic-ginger mixture. Stir very briefly,
about 30 seconds, and add the meat. Break
up the meat with a wooden spoon and
brown for about 2 minutes. Add the stock
mixture and heat to a simmer. Stir in the
noodles, cover, and cook gently until the
liquids are absorbed, about 3 minutes. Add
the cilantro and mix well. Transfer to a
heated serving bowl.

Thai Fried Noodles

Serves 4

½ pound flat Thai dried noodles
¼ cup vegetable oil
2 tablespoons chopped garlic
½ pound ground pork

Seasonings

½ cup chopped peanuts
*2 tablespoons chopped sweet pickled
    radish (available in Asian markets)*
*¼ pound firm tofu, rinsed, patted dry,
    and cut into ½-inch cubes*

(continued)

2 tablespoons fish sauce
2 teaspoons sugar
$1/2$ teaspoon dried hot red pepper flakes
Juice of $1/2$ lime
4 scallions, sliced, with green tops

Condiments
1 cup bean sprouts
3 tablespoons fish sauce
*2 tablespoons finely slivered mixed fresh
    red and green chili peppers*
Lime wedges

In a large pot, bring 4 quarts of water to a boil. Add 1 tablespoon salt. Add the noodles, stir to separate, and cook about 5 minutes, until *al dente*. Drain well and set aside.

In a small bowl, mix together all the seasonings. Set aside.

In a wok or heavy skillet, heat the oil over medium heat. Add the garlic and stir-fry until golden. Add the pork and stir-fry, breaking it up, until lightly browned, about 3 minutes. Add the noodles, stir, and add the seasonings. Continue stir-frying for about 4 minutes until the meat is cooked and the flavors are blended.

Transfer to a warm serving dish. Serve the condiments in separate small bowls on the side.

Crispy Fried Noodles

Serves 6

3 to 4 cups vegetable oil for deep frying
$1/4$ pound rice vermicelli

Syrup
$1/4$ cup water
$1/4$ cup fresh lime juice
$1/4$ cup sugar

$1/4$ cup vegetable oil
2 tablespoons minced onion
1 tablespoon minced garlic
6 ounces ground pork
1 tablespoon tomato paste
3 tablespoons fish sauce
$1/2$ cup bean sprouts
1 tablespoon chopped fresh cilantro
*2 scallions, cut into 1-inch lengths, green
    tops included*
1 teaspoon dried hot red pepper flakes
6 lime wedges

In a wok or heavy skillet, heat the oil over high heat. When it is hot, add the noodles. As soon as they puff up, turn them over and quickly fry on the other side. Do not let the noodles brown. Using a slotted spoon, immediately remove the noodles and drain on paper towels.

Make the syrup: In a small saucepan, combine the water, lime juice, and sugar.

Cook over medium heat, stirring to dissolve the sugar, until the mixture thickens to a syrup. Remove from the heat.

Heat 1 tablespoon vegetable oil in a skillet. Add the onion and stir-fry until translucent, about 3 minutes. Add the garlic and cook until golden, about 1 minute. Add the ground pork and stir-fry until no longer pink, about 3 minutes. Add the tomato paste and fish sauce and stir-fry for 3 minutes more.

Place the noodles in a large bowl and pour the syrup and the pork mixture over them at the same time. Mix thoroughly.

Add the bean sprouts, cilantro, and scallions, and mix very gently with the noodles. Serve with the lime wedges.

Noodle Pancake with Grilled Shrimp Salad

Serves 4

Marinade

½ cup olive oil
⅓ cup Asian sesame oil
¼ cup bottled teriyaki sauce
2 tablespoons sherry vinegar
2 teaspoons minced fresh ginger
1 clove garlic, minced

1 pound large shrimp in their shells

Noodle Pancake

½ pound angel hair pasta
½ cup hoisin sauce
1 small yellow onion, thinly sliced
Pinch of dried hot red pepper flakes
2 eggs, lightly beaten
Salt and freshly ground pepper to taste
Vegetable oil for frying
⅓ cup red miso
1 cup mayonnaise
2 tablespoons soy sauce
1 tablespoon sherry vinegar
1 clove garlic, minced
¼ cup chopped fresh cilantro
½ teaspoon each ground cumin, coriander, and turmeric
Pinch each of ground nutmeg and cinnamon
Salt and freshly ground pepper to taste
1 cucumber, peeled, seeded, and finely diced
¼ cup thinly sliced radishes
6 lettuce leaves, trimmed to fit wedges

Make the marinade: In a large bowl combine all the ingredients and mix well. Add the shrimp, stir to coat, and marinate for 2½ hours at room temperature or overnight in the refrigerator.

Make the noodle pancake: In a large pot, bring at least 4 quarts of water to a boil. Add 1 tablespoon salt. Add the pasta, stir to separate, and cook until *al dente*. Do not overcook. Drain the noodles and let cool to room

(continued)

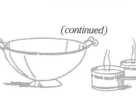

temperature. Place in a large bowl and add the hoisin sauce, onion, red pepper flakes, eggs, salt, and pepper; mix well. Pour $1/2$ inch of vegetable oil into a large skillet. Place over high heat; when the oil is hot, add the noodles and spread them to the sides of the pan, making an even layer. Cook the noodles over low heat until golden brown on one side. Turn the noodles out onto a plate and slide them back into the skillet, browned side up. Cook until the second side is golden brown. Set aside.

Preheat a broiler (or a charcoal or gas grill). Broil or grill the shrimp, positioning them close to the heat source and turning them once, until the shells are opaque, about 3 minutes total, depending upon their size. Remove from the heat and let cool. Peel the shrimp and chop into bite-sized pieces.

In a large bowl, mix together the *miso*, mayonnaise, soy sauce, vinegar, garlic, spices, salt, and pepper; mix well. Add the cucumber and radishes and again mix well. Add the chopped shrimp and toss and stir to combine. Taste and adjust the seasoning.

Slice the pancake into 6 wedges. Place a lettuce leaf on each wedge and top with the shrimp mixture.

Spicy Cold Soba Noodles

Serves 6

$1/3$ cup soy sauce
1 tablespoon molasses
$1/4$ cup Asian sesame oil
$1/4$ cup tahini
$1/4$ cup firmly packed brown sugar
$1/4$ cup chili oil
3 tablespoons red wine vinegar
$1/2$ bunch scallions, including green tops, sliced
$1/2$ pound soba noodles
$1/2$ cup diced red bell pepper
Salt to taste

Place the soy sauce in a saucepan over high heat and heat until reduced by half. Reduce the heat to low, stir in the molasses, and warm briefly. Transfer to a large bowl. Add the sesame oil, tahini, brown sugar, chili oil, vinegar, and scallions, and whisk to combine.

In a large pot, bring plenty of water to a rolling boil. Add $1^1/2$ teaspoons salt. Add the noodles and stir to separate, and cook until they just begin to soften, about 3 minutes. Begin testing for doneness after 2 minutes.

Drain the noodles, immerse in cold water, and drain again. Rinse well with cold water. Add to the sauce in the bowl, toss to coat evenly, cover, and chill before serving.

Rice Noodles with Broccoli and Almonds

Serves 4

3/4 pound fresh rice noodles
4 teaspoons oyster sauce
1 tablespoon fish sauce
1 tablespoon water
1/2 teaspoon cornstarch
3 tablespoons oil
1 teaspoon minced garlic
1/2 pound boneless pork, cut into thin strips
1/2 pound boneless, skinless chicken breast, cut into thin strips
2 teaspoons soy sauce
2 cups sliced broccoli, blanched and well drained
1/2 cup whole almonds
3/4 cup chicken stock

Place the noodles in a colander and pour hot water over them to soften them slightly. Separate the noodles, draining well.

In a small bowl, combine the oyster sauce, fish sauce, and water. Add the cornstarch and stir to dissolve.

To blanch broccoli: Bring a large pot of salted water to boil. Add broccoli and blanch 2 minutes. Drain and rinse under cold water. Drain again and pat dry.

In a wok or deep skillet, heat 2 tablespoons of the oil over medium-high heat. Add the garlic, chicken, and pork and stir-fry until

meat is no longer raw. Add the drained noodles and stir-fry until slightly browned. Stir in the soy sauce and toss to color noodles evenly. Add the broccoli, oyster sauce mixture, almonds, and stock and cook, stirring and scraping the pan, until the sauce is thick and reduced by half. Transfer to a warm serving platter.

Egg Noodle Stir-Fry with Chicken

Serves 4

3/4 pound thick egg noodles such as Chinese noodles or fettuccine
1/2 teaspoon Asian sesame oil
1 egg white
1 teaspoon soy sauce
1 teaspoon cornstarch
2 chicken skinless, boneless breasts, diced
1 tablespoon vegetable oil
1/2 cup diced onion
1 tablespoon minced garlic
1 tablespoon minced fresh garlic
1 1/2 cups chicken stock
1 tablespoon fish sauce
1/4 teaspoon freshly ground pepper
1/4 cup snow peas
1/4 cup sliced bamboo shoots
1/4 cup shredded carrots

(continued)

In a small bowl, combine the egg white, soy sauce, and cornstarch, mixing well. Add the chicken, stir, and let marinate for 30 minutes.

In a large pot, bring 4 quarts of water to a rolling boil. Add 1 tablespoon salt. Add the noodles, stirring to separate the strands, and cook until almost *al dente*. Check for doneness frequently. They will cook further when combined with other ingredients, so they should not be fully cooked at this point. If the noodles are fresh, they will be done very quickly. Dried noodles will take longer. Drain the noodles and immerse in cold water. Drain thoroughly again. Place in a bowl and stir with the sesame oil to prevent them from sticking together.

In a wok or deep skillet, heat the vegetable oil over medium heat. Drain the chicken and add to the pan. Stir-fry until the meat is just firm. Using a slotted spoon, transfer to a plate.

Add the onion, garlic, and ginger to the pan and stir-fry briefly. Add the stock, fish sauce, and pepper, bring to a boil, and cook until reduced by half. Add the noodles, snow peas, bamboo shoots, and carrots and return the chicken to the pan. Cook until the noodles have absorbed most of the liquid.

Transfer to a platter and serve.

Rice Noodles with Pork and Shrimp

Serves 4

1/2 pound rice stick noodles
1/2 pound shrimp, preferably with heads on
1 1/2 cups chicken stock
2 tablespoons vegetable oil
2 tablespoons minced garlic
1/2 cup finely chopped onion
1/2 pound pork loin, finely minced
Soy sauce to taste
Freshly ground pepper to taste
1 cup sliced napa cabbage or any Chinese cabbage
1/2 cup shredded carrots
1/2 cup snow peas
Chopped fresh cilantro for garnish

Place the rice sticks in a bowl and add warm water to cover; let stand until soft, about 15 minutes.

Meanwhile, peel and devein shrimp, reserving the heads and shells. Place the shells and heads in a saucepan with the chicken stock. Bring to a boil, reduce the heat, and simmer 10 minutes. Strain and set the broth aside.

Drain the noodles.

In a wok or deep skillet, heat the oil over high heat. Add the garlic and onion and stir-fry until soft, about 2 minutes. Add the pork, and cook until just browned. Add the shrimp, and stir-fry just until the shrimp begin to turn

pink, 1 or 2 minutes. Add the stock, bring to a boil, and simmer for about 5 minutes. Season with soy sauce and pepper.

Add the rice sticks and cook over medium heat, stirring, until noodles have absorbed most of the stock. Add the cabbage, carrots, and snow peas, and cook until the mixture is nearly dry. Transfer to a warm serving plate and garnish with cilantro.

Two Noodles Stir-Fry

Serves 4

¼ pound rice stick noodles
¾ pound thin egg noodles
1 cup water
1 cup chicken stock
1 tablespoon soy sauce
½ pound pork shoulder, in one piece
½ pound shrimp in the shell
2 tablespoons vegetable oil
3 cloves garlic, unpeeled, crushed
2 cups bean sprouts
¼ cup thinly sliced scallions, including
    green part

Place the rice sticks in a bowl and add warm water to cover; let stand until soft, about 15 minutes. Drain thoroughly.

In a large saucepan, bring 3 quarts of water to a rolling boil. Add 1 teaspoon salt.

Add the egg noodles, stir to separate, and cook until almost *al dente*. Check frequently for doneness. They will cook further when combined with other ingredients, so they should not be fully cooked at this point. Drain the noodles, place in a bowl. Toss with a bit of oil to prevent them from sticking together.

In a large saucepan, combine the 1 cup water, stock, soy sauce, and pork. Bring to a boil, reduce the heat, and simmer until the meat is tender. Remove the meat and return the stock to a boil. Add the shrimp and cook for 2 to 3 minutes until they turn pink. Drain, reserving the stock. Peel the shrimp and then devein. For additional flavor, add the shrimp shells to the stock and simmer for 10 minutes longer.

Bring the stock to a boil and cook until reduced by half. Strain the stock and set aside. (The recipe can be prepared several hours ahead up to this point.)

Slice the pork into thin, bite-sized pieces. In a wok or deep skillet, heat the oil over high heat. Add the garlic and stir-fry until golden, then remove the garlic cloves with a slotted spoon and discard. Add the egg noodles and rice sticks and stir-fry until they are lightly browned. Add the reserved stock, cover, and cook for 2 minutes. Remove the cover, add the pork, shrimp, and bean sprouts, and continue stirring and cooking until noodles have absorbed most of the liquid. Transfer to a warm serving platter and sprinkle with the scallions.

(continued)

Vietnamese Grilled Steak with Noodles

Serves 4

Sauce

6 tablespoons white wine vinegar
2 tablespoons water
3 tablespoons soy sauce
2 cloves garlic, minced
2 tablespoons sugar
¼ teaspoon dried hot red pepper flakes
½ teaspoon salt
¼ teaspoon anchovy paste

1 pound capellini
1 flank steak, about 1 pound
Salt and freshly ground pepper to taste
¼ cup packed, shredded fresh mint leaves
    or 1 teaspoon dried mint
1 cup bean sprouts
1 red bell pepper, seeded and julienned
Mint sprigs for garnish

Make the sauce: In a bowl, whisk together the vinegar, water, soy sauce, garlic, sugar, pepper flakes, salt, and anchovy paste until well blended and smooth.

In a large pot, bring at least 4 quarts of water to a rolling boil. Add 1 tablespoon salt. Add the noodles, stir to separate, and cook until *al dente*. Begin checking for doneness in just a few minutes. Drain, rinse with cold water, and drain thoroughly. Place in a large bowl, add the sauce and the mint, and toss well.

Preheat a broiler (or a charcoal or gas grill). Season the steak with salt and pepper and place in the broiler (or on a grill). Cook, turning once, until done as desired. Transfer to a cutting board and let stand for 5 minutes before slicing very thin.

To serve, divide the noodles among 4 bowls. Mound the steak slices over them, dividing evenly. Surround with bean sprouts and bell pepper strips. Garnish with a sprig of mint, if available.

Crispy Tofu with Soba Noodles

Serves 4

3 tablespoons vegetable oil
½ pound firm tofu, rinsed, patted dry,
    and cut into ½-inch cubes
Salt and freshly ground pepper to taste
4 carrots, julienned
½ pound fresh shiitake mushrooms
3 scallions, thinly sliced,thinly sliced, green
    parts included
2 tablespoons minced fresh ginger
1 Bosc pear, peeled, cored, and julienned
¼ cup water
1 tablespoon soy sauce
2 tablespoons seasoned rice vinegar
2 tablespoons Asian sesame oil
½ pound soba noodles

In a wok or deep skillet, heat 1 tablespoon of the vegetable oil over medium heat. Add the tofu and sauté on all sides until browned. Remove with slotted spoon to paper toweling to drain. Season with salt and pepper.

Add the remaining 2 tablespoons oil to the pan over high heat. Add the carrots. Stir-fry until almost tender, just a few minutes, then add the mushrooms, scallions, ginger, and pear. Stir-fry until the vegetables are cooked but not soft.

Meanwhile, bring at least 4 quarts of water to a rolling boil. Add 1 tablespoon salt. Add the noodles, stir to separate the strands, and cook until almost *al dente*. They will cook further when combined with other ingredients, so they should not be fully cooked at this point.

While the noodles are cooking, add to the wok or skillet the ¼ cup water, soy sauce, vinegar, and sesame oil, mixing well with the vegetables. Bring to a simmer.

When the noodles are ready, drain thoroughly and add to the soy mixture. Add more water if the noodles seem to dry. Cook until the liquid is absorbed and the noodles and sauce are evenly combined. Transfer to a warm serving platter and top with the tofu.

Vegetables and Bean Threads

Serves 4 *as side dish*

> ½ pound bean thread noodles
> Boiling water, to cover
> 3 tablespoons vegetable oil
> 1 tablespoon minced fresh garlic
> 1 carrot, julienned
> 1 large red bell pepper, seeded and
>   julienned
> 2 cloves garlic, minced
> ¼ pound snow peas, julienned
> 4 scallions, shredded, including green parts
> 2 tablespoons Asian sesame oil
> 1 teaspoon sugar
> 1 teaspoon salt
> 2 tablespoons sesame seeds, toasted

Place the bean thread noodles in a bowl and add warm water to cover. Let stand for 5 minutes, drain, rinse in cold water, drain again, and pat dry. Place in the bowl again and add 1 tablespoon of the sesame oil. Toss to coat and set aside.

In a small bowl, mix together the remaining 1 tablespoon sesame oil, cilantro, sugar, and salt. Set aside.

In a wok or deep skillet, heat the vegetable oil over high heat. Add the ginger and stir-fry briefly. Add the carrot and stir-fry until tender-crisp, just a few minutes. Add the bell pepper and garlic and cook for 1 minute. Add the snow peas and scallions and stir-fry

(continued)

for 2 minutes. Add the cilantro and sesame oil mixture and lower heat. Add the bean threads and toss to heat through.

Chinese Noodle Salad with Spicy Sesame Dressing

Serves 4

Spicy Sesame Dressing
3 tablespoons vegetable oil
4 scallions, white and green parts sliced
    separately
3 cloves garlic, minced
1 tablespoon minced fresh ginger
2 small dried chili peppers, preferably
    Asian, finely cut with scissors
6 tablespoons unseasoned rice vinegar
6 tablespoons soy sauce
2 tablespoons sugar
2 tablespoons tahini
2/3 to 1 cup chicken stock
2 teaspoons Asian sesame oil

3/4 pound fresh or dried Chinese egg
    noodles or other egg noodles such as
    fettuccine
Asian sesame oil, to coat
1 pound skinless, boneless chicken breast,
    cooked and shredded
3/4 cup julienned carrot

3/4 cup peeled, seeded, and diced
    cucumber
3/4 cup diced jicama
2 tablespoons toasted sesame seeds

Make the sauce: In a saucepan, heat the vegetable oil over medium heat. Add the white part of the scallions, garlic, ginger, and chilies and cook until the garlic is golden but not brown. Remove from the heat and add the vinegar, soy sauce, tahini, and 2/3 cup chicken stock. Return to the heat and simmer, stirring, for 2 minutes. If the sauce is too thick, add more stock. Add the sesame oil and stir well. Remove from the heat and let cool to room temperature.

In a large pot, bring at least 4 quarts of water to a rolling boil. Add 1 tablespoon salt. Add the noodles, stir to separate the strands, and cook until *al dente*. If the noodles are fresh, they will cook very quickly. Check for doneness frequently. If the noodles are dried, they will take longer. When the noodles are *al dente*, drain and immediately rinse them with cold water. Drain again thoroughly, then place them in a bowl and toss with a bit of sesame oil to coat. Let cool to room temperature or cover and chill.

In a large bowl, combine the noodles with the chicken, carrot, cucumber, and jicama. Add the sauce and toss well, gently turning all the noodles so that they are covered evenly. Transfer to a platter and top with sesame seeds and the greens of the scallions.

Curry Rice Noodles with Chicken and Shrimp

Serves 4

³/₄ pound dried rice stick noodles
1 stalk lemongrass
2 fresh green chili peppers, seeded and
*   sliced*
¹/₂ cup almonds
1 teaspoon ground turmeric
1 teaspoon minced fresh ginger
3 tablespoons vegetable oil
1¹/₂ pounds chicken parts, skinned and
*   seasoned with salt and pepper*
¹/₄ cup sliced shallots
1¹/₂ tablespoons soy sauce
1¹/₂ cups coconut milk
1¹/₂ cups water
1 bay leaf
1¹/₂ pounds shrimp, peeled and deveined
Fresh basil leaves

In a blender or small food processor, grind together the lemongrass, chilies, almonds, turmeric, garlic, and ginger.

In a large skillet, heat 1 tablespoon of the oil over high heat. Add the ground mixture and stir-fry for about 2 minutes. Add the chicken parts and cook until chicken is lightly browned on both sides.

Add the soy sauce, coconut milk, water, and bay leaf and bring to a boil. Reduce the heat, cover partially, and simmer until the chicken is tender, 30 to 45 minutes. Remove

the chicken with a slotted spoon. (Let cool until it can be handled, then remove the meat from the bones and shred it.) Add shrimp to the sauce. Cook, stirring, until the shrimp turn pink, 3 minutes or less. When shredded, turn chicken to the sauce.

Meanwhile, in a large pot, bring at least 4 quarts of water to a rolling boil. Add 1 teaspoon salt. Add the noodles, stir to separate the strands, and cook until *al dente*. Check frequently for doneness. If the noodles are fresh, they will be done almost immediately. If they are dried, they will take about 3 minutes. Drain the noodles.

Transfer the noodles to a large bowl, and spoon sauce over them, mounding the chicken and shrimp on top. (Individual bowls can be used as well.) Garnish with basil leaves.

Egg Noodles with Asparagus and Pork

Serves 4

¹/₂ pound pork tenderloin, partially frozen
2 tablespoons soy sauce
1 teaspoon sugar
3 tablespoons vegetable oil
³/₄ pound asparagus, trimmed and cut on
*   the diagonal into 1-inch pieces*
¹/₂ cup sliced onions

(continued)

³/₄ pound thin egg noodles
2 teaspoons minced and mashed fresh
  ginger
1 teaspoon minced garlic
1 tablespoon cornstarch
1 cup chicken stock

Thinly slice the pork across the grain (if it is partially frozen, it will be easier to cut). Combine 1 tablespoon of the soy sauce and the sugar in a dish large enough to hold the pork. Stir well, add the pork, toss to coat, and set aside.

In a wok or deep skillet, heat 1 tablespoon of the oil over medium heat. Add the asparagus and stir-fry for 2 minutes. Add the water, cover, and cook until the asparagus is nearly cooked to desired doneness, 3 or 4 minutes. Transfer the asparagus to a plate and set aside.

Rinse and dry the pan. Add 1 tablespoon of the oil to the pan and place over high heat. Add the onion and stir-fry until almost tender, about 3 minutes. Transfer to the plate holding the asparagus.

In a large pot, bring at least 4 quarts of water to a rolling boil. Add 1 tablespoon salt. Add the noodles, stir to separate, and cook until *al dente*. The noodles will need only a short time to cook. Check for doneness within 1 minute. Drain quickly. If the rest of the dish is not yet assembled, place the noodles in a warm bowl and stir in a bit of oil to keep them from sticking together.

Heat the remaining 1 tablespoon oil in the pan over high heat. Add the pork, ginger, and garlic and stir-fry just until the pork changes color. Add the remaining 1 tablespoon soy sauce and return the asparagus and onion to the pan. Stir-fry for 1 minute.

In a small bowl, stir the cornstarch into the stock until dissolved. Pour into the pan and cook over high heat, stirring constantly, until the meat is evenly coated. Immediately pour the mixture over the noodles and toss gently.

Seafood Lo Mein

Serves 4

6 small squid, cleaned and sliced
6 sea scallops, sliced in half horizontally
¹/₄ pound white fish such as snapper or
  cod, cut into strips
12 large shrimp, peeled and deveined
1 teaspoon minced fresh ginger
1¹/₂ tablespoons soy sauce
3 scallions
6 tablespoons vegetable oil
¹/₂ cup sliced bamboo shoots
1 cup napa cabbage or other Chinese
  cabbage
1 cup bean sprouts
1 pound fresh or dried thick egg noodles
1 tablespoon cornstarch
1¹/₂ cups chicken stock

In a bowl, combine the squid, scallops, fish, shrimp, ginger, and soy sauce. Mix well and set aside. Cut the white part of the scallions into 1½-inch lengths; thinly slice the green tops. Set aside separately.

In a wok or deep skillet, heat 2 tablespoons of the oil over high heat. Add the bamboo shoots, cabbage, and bean sprouts, and white part of scallions and stir-fry briefly until wilted. Remove with slotted spoon to a plate.

Add the seafood and ginger to the pan and stir-fry for about 2 minutes, until the fish is barely done. Remove to the plate holding the vegetables.

In a large pot, bring at least 4 quarts of water to a rolling boil. Add 1 tablespoon salt. Add the noodles, stir to separate, and cook until almost *al dente*. Check for doneness immediately. They will be ready in less than 2 minutes. Drain.

Heat the remaining 4 tablespoons oil to the pan and place over high heat. Add the noodles and cook and stir until some begin to brown lightly, about 2 minutes. Turn the noodles over and cook on the other side until lightly browned.

In a small bowl, stir the cornstarch into the stock until dissolved. Return the vegetables and seafood to the pan and pour the chicken stock mixture over all the ingredients. Cook, stirring constantly, until the sauce coats the noodles. Transfer to a large warm serving bowl and garnish with the green scallion slices.

Squeamish About Squid

Eek! A squid! Some creatures of the sea have a beauty of their own. An elegantly proportioned salmon. A formidable lobster. But squid, or *calamari* in Italian, *calmers* in French, *calamares* in Spanish, and *kalamaria* in Greek, are just plain ugly. That may explain why squid are more popular in American restaurant kitchens than they are in home kitchens.

Squid can be anywhere from 1 inch to 60 feet long, but luckily, the home cook usually only deals with those about 6 inches in length. They are easy to clean. Just remove the head and interior matter, then pull off the beak and outer skin. Squid, no matter what they look like, offer all the pleasures of ocean foods, an interesting texture and a truly distinct taste.

Cold Noodles and Crabmeat in Peanut Sauce

Serves 4

Sauce

¹/₄ cup dry-roasted peanuts
2 cloves garlic
¹/₂ cup vegetable oil
Dash salt
1 tablespoon Chinese hot chili sauce with garlic, or to taste
¹/₄ cup unseasoned rice vinegar
1 tablespoon sugar
4 teaspoons soy sauce

³/₄ pound fresh or dried egg noodles
2 teaspoons Asian sesame oil
One 6-ounce can lump crabmeat, or ¹/₂ pound fresh-cooked lump crabmeat
1 scallion, sliced, including green part
¹/₄ cup dry-roasted peanuts, chopped
2 tablespoons chopped fresh cilantro leaves

Make the sauce: In a small food processor or blender, combine the garlic and peanuts and process until ground. Add the vegetable oil, salt, chili sauce, vinegar, sugar, and soy sauce. Process until blended.

In a large pot, bring at least 4 quarts of water to a rolling boil. Add 1 tablespoon salt. Add the noodles, stir to separate the strands, and cook until *al dente*. Check almost immediately for doneness. If the noodles are fresh, they will be ready in about 1 minute. Dried noodles will take longer. Drain the noodles and rinse with cold water. Transfer to a bowl and toss with the sesame oil to coat.

Combine the peanut sauce with the noodles and toss to combine. Sprinkle with chopped peanuts, sliced scallion, and coriander.

Smothered Noodles

Serves 6

10 ounces rice vermicelli, or 1³/₄ pounds
    fresh flat Thai noodles
1 pound pork cutlets, cut into ¹/₂-inch
    cubes
1 tablespoon sake
¹/₂ pound broccoli

Seasonings
1 tablespoon brown bean paste
3 tablespoons cornstarch dissolved in ¹/₄
    cup water
1¹/₂ tablespoons sugar
1 tablespoon fish sauce
¹/₂ teaspoon freshly ground pepper
¹/₂ teaspoon salt

¹/₂ cup vegetable oil
3 tablespoons soy sauce
2 teaspoons chopped garlic
¹/₂ pound fresh shrimp, peeled, deveined,
    and butterflied
2¹/₂ cups boiling water to be used as part
    of sauce

If using rice vermicelli, place in a bowl and add boiling water to cover; let soak until soft, about 10 minutes. Drain.

Place the pork in a bowl and add the sake. Let marinate for 5 minutes. Cut the broccoli into small florets and slice the stems; set aside.

Make the seasonings mixture: In a small bowl, stir together all the ingredients.

In a wok or a deep skillet, heat ¹/₄ cup of the vegetable oil over high heat. Add the drained or fresh noodles and the soy sauce and stir-fry for about 3 minutes. Remove the noodles to a large serving bowl and keep warm.

Heat the remaining ¹/₄ cup oil in the pan over medium-high heat. Add the garlic and stir-fry until golden. Add the pork and stir-fry for 4 minutes. Add the shrimp, broccoli, seasonings mixture, and 2¹/₂ cups boiling water and cook, stirring, until the sauce thickens, about 4 minutes.

Pour sauce over noodles in serving bowl. Toss to combine well and serve.

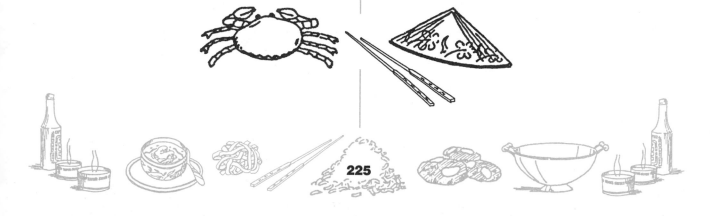

CHAPTER 13

THE GLOBAL VILLAGE: ETHNIC PASTAS

Around the world, wherever wheat is grown, pasta is eaten—only the forms and flavorings are different. Orzo, the diminutive rice-shaped pasta, is a favorite in Greece. Kasha is the preferred form in Russia. Spaetzle, driblets made by pushing dough through a colander, is eaten in Germany. Couscous, grains of semolina flour, the tiniest pasta of all, is the choice of North Africa. Pasta packages have ethnic origins, too. Pierogi are Polish dumplings, while kreplach are Jewish. Sauces, too, have ethnicity. The French recipe here, mussels and fusilli, is, characteristically, a cream-based sauce. The Portuguese offering includes their often used anchovies. The Indian, of course, is laced with curry. And the Italians, to whom pasta is simply food, native or not, have their own ethnic version—gnocchi, pasta made from potatoes.

Gnocchi Café des Artistes

Chef Andrew Berman
Café Des Artistes
Key West, Florida

Serves 4

Gnocchi
4 potatoes, peeled and diced
1 egg yolk
Pinch of salt
Pinch of white pepper
1 cup flour

Sauce
2 cups heavy cream
1 cup freshly grated Parmesan cheese
Salt and white pepper to taste
2 tablespoons Stolichnaya vodka

Four 2-ounce pieces smoked salmon
1 ounce Sevruga caviar

Make the gnocchi: Peel and dice the potatoes. In a saucepan, combine the potatoes with salted water to cover generously. Bring to a boil, and boil until tender. Drain and transfer to a large bowl. Mash the potatoes very well. Let cool to room temperature. Using an electric mixer on high speed, beat

together the potatoes, egg yolk, salt, and pepper for 10 seconds.

Reduce the speed to low and gradually add the flour. Mix for 10 to 20 seconds until the mixture just forms a dough.

Turn out the dough onto a work surface and divide into quarters. Cover 3 portions with a damp towel. Roll out the remaining quarter in a long cylinder. Cut into 1-inch pieces. Shape the pieces into bullet shapes. Repeat with other dough portions. Cover with damp towel while making sauce.

Make the sauce: In a saucepan, bring the cream to a boil. Add the cheese, stirring until melted. Reduce the heat to medium and continue stirring until the sauce thickens. Season with salt and pepper. Stir in the vodka and set aside.

In a large pot, bring at least 4 quarts of water to a boil. Add 1 tablespoon salt. Add the gnocchi. Within a minute or two they should all float, indicating that they are done. Remove the dumplings with a slotted spoon and toss them into the sauce.

Divide the dumplings and sauce among shallow bowls. Arrange each piece of smoked salmon into a flower, and set it in the middle of a serving of gnocchi. Top each flower with a $1/4$-ounce caviar. Serve immediately.

Polish Pierogi

Makes 4 dozen

Cheese Filling
$1^1/_2$ pounds farmer cheese or cottage cheese
2 eggs, beaten
Salt and freshly ground pepper to taste, or a mixture of sugar and ground cinnamon to taste

Potato Filling
2 cups mashed potatoes
1 cup grated sharp cheddar cheese
2 tablespoons chopped frozen or fresh chives
$1/_2$ teaspoon freshly ground pepper
$1/_2$ teaspoon onion powder

Dough
2 cups all-purpose flour
1 egg, beaten
$1/_2$ teaspoon salt
$1/_3$ cup water, or as needed

For serving
Butter
$3/_4$ cup cooked diced bacon, kept warm
$1/_2$ cup cooked diced onion, kept warm
Sour cream

(continued)

Choose either the cheese filling or the potato filling. For the cheese filling, stir together the cheese and eggs in a bowl and season with salt and pepper for a savory flavor or cinnamon and sugar for a sweet flavor. For the potato filling, stir together the potatoes, cheese, chives, pepper, and onion powder.

Make the dough: In a bowl, stir together the flour, egg, and salt. Stir in the $^1/_3$ cup water until stiff dough forms. If dough is too dry, slowly add up to 3 tablespoons additional water. Shape into a ball. Cover with an inverted bowl and let sit for 20 minutes. Divide the dough in half. On a lightly floured board, roll out each half paper-thin. Using a round cookie or biscuit cutter, cut dough in 2 inch rounds.

To fill the pierogi, place about 1 teaspoon filling on half of each circle. Moisten the circle edges with water. Fold over the unfilled side and seal the edges. In a large pot, bring at least 4 quarts of water to a rolling boil. Add the pierogi and cook until they rise to the surface, 3 to 5 minutes. Using a slotted spoon, gently remove from the water. Place in a single layer on a dish.

If serving cheese-filled pierogi, melt unsalted butter and drizzle over the top, or, in a large skillet, sauté the cooked pierogi in butter until golden on both sides. If serving potato-filled pierogi, sauté them in butter until golden, then serve on a warm platter and top with cooked bacon and onion. Pass the sour cream at the table.

White Truffle Gnocchi

Chef Hidemasa Yamamoto
The Ritz Carlton
Washington, D.C.

Serves 6

> *1 potato*
> *1 egg*
> *Salt and white pepper to taste*
> *One 2$^1/_2$-ounce jar sliced white truffles, drained*
> *1$^1/_2$ cups freshly grated Parmesan cheese*
> *1 cup all-purpose flour*
> *$^3/_4$ cup white truffle flour*
> *$^1/_2$ cup unsalted butter*
> *$^1/_4$ cup chopped fresh parsley*
> *$^1/_2$ cup freshly grated Parmesan*

Boil potato in skin until tender. Remove skin and pass through fine, mesh sieve. Add whole egg to potato. Knead in cheese, all-purpose flour, and truffle flour. Add sliced truffle, parsley, salt, and pepper. Roll dough $^1/_2$-inch round log and slice into $^1/_2$-inch pieces. To shape, roll dough pieces on the tines of a fork.

In a large pot, bring at least 4 quarts of water to a rolling boil. Add 1 tablespoon salt. Add the gnocchi and cook until they rise to the top, about 4 to 5 minutes. Using a slotted spoon, remove the gnocchi from the pot. Place in an ice water bath. When serving, immerse in boiling water. Then toss in lightly

browned butter and chopped Italian parsley. (To brown butter, cook over low heat, stirring constantly, until golden. It will bubble, but do not allow it to burn.)

Place in a serving bowl. Top with grated Parmesan cheese and fresh sliced white truffle.

Gnocchi... Potato Pasta

Gnocchi, while included in this book, are actually an Italian creation that look and taste like pasta, but are not. Gnocchi are made from potatoes. The word *gnocchi* (pronounced nyah-keeh) means "lumps," and they are actually dumplings made of mashed potatoes, flour, and eggs. The dough is rolled by hand into a narrow sausage shape and then cut into pieces an inch or two long; the pieces are imprinted with the tines of a fork and then poached gently in boiling water. A hint for hitting the right texture is to mash the potatoes ahead of time and let them stand, covered with a cloth, for a few hours so they lose some of their moisture. Add the flour and eggs just before cooking.

Greek Pastitsio

Serves 6

1 pound lasagna noodles
2 tablespoons olive oil
2 pounds ground lamb
½ cup chopped parsley
1 onion, chopped
5 cloves garlic, minced
½ teaspoon ground cinnamon
One 8-ounce can tomato sauce
½ cup red wine
¼ cup butter, at room temperature, cut into pieces
3 eggs, beaten
1 cup freshly grated Parmesan cheese
4 cups béchamel sauce (see Chapter 4), flavored with a pinch of ground cinnamon

Preheat the oven to 350°.

In a large, deep skillet, heat the oil over medium heat. Add the lamb and brown, breaking it up with a wooden spoon, about 5 minutes. Add the onion and garlic and sauté until softened, about 3 minutes. Drain. Add the parsley, cinnamon, tomato sauce, and wine. Let simmer over medium-low heat for 30 minutes.

In a large pot, bring at least 4 quarts of water to a rolling boil. Add 1 tablespoon salt. Place the noodles in the boiling water carefully, sliding them down gently into the water

(continued)

and stirring to prevent them from sticking to each other or to the pot. Cook until not quite *al dente*. They will cook further when baked. Drain and quickly transfer to a large bowl. Add butter, eggs, and ½ cup of the Parmesan, and toss well.

Place half of the noodles in the bottom of a large casserole dish. Top with the meat sauce, and cover with the rest of the noodles. Pour the béchamel evenly over the top. Top evenly with cheese. Bake until top is golden and bubbling, almost 1 hour.

Potato Gnocchi with Mushroom Sauce

Chef Tony Mantuano
Tuttaposto
Chicago, Illinois

Serves 4

Gnocchi
1 pound potatoes, peeled, cooked in
*   boiling water, then ground or riced*
1 egg yolk
1 cup all-purpose flour
Salt and pepper to taste

Mushroom Sauce
2 tablespoons unsalted butter
1½ pounds assorted fresh mushrooms
*   such as cremino, shiitake, and oyster,*
*   cleaned*
½ cup finely diced yellow onion
½ cup finely diced zucchini
2 tablespoons garlic puréed in
*   1 tablespoon olive oil*
1 cup chicken stock
½ cup veal stock

1 cup Romano cheese, freshly grated

To make gnocchi: Mix ingredients, folding flour in last. Knead briefly to dough consistency. Divide into 3 or 4 portions. Roll each into a rope like cylinder. Cut into 1-inch sections. Roll each piece on tines of a fork to shape gnocchi. Refrigerate until use.

Make the sauce: In a saucepan, melt 1 tablespoon of the butter over medium heat. Add all of the mushrooms, onion, zucchini, and garlic. Sauté until golden. Add the chicken and veal stock and bring to a simmer.

Cook gnocchi in boiling water until they float, about 3 minutes. Drain well. Transfer to a bowl and toss with remaining 1 tablespoon of butter. Place in serving bowls and spoon sauce over gnocchi. Sprinkle with all the Romano cheese.

Russian Kasha with Mushrooms and Onions

Serves 4

1 cup kasha (roasted buckwheat groats)
1 egg, lightly beaten
5 tablespoons unsalted butter
1 large onion, minced
2 scallions, finely chopped, white part only
1 clove garlic, minced
2 cups beef stock
Salt and freshly ground pepper to taste
½ pound fresh mushrooms, chopped
3 tablespoons chopped parsley
2 tablespoons sour cream

In a small bowl, mix together the kasha and egg. Transfer to a dry skillet and stir gently over medium heat until the grains separate and the mixture is dry, 3 to 4 minutes.

In a 2½-quart saucepan, heat 3 tablespoons of the butter over medium-low heat. Add the onion, scallions, and garlic and sauté until soft, about 3 minutes. Add the kasha and stock to the onion mixture, season with salt and pepper, cover, and simmer until the kasha is tender and the liquid is absorbed, about 15 minutes.

Meanwhile, heat the remaining 2 tablespoons butter in a small skillet. Add the mushrooms and sauté until the mushrooms are tender and all the liquid has evaporated.

When the kasha is tender, stir in the cooked mushrooms, parsley, and sour cream. Transfer to a warm serving bowl.

Mushroom Barley-Shaped Pasta Pilaf

Corporate Chef Alan Kaplan
Prestige Caterers
Queens Village, New York

Serves 6 *as a side dish*

1 pound barley-shaped pasta
½ cup corn oil
4 cups chicken stock
1 teaspoon onion powder
1 cup chopped onion
Salt and freshly ground pepper to taste

Preheat the oven to 350°.

Place the barley pasta into a 3-inch-deep baking dish. Drizzle ¼ cup of the oil over the pasta and toss to coat well. Place in the oven and bake until the pasta is well browned. The more color the better. The top of the pasta should be almost burned. The color will fade when the liquid is added.

Meanwhile, pour the chicken stock into a saucepan on the stovetop and bring to a boil. Remove the browned pasta from the oven and sprinkle onion powder over the top. Pour the hot liquid over the top. Mix well with a fork. Cover tightly with aluminum foil and return to the oven for 20 minutes, or until all liquid is absorbed.

Meanwhile, heat the remaining ¼ cup oil in a saucepan over medium heat. Add the onion and sauté until translucent. Continue to

(continued)

cook until medium brown, which brings out the sweetness of the onion.

Remove the pasta from the oven. Add the onion. Fluff with fork. Season with salt and pepper and transfer to a warm serving bowl.

Couscous Who?

Couscous is the tiniest pasta of all, semolina flour and water formed into ricelike specks. But the texture turns out to be wonderful in combination with vegetables and meats, fruits and sauces. A North African staple, couscous is usually served as the pasta that mixes with a stew or ragout of meat or poultry. It combines so well with vegetables that it's often used as an anchor for vegetarian main dishes. And, couscous even comes as dessert, sweetened with fruit and honey, cream and sugar. Originally, this unusual pasta needed to be cooked for hours in a steamer aptly called a *couscoussière*. But today, it's packaged as a precooked product and is practically an instant food. Just boil water, stir in couscous, wait a few minutes, and it's ready.

Moroccan Couscous

Serves 4

2 navel oranges, peeled and sectioned
1/4 cup red onion, chopped
1/2 teaspoon sugar
1/4 teaspoon ground cinnamon

1 cup chicken stock
1 cup water
2 tablespoons unsalted butter
3 strips orange zest, each 1 inch long
1 bay leaf
1 teaspoon salt
1/2 teaspoon ground cumin
1/2 teaspoon ground coriander
1/8 teaspoon ground turmeric
1/8 teaspoon ground allspice
1/8 teaspoon ground nutmeg
Dash Tabasco sauce
1 1/4 cups instant couscous
1 tablespoon chopped fresh cilantro
1/4 cup chopped roasted, unsalted peanuts

In a small bowl, combine the orange segments, onion, sugar, and cinnamon.

In a saucepan, combine the chicken stock, water, butter, orange zest, bay leaf, salt, cumin, coriander, turmeric, allspice, nutmeg, and Tabasco. Bring to a boil and stir in the couscous. Cover and remove from the heat. Let stand until the liquid is absorbed, about

5 minutes. Be careful not to let rest too long. Fluff the couscous with a fork to separate the grains. Remove the orange zest and bay leaf and discard.

Transfer the couscous to a serving bowl. Toss gently with the orange mixture. Sprinkle with the cilantro and nuts.

Armenian Egg Noodles with Spinach and Cheese

Serves 4

Two 10-ounce packages frozen spinach, thawed and squeezed of all excess moisture
3 tablespoons olive oil
1 large onion, finely chopped
3 tablespoons fine dried bread crumbs
3 eggs
1/2 pound feta cheese, crumbled
3/4 cup cottage cheese
1/4 cup freshly grated imported Parmesan cheese, plus additional 2 tablespoons Parmesan cheese
Salt to taste
12 medium-wide dried egg noodles
1/4 cup unsalted butter, at room temperature

Preheat the oven to 375°.

In a large, heavy skillet, heat the oil over medium heat. Add the garlic and onion and sauté until soft but not browned. Add the spinach and cook briefly, stirring frequently, just until soft. Stir in the bread crumbs, remove from the heat, and set aside.

In a large bowl, beat the eggs lightly. Add the feta cheese, cottage cheese, and 1/4 cup Parmesan cheese and stir well. Add the spinach mixture and again stir well. Taste and add salt if needed. Set aside.

In a large pot, bring at least 4 quarts of water to a rolling boil. Add 1 tablespoon salt. Place the noodles in the water, gently pushing them down and stirring so that they do not break or stick together or to the pot. Cook until not quite *al dente*. They will continue to cook in the casserole. Drain and immediately return to the cooking pot. Toss with 2 table-spoons of the butter.

Lay half of the noodles on the bottom of a buttered 9-by-9-by-2-inch baking pan. Spread evenly with the spinach-cheese mixture. Cover with the remaining noodles and dot with the remaining 2 tablespoons butter. Sprinkle evenly with the 2 tablespoons Parmesan cheese.

Bake for 30 minutes. Uncover and continue to bake until golden brown, about 15 minutes. Remove from the oven and let cool for 5 minutes. Cut into squares to serve.

Greek Orzo with Goat Cheese

Serves 4

3 tablespoons pine nuts
2 yellow zucchini, diced
2 tablespoons butter
1 tablespoon olive oil
1 large shallot, finely chopped
1/2 pound fresh mushrooms, cut into
 1/4-inch dice
1 green bell pepper, seeded and diced
1/4 cup chopped sun-dried tomatoes
2 tablespoons heavy cream
1/4 pound fresh goat cheese
1 cup orzo
1/4 cup Parmesan cheese, grated
2 tablespoons finely chopped fresh basil
Salt and freshly ground pepper to taste

Preheat the oven to 350°. Spread the pine nuts on a baking sheet and toast until lightly browned, about 5 minutes. Set aside.

Squeeze the zucchini in paper towels to remove as much liquid as possible.

In a skillet, melt the butter with the olive oil over medium heat. Add the shallot and sauté until softened, about 2 minutes. Add the zucchini and continue to sauté for about 3 minutes. Add the mushrooms and sauté for 3 more minutes, or until tender. Add sun-dried tomatoes and heat through.

In a small saucepan, combine the cream and goat cheese over low heat and stir until softened.

Meanwhile, bring at least 4 quarts of water to a rolling boil. Add 1 tablespoon salt. Add the orzo, stir to separate, and cook until *al dente*. Drain well.

In a large warm serving bowl, combine the sautéed vegetables, orzo, warmed goat cheese, Parmesan cheese, and basil. Mix gently but thoroughly. Stir in the pine nuts. Season with salt and pepper and serve.

Dumplings for Soup: Kreplach Dough and Meat Filling

Makes 24

Dough
2 cups sifted all-purpose flour
1/4 teaspoon salt
2 eggs
2 tablespoons water

Filling
3 tablespoons oil
3/4 pound ground beef
1 onion, grated
2 tablespoons chopped parsley
1/2 teaspoon freshly ground pepper
1/2 teaspoon salt, or to taste

For serving

Clear soup, optional
Butter, optional

Make the dough: Sift together the flour and salt onto a flat surface. Make a well in the center. Place the eggs and water in the well. Quickly blend the eggs and water with a fork. Then, with your hands, work the flour into the eggs until a dough forms. Knead until smooth and elastic. Cover with a damp kitchen towel while preparing the filling.

Make the filling: In a large skillet, heat the oil over medium heat. Add the meat and brown well, breaking it up with a wooden spoon, about 5 minutes. Add the onion, parsley, salt, and pepper and sauté for about 10 minutes. Remove from the heat and cool for 15 minutes.

On a lightly floured surface, roll the dough as thin as possible. Using a pastry wheel or sharp knife, cut into 2-inch squares. Place a heaping teaspoonful of meat mixture on each square. Fold the dough over the filling to form a triangle, and seal the edges well.

The dumplings may be prepared several ways. They may be dropped into a boiling clear soup, and for 15 minutes, and served in the soup. They may be cooked in plenty of boiling water and served tossed in butter and lightly salted. Dumplings may also be sautéed on both sides in butter until golden.

German Spaetzle

Serves 4

2¹/₂ cups all-purpose flour
1 teaspoon salt
¹/₄ teaspoon freshly ground pepper
¹/₄ teaspoon freshly grated nutmeg
3 eggs, beaten, plus 2 egg yolks
About ¹/₂ cup milk
2 tablespoons unsalted butter (optional)

In a large bowl, stir together the flour, salt, pepper, and nutmeg. Stir in the eggs and egg yolks and ¹/₄ cup of the milk until a thick, smooth dough forms. Gradually add more milk as needed to achieve the correct consistency.

In a large saucepan, bring at least 4 quarts of water to a rolling boil. Add 1 tablespoon salt. Hold a large-holed colander over the water and push about ¹/₄ cup dough at a time through the holes to make the dumplings. Cook for about 5 minutes. They will float when they are cooked. Remove with a slotted spoon. Repeat until all dough is cooked.

The spaetzle may be sautéed in butter in a large skillet and served as a side dish, but they are more often paired with a dish such as goulash in which the gravy or sauce is spooned over them.

Jewish Noodle Pudding

Serves 8

1 pound dried broad egg noodles
1/2 pound dried apricots, diced
1 apple, peeled, cored, and diced
1/4 cup crushed drained pineapple
3/4 cup golden raisins
6 eggs
2 cups (1 pint) sour cream
2 cups (1 pound) cottage cheese
1 cup milk
1/2 cup unsalted butter, melted
3/4 cup sugar
1 tablespoon vanilla extract
Cornflake crumbs

Preheat the oven to 350°. Grease a 9-by-13-inch baking dish.

In a large saucepan, bring at least 4 quarts of water to a rolling boil. Add 1 tablespoon salt. Add the noodles, stir to separate, and cook until *al dente*. Drain.

In a large bowl, combine the noodles, apricots, apple, pineapple, and raisins. Beat the eggs and combine, in a large bowl, with the sour cream, cottage cheese, milk, and melted butter. Using an electric mixer, beat until well blended and creamy. Add the sugar and vanilla and mix thoroughly. Pour the sour cream mixture over the noodles and combine well. Transfer the mixture to the prepared dish. Sprinkle the cornflake crumbs evenly over the top. Bake until set and golden brown, about 1 hour. Serve at once or reheat when ready to serve.

Marisa's Noodles

Serves 6

1/2 pound fine egg noodles
1 cup small-curd cottage cheese
1 egg, beaten
1 1/2 cups sour cream
3/4 cup finely minced onion
1 clove garlic, finely minced
3 drops Tabasco sauce
Salt and freshly ground pepper to taste
1/2 cup sour cream
1/2 cup freshly grated Parmesan cheese

Preheat the oven to 350°. Grease a 1 1/2-quart baking dish.

In a large pot, bring at least 4 quarts of water to a rolling boil. Add 1 tablespoon salt. Add noodles, stir to separate, and cook until *al dente*. Drain.

In a large bowl, mix together the cottage cheese, egg, 1 cup of the sour cream, onion, garlic, Tabasco, salt, and pepper. Add the noodles and mix well. Transfer to the prepared baking dish. Bake for 20 minutes. Remove from oven, spread the remaining 1/2 cup sour cream and the Parmesan cheese over the noodles. Return to the oven and bake until top is golden and bubbling, about 10 minutes longer. Allow to rest for 10 minutes before cutting.

Portuguese Green Noodles with Anchovies

Serves 4

1 pound fresh or dried spinach egg
    noodles
1/4 cup unsalted butter
1 teaspoon freshly ground pepper
1/2 cup olive oil
4 large cloves garlic, cut in half
Two 2-ounce cans anchovy fillets, drained

In a large pot, bring at least 4 quarts of water to a rolling boil. Add 1 tablespoon salt. Add the noodles, stir to separate, and cook until *al dente*. If the noodles are fresh, they will cook very quickly, so check for doneness almost immediately. Drain and transfer to a warm bowl. Toss with the butter.

In a large, deep skillet, heat the olive oil over medium heat. Add the garlic and sauté until browned. Remove with a slotted spoon and discard. Reduce the heat to low. Add 1 can of the anchovies and cook until disintegrated. Cut the anchovies from the other can into 1/2-inch pieces. Gently stir them into the skillet.

Carefully add the pasta a little at a time to the anchovy sauce, tossing until all the noodles are glazed. Season with pepper to taste. Transfer to a warm platter.

French Fusilli with Mussels

Serves 4

3/4 pound fusilli
2 shallots, minced
1/2 cup minced onions
2 cloves garlic, minced
2 tablespoons chopped parsley
1 cup dry white wine
4 peppercorns, crushed
2 tablespoons unsalted butter
2 tablespoons all-purpose flour
2 egg yolks
1/2 cup heavy cream
1 cup freshly grated Asiago cheese

In a pot large enough to accommodate the mussels, combine the shallots, onion, garlic, 1 tablespoon of the parsley, wine, and peppercorns. Add the mussels and place over high heat. Cover and cook until the mussels open, 4 to 6 minutes. Remove from the heat. Remove the mussels with a slotted spoon, reserving the liquid in the pot. Discard any mussels that did not open. Remove the others from their shells and place in a warm bowl; cover to keep warm.

Bring the liquid in the pot to a boil and cook for 3 minutes. Pour through a fine-mesh sieve and reserve.

In a saucepan, melt the butter over medium heat. Add the flour and cook, stirring constantly until smooth and tawny in color. Remove from the heat and stir in the strained

(continued)

liquid. Return to low heat and cook briefly until the sauce is smooth. Remove from the heat.

In a small bowl, beat together the egg yolks and cream and stir into the sauce. Warm the sauce over a low heat, but do not boil or it will curdle. Add half of the mussels.

Meanwhile, in a large pot, bring at least 4 quarts water to a rolling boil. Add 1 tablespoon salt. Add the pasta, stir to separate, and cook until *al dente*. Drain.

Pour the sauce over the pasta and toss. Transfer to a warm platter and place the mussels over the pasta. Sprinkle with the remaining 1 tablespoon parsley. Serve the cheese at the table.

Hungarian Goulash and Noodles

Serves 6

1 pound veal shoulder, cut into 1 1/2-inch cubes
1 pound pork loin, cut into 1-inch cubes
1 teaspoon paprika
1 teaspoon salt
1 pound egg noodles
4 small white onions, coarsely chopped
1/4 cup unsalted butter
2 tablespoons flour
4 cups beef stock
Salt and freshly ground pepper to taste

Sprinkle the veal and pork cubes with paprika and salt and set aside.

In a large, deep skillet, melt the butter over medium heat. Add the onion and sauté until soft, about 3 minutes. Add the veal and pork and cook, turning as needed, until the meat loses its surface color, about 15 minutes. Add the beef stock, salt, and pepper, and sprinkle the flour over the mixture. Mix thoroughly. Cover and simmer over moderately low heat for 1 hour. Stir occasionally and check for doneness. The meat should be tender and the sauce thickened.

When the meat is nearly ready, in a large pot, bring at least 4 quarts of water to a rolling boil. Add 1 tablespoon salt. Add the noodles, stirring to separate, and cook until *al dente*. Drain. Place the noodles in a large warm serving bowl, add the meat and its gravy, and toss well.

German Sautéed Cabbage and Noodles

Serves 6 *as a side dish*

4 cups finely shredded cabbage
1 tablespoon salt
1 pound broad noodles such as pappardelle
1/2 cup unsalted butter
1 teaspoon sugar
Freshly ground pepper to taste

Place the cabbage in a colander and sprinkle with the salt. Let stand for 15 minutes. Drain well.

In a large, deep skillet, melt the butter over medium heat. Add the cabbage, sugar, and pepper. Stir to blend, cover, and cook over low heat until the cabbage is tender but not mushy, about 45 minutes.

Meanwhile, in a large pot, bring at least 4 quarts of water to a rolling boil. Add 1 tablespoon salt. Add the noodles, stir to separate, and cook until not quite *al dente*. Check frequently for doneness. Drain.

Add the noodles to the skillet with the cabbage, toss to combine, and cook briefly. Transfer to a warm platter.

Indian Farfalle with Curried Chicken

Serves 6

1/4 cup butter
1 cup chopped onion
1/2 cup chopped celery
1 apple, peeled, cored, and chopped
1/2 teaspoon dry mustard
1 bay leaf
2 to 3 teaspoons curry powder
3 tablespoons all-purpose flour
One 16-ounce can plum tomatoes, drained and chopped

1 cup chicken stock
1/2 cup cashews, coarsely ground
1/2 cup half-and-half
Salt and freshly ground pepper to taste
3 cups cubed cooked chicken (1-inch cubes)
1 pound farfalle

In a deep, heavy skillet, melt the butter over medium heat. Add the onion, celery, and apple and sauté until soft. Stir in the mustard, bay leaf, curry powder, and flour and cook for 3 minutes, stirring constantly. (The amount of curry depends on the brand and taste.) Blend in the tomatoes and chicken stock and cook until the sauce thickens, about 10 minutes. Reduce heat, add the cashews and half-and-half, and simmer briefly. Add the salt and pepper and stir in the cooked chicken. Simmer until heated through.

Meanwhile, in a large pot, bring at least 4 quarts of water to a rolling boil. Add 1 tablespoon salt. Add the farfalle, stir to separate, and cook until *al dente*. Drain.

Immediately add the pasta to the chicken and sauce in the skillet and toss well. Serve in warm soup bowls.

CHAPTER 14

COOL NOODLES:
PASTA SALADS

GOSH, THESE GUYS REALLY ARE COOL

I n the history of *maccheroni*, cold was not a virtue—until the pasta salad. Noodles rinsed in cool water maintain their integrity no matter *what* they are mixed with. Sauced with peanuts, flavored with fruit and oils, paired with seafood or chicken or meat, fresh vegetables or greens, pasta at room temperature has a satisfying assertiveness. In fact, it is important never to dress a pasta salad until serving, because, left to stand, the noodles will absorb too much of the dressing. The recipes here feature the full gamut: from Asian noodles to fresh, dried, and stuffed pastas, all with dressings heightened by coolness.

Cajun Pasta Salad

Chef Roger M. Jamison
Painted Plates
St. Louis, Missouri
Serves 4 to 6

Dressing
2 eggs
³/₄ cup red wine vinegar
1 tablespoon Cajun spice (store-bought or homemade)
¹/₂ teaspoon sugar
1 cup safflower oil

Meat and Vegetables
1 red onion, julienned
1 cup Madeira wine
1 cup diced crispy sautéed andouille sausage, cooled

1 large cucumber, peeled, seeded, and diced
1 firm tomato, diced
1 head romaine lettuce, shredded
1 pound cooked crawfish meat or bay shrimp, chilled

1 pound ditalini, cooked
Freshly grated cheese of choice (optional)

Make the dressing: In blender, combine the eggs, vinegar, Cajun spice, and sugar. Cover and blend on low speed until mixed. Then increase the speed to medium and finally to high. Remove the lid and slowly add the safflower oil in a thin, steady stream, blending until it is incorporated and a smooth dressing forms.

Prepare the meat and vegetables: Heat a dry nonstick skillet over medium heat. Add

the onion and let the natural juices and sugar of the onion turn the pieces brown. (This is known as caramelizing.) When browned, add the wine and reduce over moderately low heat by two-thirds. Remove from the heat and let cool. Ready the andouille, cucumber, tomato, lettuce, and shellfish.

Cook the pasta: In a large pot, bring at least 4 quarts of water to a rolling boil. Add 1 tablespoon of salt. Add pasta, stirring to separate. Cook until *al dente*. Drain, rinse in cold water, and drain again.

Place the romaine on a large salad platter. In a mixing bowl, combine the pasta, crawfish or bay shrimp, tomato, cucumber, andouille, and caramelized onion and mix well. Gradually add the dressing and toss to coat all the ingredients. Add only as much dressing as you like, to taste, and reserve the remainder for another use. Spoon the salad onto the lettuce. Top with grated cheese, if desired.

Lemony Conchiglie Salad

Serves 4

> 4 tomatoes, peeled, seeded, and diced
> 4 scallions, white part only, sliced
> 1 large cucumber, peeled, seeded, and diced
> 1 red bell pepper, seeded and diced
> 1 teaspoon salt
> $2/3$ cup olive oil
> 1 clove garlic, minced
> $1/2$ teaspoon paprika
> 1 teaspoon sugar
> $1/4$ teaspoon ground cumin
> $1/4$ teaspoon ground coriander
> $1/4$ teaspoon dry mustard
> Grated zest of 2 lemons
> $1/4$ cup fresh lemon juice
> 2 cups conchiglie shells

In a bowl, combine the tomatoes, scallions, cucumber, and red pepper. Cover and chill.

In a blender or food processor, combine all the remaining ingredients except the pasta and process until smooth. Transfer to a bowl, cover, and chill.

Meanwhile, in a large pot, bring at least 4 quarts of water to boil. Add 1 tablespoon salt. Add the pasta, stir to separate, and cook until *al dente*. Drain and rinse with cold water. (If the pasta is to remain standing without the sauce, toss it with a bit of olive oil.)

In a large bowl, combine the vegetables and the sauce. Add the pasta and toss well.

Pasta Salad with Smoked Chicken and Oven-Dried Tomatoes

Chef Stephan Pyles
Star Canyon
Dallas, Texas

Serves 6 to 8

2 tablespoons chopped fresh cilantro
1 tablespoon chopped fresh thyme
2 tablespoons chopped fresh basil
2 cloves garlic, minced
2 shallots, minced
1 tablespoon dry white wine
2 tablespoons white wine vinegar
1 tablespoon balsamic vinegar
1/2 cup plus 3 tablespoons olive oil
1/4 cup corn oil
Salt and freshly ground pepper to taste
9 ounces dried pasta such as fusilli
    or penne
1/2 cup cooked black beans
1/2 red bell pepper, seeded and cut into
    1/4-inch-wide strips
2 yellow bell peppers, seeded and cut into
    1/4-inch-wide strips
1 small carrot, coarsely chopped
5 tomatillos, husked and diced
1/4 pound fresh mozzarella cheese, diced
1/2 pound smoked chicken breast meat,
    diced
1 cup oven-dried cherry tomatoes

In a bowl, combine the cilantro, thyme, 1 tablespoon of the basil, half of the garlic, and the shallots. Mix well, then whisk in the wine and both vinegars. Slowly drizzle in the 1/2 cup olive oil and all the corn oil, whisking constantly. Season the vinaigrette with salt and pepper, and set aside.

In a large pot, bring at least 4 quarts water to a rolling boil. Add 1 tablespoon salt. Add the pasta, stir to separate, and cook until *al dente*. Drain and place in a large serving bowl. Add the remaining 3 tablespoons olive oil and toss well. Set aside to cool.

When the pasta is thoroughly cool, add the black beans, bell peppers, carrot, tomatillos, mozzarella, smoked chicken, dried tomatoes, and the remaining basil and garlic. Toss with the reserved vinaigrette and adjust the seasoning. Cover and refrigerate to chill slightly, about 20 minutes.

Ham and Vegetable Noodle Salad with Peanut Sauce

Serves 6 to 8

Peanut Sauce
1 tablespoon minced fresh ginger
1 tablespoon minced garlic
1 tablespoon finely chopped scallion
6 tablespoons creamy peanut butter

3 tablespoons soy sauce
¼ cup red wine vinegar
1 tablespoon Chinese chili sauce
1 teaspoon sugar
1 tablespoon Asian sesame oil
2 tablespoons vegetable oil
1 teaspoon hot dry mustard
½ teaspoon salt
½ cup chicken stock

1 cup julienned carrots
1 cup snow peas, julienned
¼ pound cooked ham, julienned
1 cup bean sprouts
1 cup julienned scallions
1 cup julienned red bell pepper
1 pound thin fedelini
2 tablespoons vegetable oil

Make the peanut sauce: In a bowl or food processor, combine all the ingredients and stir to mix well. When ready to use, stir well again. You will have almost 2½ cups.

Place the carrots and snow peas in a sieve or colander and douse with boiling water. Drain and pat dry. Cover and refrigerate until needed. Ready the ham, bean sprouts, scallions, and bell pepper, cover, and refrigerate.

In a large pot, bring at least 4 quarts of water to a rolling boil. Add 1 tablespoon salt. Add the pasta, stir to separate, and cook until *al dente*. Drain, rinse, and drain again. While the noodles are still warm, place in a bowl

and toss with the oil to coat. (The noodles can be chilled and brought back to room temperature before serving.)

To serve, place the noodles in a large bowl. Add the vegetables and ham and toss well. Gradually add the dressing and toss to coat. Judge the amount of dressing to taste.

Rooting For Ginger

Ginger is the flavoring we all know from gingersnap and gingerbread (the first is said to have been baked in the year 2,800 B.C.), but it is much, much more. A key ingredient in Asian cooking, the knobby brown rhizome is now a staple in Western supermarkets and is used in everything from meats to salads. "Hands" of ginger, as the bulbous pieces are called, can be kept in the refrigerator in a plastic bag. But since only a small amount is usually used at a time, it can also be stored, in plastic, in the freezer. After a quick immersion in hot water, the skin comes off easily and the ginger can be readily chopped.

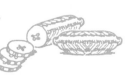

Randi's Bok Choy Chicken Salad

Randi Subarsky
Michael Subarsky Fine Catering
Closter, New Jersey

Serves 4

3 tablespoons soy sauce
1/2 cup sugar
1/3 cup white vinegar
3/4 cup olive oil
2 pounds skinless, boneless, thinly sliced
    chicken breasts
3/4 cup slivered blanched almonds
3/4 cup unsalted, shelled sunflower seeds
One 3-ounce package ramen noodles,
    crushed
2 heads bok choy, chopped
4 scallions, chopped
1/2 teaspoon paprika
1/2 teaspoon poultry seasoning

In a small bowl, stir together the soy sauce, sugar, vinegar, and oil until the sugar dissolves.

Cook chichen one of two ways. Season with paprika and poultry seasoning and grill whole breasts on medium hot-grill. Slice when cool. Or slice and sauté in 1 tablespoon of olive oil until just tender. Keep warm or at room temperature.

In a small bowl, combine the almonds, sunflower seeds, and noodles and stir until well mixed. In a large bowl, combine the chicken, bok choy, and scallions and stir to mix. Add the almond mixture and the soy mix and stir and toss to mix well. Allow to stand 1/2 hour before serving.

Chili-Pepper Penne Salad

Serves 4

1 pound hot-pepper pasta
1 avocado, pitted, peeled, and diced
1/2 cup julienned red onion
1 cup seeded and sliced Anaheim chili
    pepper
1 cup diced tomato
1/2 cup peeled, seeded, and sliced
    cucumber
1/2 cup soy sauce
1/2 cup fresh lime juice
1/3 cup red wine vinegar
1/3 cup extra virgin olive oil
1 tablespoon finely minced onion
1/2 teaspoon finely chopped garlic
1/4 cup chopped fresh cilantro
1/4 teaspoon salt
1/4 teaspoon freshly ground pepper

In separate mixing bowl, whisk together soy sauce, lime juice, and vinegar. Gradually whisk in the olive oil. Blend in the onion,

garlic, cilantro, salt, and pepper and continue to mix well.

In a large pot, bring at least 4 quarts of water to a rolling boil. Add 1 tablespoon salt. Add the pasta, stir to separate, and cook until *al dente*. Drain. Rinse until cool and drain again.

Transfer the pasta to a large serving bowl, and toss with vegetables. Toss with dressing to coat.

Lo Mein Pasta Salad with Flash-Fried Soft-Shell Crab

Chef Daniel Bonnot
Bizou * Chez Daniel
New Orleans, Louisiana

Serves 8

Lo Mein Sauce
1 teaspoon minced garlic
1 teaspoon minced fresh ginger
1 serrano chili pepper, seeded and minced
1 cup soy sauce
¼ cup dry sherry
¼ cup oyster sauce
¼ cup honey
Pinch of dried hot red pepper flakes
2 scallions, sliced thinly, green part included
1 cup firmly packed brown sugar

Pasta
2 pounds soba noodles or angel hair pasta
1 tablespoon vegetable oil
¼ head red cabbage, julienned
1 head broccoli, cut into very small florets
¼ pound snow peas, julienned
2 scallions, thinly sliced, green part included
1 carrot, julienned or shredded

Soft-Shell Crab
8 large soft-shell crabs
4 cups (1 quart) buttermilk
1 cup Asian bread crumbs (called panko, *these are coarser crumbs sold in Asian markets)*
1 cup flour
1 tablespoon salt
1 teaspoon freshly ground black pepper
1 teaspoon paprika
4 quarts oil, preferably peanut

Toasted sesame seeds (optional)

Make the sauce: Combine all the ingredients in a large saucepan. Bring to a boil, reduce to a simmer, and cook for 5 minutes. Allow to cool.

Make the pasta: Meanwhile, in a large pot, bring at least 4 quarts water to a rolling boil. Add 1 tablespoon salt. Add the pasta, stir to separate, and cook *less than al dente*. Drain.

(continued)

The pasta should be undercooked. It will cook further in the sauce.

In a very large sauté pan heat the oil over high heat. Add the cabbage, broccoli, snow peas, scallions, and carrot. When slightly limp, add the sauce and bring to a boil. Reduce the sauce by half and add the pasta. Add the pasta to absorb all of the sauce. When the sauce is absorbed, transfer the contents of the pan to a bowl, cover, and cool rapidly in the refrigerator.

Prepare the crab: In a bowl, combine the buttermilk, flour, salt, black pepper, and paprika. This mixture should be a very pasty butter. Dip 1 soft-shell crab in the buttermilk mixture, then dip the same crab in the bread crumbs. Follow this procedure for each crab. Fill a large pot with the oil and heat to 350° on a deep-fat frying thermometer. When the oil is ready, carefully slip the crabs into the pot, in batches. Do not crowd the pan or the oil temperature will drop. Fry the crabs golden brown, about 3 minutes. Using a slotted spoon or tongs, transfer to paper towels to drain briefly.

To serve, place a small mound of the pasta mixture in the middle of each individual plate. Place 1 crab on top of each mound. Sprinkle with toasted sesame seeds, if desired.

Marinated Beef and Pasta Salad

Serves 6 to 8

> 2 cups flank steak grilled and cut in
>   1-inch julienne strips
> 3 tablespoons fresh lemon juice
> 2 tablespoons red wine vinegar
> 2 tablespoons Dijon-style mustard
> 2 tablespoons vegetable oil
> 1/2 cup chopped fresh parsley
> 1 tablespoon chopped fresh oregano
> 1 tablespoon chopped fresh thyme
> 1 cup sliced fresh mushrooms
> 2 cups snow peas, cut in half on the
>   diagonal
> 1 red bell pepper, seeded and julienned
> 1 yellow bell pepper, seeded and julienned
> 1 pound cavatappi
> Salt and pepper to taste

Score the steak at an angle crosswise with a sharp knife. Grill over a hot grill or under a broiler, turning once. Cut in very thin strips crosswise, against the grain.

In a large bowl, whisk together the lemon juice, vinegar, and mustard. Gradually whisk in vegetable oil. Stir in the parsley, oregano, and thyme. Add the beef and marinate for 2 to 6 hours. During the last hour, add the mushrooms, snow peas, and bell peppers and mix well.

In a large pot, bring at least 4 quarts of water to a rolling boil. Add 1 tablespoon salt. Add the pasta, stir to separate, and cook until *al dente*. Drain. Rinse until cool and drain again.

Transfer the pasta to a large serving bowl. Add the meat, vegetables, and marinade and toss well. Add salt and pepper to taste. Serve chilled or at room temperature.

Bay Shrimp Salad

Chef Robert Boone
Stephens
An American Café
Albuquerque, New Mexico

Serves 4

1 pound tortiglioni
3 tomatoes
¹/₄ cup balsamic vinegar
2¹/₂ tablespoons rice vinegar
1¹/₄ tablespoons chopped fresh basil
1¹/₄ tablespoons chopped fresh tarragon
1¹/₂ teaspoons Dijon-style mustard
¹/₂ cup olive oil
³/₄ pound bay shrimp, peeled and deveined
1 pound mixed baby greens
8 tomato wedges

4 canned whole artichoke hearts,
*   quartered*
4 canned whole hearts of palm, quartered
8 fresh chives

To cook shrimp: Bring 2 quarts of water to boil. Add 1 tablespoon of salt. Add shrimp. After the water returns to a boil, cook *briefly*, just until the shrimp turn pink.

In a large pot, bring at least 4 quarts water to a rolling boil. Add 1 tablespoon salt. Add the pasta, stir to separate, and cook until *al dente*. Drain.

Grill tomatoes until they are black all around the outside. To grill, cut in half and place under a broiler or on a grill, skin side to the fire. Or hold, on a long skewer, over the flame of a gas burner. The blackened skin is included in the recipe.

Place the tomatoes in a food processor with the balsamic vinegar, rice vinegar, basil, mustard; process until smooth. Slowly add the oil, processing until fully incorporated. Transfer to a large bowl and add the bay shrimp and tortiglioni. Toss to distribute all the ingredients evenly. Divide the mixed greens among 4 individual salad plates. Arrange the tomato wedges, artichoke hearts, and hearts of palm around the outside of the greens. Mound an equal amount of the pasta mixture in the center of each plate. Stick 2 chives in the top of each salad so they appear to shoot out from it.

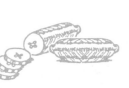

Orange Pasta Salad

Serves 8

*3 whole boneless, skinless chicken breasts,
   cooked and cooled*
1 cup chicken stock
1 pound wagon wheel pasta
*1¼ cups red or white seedless grapes, cut
   in half*
*1 large cucumber, peeled, seeded, and cut
   into chunks*
6 scallions, sliced, including green part
*2 cups drained canned mandarin orange
   segments*
*⅓ cup pecan halves, toasted and coarsely
   chopped*

Orange Vinaigrette
¼ cup vegetable oil
¼ cup white wine vinegar
¾ cup orange juice concentrate, thawed
1 teaspoon salt
½ teaspoon freshly ground pepper

1 head lettuce, leaves separated

To cook the chicken breasts: Preheat oven
to 325°. Cut into 6 breast halves. Place in an
ovenproof dish and pour chicken stock over.
Loosely cover with tinfoil. Cook until chicken
is just tender. Timing depends on size. Let
cook and cut into 1-inch cubes.

To prepare pasta: Bring at least 4 quarts of
water to boil. Add 1 tablespoon of salt. Add

wagon wheels and stir to separate. Cook until
al dente. Drain.

In a large bowl, stir together the pasta,
chicken, grapes, cucumber, scallions, and all
but 8 to 10 of the mandarin segments. In a
small bowl, whisk together all the vinaigrette
ingredients. Pour the vinaigrette into the pasta
mixture and toss the salad gently. On a large
platter, make a bed of the lettuce leaves.
Mound the salad on top of the lettuce and
garnish with remaining mandarin segments.

Chicken and Avocado with Spicy Tomato Salsa Over Linguine

Serves 6

Salsa
1½ pounds tomatoes, chopped
2 tablespoons minced red onion
*1 jalapeño or serrano chili pepper, or to
   taste, seeded and minced*
¼ cup chopped fresh cilantro
1 tablespoon red wine vinegar
Salt and freshly ground pepper to taste

3 cups chicken stock
3 boneless, skinless, whole chicken breasts
1 pound linguine
Salt to taste
2 avocados
Lemon juice

Make the salsa: In a small bowl, combine all ingredients and mix well. Set aside.

In a large skillet, bring the chicken stock to a boil. Add the chicken breasts and reduce the heat to a simmer. Poach the breasts until tender, about 10 minutes; the timing depends on the size. Drain, pat dry, and dice. Set aside.

In a large pot, bring at least 4 quarts of water to a rolling boil. Add 1 tablespoon salt. Add the pasta, stir to separate, and cook until *al dente*. Drain thoroughly. Rinse with cold water and drain again.

Pit, peel, and dice 1 avocado and place in a large serving bowl. Add the salsa and chicken and stir to mix. Carefully add the cooled pasta and toss well. Season to taste with salt. Pit, peel, and slice the remaining avocado $1/2$ inch thick. Dip slices in lemon juice to prevent discoloring. Garnish the salad with the avocado slices, arranging them around the outside edge of the bowl.

Asian Noodle Salad with Spicy Peanut Sauce

Serves 6

Spicy Peanut Sauce
$1/2$ cup chunky peanut butter
2 tablespoons unseasoned rice vinegar
1 tablespoon soy sauce

2 teaspoons sugar
1 tablespoon vegetable oil
1 tablespoon Asian sesame oil
6 scallions, including green tops, chopped
$1/2$ teaspoon dried hot red pepper flakes
$2/3$ cup plain yogurt
1-inch piece fresh ginger, peeled
1 clove garlic
$1/4$ teaspoon salt
1 pound spaghettini
1 tablespoon kosher salt
1 tablespoon Asian sesame oil
2 carrots, thinly sliced
1 red bell pepper, seeded and cut
   into strips 3 inches long and
   $1/4$ inch wide
Chopped fresh cilantro for garnish

Make the sauce: Combine all the sauce ingredients in a blender or food processor and process until smooth. Pour into a bowl, cover, and chill.

In a large pot, bring at least 4 quarts of water to a rolling boil. Add 1 tablespoon salt. Add the spaghettini, stir to separate, and cook until *al dente*. Drain, rinse under cold water until cool, and drain again. Place in a bowl, add the sesame oil, toss well, cover, and chill.

When ready to serve, transfer the noodles to a large serving bowl. Add the carrots and bell pepper and toss well. Add the sauce and toss thoroughly so that the noodles are evenly coated. Sprinkle with cilantro.

Pasta with Asparagus and Prosciutto in Balsamic Vinaigrette

Serves 2 to 4

Balsamic Vinaigrette

$1/2$ tablespoon olive oil
$1/2$ large red onion, thinly sliced
2 shallots, minced
$2^1/2$ tablespoons balsamic vinegar
1 teaspoon salt
$1/2$ teaspoon freshly ground pepper
Scant $1/3$ cup virgin olive oil

$1/2$ pound fusilli
1 tablespoon olive oil
1 tablespoon virgin olive oil
1 pound asparagus, trimmed and cut
    on the diagonal into 1-inch pieces
4 thin slices prosciutto, julienned
$1/3$ cup pine nuts, toasted
1 teaspoon grated lemon zest

Make the vinaigrette: In a small saucepan, heat the $1/2$ tablespoon olive oil over medium heat. Add the onion slices and sauté until lightly browned. Place in the bottom of a bowl and add all the remaining vinaigrette ingredients; mix well. Set aside.

In a large pot, bring at least 4 quarts water to a rolling boil. Add 1 tablespoon salt. Add the pasta, stir to separate, and cook until *al dente*. Drain. Rinse under cold water until cool and drain again. Transfer to a large serving bowl and toss with the 1 tablespoon olive oil.

In a saucepan, bring a small amount of water to a boil; add salt to taste and the asparagus. Cook until tender-crisp. Drain.

Add the asparagus and prosciutto to the fusilli and toss gently. Add the vinaigrette and toss to coat the pasta completely. Sprinkle with the pine nuts and lemon zest.

Vintage Vinegar

Vinegar was first made from spoiled wine more than 5,000 years ago, but balsamic vinegar comes to us only from the area around Modena and Reggio Emilia in Italy, where the production of vinegar is taken as seriously as the making of wine. Balsamic is made only from the Trebbiano grape and is aged in a series of casks made of different woods. The vinegar is dark brown and has a wonderful complex taste and aroma—pungent, sweetish, with a slight sharpness, but still mellow. It can be used in any number of ways in cooking and in salads, but should always be added sparingly.

Herbed Couscous Salad

Serves 6

1 cup water
1 cup instant couscous
1 teaspoon salt
1 large red bell pepper, seeded and finely diced
2 serrano chili peppers, or to taste, seeded and minced
1 large ripe tomato, seeded and chopped
2 large carrots, coarsely shredded
6 scallions, including green tops, minced
2 cloves garlic, mashed
2 tablespoons chopped fresh basil
1/3 cup chopped fresh cilantro
1/3 cup chopped fresh mint
2 tablespoons white wine vinegar
1/3 cup virgin olive oil
Salt and freshly ground pepper to taste
3 ounces fresh goat cheese, crumbled

In a 2-quart saucepan, bring the water to a boil. Add the couscous and salt and stir well. Remove from the heat, cover, and let stand until the liquid is absorbed, about 5 minutes. Using a fork, fluff up the couscous until there are no lumps. Transfer to a large bowl.

Add the bell pepper, chilies, tomato, carrots, scallions, garlic, basil, cilantro, mint, vinegar, and oil to the warm couscous and mix well with a fork to separate the grains. Add the salt and fresh pepper, cover, and chill for 10 minutes. Sprinkle with the cheese just before serving.

Radiatori with Shrimp and Artichokes in Parmesan Vinaigrette

Serves 6

1 pound shrimp, peeled and deveined
2 cloves garlic, sliced

Parmesan Vinaigrette
1/3 cup white wine vinegar
1 tablespoon Dijon-style mustard
1 teaspoon minced garlic
2 teaspoons minced shallot
1/2 cup olive oil
1/2 cup vegetable oil
1 teaspoon freshly ground pepper
Dash Tabasco sauce
1/4 cup freshly grated Parmesan cheese

3/4 pound radiatori
One 10-ounce package frozen artichoke hearts, cooked and drained
1 bunch fresh spinach, cleaned, stems removed, and leaves torn into bite-sized pieces

In a saucepan, bring 3 quarts of water to a boil. Add 1 tablespoon salt. Add the shrimp and garlic and cook just until turning pink, 2 or 3 minutes. Drain and let cool.

Make the vinaigrette: In a bowl, whisk together the vinegar, mustard, garlic, and shallot. Gradually whisk in the oils. Add the pepper and Tabasco, then stir in the Parmesan cheese.

(continued)

In a large pot, bring at least 4 quarts of water to a rolling boil. Add 1 tablespoon salt. Add the pasta, stir to separate, and cook until *al dente*. Drain. Rinse under cold water until cool and drain again.

Transfer the pasta to a large serving bowl. Add the shrimp, artichoke hearts, and spinach. Toss well. Add the vinaigrette and toss thoroughly to coat the pasta.

Couscous Salad with Raspberry Vinaigrette

Serves 6 to 8

2$^1/_4$ cups water
1 tablespoon olive oil
1$^1/_2$ cups instant couscous

Dressing
3 tablespoons raspberry vinegar
2 tablespoons fresh lime juice
1 teaspoon finely chopped lime zest
1 clove garlic, minced
$^1/_4$ teaspoon ground ginger
$^1/_4$ teaspoon salt
$^1/_8$ teaspoon cayenne pepper
$^1/_2$ cup plus 2 tablespoons olive oil
Salt and freshly ground black pepper

$^1/_3$ cup chopped walnuts
$^1/_2$ cup frozen tiny peas, thawed
Boiling water, as needed
2 zucchini, finely diced
1 carrot, finely diced
1 tablespoon finely chopped flat-leaf
    parsley

In a saucepan, bring the water and olive oil to a boil. Pour the couscous into the pan, remove from the heat, cover, and let stand until all the liquid is absorbed, about 5 minutes. Using a fork, fluff up the couscous until there are no lumps. Keep stirring occasionally until the couscous cools. Transfer to a large serving bowl.

Make the dressing: Combine the raspberry vinegar, lime juice, lime zest, garlic, ginger, salt, and cayenne in a bowl. Whisk until well combined. Slowly add the olive oil, whisking constantly until incorporated. Add the salt and black pepper. Set aside.

Preheat the oven to 350°. Toast the walnuts until lightly browned, about 5 minutes. Set aside.

Place the peas in a sieve and douse with boiling water. Drain. Add the peas, zucchini, carrot, 1 tablespoon of the parsley, and 2 tablespoons of the walnuts to the couscous. Toss well. Add the dressing to the couscous and toss again thoroughly. Garnish with the remaining parsley and walnuts.

Orecchiette with Broccoli in Saffron Vinaigrette

Serves 6 *as a side dish*

Dressing

1/4 cup red wine vinegar
1/2 teaspoon saffron threads
2 tablespoons fresh lemon juice
2 teaspoons Dijon-style mustard
1 clove garlic, minced
1/2 cup olive oil
1/2 teaspoon salt
1/4 teaspoon freshly ground pepper

2 cups broccoli florets
3/4 pound orecchiette
3 tablespoons freshly grated Parmesan
    cheese
1 large red bell pepper, seeded and cut
    into 1-inch dice
2 tablespoons finely chopped parsley

Make the dressing: Pour the vinegar into a small saucepan. Add the saffron threads and bring to a simmer over medium heat. Immediately remove from the heat and let cool. The saffron will infuse the vinegar.

In a bowl, combine the cooled vinegar and saffron, lemon juice, mustard, and garlic. Whisk in the olive oil. Add the salt and pepper. Adjust the seasoning. Set aside.

Bring a large pot of salted water to a boil. Add the broccoli and blanch for 2 minutes.

Drain and rinse under cold water. Drain again and pat dry.

In a large pot, bring at least 4 quarts water to a rolling boil. Add 1 tablespoon salt. Add the pasta, stir to separate, and cook until *al dente*. Drain and rinse under cold water until cool and drain again. Transfer to a large serving bowl.

Pour the dressing over the pasta and toss well. Add the Parmesan cheese and red pepper and mix again. Taste for seasoning. Garnish with the parsley.

Tortellini with Prosciutto and Mesclun

Serves 4

2 tablespoons olive oil
1/2 cup onion, minced
1/4 pound thinly sliced prosciutto, cut into
    narrow strips
1/2 cup peeled, seeded, and chopped
    tomato
2 tablespoons chopped fresh basil
1/2 teaspoon dried oregano
2 tablespoons balsamic vinegar
1 teaspoon salt
Freshly ground pepper to taste
1 pound cheese tortellini

(continued)

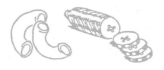

2 cups mesclun *(mixture of frisée, arugula, mâche, oak-leaf lettuce, and similar greens)*
½ cup freshly grated Parmesan cheese

In a large skillet, heat the oil over high heat. Add the onion, prosciutto, tomato, basil, and oregano and sauté for 2 minutes. Stir in the vinegar and remove from the heat. Add the salt and pepper. Transfer to a large bowl.

In a large pot, bring at least 4 quarts water to a rolling boil. Add 1 tablespoon salt. Add the pasta, stir to separate, and cook until *al dente*. Drain. Rinse under cold water until cool and drain again. Immediately transfer to the bowl holding the prosciutto mixture.

Add the *mesclun* and the Parmesan to the bowl and toss well.

Citrus-Scented Orzo with Sesame Dressing

Serves 8 to 10 *as a side dish*

Dressing
¾ cup vegetable oil
¼ cup light sesame oil (Asian)
½ cup rice vinegar

1 tablespoon fresh lemon juice
1 teaspoon soy sauce
1 teaspoon grated lemon zest
1 teaspoon grated orange zest
2 tablespoons thinly sliced scallions, white part only
1 teaspoon grated fresh ginger
½ teaspoon minced garlic
1 teaspoon freshly ground pepper
1 teaspoon salt
1½ tablespoons sugar
1 tablespoon finely chopped fresh cilantro

1 pound orzo
2 cups shredded carrots
2 cups raisins
1 cup unsalted, shelled sunflower seeds

Make the dressing: Combine all the ingredients in a large bowl, and stir to mix well. Set aside.

In a large pot, bring at least 4 quarts water to a rolling boil. Add 1 tablespoon salt. Add the pasta, stir to separate, and cook until *al dente*. Drain. Rinse under cold water until cool and drain again.

Add the pasta to the bowl holding the dressing. Stir in the carrots, raisins, and sunflower seeds and serve.

Gemelli with Grilled Shrimp and Fruit Salsa

Serves 4

Fruit Salsa
1 cup diced pineapple
1 cup diced mango
2 tablespoons minced red onion
1 tablespoon fresh lime juice
1 jalapeño chili pepper, seeded and
    minced
3 tablespoons vegetable oil
¹/₂ cup chopped fresh cilantro

¹/₂ cup olive oil
1 tablespoon white wine vinegar
1 clove garlic
¹/₂ teaspoon ground cumin
Salt and freshly ground pepper to taste
16 extra-large shrimp, peeled and deveined
¹/₂ pound gemelli
Vegetable oil, as needed

Make the salsa: In a large bowl, combine all the ingredients, and stir to mix well. Cover and refrigerate for several hours. Bring back to room temperature before serving.

In a large bowl, combine the olive oil, vinegar, garlic, cumin, salt, and pepper. Mix well. Add the shrimp, cover, and marinate for 3 hours in the refrigerator.

Preheat the broiler, or prepare a charcoal fire. Remove the shrimp from the marinade and place on a broiler pan or grill rack. Broil or grill, turning once, until cooked through, about 4 minutes. Remove from broiler or grill and set aside.

In a large pot, bring at least 4 quarts water to a rolling boil. Add 1 tablespoon salt. Add the pasta, stir to separate, and cook until *al dente*. Drain. Rinse under cold water until cool and drain again.

Transfer the pasta to a large bowl and toss with a bit of vegetable oil to coat. Add the shrimp and toss to mix. Season with salt and pepper. Add the salsa and toss well.

CHAPTER 15

SALT OF THE EARTH:
PASTA AND BEANS

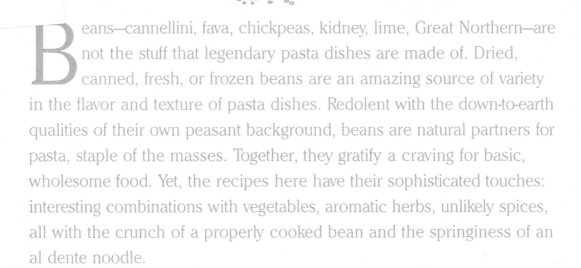

Beans—cannellini, fava, chickpeas, kidney, lime, Great Northern—are not the stuff that legendary pasta dishes are made of. Dried, canned, fresh, or frozen beans are an amazing source of variety in the flavor and texture of pasta dishes. Redolent with the down-to-earth qualities of their own peasant background, beans are natural partners for pasta, staple of the masses. Together, they gratify a craving for basic, wholesome food. Yet, the recipes here have their sophisticated touches: interesting combinations with vegetables, aromatic herbs, unlikely spices, all with the crunch of a properly cooked bean and the springiness of an al dente noodle.

Orecchiette with Broccoli, Chickpeas, Onions, and Tomatoes

Serves 4

1/2 cup dried chickpeas, or 1 1/2 cups canned chickpeas, drained and well rinsed
2 teaspoons salt, if using dried chickpeas
5 tablespoons olive oil
3/4 pound orecchiette
1 large head broccoli, cut into small florets (about 3 cups)
Ice water, to cover
1/2 cup diced red onion
2 tablespoons finely minced garlic
One 28-ounce can plum tomatoes, drained and diced
Salt and freshly ground black pepper
1/2 cup freshly grated pecorino romano cheese

If using dried chickpeas, in a large bowl, place the chickpeas in 2 1/2 cups water and refrigerate overnight. Drain and rinse. Place the chickpeas in a small saucepan and add water to cover. Bring to a boil over medium heat, then reduce the heat, cover, and simmer until the chickpeas are tender but not mushy, about 1 hour. During the last 15 minutes, add the 2 teaspoons salt. Drain and place in a bowl; toss with 1 tablespoon of the olive oil. Let cool.

Blanch the broccoli florets in boiling salted water for 2 minutes. Drain and immerse in ice water. Drain well.

In a large pot, bring at least 4 quarts water to a rolling boil. Add 1 tablespoon salt. Add the orecchiette, stir to separate, and cook until *al dente*.

Meanwhile, heat the remaining 4 table-spoons olive oil in a large skillet over

medium heat. Add the onion and cook until translucent, about 5 minutes. Add the chickpeas and garlic and cook briefly. Add the tomatoes and broccoli and cook until warmed through. Season with salt and pepper.

Drain the pasta and transfer to a warmed serving bowl. Add the sauce and toss well. Sprinkle with the cheese.

Orzo Pasta with Young Fava Beans in Cream and Curry Leaves

Chef Christophe Vessaire
The Grapevine Café
Atlanta, Georgia

Serves 4

5$\frac{1}{2}$ *pounds small fava beans*
$\frac{3}{4}$ *cup heavy cream*
Salt to taste
1 sprig fresh savory
1 pound orzo
Freshly ground black pepper to taste
1 tablespoon parsley
4 curry leaves, julienned

Shell the fava beans, immerse in boiling water for 1 minute, then slip each bean out of its tough skin. Set aside.

Pour the cream into a shallow pan; add the salt and savory, and bring to a boil. Add the fava beans and boil, uncovered, for 5 minutes. Check that the beans are done; they should be tender but not falling apart. Remove the savory and discard.

Bring at least 4 quarts of water to a rolling boil. Add 1 tablespoon of salt. Add orzo, stirring to separate. Boil until *al dente*. Drain. Place the pasta in a warm serving bowl.

Add the sauce, the fava beans, season with salt and pepper. Toss well. Sprinkle with the parsley and curry leaves.

Note: Fresh cilantro may be substituted for curry leaves, if unavailable.

Mexican Pasta and Bean Medley

Serves 4

$\frac{1}{2}$ *pound rotini*
One 16-ounce can black beans, well rinsed
    and drained
One 16-ounce can cannellini beans, well
    rinsed and drained
One 11-ounce can corn kernels, drained

(continued)

1 cup chopped red onion
¹/₄ cup finely diced red bell pepper
¹/₄ cup finely chopped green bell pepper
¹/₄ cup chopped fresh cilantro
¹/₂ cup chopped fresh parsley
¹/₄ cup red wine vinegar
1 tablespoon Dijon-style mustard
2 cloves garlic, minced
1¹/₂ teaspoons ground cumin
¹/₂ teaspoon freshly ground pepper
¹/₄ cup vegetable oil

In a large pot, bring at least 4 quarts water to a rolling boil. Add 1 tablespoon salt. Add the rotini, stir to separate, and cook until *al dente*. Drain. Rinse with cold water until cool and drain again.

In a large bowl, combine the pasta, all the beans, corn, onion, bell peppers, cilantro, and parsley. In a separate bowl, combine the vinegar, mustard, garlic, cumin, and pepper. Slowly whisk the oil into the vinegar mixture. Add the vinegar mixture to the pasta and stir well. Cover and chill well before serving.

Gazpacho Pasta with Cannellini Beans

Serves 4

1 pound radiatori or ruffled pasta
3 large, ripe tomatoes, finely diced
2 cucumbers, peeled, seeded, and finely diced
1 red onion, diced
2 cups vegetable juice
3 tablespoons red wine vinegar
One 16-ounce can cannellini beans, rinsed well and drained
¹/₄ cup chopped fresh parsley
Salt and freshly ground pepper to taste
1 tablespoon butter
¹/₂ cup fresh bread crumbs

In a large pot, bring at least 4 quarts water to a rolling boil. Add 1 tablespoon salt. Add the pasta, stir to separate, and cook until *al dente.* Drain. Rinse under cold water until cool and drain again.

In a large bowl, stir together the tomatoes, cucumbers, onion, vegetable juice, vinegar, beans, parsley, salt, and pepper. Add the pasta and toss to coat evenly.

In a small sauté pan, melt the butter over medium heat. Add the bread crumbs and toss to coat with butter, stirring constantly.

Just before serving, sprinkle the toasted crumbs over pasta.

Orecchiette with Seafood, Rapini, and White Beans

Chef Cary Neff
Cary Restaurant and Bar
Philadelphia, Pennsylvania

Serves 4

> 1 pound rapini *(broccoli rabe)*, tough
>   stems removed
> ¹/₄ cup olive oil
> 2 teaspoons minced garlic
> ¹/₂ pound rock shrimp
> ¹/₄ pound cleaned squid bodies, cut into
>   rings
> 6 ounces fish fillet such as salmon, tuna,
>   or tilapia, cubed
> 1 cup cooked cannellini beans, well rinsed
>   and drained, reserving ¹/₂ cup of liquid
> ¹/₈ teaspoon dried hot red pepper flakes
> 1 teaspoon each chopped fresh parsley,
>   tarragon, and thyme
> Juice from 1 lemon
> Salt and freshly ground pepper to taste
> ¹/₄ cup freshly grated pecorino romano
>   cheese
> 1 pound orecchiette
> 1 tablespoon bread crumbs

Blanch the *rapini* in boiling water for about 2 minutes. Rinse under cold running water, drain, and chop into small pieces. Set aside.

In a large, heavy skillet, heat olive oil over medium heat. Add the garlic and sauté until translucent, about 2 minutes; do not allow to brown. Add the shrimp, squid, and fish. Cook until all the seafood is firm. Add the beans and ¹/₂ cup of the liquid reserved from cooking the beans. Bring to a boil. Add the herbs and lemon juice and season with salt and pepper.

Meanwhile, in a large pot, bring at least 4 quarts of water to a rolling boil. Add 1 tablespoon salt. Add the pasta, stir to separate, and cook until *al dente*. Drain.

Add the pasta and rapini to seafood. Raise heat and gently toss until combined. Transfer to warm serving bowl. Drizzle with 1 tablespoon olive oil and top with grated cheese, and 1 tablespoon bread crumbs.

White Bean and Pasta Bake

Serves 4

> ¹/₄ pound ground turkey
> 1 cup diced onion
> 2 cups chopped broccoli
> 1 teaspoon marjoram
> 1 teaspoon tarragon
> One 16-ounce can Italian plum tomatoes,
>   drained and chopped

(continued)

One 15½-ounce can cannellini beans, well
    rinsed and drained
1½ cups chicken stock
Salt and freshly ground black pepper
½ pound spirals
1 tablespoon bread crumbs
¼ cup freshly grated Parmesan cheese

Preheat oven to 350°.

Place the turkey in a large skillet over
medium heat and cook, breaking it up with
a wooden spoon, until browned, about
5 minutes. Pour off almost all the liquid.
Add onion and cook just until it begins to
soften. Add the broccoli, marjoram, and
tarragon and cook briefly, stirring constantly.
Add the tomatoes, bring quickly to a boil,
and remove from the heat. Stir in the beans
and chicken stock and season with salt and
pepper.

In a large pot, bring at least 4 quarts
water to a rolling boil. Add 1 tablespoon salt.
Add the pasta, stir to separate, and cook until
not quite *al dente*. The white core of the
pasta should still be visible. Drain.

In a large bowl, combine the turkey
mixture with the pasta. Mix well. Transfer to a
1½-quart baking dish. In a small bowl, mix
together the bread crumbs and Parmesan
cheese and sprinkle evenly over the dish.

Place in the oven and bake until heated
through and the top is lightly browned, about
20 minutes.

Fiesta Pasta

Michael Meehan
Tupelo Honey
Sea Cliff, New York

Serves 4 as an appetizer

¾ pound fresh or dried pasta
1 Anaheim chili pepper or bell pepper,
    seeded and diced
½ cup vegetable stock
1 teaspoon olive oil
Kernels from 2 ears of corn
½ cup cooked red kidney beans
1 teaspoon unsalted butter (optional)
Salt and freshly ground pepper to taste

Garnish
¼ pound fresh goat cheese
½ red bell pepper, seeded and diced
Fresh cilantro leaves

In a large sauté pan or wok, heat the oil
over high heat. Add the chili or bell peppers
and corn and "sweat" for 30 seconds. Add
the vegetable stock. When the mixture
reaches a boil, reduce the heat to a simmer
and add the beans, butter (if using), salt, and
pepper. Keep warm.

In a large pot, bring at least 4 quarts
water to a rolling boil. Add 1 tablespoon salt.
Add the pasta, stir to separate, and cook until
al dente. The fresh pasta will take only 2 to 3
minutes; the dried pasta will take at least

twice that amount. Drain noodles and add to vegetable and bean mix. Serve immediately.

Divide evenly among 4 bowls. Crumble the goat cheese over the tops and garnish with the bell pepper and cilantro leaves.

Switching One Bean For Another

Borlotti and cannellini are the preferred beans of Italian cuisine. Borlotti are from the same family tree as kidney beans, whose red color they share with more interesting variations. Found in shades from pale pink to dark red, borlotti are always speckled. They may be bought fresh in specialty stores or canned, packed in brine. The latter should be rinsed before use. Their cousins, kidney beans, can stand in as a substitute.

If dried beans are called for in an Italian recipe, small, white, elongated cannellini are generally the beans of choice. Cannellini come in a canned version, too. If a search for either leaves you beanless, white navy beans can be used in their place.

Bow Ties with Black Beans and Cherry Tomatoes

Serves 4

2 teaspoons olive oil or vegetable oil
2 cloves garlic, finely chopped
1 bunch scallions, trimmed and thinly sliced, including green tops
1½ teaspoons ground cumin
1½ tablespoons fresh lemon juice
One 15-ounce can black beans, well rinsed and drained
Salt and freshly ground pepper to taste
¾ pound bow ties
8 cherry tomatoes, quartered
2 tablespoons chopped fresh cilantro

In a saucepan, heat the oil over medium heat. Add the garlic and sauté until soft, just a few minutes. Do not allow to brown. Add the scallions and cumin and cook briefly. Remove from the heat and stir in the lemon juice. Add the beans and toss to coat. Season with salt and pepper.

In a large pot, bring at least 4 quarts water to a rolling boil. Add 1 tablespoon salt. Add the pasta, stir to separate, and cook until less than *al dente*. The pasta should be undercooked. Before draining, reserve ½ cup of the cooking water. Then drain and return the pasta to the pot.

Add the reserved pasta water to the black bean mixture, stir, and add to the pasta. Bring

(continued)

to a boil over medium heat and cook until the sauce is thick enough to coat the pasta. Remove from the heat. Carefully stir in the cherry tomatoes and cilantro just before serving.

Linguine with Beef and Black Bean Chili

Serves 4 to 6

2 tablespoons vegetable oil
1 pound ground beef
3/4 cup finely diced onion
1 jalapeño chili pepper, seeded and thinly
    sliced
2 tablespoons chili powder
1 tablespoon ground cumin
2 cloves garlic, finely chopped
One 16-ounce can black beans, well rinsed
    and drained
One 15-ounce can crushed tomatoes
2 tablespoons chopped fresh cilantro
2 cups water
Salt and freshly ground pepper to taste
1 pound linguine

In a large, deep skillet, heat the oil over medium heat. Crumble the meat into the skillet and cook, stirring with a wooden spoon to break it up, until the meat begins to brown, about 5 minutes. Add the onion,

jalapeño, chili powder, cumin, and garlic and cook until the onion changes color. Add the beans, tomatoes, cilantro, and water. Bring to a boil, reduce the heat to low, cover, and simmer for 15 minutes to blend the flavors. Season with salt and pepper.

In a large pot, bring at least 4 quarts water to a rolling boil. Add 1 tablespoon salt. Add the pasta, stir to separate, and cook until *al dente*. Drain and return to the pot. Add the bean mixture and stir over medium heat until the sauce simmers and the pasta is glazed with the sauce.

Tagliatelle with Cannellini and Tomato Sauce

Serves 4 to 6

1 tablespoon olive oil
3 cloves garlic, minced
2 pounds fresh tomatoes, peeled, seeded,
    and chopped, or one 28-ounce can
    plum tomatoes, with juice, chopped
1 teaspoon sugar
1 teaspoon dried oregano
2 cups well rinsed and drained canned
    cannellini beans or drained cooked
    cannellini beans
Salt and freshly ground pepper to taste
1 pound tagliatelle
1/2 cup freshly grated Parmesan cheese

In a deep skillet, heat the olive oil over medium heat. Add the garlic and sauté until soft, about 3 minutes. Do not allow the garlic to brown. Immediately add the tomatoes, sugar, and oregano. Cook vigorously for a few minutes, and then lower the heat to a simmer and cook until the sauce thickens, about 20 minutes. Stir in the beans and warm through. Season with salt and pepper.

Meanwhile, in a large pot, bring at least 4 quarts of water to a rolling boil. Add 1 tablespoon salt. Add the pasta, stir to separate, and cook until *al dente*. Drain. Transfer the pasta to a warm serving bowl. Pour the sauce over the top and toss well. Sprinkle with the cheese.

Gemelli with Fava Beans and Bacon

Serves 4 to 6

8 strips thick-cut bacon, cut into
*   ¹⁄₂-inch squares*
2 pounds young fava beans
¹⁄₂ cup red onion, diced
¹⁄₄ cup green bell pepper, diced
¹⁄₄ cup chopped parsley
¹⁄₄ cup unsalted butter
2 tablespoons shredded fresh basil leaves
Salt and freshly ground pepper
*   to taste*

1 pound gemelli
¹⁄₃ cup freshly grated pecorino romano
*   cheese*

Shell the fava beans, immerse in boiling water for 1 minute, then slip each bean out of its tough skin.

In a skillet, sauté the bacon over high heat. When it is crisp, remove with a slotted spoon and drain on paper towels. Discard all but 1 tablespoon of the bacon drippings. Add green onion and sauté 1 minute. Add the onion to the pan. Sauté just until the red begins to change color. Remove from the heat.

Cook the fava beans in salted boiling water for 5 to 10 minutes, depending on their size. They should be soft but not mushy. Drain and toss with the butter in a small bowl. Add the bacon and onion and mix well. Keep warm.

Meanwhile, in a large pot, bring at least 4 quarts of water to a rolling boil. Add 1 tablespoon salt. Add the pasta, stir to separate, and cook until *al dente*. Reserve 1/2 cup of the pasta cooking water. Drain.

Transfer the pasta to a large, warm serving bowl. Add the fava mixture and the basil and toss to mix well. Season with salt and pepper. Add the cheese and toss again.

Rigatoni with Borlotti Beans and Sausage

Serves 4

> *1 cup dried borlotti or cranberry beans,*
> *soaked overnight in water to cover*
> *1 pound fresh sweet Italian sausages,*
> *casings removed*
> *3 tablespoons olive oil*
> *3/4 cup chopped onion*
> *2 cloves garlic, crushed*
> *1 bay leaf, crumbled*
> *1 teaspoon dried thyme*
> *1 1/4 cups red wine*
> *2 tablespoons tomato paste*
> *Salt and freshly ground pepper*
> *1/2 pound rigatoni*

Drain the beans and place in a large pot with a generous amount of fresh water. Bring to a boil and boil for 10 minutes. Reduce the heat to low, cover partially, and simmer until just tender but not mushy, about 30 minutes. Drain.

Place the sausage in a deep skillet over medium heat. Break up into chunks with a wooden spoon and cook until fully browned, 5 to 10 minutes. Drain off the fat. Add the olive oil to the pan. When it is hot, add the onion, garlic, bay leaf, and thyme. Cook just until the onion is translucent. Add the wine and tomato paste, stir well, bring to a boil, and then reduce the heat. Season with salt and pepper, cover, and simmer for 1 hour. Add the beans during the last 15 minutes.

Check the beans for doneness and cook more if necessary. (If the mixture becomes too thick, add some of the pasta cooking water a little at a time, stirring constantly.)

Meanwhile, in a large pot, bring at least 4 quarts of water to a rolling boil. Add 1 tablespoon salt. Add the pasta, stir to separate, and cook until *al dente.* Reserve 1 cup of the pasta cooking water. Drain.

Transfer the pasta to a large warm serving bowl. Add the sausage-bean mixture and toss well.

Little Tubes and Beans

Serves 4

> *2 tablespoons olive oil*
> *1 cup onions, minced*
> *2 cloves garlic, minced*
> *One 28-ounce can Italian plum tomatoes,*
> *with juice, chopped*
> *2 tablespoons tomato paste*
> *One, 15-ounce can cannellini beans,*
> *undrained*
> *1 tablespoon dried basil*
> *1 teaspoon salt*
> *Dash dried hot red pepper flakes*
> *1 cup warm water*
> *Freshly ground pepper to taste*
> *1/3 cup freshly grated Parmesan cheese*
> *3/4 pound tubetti*

In a deep skillet, heat the olive oil over medium heat. Add the onions and garlic and sauté until soft, about 5 minutes. Do not allow the garlic to brown. Add the tomatoes, stir in tomato paste, and cook for a few minutes. Reduce the heat to low and simmer, uncovered, until the sauce thickens, 15 to 20 minutes. Add the undrained beans, basil, 1 teaspoon salt, and red pepper flakes. Cover and simmer until thick, about 30 minutes. Check frequently for thickness. If the mixture becomes too thick, add warm water accordingly. Add pepper to taste.

Meanwhile, in a large pot, bring at least 4 quarts of water to a rolling boil. Add 1 tablespoon salt. Add the pasta, stir to separate, and cook until *al dente*. Drain. Transfer the pasta to a large warm serving bowl. Add the tomato-bean mixture and toss well. Add the Parmesan cheese and toss again.

Chicken and Black Bean Salad Over Spirals

Serves 4

> 1 pound boneless, skinless chicken breast
> 1/2 cup chicken stock
> Salt and freshly ground black pepper
>   to taste
> 1/2 teaspoon dried oregano

1/4 cup olive oil
Zest and juice (1/4 cup) of 2 lemons
2 cups drained cooked black beans, or
   one 16-ounce can black beans, rinsed
   well and drained
1/2 teaspoon dried hot red pepper flakes
   (optional)
2 large tomatoes, seeded and chopped
3/4 pound spirals

Preheat the oven to 325°. Place the chicken breast and stock in a small baking dish. Sprinkle the breast on both sides with salt, pepper, and oregano. Cover with aluminum foil. Bake briefly, turning once, until the breast is just cooked through yet still moist. Remove from the oven, let cool, and cut into 1/2-inch cubes.

In a large bowl, combine the olive oil, lemon zest, and juice. Add the black beans and chicken and stir well to combine. Add the red pepper flakes and tomatoes and fold in gently.

Meanwhile, in a large pot, bring at least 4 quarts of water to a rolling boil. Add 1 table-spoon salt. Add the pasta, stir to separate, and cook until *al dente*. Drain. Rinse with cold water until cool and drain again.

In a large bowl, combine the pasta with the chicken-bean mixture. Serve at room temperature or cover and chill before serving.

Bucatini with Lima Beans
Serves 4 to 6

2 tablespoons olive oil

Four 4-inch sweet Italian sausages, sliced

1 large onion, thinly sliced

2 cloves garlic, minced

One 28-ounce can Italian plum tomatoes,
with juice, chopped

1 tablespoon dried basil

$^1/_2$ pound bucatini or spaghetti, broken into
1-inch pieces

2 cups lima beans, cooked

Salt and freshly ground pepper to taste

$^1/_3$ cup freshly grated Parmesan cheese

Preheat the oven to 375°. Butter a 9 x 9-inch baking dish.

In a deep skillet, heat the oil over medium heat. Add the sausages and brown on all sides until partially cooked. Remove with a slotted spoon to a plate and drain almost all the drippings from the pan. Add the onion and cook until just wilted. Remove with the slotted spoon to the plate. Add the garlic and cook until soft. Do not allow the garlic to become brown. Add the tomatoes and cook for a few minutes, then reduce the heat and simmer, uncovered, until the sauce thickens, 15 to 20 minutes. Stir in the basil. Add salt and pepper to taste.

Meanwhile, in a large pot, bring at least 4 quarts of water to a rolling boil. Add 1 tablespoon salt. Add the pasta, stir to separate, and cook until less than *al dente*. Drain. The pasta should be undercooked.

In a large bowl, combine the pasta, lima beans, tomato sauce, onion, and sausage. Season with salt and pepper.

Transfer the mixture to the prepared baking dish. Sprinkle the Parmesan cheese evenly over the top. Bake, uncovered, until the mixture bubbles, about 15 minutes.

Bean Cuisine

Dried beans are not for spur-of-the-moment, let's-see-what's-in-the-cupboard cooks. Many require hours of soaking. (Only fish seem to need more time in water.) To prepare dried beans, if you *can* plan ahead, soak them overnight. Simply immerse beans in cold water to cover by about 2 inches. Cover, ignore for about 12 hours, and then rinse before using. If you can manage just a couple of hours of advanced preparation, place the beans in a saucepan with cold water to cover, bring to a boil, boil for 2 minutes, turn off the heat, and let them stand for an hour. Drain and use. No matter which method time allows, it's important to discard the soaking water and start fresh for the rest of the recipe.

Orecchiette with Fava Beans and Sage

Serves 4 to 6

2 cups dried fava beans, soaked for
    6 hours or overnight in water to cover
1 onion, cut into quarters
1 bay leaf
2 teaspoons salt, plus salt to taste
3 tablespoons olive oil
2 cloves garlic, minced
1/2 cup packed fresh sage leaves, shredded
Juice of 1 lemon
Freshly ground pepper to taste
1 pound orecchiette
1/2 cup freshly grated Parmesan cheese

Drain the beans and place in a large pot with a generous amount of fresh water. Bring to a boil, reduce the heat, add the onion, bay leaf, and 2 teaspoons salt, and simmer until tender but not mushy, about 1 1/2 hours. Drain, reserving 1/2 cup of the liquid and discarding the onion and bay leaf.

In a large skillet, heat the oil over medium heat. Add the garlic and sauté until just soft, about 3 minutes. Add the sage and lemon juice and cook for 1 minute. Remove from the heat, stir in the beans, and season with salt and pepper. Keep warm.

Meanwhile, in a large pot, bring at least 4 quarts of water to a rolling boil. Add 1 tablespoon salt. Add the pasta, stir to separate, and cook until *al dente*. Drain.

In a large serving bowl, combine the beans and pasta. Add the bean liquid and stir gently. Add the Parmesan cheese and toss well.

Ditalini with Beans

Serves 4

2 cups dried Great Northern beans,
    soaked for 6 hours or overnight in
    water to cover
1 teaspoon salt, plus salt to taste
1/4 cup olive oil
1 cup chopped onion
2 stalks celery, chopped
6 tomatoes, peeled, seeded, and chopped
2 tablespoons chopped flat-leaf parsley
2 tablespoons chopped fresh basil
2 to 4 jalapeño chili peppers, or to taste,
    seeded and minced
3/4 pound ditalini

Drain the beans and place in a large pot with a generous amount of water. Add the salt, bring to a boil, reduce the heat, and simmer for about 1 hour. The beans should be firm, not mushy.

In a large saucepan, heat the oil over medium heat. Add the onion and celery and cook until soft. Add the tomatoes, parsley, and basil. Season with salt. Simmer

(continued)

uncovered, stirring occasionally, for 15 minutes to blend the flavors. Add the beans and jalapeños to taste and stir thoroughly.

Meanwhile, in a large pot, bring at least 4 quarts of water to a rolling boil. Add 1 table-spoon salt. Add the pasta, stir to separate, and cook until *al dente*. Drain.

Return the pasta to the pot and add the beans and tomato sauce. Combine well and heat through before serving.

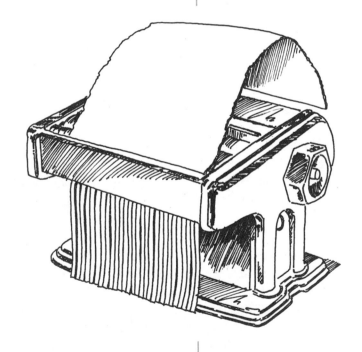

CHAPTER 16

THE THIN LINE:
LOW FAT PASTA

onventional wisdom tells us that pasta is a natural low-fat food—the fat is in the sauce. For once, conventional wisdom is correct. According to the National Pasta Association, 1 2-ounce portion of pasta, the recommended serving size, has only 211 calories and 1 gram fat. Even if 4 ounces is a more realistic helping, pasta is a caloric bargain. To keep the sauces in the same category takes some awareness, but with a few commonsense techniques, calories can be kept down without sacrificing taste and texture.

For Meats, Seafood, and Poultry:

- Choose the leanest cuts and remove as much fat as possible before cooking.
- Broil, bake, or grill instead of frying.
- Poach poultry or fish in stock, lemon juice, or wine with seasoning

For Vegetables:

- Steam vegetables rather than stir-fry.
- Use vegetable oils for cooking rather than butter.
- Substitute low-fat versions of sour cream and yogurt in recipes.

For Milk and Cheese:

- Substitute low-fat milk for cream and evaporated skim milk for regular.
- Use low-fat cheeses in pasta salads and recipes.
- Use Parmesan cheese frugally.

To Improve Sauces with Low-Fat Ingredients:

- Mix flour with low-fat milk, evaporated skim milk, or stock.
- Increase the stock and reduce the oil in recipes.
- Use cornstarch, dissolved in liquid, to thicken stir-fry sauces quickly.
- Purée low-fat ricotta or low-fat sour cream to enrich a cream sauce.

It is also good to remember that the pasta itself is delicious, nutty in flavor, chewy, and pleasantly filling. Digging into a hot dish of noodles with just a touch of olive oil, salt, and garlic is so satisfying that it seems possible to sacrifice everything that the more fattening ingredients have to offer.

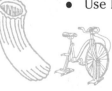

New Wave Bow Ties

Corporate Chef Alan Kaplan
Prestige Caterers
Queens Village, New York

Serves 4

*1 pound new bow-tie pasta (squeezed
    ends, not round)*
2 tablespoons extra virgin olive oil
4 scallions, cut into 2½-inch strips
Ice water, to cover
¼ cup sliced ripe black olives
2 teaspoons finely chopped garlic
1 teaspoon balsamic vinegar
*1 pound thinly sliced smoked salmon,
    cut into 2½-inch-long strips*
Salt and white pepper to taste

Cut the scallions into thin strips about
2½ inches long. Place in a bowl of ice water
to cover and let stand for about 3 hours, or
until the scallions curl.

In a large pot, bring at least 4 quarts
water to a rolling boil. Add 1 tablespoon salt.
Add the pasta, stir to separate, and cook until
al dente. Rinse, drain, and place in a stainless steel bowl.

Drain the scallions and add to the pasta
along with the garlic, vinegar, and the
remaining 5 teaspoons oil. Fold, do not mix,
as this will break the pasta. Add the salmon
and fold in.

Season with salt and pepper, cover, and
chill well before serving.

Spicy Cucumber Raita with Gemelli

Serves 4 to 6

*2 medium cucumbers, peeled, seeded, and
    coarsely grated*
2 tablespoons minced onion
1 teaspoon salt
*2 cups plain yogurt (low-fat rather than
    nonfat)*
1 clove garlic, minced
1 scallion, chopped, including green parts
1 tomato, finely chopped
2 tablespoons freshly squeezed lime juice
2 tablespoons minced fresh mint
1 teaspoon ground cumin
*Salt and freshly ground black pepper to
    taste*
1 tablespoon vegetable oil
1 pound gemelli
Mint sprigs for garnish

In a nonmetallic bowl, combine the grated
cucumber and onion. Sprinkle with salt and
allow to stand for 15 minutes. Drain and
squeeze out all the moisture.

Whisk yogurt until creamy. Add cucumber
and onion, garlic, scallion, tomato, lime juice,
mint, and cumin. Mix thoroughly. Add salt
and pepper to taste. Chill 2 hours or
overnight.

Bring at least 4 quarts of water to a rolling
boil. Add 1 tablespoon of salt. Add pasta and
cook until *al dente*. Drain. Transfer to a large

(continued)

serving bowl and toss with 1 tablespoon of oil. Cool to room temperature, stirring occasionally. Pour sauce over pasta, toss well, garnish with mint sprigs, and serve.

Fedelini with Shrimp and Snow Peas

Serve s 4

1/4 cup fresh lemon juice
Zest of one lemon
2 teaspoons cornstarch
2 tablespoons olive oil
3 cloves garlic, minced
4 scallions, thinly sliced
1 teaspoon grated fresh ginger
1/2 pound snow peas, cut on the
*   diagonal*
1 pound medium shrimp, peeled and
*   deveined*
1 cup fish stock or salt-reduced chicken
*   stock, defatted*
1/2 cup dry white wine
1/4 cup chopped parsley
Salt and freshly ground pepper
3/4 pound fedelini

Place the lemon juice and zest in a small bowl and stir in the cornstarch until it dissolves.

In a large, deep skillet, heat the oil over medium heat. Add the garlic, scallions, ginger, and snow peas and sauté until beginning to soften, about 3 minutes. Add the shrimp and sauté just until they turn pink, 2 to 3 minutes. Stir in the stock, wine, and parsley and bring to a simmer. Add the lemon juice mixture and continue to simmer until the sauce begins to thicken. Season with salt and pepper.

Meanwhile, in a large pot, bring at least 4 quarts of water to a rolling boil. Add 1 tablespoon salt. Add the pasta, stir to separate, and cook until just *al dente*. Drain.

Transfer the pasta to a warm serving bowl. Add the sauce and toss thoroughly.

Mother's Fresh Orecchiette with Rapini

Chef Aldo Saad
Tuscany il Restaurant
West Lake Village, California

Serves 6 as an appetizer

Pasta
(See Chapter 3 for more detailed
    directions)
3 cups durum wheat semolina
1 cup water

Sauce

¹/₂ cup extra virgin olive oil
4 cloves garlic, chopped
2 dried chili peppers
3 anchovies fillets, rinsed and drained
1 pound rapini (broccoli rabe), tough stems removed
1 tablespoon salt

Make the pasta: Make a well on the counter with the semolina, add the water, a little at a time, and with a fork incorporate the semolina slowly. As soon as the dough starts to form, knead it, using the palm of your hand, stretching and folding the dough over with the other hand until it forms a ball with a smooth and elastic texture. Let the dough rest covered with a kitchen towel for about 15 minutes. Cut into 4 portions, working with 1 at a time. Using the palms of both hands, make each portion into a snakelike strand ¹/₄ inch thick. Cut the strand into ¹/₄-inch pieces. Turn each piece over your thumb to flatten it and create the orecchiette shape. Spread over a floured board and let dry for 1 hour.

In a large sauté pan, heat the oil, garlic, and peppers until the garlic is golden brown. Remove the peppers. Add the anchovies and mash them with a fork until they almost dissolve.

In a large pot, bring plenty of water to boil. Add salt, then add at one time the orecchiette and *rapini*. Boil gently for 15 minutes,

until the pasta and *rapini* are semisoft to the bite. Drain, reserving ¹/₂ cup of cooking liquid. Return the pasta to the pot. Moisten the pasta with the liquid. Toss the orecchiette with the sauce and serve immediately.

Spaghettini with Winter Vegetables

Serves 4

¹/₂ cup low-fat skim milk
¹/₃ cup reduced-fat sour cream
1¹/₂ tablespoons Dijon-style mustard
¹/₄ teaspoon salt
¹/₄ teaspoon freshly ground pepper
¹/₄ cup freshly grated Parmesan cheese
³/₄ pound spaghettini
2 cups broccoli florets
2 carrots, sliced on the diagonal
6 ounces sliced bacon, fried until crisp, well drained, and crumbled

In a saucepan, whisk together the milk, sour cream, mustard, salt, pepper, and half of the Parmesan cheese. Place over medium-low heat, stirring to heat through and form a sauce. Keep warm.

In a large pot, bring at least 4 quarts water to a rolling boil. Add 1 tablespoon salt. Add the pasta, stir to separate, and cook until *al dente*. Check for doneness early in the

(continued)

cooking, and add the broccoli and carrots during the last few minutes of cooking time. Drain.

Transfer the pasta, broccoli, and carrots to a warm serving bowl. Add the sauce, bacon, and the remaining Parmesan and toss well.

Mix and Match Vegetables

Few recipes are carved in stone, and those with a variety of vegetables least of all. Today, with vegetables grown all over the world and flown to your local supermarket while you brush your teeth, most crops are available almost daily year-round. Still, it is more economical to use vegetables in season, and to purchase those that are grown locally. Fresher *is* better. So feel free to make changes in the recipes that suit your taste and the seasons. Interchange types of peppers, substitute broccoli for its bitter cousin rapini (broccoli rabe), use green beans as an alternative to asparagus, choose yellow squash over zucchini, try a variety of mushrooms, use sugar snap peas whenever you can get them fresh, and, most of all, cook what you like best.

Pasta Alla E.M.I.

Chef Emilio Baglioni
Restaurant E.M.I.
Hollywood, California

Serves 6

½ cup white part of leeks, diced
4 cloves garlic, crushed
2 tablespoons virgin olive oil
½ teaspoon dried hot red pepper flakes
½ cup dry Italian white wine
One 10-ounce can Italian plum tomatoes, seeded, diced, and drained
2 bay leaves
8 fresh basil leaves, minced
1 pound capellini or thin spaghetti

In a large skillet, sauté the leeks and garlic in the oil with the pepper flakes together for 2 minutes. Add the wine and cook for 1 minute. Add the tomatoes and bay leaves and cook for 5 minutes. Add the basil and toss thoroughly. Remove the bay leaves and set aside.

In a large pot, bring at least 4 quarts water to a rolling boil. Add 1 tablespoon salt. Add the pasta, stir to separate, and cook until just *al dente*. Drain. Add the pasta to the sauce and cook for another 2 minutes, combining the pasta and sauce thoroughly. Serve immediately without cheese.

Serve the sauce over fish, chicken, or veal instead of pasta.

Add mushrooms for variety.

Penne with Chicken, Broccoli, and Rosemary

Serves 4

1 tablespoon olive oil
1 clove garlic, minced
2 shallots, minced
¹/₂ teaspoon dried rosemary
*1 pound boneless, skinless chicken breast
    meat, trimmed of fat and cut into thin
    bite-sized strips*
2 cups small broccoli florets
¹/₂ cup salt-reduced chicken stock, defatted
¹/₄ cup white wine
2 tablespoons chopped fresh parsley
³/₄ pound penne
Salt and freshly ground pepper to taste
*2 tablespoons freshly grated Parmesan
    cheese*

In a large, deep skillet, heat the oil over medium heat. Add the garlic, shallots, and rosemary and sauté for 1 minute. Add the chicken and sauté, tossing well, until lightly browned, about 3 minutes. Add the broccoli, chicken stock, wine, and parsley and simmer until heated through.

Meanwhile, in a large pot, bring at least 4 quarts of water to a rolling boil. Add 1 tablespoon salt. Add the pasta, stir to separate, and cook until not quite *al dente*. Drain.

Transfer the pasta to the skillet holding the chicken and raise the heat to high. Bring to a boil, stirring, until the liquid reduces enough

to glaze the pasta lightly. Season with salt and pepper.

Remove to a warm platter and sprinkle with the Parmesan.

Penne con Verdure
**Chefs Vincent and Joseph Gismondi
Arturo's Ristorante
Boca Raton, Florida**

Serves 4

2 tablespoons olive oil
4 cloves garlic, minced
2 tablespoons chopped onion
*5 vine-ripened tomatoes, peeled, seeded,
    and chopped*
Salt and freshly ground pepper to taste
4 fresh basil leaves, coarsely chopped
1 eggplant, diced
1 zucchini, diced
1 yellow bell pepper, cut into strips
1 red bell pepper, cut into strips
12 asparagus, trimmed and diced
6 fresh mushrooms, sliced
1 pound penne
Freshly grated Parmesan cheese for serving

In a medium skillet, sauté the garlic and onion until the garlic is golden in color. Add the tomatoes and simmer for 5 minutes. Add

(continued)

the basil. Remove the pan from the heat. In a large skillet sauté the 6 vegetables in oil until crisp-tender. Add the tomatoes, salt, and freshly ground pepper and set aside.

In a large pot of boiling salted water, cook the penne until *al dente*. Drain the pasta and add it to the sauce. Cook for 2 minutes, tossing to combine, and serve at once with grated Parmesan cheese.

Linguine with Asparagus and Garlic Chicken Stir-Fry

excellent *April 02 (Heather)*

Serves 6

2 tablespoons olive oil
1 pound boneless, skinless chicken breasts, cut into slivers
1 pound asparagus, trimmed and cut on the diagonal into 1-inch pieces
2 red bell peppers, seeded and diced
4 cloves garlic, minced
¼ cup teriyaki sauce *(more?)*
1 cup salt-reduced chicken stock, defatted
1 pound linguine

used soy, molasses, wine, ginger

In a wok or large, deep skillet, heat 1 tablespoon of the oil over high heat. Add chicken and stir-fry until firm, about 4 minutes. Remove the chicken to a plate. Add the remaining 1 tablespoon oil to the

pan. Add the asparagus and bell peppers and stir-fry until tender-crisp. Add the garlic and stir-fry for 30 seconds. Stir in the teriyaki sauce and chicken stock.

Meanwhile, in a large pot, bring at least 4 quarts of water to a rolling boil. Add 1 tablespoon salt. Add the pasta, stir to separate, and cook until not quite *al dente*. Drain.

As the pasta finishes cooking, return the chicken to the pan holding the asparagus and heat through. Add the drained pasta and toss with the chicken and sauce until the noodles are glazed. Transfer to a warm platter.

Tonnarelli with Curried Vegetables

Serves 4

1 tablespoon vegetable or peanut oil
1 small onion, diced
6 scallions, thinly sliced
1 tablespoon chopped garlic
1 jalapeño pepper, seeded, if desired, and finely chopped
1 tablespoon curry powder, or to taste
1 large, ripe tomato, cut into ½-inch cubes, with juice
1 tablespoon soy sauce
½ cup grated carrot
½ cup diced zucchini

½ cup broccoli florets
½ cup green peas
¾ pound tonnarelli
2 tablespoons honey
½ cup raisins

In a large skillet, heat the oil over medium heat. Add onion, scallions, garlic, and jalapeño and sauté until the onion is wilted and begins to brown, about 4 minutes. Stir in the curry powder and cook for 1 minute. Add the tomato and soy sauce, reduce the heat to low, and cook until the tomato begins to give off liquid. Stir in the carrot, zucchini, broccoli, and peas and cook until the vegetables are tender, 3 to 5 minutes. Remove from the heat.

Meanwhile, in a large pot, bring at least 4 quarts of water to a rolling boil. Add 1 tablespoon salt. Add the pasta, stir to separate, and cook until *al dente*. Remove ½ cup of the pasta cooking water. Drain.

Just before draining the pasta, stir the reserved pasta water into the curry mixture. Return the skillet to low heat and heat through.

Transfer the pasta to a large, warm bowl. Add the curry mixture and stir well. Fold in the honey and raisins.

Pasta with Yellow Summer Squash and Roasted Garlic

Serves 4

8 cloves garlic, peeled
½ teaspoon dried thyme
½ teaspoon dried basil
2 tablespoons olive oil
3 yellow squashes, coarsely grated
1 pound rotini
Salt and freshly ground pepper to taste

Preheat the oven to 450°.

Place the whole garlic cloves in the center of a large piece of aluminum foil. Sprinkle with the thyme and basil. Pour the oil over the garlic and herbs. Make a sealed packet, place in the center of the oven, and bake until the garlic is soft, 20 to 30 minutes.

Meanwhile, in a large pot, bring at least 4 quarts of water to a rolling boil. Add 1 tablespoon salt. Add the pasta, stir to separate, and cook until *al dente*. Two minutes before the pasta is done, add the squash to the pasta cooking water. Remove ½ cup of the pasta cooking water, then drain the pasta and squash.

Place the pasta and squash in a warm serving bowl. Remove the garlic from the foil, place in a small bowl, and mash lightly with a spoon. Add a little bit of the reserved pasta water to form a thick but slightly liquid sauce. Add to the pasta and squash, toss well, and season with salt and pepper.

Capellini with Super-Low-Fat Tomato Sauce

Serves 4

One 28-ounce can Italian plum tomatoes,
    with juice
1/2 cup diced onion
2 cloves garlic, finely chopped
1 teaspoon dried basil
1 teaspoon dried parsley
1 teaspoon dried oregano
1/4 to 1/2 teaspoon dried hot red pepper
    flakes
Salt to taste
1 pound capellini

In a 2-quart saucepan, combine the tomatoes, onion, garlic, basil, parsley, oregano, and red pepper flakes. Place over medium heat and bring to a boil. Reduce the heat to moderately low and simmer until the liquid is reduced by half, 10 to 20 minutes. Season with salt. Remove from the heat. In a food processor or blender, purée small quantities of the sauce to desired consistency, using quick on-off pulses for a chunky sauce, and processing continuously for a smoother sauce.

Meanwhile, in a large pot, bring at least 4 quarts of water to a rolling boil. Add 1 tablespoon salt. Add the pasta, stir to separate, and cook until *al dente*. Drain.

Transfer the pasta to a warm bowl. Add the tomato sauce and toss well.

Southwestern Radiatori

Serves 4

3 tomatoes, minced
3 scallions, thinly sliced
1/2 cup fresh lime juice
1 teaspoon salt
2 teaspoons olive oil
2 cloves garlic, minced
1 small red onion, chopped
1 jalapeño chili pepper, seeded and
    minced
1 large red bell pepper, seeded and
    julienned
1 large green bell pepper, seeded and
    julienned
1/2 teaspoon ground cumin
1/2 teaspoon chili powder
1 pound radiatori
2 tablespoons chopped fresh cilantro

Place the tomatoes and scallions in a large bowl. Stir in the lime juice and salt. Set aside.

In a large, deep skillet, heat the oil over medium heat. Add the garlic and sauté until soft. Add the onion and jalapeño and sauté for 2 to 3 minutes. Add the red and green peppers and sauté until tender-crisp. Add the tomatoes and scallions, cumin, and chili powder, and cook until the sauce thickens slightly.

Meanwhile, in a large pot, bring at least 4 quarts of water to a rolling boil. Add

1 tablespoon salt. Add the pasta, stir to separate, and cook until *al dente*. Drain.

Add the pasta to the sauce in the skillet and toss well. Transfer to a warm serving bowl and sprinkle with the cilantro.

Fettuccine with Light Alfredo Sauce

Serves 4

1 pound fettuccine
1 cup evaporated skim milk
$^1/_2$ cup freshly grated Parmesan cheese
$^1/_2$ cup finely chopped parsley
$^1/_4$ teaspoon white pepper
White pepper to taste
Pinch of dried hot red pepper flakes
   (optional)

In a large pot, bring at least 4 quarts water to a rolling boil. Add 1 tablespoon salt. Add the pasta, stir to separate, and cook until *al dente*. Drain and transfer to a warm bowl.

Meanwhile, heat the milk in a deep saucepan over medium heat. Simmer but do not boil. Add the Parmesan cheese and parsley. As soon as the cheese has melted and the sauce is thick and creamy, remove from the heat and toss with the pasta. Season with white pepper and the red pepper flakes (if using).

Ziti with Chicken, Pineapple, and Mint

Serves 4

$^3/_4$ pound ziti
1 pound boneless, skinless chicken breasts
1 tablespoon vegetable oil
$^1/_4$ cup dry white wine
$^1/_4$ teaspoon cayenne pepper
1 bunch scallions, cut on the diagonal
   into 1-inch lengths
$1^1/_2$ cups pineapple juice
1 tablespoon soy sauce
1 tablespoon grated fresh ginger
1 tablespoon honey
1 tablespoon orange juice
1 tablespoon margarine
One 15-ounce can mandarin oranges,
   drained
1 tablespoon chopped fresh mint

Preheat the oven to 350°.

Place the chicken in a baking dish. Brush it with oil and sprinkle with the wine and cayenne. Cover with aluminum foil and bake until cooked through, about 15 minutes. Do not overcook. During the last 2 to 3 minutes, place the scallions in the baking dish. Remove from the oven, let cool slightly, and cut into bite-sized pieces. Reserve the scallions.

In a small saucepan, combine the pineapple juice, soy sauce, ginger, and honey. Bring to a boil over medium-high heat and

(continued)

cook until reduced by half, about 20 minutes. Add the orange juice and remove from the heat. Whisk in the margarine. Add chicken to the sauce and stir to coat.

Meanwhile, in a large pot, bring at least 4 quarts of water to a rolling boil. Add 1 tablespoon salt. Add the pasta, stir to separate, and cook until *al dente*. Drain. Carefully fold in the mandarin oranges and mint.

Transfer the pasta to a warm serving bowl. Pour over sauce, top with the scallions, and toss well.

Fusilli with Fresh Herbs and Ricotta

Serves 4

> 1 pound fusilli
> One 15-ounce container low-fat ricotta cheese
> $^2/_3$ cup low-fat (1%) milk
> $^1/_4$ cup freshly grated Parmesan cheese
> 1 tablespoon olive oil
> $^3/_4$ cup chopped onion
> $^1/_2$ cup chopped fresh basil
> $^1/_4$ cup chopped scallions, including green parts
> $^1/_4$ cup chopped parsley
> Salt and freshly ground pepper to taste

In a food processor or blender, combine the ricotta, milk, and Parmesan and process until smooth. Set aside.

In a large, deep skillet, heat the oil over medium heat. Add the onion and sauté until nearly browned. Add the garlic and cook until soft. Add the ricotta mixture and fold in the basil, chives, and parsley. Cook until heated through. Season with salt and pepper.

Meanwhile, in a large pot, bring at least 4 quarts of water to a rolling boil. Add 1 tablespoon salt. Add the pasta, stir to separate, and cook until *al dente*. Drain.

Add the pasta to the skillet holding the ricotta mixture and toss well so that the pasta is coated. Transfer to a warm serving bowl.

Vermicelli with Tuna, Anchovies, and Capers

Serves 4 to 6

> 2 tablespoons olive oil
> $^1/_2$ cup chopped onion
> 1 clove garlic, minced
> One 16-ounce can Italian plum tomatoes, drained
> 3 tablespoons capers, drained
> 12 anchovy fillets, chopped

2 tablespoons margarine, at room
   temperature
One 6½-ounce can water-packed tuna
1 pound vermicelli
2 tablespoons chopped parsley

In a large, deep skillet heat the oil over
medium heat. Add the onion and cook until
soft, about 5 minutes. Add the garlic and
sauté briefly. Add the tomatoes, breaking them
up with a wooden spoon, cover, and simmer
for 10 minutes. Remove from the heat and
keep warm.

Place the anchovies in a small bowl and
mash them with a spoon. (Or process them
in a mini food processor.) Add the
margarine and work it into the anchovies.
Reserve. Break up the tuna into small
pieces; reserve.

In a large pot, bring at least 4 quarts
water to a rolling boil. Add 1 tablespoon salt.
Add the pasta, stir to separate, and cook until
al dente. Remove ½ cup of the pasta cooking
water. Drain.

Stir a bit of the cooking water into the
anchovy butter until it is thick and smooth
but no longer a paste. Add to the skillet
holding the tomatoes and stir to blend. Add
the tuna and capers, return to the heat, and
reheat to serving temperature.

Add the pasta to the sauce in the skillet
and toss until coated. Transfer to a warm
serving bowl and sprinkle with the parsley.

Gemelli with Eggplant and Tomatoes

Serves 4

2 tablespoons olive oil
¾ cup chopped onion
3 cloves garlic, minced
¾ pound eggplant, cut into ½- to 1-inch
   cubes
2 tablespoons balsamic vinegar
½ cup salt-reduced chicken stock, defatted
One 16-ounce can Italian plum tomatoes,
   with juice
1 tablespoon tomato paste
½ teaspoon dried oregano
2 tablespoons chopped fresh basil
Pinch of dried hot red pepper flakes
Salt to taste
¾ pound gemelli

In a large, deep skillet, heat the oil over
medium heat. Add the onion and sauté until
soft, about 5 minutes. Add the garlic and
sauté briefly. Add the eggplant, vinegar, and
chicken stock. Cover and cook until the
eggplant is tender, about 10 minutes. Add
the tomatoes, breaking them up with a
wooden spoon, the tomato paste, and
oregano. Cook, uncovered, until the sauce
thickens slightly. Stir in the basil, red pepper
flakes, and salt.

Meanwhile, in a large pot, bring at least
4 quarts of water to a rolling boil. Add
1 tablespoon salt. Add the pasta, stir to

(continued)

separate, and cook until *al dente*. Drain. Transfer the pasta to a large warm bowl and add the sauce. Toss well.

Turkey and Spinach Fettuccine Casserole

Serves 4

2 teaspoons olive oil
³/₄ pound fresh mushrooms, sliced
*³/₄ pound turkey breast meat, cut into
    ¹/₂-inch-wide strips*
¹/₂ cup dry white wine
3 tablespoons all-purpose flour
2 cups low-fat (1%) milk
¹/₂ teaspoon dried marjoram
¹/₂ cup freshly grated Parmesan cheese
Salt and freshly ground pepper to taste
³/₄ pound spinach fettuccine
3 tablespoons slivered almonds

Preheat the oven to 400°.

In a large, deep skillet, heat the oil over medium heat. Add the mushrooms and cook until they begin to soften, just a few minutes. Add the turkey and sauté just until browned. Add the wine and cook for 3 minutes. Stir in the flour, mixing thoroughly. Gradually add the milk, stirring constantly. Continue to stir until the mixture has thickened slightly. Stir in the marjoram and half

of the Parmesan cheese until blended. Season with salt and pepper.

In a large pot, bring at least 4 quarts water to a rolling boil. Add 1 tablespoon salt. Add the pasta, stir to separate, and cook until not quite *al dente*. Drain.

Add the pasta to the turkey mixture in the skillet and mix well. Pour the contents of the skillet into an 11-by-7-inch greased baking dish. Top evenly with the remaining Parmesan cheese and sprinkle with the almonds. Bake until heated through and the top is lightly browned, almost 20 minutes.

Baked Ziti with Meat

Serves 4

2 tablespoons olive oil
1 cup chopped onion
4 cloves garlic, minced
¹/₂ pound lean ground beef
¹/₂ cup dry white wine
One 28-ounce can crushed tomatoes
¹/₂ teaspoon dried basil
¹/₂ teaspoon dried oregano
1 tablespoon tomato paste
2 tablespoons all-purpose flour
¹/₂ cup low-fat (1%) milk
*Salt and freshly ground pepper
    to taste*
³/₄ pound ziti

1 cup shredded part-skim mozzarella
   cheese
$^1/_2$ cup freshly grated pecorino romano
   cheese

Preheat the oven to 400°.

In a large skillet, heat the oil over medium heat. Add the onion and sauté until soft, about 5 minutes. Add the garlic and sauté briefly. Stir in the beef, breaking it up with a wooden spoon, and brown on all sides. Drain off the oil from the pan. Stir in the wine and deglaze the pan by scraping up browned bits. Add the tomatoes, basil, oregano, and tomato paste, stirring to blend. Cook for 3 minutes. Add the flour and stir well until combined. Gradually add the milk and cook until slightly thickened. Season with salt and fresh pepper.

Meanwhile, in a large pot, bring at least 4 quarts of water to a rolling boil. Add 1 tablespoon salt. Add the pasta, stir to separate, and cook until not quite *al dente*. Drain.

Transfer the pasta to a large warm bowl. Add the meat mixture, tossing well. Transfer to a 3-quart greased baking dish. Bake until heated through, about 15 minutes. Distribute the mozzarella evenly over the top and sprinkle with the *pecorino romano*. Return to the oven until the cheese has melted and the top has browned lightly, about 5 minutes.

Tagliatelle with Salmon

Serves 4

$^3/_4$ pound fettuccine
1 cup reduce-salt chicken stock, defatted
$^1/_2$ cup dry white wine
1 pound salmon fillets, skinned and cut
   into 12-inch pieces
1 tablespoon vegetable oil
3 shallots, minced
6 scallions, thinly sliced, white part only
One 16-ounce can Italian plum tomatoes,
   drained
2 tablespoons tomato paste
$^1/_2$ cup evaporated nonfat milk
1 tablespoon fresh lemon juice
$^1/_4$ cup snipped fresh dill, plus sprigs for
   garnish

In a large skillet, combine the stock and wine and bring to a boil over high heat. Reduce to a gentle simmer and add the salmon. Cover and cook until the fish is opaque throughout, about 5 minutes. Remove the fish with a slotted spoon. Set aside on a plate; cover to keep warm. Reserve $^1/_2$ cup of the cooking liquid.

In a large skillet, heat the oil over medium heat. Add the shallots and scallions and sauté until soft, about 5 minutes. Add the tomatoes, breaking them up with a wooden spoon. Stir in the tomato paste, milk, lemon juice, the reserved cooking liquid, and snipped dill. Simmer until thickened. Return the fish to the pan and heat through.

(continued)

Meanwhile, in a large pot, bring at least 4 quarts of water to a rolling boil. Add 1 tablespoon salt. Add the pasta, stir to separate, and cook until *al dente*. Drain.

Transfer the pasta to a warm serving bowl. Add the sauce and toss gently. Garnish will dill sprigs.

Orecchiette with Summer Tomato Sauce and Olives

Serves 4

1¹/₂ pounds tomatoes, peeled, seeded, and
chopped into ¹/₂-inch pieces
1 teaspoon minced garlic
3 tablespoons olive oil
2 tablespoons shredded fresh basil leaves
Freshly ground pepper to taste
¹/₃ cup Kalamata olives, pitted
1 pound orecchiette

In a large bowl, combine the tomatoes, garlic, oil, basil, and pepper. Stir well and let stand at room temperature for at least 30 minutes.

In a large pot, bring at least 4 quarts water to a rolling boil. Add 1 tablespoon salt. Add the pasta, stir to separate, and cook until *al dente*. Drain.

Stir the olives into the tomato mixture. Add the pasta and toss well.

Ruoti with Sweet-and-Sour Chicken

Serves 4

One 8-ounce can pineapple chunks in
unsweetened juice
1¹/₂ tablespoons tomato paste
2 tablespoons cider vinegar
2 tablespoons soy sauce
1 tablespoon sugar
2 teaspoons cornstarch
³/₄ pound ruoti
2 tablespoons vegetable oil
1 pound boneless, skinless chicken breasts,
cut into ¹/₂-inch-wide slices
3 cloves garlic, minced
2 teaspoons grated fresh ginger
¹/₂ cup chopped onion
¹/₂ cup chopped green bell pepper
2 cups bok choy or other Chinese
cabbage, thinly sliced
4 scallions, thinly sliced, including green part
2 tablespoons chopped fresh cilantro

Drain the pineapple, reserving ¹/₂ cup of the juice. Place the juice in a small bowl. Add the tomato paste, vinegar, soy sauce, sugar, and cornstarch and stir well. Reserve. Reserve the pineapple chunks separately.

In a wok or large, deep skillet, heat the oil over high heat. Add the chicken and stir-fry until firm and lightly browned. Add the garlic, ginger, onion, and bell pepper and

sauté until soft, about 3 minutes. Add the bok choy and stir-fry until tender-crisp.

Reduce heat to medium. Stir the tomato-pineapple mixture and add it to the pan. Add pineapple chunks and stir constantly so that the sauce coats the contents as it thickens. Add the scallions.

Meanwhile, in a large pot, bring at least 4 quarts of water to a rolling boil. Add 1 tablespoon salt. Add the pasta, stir to separate, and cook until *al dente*. Drain.

Transfer the pasta to a large warm serving bowl. Pour the sauce over the pasta and toss to mix well. Sprinkle with the cilantro.

Shells with Scallops and Sun-Dried Tomato Pesto

Serves 4

1 cup water
¹/₂ cup dry-packed sun-dried tomatoes
1 clove garlic
2 tablespoons pine nuts
2 tablespoons freshly grated Parmesan cheese
2 tablespoons olive oil
¹/₄ teaspoon salt
¹/₄ cup dry white wine
2 teaspoons cornstarch
1 pound bay scallops

¹/₂ cup reduced-salt chicken stock or fish stock
³/₄ pound medium shells
2 tablespoons chopped parsley

In a saucepan, bring the water to a boil. Add the tomatoes and cook until softened, about 4 minutes. Add the garlic and cook for another 2 minutes. Pour the mixture into a food processor or blender. Add the pine nuts, cheese, 1 tablespoon of the oil, and salt and blend until smooth to form a tomato pesto. Reserve.

In a small bowl, stir together the wine and cornstarch. Reserve.

In a large, deep skillet, heat the remaining 1 tablespoon oil over medium heat. Add the garlic and cook until soft. Add the scallops and cook until slightly firm. Add the chicken stock and cook for 1 minute. Stir in the tomato pesto. Heat through. Stir the cornstarch mixture and add to the skillet. Cook, stirring constantly, until the sauce thickens slightly, about 1 minute.

Meanwhile, in a large pot, bring at least 4 quarts of water to a rolling boil. Add 1 tablespoon salt. Add the pasta, stir to separate, and cook until *al dente*. Drain.

Transfer the pasta to the skillet and toss so the pasta is glazed with the sauce. Transfer to a warm serving bowl. Sprinkle with the parsley.

CHAPTER 17

PASTA ON THE RUN:
QUICK AND EASY PASTA

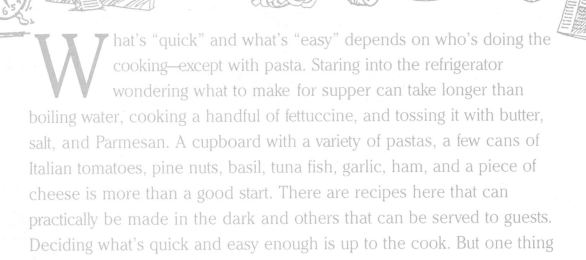

W hat's "quick" and what's "easy" depends on who's doing the cooking—except with pasta. Staring into the refrigerator wondering what to make for supper can take longer than boiling water, cooking a handful of fettuccine, and tossing it with butter, salt, and Parmesan. A cupboard with a variety of pastas, a few cans of Italian tomatoes, pine nuts, basil, tuna fish, garlic, ham, and a piece of cheese is more than a good start. There are recipes here that can practically be made in the dark and others that can be served to guests. Deciding what's quick and easy enough is up to the cook. But one thing is for sure: Pasta offers the possibilities.

Tomato-Basil Pasta

Serves 3

³⁄₄ pound tomato fettuccine
¹⁄₄ cup extra virgin olive oil
2 cloves garlic, minced
2¹⁄₂ cups diced tomatoes
¹⁄₃ cup chopped fresh basil
Salt and freshly ground pepper to taste
³⁄₄ cup chicken stock
¹⁄₄ cup freshly grated Parmesan cheese

In a large, deep skillet, heat the oil over medium heat. Add the garlic and sauté until soft. Add the tomatoes and basil and season with salt and pepper. Sauté for about 5 minutes. Add the chicken stock and bring to a simmer.

In a large pot, bring at least 4 quarts water to a rolling boil. Add 1 tablespoon salt.

Add the pasta, stir to separate, and cook until *al dente*. Drain.

Combine pasta with the sauce in the skillet. Stir to combine well. Top with Parmesan and serve.

Crawfish and Tasso Pasta

Chef Greg Sonnier
Gabrielle Restaurant
New Orleans, Louisiana

Serves 4

2 tablespoons unsalted butter
¹⁄₂ cup julienned tasso or good-quality
*   smoked ham*
¹⁄₃ cup sliced scallion tops

¹/₂ pound peeled crawfish tails
¹/₂ pound spaghetti, fusilli, or linguine
1 cup light cream or half-and-half
¹/₄ cup Creole mustard or other whole-grain mustard

In a large skillet, melt the butter over medium heat. Add the tasso and scallions and sauté for about 5 minutes, continuously stirring and scraping the bottom of the pan. Add the crawfish and sauté for 30 seconds. Slowly stir in the cream and mustard; mix well and cook for about 2 minutes to reduce the liquid. Toss in cooked pasta and serve.

Spaghetti with Meat Sauce

Serves 4

¹/₄ cup unsalted butter
1 clove garlic, minced
1 cup chopped onion
¹/₂ cup chopped green bell pepper
1 pound ground beef
2 cups canned Italian plum tomatoes, diced
1 teaspoon dried oregano
1¹/₂ teaspoons salt
Freshly ground pepper to taste
1 pound spaghetti
¹/₂ cup freshly grated Parmesan cheese

In a large, deep skillet, melt the butter over medium heat. Add the garlic, onion, and bell pepper and sauté until they just soften. Add the meat, breaking it up with a wooden spoon, and cook until browned, about 5 minutes. Add the tomatoes and oregano, stir, and season with the salt and pepper. Reduce heat to low, cover and simmer for 1 hour.

When the sauce is nearly ready, bring at least 4 quarts of water to a rolling boil in a large pot. Add 1 tablespoon salt. Add the pasta, stir to separate, and cook until *al dente*. Drain.

Transfer the pasta to the skillet and toss with the sauce, combining thoroughly. Transfer to a warmed serving dish and top with the Parmesan cheese.

Capellini Pescatore

Chef Salvador Medina
Lombardi's at Underground
Atlanta, Georgia

Serves 6

3 tablespoons extra virgin olive oil
1 clove garlic, minced
2 shallots, minced
2 cups diced, fresh, or canned Italian plum tomatoes, with juice
1 teaspoon dried basil
¹/₄ teaspoon dried oregano

(continued)

½ *pound salmon fillet, skinned and cut into 1-inch pieces*
½ *pound bay scallops*
½ *pound medium shrimp, peeled and deveined*
Salt and freshly ground pepper to taste
1 pound linguine

In a large, deep skillet, heat the oil over medium heat. Add the garlic and shallots and sauté until soft, about 3 minutes. Add the tomatoes, basil, and oregano and simmer for 5 minutes. Add the salmon and cook until the fish begins to look opaque. Add the scallops and cook for 2 minutes. Add the shrimp and cook, stirring, until pink, about 3 minutes. Season with salt and pepper.

Meanwhile, in a large pot, bring at least 4 quarts of water to a rolling boil. Add 1 tablespoon salt. Add the pasta, stir to separate, and cook until *al dente*. Drain.

Transfer the pasta to a large warm serving bowl.

Vermicelli and Peanut Sauce Stir-Fry

Serves 4

Sauce
3 tablespoons creamy peanut butter
⅓ *cup fresh lime juice*
¼ *cup soy sauce*

¼ *cup chicken stock*
Freshly ground pepper to taste

1 pound vermicelli
Vegetable oil for pasta, if needed, plus 1 teaspoon
2 cups broccoli florets
1 large red bell pepper, seeded and finely julienned
1 large cucumber, peeled and finely julienned
1 bunch scallions, cut on the diagonal into ½-inch lengths
½ *teaspoon dried hot red pepper flakes, or to taste*

Make the sauce: In a small bowl, whisk together the peanut butter, lime juice, soy sauce, and stock. Season with pepper.

In a large pot, bring at least 4 quarts water to a rolling boil. Add 1 tablespoon salt. Add the pasta, stir to separate, and cook until *al dente*. Drain. Transfer to a warm bowl and toss with a bit of the oil if the sauce is not ready.

Meanwhile, place a large, deep skillet or a wok over high heat and heat the oil. Add the broccoli and bell pepper and stir-fry briefly. The vegetables should remain crisp. Add the cucumber, scallions, and red pepper flakes and stir-fry for 2 minutes.

Add the sauce mixture to the pan and bring to a boil. Adjust the seasoning. Add the pasta and toss to combine with the sauce and vegetables. Transfer to a warm serving bowl.

Ziti with Shrimp and Arugula

Chef Norman J. Leclair
Red Rooster Tavern
Kingston, Rhode Island

Serves 4

6 ounces ziti or other tubular pasta
2 tablespoons olive oil
2 cloves garlic, minced
¼ teaspoon dried hot red pepper flakes
1 red bell pepper seeded, thinly sliced
1 pound medium shrimp, peeled, deveined, and tails removed
1 bunch arugula, tough stems removed and leaves chopped into bite-sized pieces
½ cup thinly sliced scallions

In a large pot, bring at least 4 quarts water to a rolling boil. Add 1 tablespoon salt. Add the pasta, stir to separate, and cook until *al dente.*

While the pasta is cooking, heat the oil in a large skillet over medium heat. Add the garlic and red pepper flakes and sauté until the garlic is golden, about 2 minutes. Add the bell pepper and shrimp and sauté until the shrimp turn pink, about 3 minutes. Remove from the heat.

Drain the pasta and return it to the pot. Add the shrimp mixture, arugula, and scallions and toss lightly to combine. Serve at

once on heated individual plates, or let cool and serve at room temperature or cold.

Ziti with Orange Asparagus Sauté

Serves 4

1 cup fresh orange juice at room temperature
1 teaspoon grated orange zest
1 teaspoon cornstarch
1 pound ziti
1 tablespoon vegetable oil
3 carrots, thinly sliced on the diagonal
1 celery stalk, thinly sliced on the diagonal
1 bunch scallions, sliced
1 pound asparagus, trimmed and cut on the diagonal into 2-inch lengths
Salt and freshly ground pepper to taste

In a small bowl, combine the orange juice, orange zest, and cornstarch and stir until cornstarch is dissolved. Set aside.

In a large pot, bring at least 4 quarts water to a rolling boil. Add 1 tablespoon salt. Add the pasta, stir to separate, and cook until *al dente.* Drain. Transfer to a warm bowl and toss with a bit of the oil if the sauce is not ready.

(continued)

Meanwhile, heat the oil in a large, deep skillet or a wok over high heat. Add the carrots and sauté for 2 minutes. Add the asparagus and scallions and cook briefly until the asparagus is tender-crisp, about 2 minutes. Stir the orange juice mixture and add to the skillet. Quickly cook over high heat to boiling so that the sauce thickens slightly.

Add the pasta to the pan and toss well. Transfer to a large, warm serving bowl.

Linguini Alle Vongole

**Owner Tony Vallone
Tony's * Anthony's * Grotto * La Griglia
Houston, Texas**

Serves 4

*1 pound linguine
7 tablespoons olive oil
1 tablespoon chopped garlic
1¾ cups chopped clams
12 fresh clams in the shell, opened
½ cup bottled clam juice
Salt and freshly ground pepper to taste
1 teaspoon dried hot red pepper flakes
½ cup chopped flat-leaf parsley*

Place clams with shells in a pot deep enough to hold 2 inches of water plus the clams. Cover tightly. After the water comes to a rolling boil over high heat, steam the clams until just opened, 3 to 5 minutes. Do not overcook.

In a large skillet, heat 5 tablespoons of the oil over medium heat. Add the garlic and sauté until golden, 1 to 2 minutes. Add the chopped clams and fresh clams and sauté for 1 minute. Add the clam juice, salt, pepper, red pepper flakes, and parsley.

In a large pot, bring at least 4 quarts water to a rolling boil. Add 1 tablespoon salt. Add the pasta, stir to separate, and cook until *al dente.* Drain.

Serve over linguine. Drizzle the remaining 2 tablespoons oil over the top.

Roasted Garlic Orzo

Serves 4

*3 large cloves garlic, unpeeled
2 tablespoons unsalted butter, at room
    temperature
¼ cup chopped flat-leaf parsley
1 cup of orzo
⅓ cup pine nuts, toasted
Freshly grated Parmesan cheese*

Preheat the oven to 450°.

Place the garlic cloves on a sheet of aluminum foil, wrap securely, and place in the middle of the oven. Bake until tender, about

25 minutes. Unwrap, let cool slightly, and remove the skins from the cloves. Transfer the garlic to a large bowl, add the butter and parsley, and mix well.

Meanwhile, in a large pot, bring at least 4 quarts of water to a rolling boil. Add 1 tablespoon salt. Add the pasta, stir to separate, and cook until *al dente*. Drain. Remove 1/2 cup of the pasta cooking water.

Add the pasta to the garlic mixture and toss well. Add enough of the reserved cooking water to melt the butter and prevent the pasta from sticking. Fold in the pine nuts. Transfer to a warm serving platter and sprinkle with the Parmesan cheese.

Fresh Spinach Fettuccine in Mussel Cream Sauce

Chef Louis Lindic
The Treehouse
Atlanta, Georgia

Serves 4

24 mussels, well scrubbed and debearded
1 tablespoon unsalted butter
2 shallots, minced
1/2 cup dry white wine
1 cup heavy cream
1 1/4 pounds fresh spinach fettuccine
Chopped parsley or tomato for garnish

Place the mussels in a saucepan with 2 inches of water. Place over high heat. Cover and steam, shaking the pan occasionally, until the mussels open, 4 to 6 minutes. Discard any that do not open. Remove the mussels from shell; reserve 6 for garnish. Strain the liquid in the pan through a fine-mesh sieve. Set aside.

In a skillet, melt the butter over low heat. Add the shallots and sauté until soft. Make sure they do not brown. Raise heat to medium, add the wine, and deglaze the pan, scraping up any browned bits. Add 1 cup of the cream, bring to a simmer, and reduce, over low heat, by half, about 20 minutes. Stir frequently to prevent sticking.

Meanwhile, in a large pot, bring at least 4 quarts of water to a rolling boil. Add 1 tablespoon salt. Add the pasta, stir to separate, and cook until *al dente*.

When sauce has reduced by half, add the shelled mussels and reheat gently. Drain the pasta and place on a warm serving platter. Pour the sauce over the pasta and garnish with the tomato or parsley, and the reserved mussels.

mmmm!

Mussels

When the adjective "sweet" is used for something from the sea, mussels always come to mind. Plump, succulent, and, yes, sweet, the mussel is one of nature's perfect foods. The mollusks are high in protein, low in fat, and they even contain carbohydrates, plus they are delicious. A true rarity, mussels are a food that tastes good and is good for you.

Mussels appear a bit daunting, but are easy to cook. The only hard part is cleaning them: Immerse them in a bowl of cold water and rub the shells together to rid them of sand and clinging particles. Then scrub the mussels with steel wool or a brush, and finally, pull off any of the "beard," the sea strands that are still attached. Steaming is the most common method of cooking, at least as a first step. The mussel liquid, flavored with wine and spices, is a wonderful accompaniment to pasta.

Tagliatelle with Lemon Vodka Sauce

Serves 4

1 pound tagliatelle
1 tablespoon unsalted butter, if needed

Lemon Vodka Sauce
1 cup heavy cream
1/2 cup vodka
Juice of 1 lemon
Finely grated zest of 1 lemon
2 tablespoons chopped fresh chives
1/2 teaspoon freshly ground pepper

2 tablespoons chopped parsley
3/4 cup freshly grated Parmesan cheese

In a large pot, bring at least 4 quarts water to a rolling boil. Add 1 tablespoon salt. Add the pasta, stir to separate, and cook until *al dente*. Drain. If the sauce is not ready at this point, reserve the pasta in a warm bowl tossed with the butter.

Make the sauce: In a large, deep skillet, combine the cream and vodka and simmer until the sauce thickens a little, about 5 minutes. Add the lemon juice, zest, chives, and pepper and cook for 1 minute, stirring constantly. Do not allow the sauce to boil.

Add the pasta to the skillet and combine with the sauce so that all the strands are well coated. Transfer to a warm serving bowl. Garnish with the parsley. Pass the Parmesan cheese at the table.

Pasta with Scallops and Champagne Cream Sauce

Serves 4

1 bottle inexpensive dry champagne
1/3 cup white wine vinegar
1/3 cup minced shallot
4 cups (1 quart) heavy cream
2 tablespoons fresh lemon juice
1 teaspoon salt
1 teaspoon freshly ground pepper
3/4 pound bay scallops
1 pound angel hair pasta
2 tablespoons chopped parsley

Combine the champagne, vinegar, and shallots in a 6-quart saucepan over high heat. Reduce to 2 cups. Add the cream and reduce to 3 1/2 cups, or until thickened to the consistency of light gravy. Be careful not to reduce too much or the butter will separate from the cream. Add the lemon juice, salt, pepper, and scallops to the sauce and heat until the scallops are cooked, 2 to 3 minutes.

Meanwhile, in a large pot, bring at least 4 quarts of water to a rolling boil. Add 1 tablespoon salt. Add the pasta, stir to separate, and cook until *al dente*. Drain.

Add the pasta to the sauce and toss to coat well and heat through. Turn out onto a warm serving platter and sprinkle with the parsley.

Orecchiette with Peas and Onions

The Moosewood Collective
Moosewood Restaurant
From *Moosewood Restaurant Cooks at Home*
Ithaca, New York

Serves 4 to 6

1 tablespoon olive oil
4 onions, cut in half through the stem and thinly sliced (about 4 cups)
4 cups fresh or frozen tiny peas
Salt and freshly ground pepper to taste
1 pound orecchiette or other small shell pasta
About 1 cup freshly grated pecorino cheese

In a large pot, bring at least 4 quarts water to a rolling boil.

Meanwhile, in a skillet or saucepan, heat the oil on medium heat. Add the onions and cook, stirring occasionally, until the onions begin to brown. Add the peas, salt, and pepper, and cook for a few minutes longer. Add 2 tablespoons of the water from the pot of boiling water to the skillet, stir, reduce the heat, and cover.

Add the pasta to the boiling water, stir well to separate, and cook until *al dente*. Drain and transfer to a warm serving bowl. Add some of the cheese and toss until melted. Top with the peas and onions. Serve the remaining grated cheese at the table.

Fettuccine with Truffles

Milos Cihelka
Formerly of The Golden Mushroom
Southfield, Michigan

Serves 6 as an appetizer

> *1 ounce black or white truffles, fresh or
> frozen only ($^1/_4$ cup fresh wild or
> domestic mushrooms may used as a
> substitute)*
> *1 tablespoon unsalted butter, or more if
> using mushrooms*
> *$^1/_2$ cup heavy cream*
> *$^3/_4$ pound fresh fettuccine*

If using black truffles, peel them. Cut the
black or white truffles into very fine threads. If
using mushrooms, slice them and sauté them
in a little butter until tender.

In a large pot, bring at least 4 quarts
water to a rolling boil. Add 1 tablespoon salt.
Add the pasta, stir to separate, and cook until
al dente. Fresh pasta will cook very quickly.
Drain.

While the noodles are cooking, place the
butter, cream, and truffles or sautéed mushrooms in a large skillet. Bring to a boil,
reduce the heat, and simmer to reduce a
little. Add the drained noodles to the skillet
and toss to coat them.

Transfer to a warm serving platter or individual plates.

Rigatoni Siciliana

Chef Scott Harris
Mia Francesca
Chicago, Illinois

Serves 4

> *1 pound rigatoni*
> *$^1/_4$ cup olive oil*
> *2 tablespoons chopped garlic*
> *2 cups tomato sauce (see classic tomato
> sauce, Chapter 4)*
> *$^1/_4$ cup chopped fresh basil*
> *2 tablespoons Alouette cheese*
> *2 tablespoons unsalted butter*
> *Pinch of dried hot red pepper flakes*
> *Salt and freshly ground pepper to taste*
> *$^1/_4$ cup freshly grated Parmesan cheese*

In a large pot, bring at least 4 quarts
water to a rolling boil. Add 1 tablespoon salt.
Add the pasta, stir to separate, and cook until
al dente. Drain.

Meanwhile, in a sauté pan, heat the oil
over medium heat. Add the garlic and sauté.
Add the tomato sauce and let reduce slightly.
Stir in the basil, Alouette cheese, butter, and
red pepper flakes.

Drain the pasta and place in a warm
serving bowl. Add the sauce, toss well, and
season with salt and pepper. Sprinkle with the
Parmesan cheese.

Truffles Explained

Nothing tastes as good and looks as bad as a truffle. Truffles are a variety of fungus that grows underground. Their season is short and harvesting is difficult, which makes them rare and, therefore, expensive. There are people who turn up their noses at truffles, literally, because their scent, which is difficult to describe, falls somewhere between unpleasant and unusual. Nevertheless, their contribution to flavors in a dish is said to be ethereal.

There are mainly two types, the Italian white, found in the Piedmont region of Italy, and the French black, which grow beneath the soil of the Périgord region of France. The white looks like a small, oddly shaped potato. The black, covered with warty knobs, is not a pretty sight. The white are difficult to keep for any length of time, but the black can be kept in a tightly closed jar in the refrigerator and covered with cognac or sherry for at least a month. Although the flavor is not the same, mushrooms are often used as a substitute.

Rigatoni alla Contadina

Owner Joey Vallone
Tony's * Anthony's * Grotto * La Griglia
Houston, Texas

Serves 4

1 pound ground Italian sausage
1 pound rigatoni
¼ cup olive oil
4 teaspoons chopped garlic
½ cup diced roasted red bell peppers
½ cup diced roasted yellow bell peppers
½ cup red wine
1 cup marinara sauce (see red wine marinara sauce, Chapter 4)
Salt and freshly ground pepper to taste
½ cup fresh basil, chopped
1 cup crumbled ricotta salata *cheese*

In a small skillet sauté sausage, breaking up with wooden spoon, until cooked. Remove with slotted spoon and drain well.

In a large skillet, heat the oil over medium heat. Add the garlic and sauté for 1 minute. Add the sausage, roasted peppers, and wine and cook for 2 to 3 minutes. Add the marinara sauce, salt, pepper, and basil.

In a large pot, bring at least 4 quarts water to a rolling boil. Add 1 tablespoon salt. Add the pasta, stir to separate, and cook until *al dente*. Drain.

(continued)

Transfer the pasta to a warm serving bowl. Add the sauce and toss well. Scatter the *ricotta salata* over the top.

Fedelini all'Amatriciana

Owner Jeff Vallone
Tony's * Anthony's * Grotto *
   La Griglia
Houston, Texas

Serves 4

> 1 tablespoon olive oil
> 1/4 pound pancetta, cut into 1/4-inch pieces
> 1 onion, finely diced
> One 35-ounce can Italian plum tomatoes, broken up by hand
> Salt and freshly ground pepper to taste
> 1 teaspoon dried hot red pepper flakes
> 6 to 8 fresh basil leaves
> 1 pound fedelini or spaghetti
> 1/4 cup pecorino romano *cheese, grated*

In a large skillet, heat the oil over medium heat. Add the pancetta and cook until crispy. Reduce the heat to moderately low, add the onion, and cook until soft. Add the tomatoes, raise the heat, and cook until the sauce thickens. Add the salt, pepper, red pepper flakes, and basil and stir to combine.

Meanwhile, in a large pot, bring at least 4 quarts water to a rolling boil. Add 1 table-spoon salt. Add the pasta, stir to separate, and cook until *al dente*. Drain.

Transfer the pasta to a warm serving bowl, add the sauce, and toss well. Sprinkle with the *pecorino romano* cheese.

Orecchiette with Rapini and Sausage

Owner Jeff Vallone
Tony's * Anthony's * Grotto *
   La Griglia
Houston, Texas

Serves 4

> 1 pound Italian sausage
> 1/4 cup olive oil
> 4 teaspoons chopped garlic
> 2 cups rapini (broccoli rabe)
> Salt and freshly ground pepper to taste
> 1 teaspoon dried hot red pepper flakes
> 1 pound orecchiette

In a small skillet, sauté sausage, breaking up with a wooden spoon, until cooked. Remove with slotted spoon and drain well.

Heat olive oil in a large skillet and add garlic. Sauté garlic for 1 minute, then add

broccoli and sausage. Cook for 5 minutes. Add salt, pepper, and red pepper.

Bring at least 4 quarts of water to a rolling boil. Add 1 tablespoon of salt. Add pasta and stir to separate. Cook until *al dente*. Drain.

Transfer pasta to warm serving bowl and toss with sauce.

Fusilli with Rapini and Sausage

Lois Ringelheim
Professional Chef
Fairfield, Connecticut

Serves 4

> *1 pound hot Italian sausage*
> *½ cup olive oil*
> *2 bunches rapini (broccoli rabe), tough*
>   *stems removed and coarsely chopped*
> *8 large cloves garlic, coarsely chopped*
> *1 cup chicken stock*
> *1 pound fusilli*
> *Dried hot red pepper flakes for garnish*
> *Freshly grated Parmesan cheese for garnish*

Preheat the oven to 375°.

Pierce the sausages with a fork and place in a baking pan. Bake until done, about 35 minutes. Remove from the oven, let cool, and slice thinly.

In a large skillet, heat ¼ cup of the oil over medium heat. Add the rapini and sauté until wilted. Add garlic, the remaining ¼ cup oil, and simmer over low heat for about 5 minutes. Add the cooked sausage slices, cover, and simmer for 5 minutes more.

Meanwhile, in a large pot, bring at least 4 quarts water to a rolling boil. Add 1 tablespoon salt. Add the pasta, stir to separate, and cook until *al dente*. Drain.

Transfer the pasta to the skillet and toss with the sauce to coat well. Place in a warm serving bowl and sprinkle with red pepper flakes and Parmesan cheese.

Penne with Artichokes and Pancetta

Chef Christophe Vessaire
The Grapevine Café
Atlanta, Georgia

Serves 4

> *6 young, small artichokes*
> *⅔ cup extra virgin olive oil*
> *2 cloves garlic, chopped*
> *¼ pound pancetta, finely julienned*
> *1 pound penne*
> *3 tablespoons freshly grated Parmesan*
>   *cheese*
> *Salt and freshly ground pepper to taste*

(continued)

Clean the artichokes, slice lengthwise into halves, quarters, or even smaller depending on size. (To clean artichokes, see Chapter 7.)

In a saucepan, heat 1/3 cup of the oil over low heat. Add the artichokes and cook, stirring occasionally, until tender, about 15 minutes. Remove from the heat and keep warm.

In a large, deep skillet, heat the remaining 1/3 cup oil over medium heat. Add the garlic and pancetta and sauté until the pancetta is browned.

Meanwhile, in a large pot, bring at least 6 quarts of water to a rolling boil. Add 1 tablespoon salt. Add the pasta, stir to separate, and cook until not quite *al dente*. Drain.

Transfer the pasta to the skillet holding the pancetta. Add the artichokes, salt, and pepper, cover, and cook for 2 more minutes over medium heat, stirring once or twice. Pour into a warm serving bowl and sprinkle with the Parmesan cheese.

Shells with Spinach and Ricotta

Serves 4

> 2 tablespoons olive oil
> Two 10-ounce packages frozen spinach, thawed and squeezed dry
> 1 tablespoon unsalted butter
> 1 cup ricotta cheese
> 1 cup half-and-half
> 1 pound medium shells
> 1/2 cup freshly grated Parmesan cheese
> Salt and freshly ground pepper to taste
> 1/4 cup thinly sliced scallions

In a large, deep skillet, heat the oil over medium heat. Add the spinach and cook, stirring constantly, until wilted. Cover and continue to cook for 3 minutes. Add the butter, ricotta, salt and pepper, and half-and-half, stir well, and simmer briefly. Do not allow to boil.

Meanwhile, in a large pot, bring at least 4 quarts of water to a rolling boil. Add 1 tablespoon salt. Add the pasta, stir to separate, and cook until *al dente*. Remove 1/2 cup of the pasta cooking water. Drain.

Transfer the pasta to the skillet holding the sauce. Add scallions. Add some of the reserved cooking water and toss thoroughly over medium heat (the sauce should not be too liquidy). Transfer to a warm serving bowl and sprinkle with the Parmesan cheese.

CHAPTER 18

SWEET TOOTH PASTA: DESSERT

Nothing is as rejuvenating as a bowl of hearty pasta on a winter night, or as refreshing as pasta with fragrant raw tomatoes on a summer afternoon. But sweet pasta, noodles with sugar and honey, cinnamon and berries, chocolate and cream, is something completely different. Pasta transforms itself into dessert when it is served as deliciously filled sweetened wontons and raviolis; couscous, warmed and spice-scented; and puddings, rich in noodles and egg. The results can be both homey and spectacular, simple to prepare, or a *tour de force* in the kitchen. Pasta alone may not be as decadent as chocolate or as comforting as custard, but few foods are as gratifying as noodles. In combination with desserts' sweet ingredients, they are all the more satisfying.

Sweet Cheese Triangles

Makes about 40 pieces

1 recipe noodle dough (see Chapter 3)

Filling
1 cup small-curd cottage cheese
2 egg yolks
1/4 teaspoon salt
1 tablespoon sugar

1 teaspoon ground cinnamon (optional)
1 egg white, lightly beaten
Sour cream or jelly for serving

Make the filling: In a large bowl, using a mixer, beat the cottage cheese until smooth. Beat in the egg yolks, then stir in the salt, sugar, and the cinnamon, if using.

Roll out the dough for ravioli. (See Chapter 3 for detailed directions.) Cut into 2-inch squares. Brush the edges of each square with the egg white. Place 1 teaspoon of filling in the center of each square. Fold into triangles and press edges together firmly to seal.

Preheat the oven to 350°. Butter a baking dish large enough to hold all the triangles.

In a large pot, bring at least 4 quarts of water to a gentle boil. Add 1 tablespoon salt. Add the triangles, in batches, and cook about 5 minutes. Test for doneness by removing one with a slotted spoon. Cut off edge with a fork. If it cuts easily, the ravioli are done. Remove with a slotted spoon and place in the prepared baking dish. Bake until golden, about 20 minutes. Serve with sour cream or jelly.

Sweet Lemon Stars with Lemon Cream Anglaise and Raspberry Coulis

**Chef Tania Lovato, CSC
Albuquerque, New Mexico**

Makes 20 to 30 pieces

Pasta Dough

2¼ cups all-purpose flour
3 eggs
½ teaspoon salt
½ cup powdered sugar
1½ teaspoons vanilla extract

Lemon Curd

Zest of 4 lemons
Juice of 4 lemons (about 1 cup)
4 eggs, lightly beaten
½ cup unsalted butter, cut into pieces
2 cups sugar

Lemon Cream Anglaise

2 cups heavy cream
1 tablespoon vanilla extract
4 egg yolks
⅓ cup granulated sugar

Filling

14 ounces mascarpone cheese or cream
    cheese
2 tablespoons granulated sugar
1 egg yolk
½ cup lemon curd

Raspberry Coulis

⅓ cup sugar
¾ pound raspberries
1 tablespoon cornstarch
1½ cups water

Oil for deep-frying

Make the dough: In a food processor, combine the flour, eggs, salt, sugar, and vanilla. Pulse until well mixed, then run the motor continuously until the mixture comes together to form a ball. Transfer to a lightly floured work surface and knead by hand briefly, adding more flour if needed. The dough should be smooth and silky. Cover the dough with plastic wrap and let rest 25 minutes. (See Chapter 3 for detailed directions.)

Make the lemon curd: Combine the lemon zest, lemon juice, beaten eggs, butter, and sugar in a heatproof bowl. Place the bowl over a saucepan of simmering water. Do not allow the bowl to touch the water. Cook, stirring occasionally, until thickened and smooth. Do not allow it to get too hot or eggs will coagulate. Remove from over the saucepan and let cool.

Make the coulis: In a saucepan, combine the raspberries, sugar, and 1 cup of the water. Bring to a simmer, and cook over low heat for 5 minutes; be careful not to let the sauce boil over. Strain through a fine-mesh sieve into a clean saucepan. In a cup, stir together the cornstarch and the remaining ¼ cup water. Place the raspberries over medium-low heat and bring to a boil. Stir in

(continued)

the cornstarch mixture and cook, stirring, until slightly thickened, 2 to 3 minutes. Remove from the heat, let cool, cover, and chill.

Make the lemon cream anglaise: In a saucepan, combine the cream, lemon zest and the vanilla bean, if using. Place over low heat and cook until hot. In a bowl, whisk together the egg yolks, sugar, and the vanilla extract, if using. Slowly add about $\frac{1}{2}$ cup of hot cream mixture, whisking constantly. Then add the egg yolk mixture to the saucepan and cook over low heat, stirring constantly, until slightly thickened. Strain through a fine-mesh sieve into a clean bowl. Nest the bowl in a bowlful of ice cubes to cool down quickly, stirring occasionally. Cover with plastic wrap, pressing directly into the surface. Refrigerate until needed.

Make the filling: In a bowl, using a mixer, beat together the cream cheese, sugar, and egg yolk. Stir in the $\frac{1}{2}$ cup lemon curd.

Make the ravioli: Divide the dough in half. Using a pasta machine, roll out half of the dough into a thin sheet. Cut the dough with a star- or circle-shaped cookie cutter $2\frac{1}{2}$ to 3 inches in diameter. Place a scant tablespoon of filling in the center of half the stars. Cover with the other half. Seal the edges with water, and press together. Continue until all pasta is gone. Place on a lightly floured baking sheet and cover with damp kitchen towel until ready to cook.

In a saucepan or deep fryer, pour in oil to a depth of 2 inches and heat to 375° on a deep-fat frying thermometer. Fry the ravioli, a few at a time, turning once until golden. Using a slotted spoon, remove and let drain on paper towels.

To serve, spoon cream anglaise on each plate. Place ravioli on each serving. Drizzle with raspberry coulis, allowing the raspberry to run into the anglaise. Serve ravioli at room temperature.

Orange Almond Pastina Soufflé

Serves 6

$\frac{1}{3}$ cup pastina
2 cups milk
$\frac{3}{4}$ cup sugar
3 tablespoons unsalted butter, melted
2 tablespoons grated orange zest
1 teaspoon almond extract
4 eggs, separated, at room temperature

Preheat oven to 350°. Grease a 2-quart baking dish.

Pour the milk into a saucepan and place over high heat until small bubbles appear along the edges of the pan. Stir in the pastina, reduce the heat to medium, and stir constantly until the pastina is softened and the mixture has thickened. Add $\frac{1}{4}$ cup of the sugar and

stir until it dissolves. Stir in the butter, orange zest, and almond extract. Remove from heat.

In a bowl, using a mixer, beat the egg yolks until well blended. Add ¼ cup of the sugar and beat until foamy.

In another bowl, using a mixer, beat the egg whites, adding the remaining ¼ cup sugar as they become foamy. Then beat until shiny but not too stiff. Fold the yolks into the pastina, blending completely. Then carefully fold in the whites just until no white streaks remain.

Pour into the prepared baking dish and place it in a larger pan. Pour hot water into the larger pan to a depth of 1 inch. Bake until set and top is golden, about 35 minutes. Serve warm or at room temperature.

Rich Roll-ups with Apricot Sauce

Lois Ringelheim
Professional Chef
Fairfield, Connecticut

Makes 16 pieces

Sauce
⅔ cup apricot jam
⅓ cup orange juice
2 tablespoons unsalted butter, melted
1 tablespoon fresh lemon juice
1½ teaspoons grated lemon zest

8 ruffle-edged lasagna noodles
1 cup (½ pound) cream cheese, softened
¼ cup plus 2 tablespoons unsalted butter, softened
¼ cup sugar
1½ teaspoons vanilla extract
2 tablespoons unsalted butter
⅓ cup chopped almonds, toasted

Preheat the oven to 350°. Butter a 9-by-13-inch baking dish.

Make the sauce: Combine all the ingredients in a blender or food processor and process until well blended. Set aside.

In a bowl, using an electric mixer or a wooden spoon, beat together the cream cheese, the ¼ cup butter, sugar, and vanilla until well blended.

To cook noodles: In a large pot, bring at least 4 quarts water to a rolling boil. Add 1 tablespoon salt. Add the pasta, stir to separate, and cook until *al dente*. Do not pour the noodles directly into a colander or they will stick together. Bring the pot to the sink and position over a colander. Run cold water into the pot as you pour the noodles out. Grab each one with your hands. Shake gently, and place on a paper towel to blot any excess moisture. (If necessary, keep moist under a lightly dampened towel until ready to fill.)

To assemble the roll-ups, spread a thin layer of the cream cheese mixture on each noodle and roll up loosely from a narrow end. Cut each roll up in half and place seam

(continued)

side down in the prepared baking dish. Dot with the additional 2 tablespoons butter. Bake until golden, about 15 minutes. Meanwhile, pour the apricot sauce into a saucepan and place over low heat until warmed to serving temperature. To serve, place the roll-ups on individual plates and spoon the warm apricot sauce over the top. Sprinkle with the almonds.

Berry Medley with Noodles

Serves 4

Juice of 1 lemon
3 tablespoons fruit-flavored brandy
2 cups mixed berries such as blueberries, strawberries, and raspberries
$1/2$ pound medium egg noodles
$1/3$ cup powdered sugar
$3/4$ cup half-and-half
$1/4$ cup walnuts, coarsely chopped and toasted

In a cup, combine the lemon juice and brandy. Place the berries in a shallow bowl and sprinkle with the sugar and lemon juice–brandy mixture. Cover and chill for 2 hours.

In a large pot, bring at least 4 quarts water to a rolling boil. Add 1 tablespoon salt. Add the pasta, stir to separate, and cook until *al dente*. Drain.

Place the half-and-half in a saucepan large enough to hold the noodles. Add the noodles and toss over low heat.

Transfer to a warm serving dish. Top with the berries and sprinkle with the nuts.

Sweet Blue Corn Ravioli Filled with Apples and Green Chili

Chef Tania Lovato, CSC
Albuquerque, New Mexico

Makes 20 to 30 pieces

Pasta Dough
$1^1/4$ cups flour
1 cup blue corn flour
3 eggs
$1/2$ teaspoon salt
$1/2$ cup powdered sugar
1 teaspoon vanilla extract
2 tablespoons butter
1 cup peeled, cored, and diced apples
$1/8$ teaspoon ground cinnamon
$1/3$ cup firmly packed brown sugar
$1/2$ cup pecans, chopped and toasted
$1/4$ cup roasted, peeled, and chopped green chili pepper (optional)
Oil for deep-frying
Cream anglaise

Make the dough: In a food processor, combine the flours, eggs, salt, sugar, and vanilla. Pulse until well mixed, then run the motor continuously until the mixture comes together to form a ball. Transfer to a lightly floured work surface and knead briefly by hand until smooth and silky, adding more flour if needed. Cover the dough with plastic wrap and let rest for 25 minutes.

In a skillet, melt the butter over moderately low heat. Add the apples and sprinkle with the cinnamon and brown sugar. Sauté until the apples are tender. Remove from the heat and let cool, then add the pecans and the chili, if using. Stir well.

Using a pasta machine, roll dough out into sheets and into raviolis. (See Chapter 3 for detailed directions.) For these ravioli, use 1 scant tablespoon of filling for each piece.

In a saucepan or deep fryer, pour in oil to a depth of 2 inches and heat to 375°. Fry the ravioli, a few at a time, turning once until golden. Remove with a slotted spoon and let drain on paper towels.

To make cream anglaise:
4 egg yolks
$1/3$ cup sugar
2 cups heavy cream
1 tablespoon vanilla

Heat cream in sauce pan. Wisk together yolks and sugar. Temper yolk mixture into cream by slowly pouring mixture into hot cream.

Heat over a low heat, stirring slowly. Do not let it boil or the yolks will coagulate. Simmer until the mixture has thickened enough to coat the back of a metal spoon. Strain. Cool in an ice bath. Add vanilla.

To serve: Spoon cream anglaise onto plates and arrange ravioli on top.

Festive Fafalline

Serves 4

$1/2$ pound fafalline
Juice of 2 oranges
Grated zest of 1 orange
$1/4$ cup unsalted butter
$1/4$ cup sugar
$1/4$ cup light cream
2 kiwi, peeled and divided into eighths
2 tablespoons flaked coconut, toasted

In a saucepan, combine the orange juice, zest, butter, sugar, and cream. Stir over low heat until the sugar dissolves and the mixture is heated through. Add the kiwi fruits.

Meanwhile, in a large pot, bring at least 4 quarts water to a rolling boil. Add 1 tablespoon salt. Add the pasta, stir to separate, and cook until *al dente*. Drain.

Add the pasta to the saucepan holding the sauce and mix gently. Pour into a serving dish and sprinkle with the coconut. Serve alone or with ice cream.

Tagliatelle with Peaches

Serves 4

> Juice of 1 orange
> Grated zest of 1 orange
> 2 tablespoons plus 1 teaspoon sugar
> ½ pound tagliatelle
> 5 tablespoons unsalted butter
> 1 tablespoon Cointreau liqueur
> 2 peaches, peeled, pitted, and sliced
> ½ teaspoon ground cinnamon
> 1 tablespoon unsalted butter
> 2 tablespoons chopped pecans, toasted

In a saucepan, combine the orange juice and zest, 4 tablespoons of the butter, and the 2 tablespoons sugar. Stir over low heat until the sugar dissolves and the mixture is heated through. Add the Cointreau, stir well, and heat through.

In a small saucepan, melt the remaining 1 tablespoon butter over low heat. Add the peaches and sprinkle with 1 teaspoon sugar. Heat through, but do not cook.

In a large pot, bring at least 4 quarts of water to a rolling boil. Add 1 tablespoon of salt. Add pasta and stir to separate. Cook until *al dente*. Drain.

Add the pasta to the orange juice mixture and toss to coat. Transfer to a warm serving dish and top with the peaches. Sprinkle with pecans.

Sweet and Spicy

The only difficult thing about cinnamon is how to spell it. Its delicate flavor is easy to add to just about any dessert. An ancient spice, one that traveled the caravan routes from East to West in biblical times, cinnamon is harvested from the bark of the cinnamon tree, which is stripped and then rolled into long "quills" called cinnamon sticks. Native to Sri Lanka, the tree is also cultivated in the West Indies and in many Southeast Asian countries. A truly international spice, cinnamon is used in many different ways—in chocolate in Mexico, in curry in India, in stews in Greece, and in fruit desserts and spice cakes just about everywhere. And, of course, with pasta.

Hot Honeyed Noodles with Bananas

Serves 4

½ pound wide egg noodles
½ cup honey
Juice of 2 lemons
Grated zest of 1 lemon
½ cup golden raisins
½ cup unsalted butter
2 bananas, sliced
2 tablespoons almonds, coarsely chopped
  and toasted

In a saucepan, combine the honey, lemon juice and zest, and raisins and heat and stir over low heat until the honey melts and the mixture is heated through.

In a small skillet, melt the butter over moderately low heat. Add the banana slices and brown lightly on both sides.

Meanwhile, in a large pot, bring at least 4 quarts water to a rolling boil. Add 1 tablespoon salt. Add the pasta, stir to separate, and cook until *al dente*. Drain.

Transfer the pasta to a warm serving bowl. Add the hot honey mixture and the bananas and toss gently. Top with the nuts.

Decadent Ravioli with Fudge Sauce

Makes 8 servings

Filling
14 ounces cream cheese, at room
  temperature
3 tablespoons sugar
1 egg yolk

Fudge Sauce
¾ cup evaporated milk
1 cup sugar
2 ounces unsweetened chocolate
¼ cup unsalted butter
1 teaspoon vanilla extract
½ teaspoon salt

Pasta dough made with 3 eggs (see
  Chapter 3) flavored with a few drops
  of sweet-flavored oil such as orange,
  lemon, or peppermint
1 egg white, slightly beaten
Melted butter for brushing
Powdered sugar

Make the filling: In a bowl, using a mixer, beat the cream cheese until soft. Beat in sugar and egg yolk until well blended and smooth.

Make the fudge sauce: In a heavy saucepan, combine the milk and sugar and bring to a rolling boil, stirring constantly. Boil and stir for 1 minute. Add the chocolate, and

(continued)

stir until melted. Beat with wire whisk over moderately low heat until smooth and all the sugar has dissolved, about 5 minutes. Remove from the heat. Beat in the butter, vanilla, and salt. (You should have about 1¹/₂ cups.)

Roll out dough as thin as possible. (See Chapter 3 for detailed directions.) Cut into 5-inch squares. Brush half of the squares with egg white. Place 3 tablespoons filling in the center of each of the squares. Top with the remaining squares. Press firmly to seal the edges. Trim with a fluted pastry wheel. (Cover squares not being used to prevent drying out. Or dust with cornstarch, stack, and cover.)

In a large pot, bring at least 4 quarts of water to a rolling boil. Add 1 tablespoon salt. Working in small batches, carefully stir in the ravioli and cook until *al dente*. Remove with a slotted spoon to a warm platter and brush with melted butter.

To serve, spoon fudge sauce onto individual plates. Top with the ravioli and sprinkle with the powdered sugar.

Heavenly Half Moons

Makes about 30 pieces

Filling
2 cups dried pitted prunes
¹/₂ cup pineapple juice
1 tablespoon grated lemon zest
¹/₄ cup granulated sugar
¹/₄ shredded coconut
¹/₄ cup walnuts, finely chopped

Pasta dough made with 3 eggs (see
Chapter 3) flavored with spice or
lemon if desired
Oil for deep-frying
1 egg white, lightly beaten
Powdered sugar

Make the filling: In a saucepan, combine the prunes, pineapple juice, orange zest, and sugar. Place over moderately low heat, bring to a simmer, and cook until reduced to the consistency of a paste.

Divide the dough into 3 portions. Working with 1 portion at a time and keeping the rest covered to prevent them from drying out, roll out the dough into a thin sheet. Using a cookie cutter 3 inches in diameter, cut out circles. Brush the edges of the circles with the egg white. Place ¹/₂ teaspoon of filling in the center of each circle. Fold over to form a half moon. Press firmly to seal the edges. Place on a lightly oiled baking sheet.

In a large saucepan or a deep fryer, pour in oil to a depth of 2 inches and heat to 375° on a deep-fat frying thermometer. Fry the half moons, 8 at a time, turning once, until golden brown on both sides. Using a slotted spoon, remove and let drain on paper towels. Arrange on a platter and sprinkle with the powdered sugar.

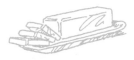

Magic Cookie Wontons

Makes about 30 pieces

Filling

2 ounces semisweet chocolate
1/2 cup unsalted butter, melted
1/2 cup powdered sugar
1/4 cup chopped walnuts
2 tablespoons shredded coconut

36 wonton skins
1 egg white
Oil for deep-frying
Powdered sugar

Make the filling: In a saucepan, melt the chocolate over low heat, stirring frequently. Remove from the heat and let cool. Whisk in the melted butter. Add the sugar and whisk or beat with a wooden spoon until well combined. Stir in the nuts and coconut.

Lay out about 10 wonton skins on a work surface. Keep the remainder covered to prevent them from drying out. Brush each wonton very lightly with the beaten egg white. Place 1 teaspoon of filling in the center of each wonton skin. Fold to form a triangle. With the center point at the top, fold back the other two corners so that the one overlaps the other. Press ends together to seal. Use additional egg white to hold, if necessary. Place on a lightly oiled baking sheet and cover with a towel. Repeat until all the filling is used up.

In a large saucepan or a deep fryer, pour in oil to a depth of 2 inches and heat to 375° on a deep-fat frying thermometer. Fry the wontons, a few at a time, turning as needed, until golden brown. Using a slotted spoon, remove and let drain on paper towels. Arrange on a warm platter and sprinkle with the powdered sugar.

From Tree To Chocolate

Chocolate is one of those objects of desire that people want so much that they don't care where it comes from. But chocolate doesn't grow on store shelves. Its origins are in the cocoa tree, and it's created, not by a concoction of the gods, but by a lengthy production process. A cocoa tree produces "beans," which are about the size of a pineapple. They contain about two hundred "pods." The beans are dried and cracked open to remove the pods, which are also dried. The pods are pressed to produce cocoa butter and then ground to make cocoa powder. The finest chocolate is made from 33 percent cocoa butter, which is very expensive; cocoa powder; and sugar. For milk chocolate, dry milk solids are substituted for part of the cocoa powder.

Double Cherry Delight Dessert Dumplings

Makes 30 pieces

¹/₃ cup sour cream
1 egg
1 egg yolk
1 teaspoon salt
1¹/₂ cups all-purpose flour
One 16-ounce can tart pitted cherries
9 tablespoons sugar
3 tablespoons cornstarch
¹/₂ teaspoon cinnamon
¹/₈ teaspoon nutmeg
1 egg white
1 large jar cherry preserves
6 tablespoons unsalted butter, melted
1 pint sour cream
Additional sugar

Make the dough: In a large bowl, with a mixer, blend ¹/₃ cup sour cream, egg, egg yolk, and salt. Gradually add flour on slow speed until the dough forms a ball. Wrap and let rest in the refrigerator for 2 hours.

Drain cherries over a bowl and collect the syrup. Reserve cherries. Pour syrup into a small saucepan and add 1 tablespoon of sugar. Bring to a boil over high heat. Reduce heat and simmer reduced to about one-third of a cup. Cool.

In a wide bowl, mix 8 tablespoons of sugar, the cornstarch, cinnamon, and nutmeg with a fork. Lightly dust a baking sheet with flour and cornstarch.

Make the dumplings: See Chapter 3 for detailed directions on rolling dough. Cut dough into 8 pieces. Cover resting dough with a damp kitchen towel. Roll one portion into a sheet. Cut out circles with a cookie cutter 3 inches in diameter.

Brush each circle with egg white. Place ¹/₄ teaspoon of preserves in the center. Roll two cherries in the sugar and spice mixture and place on top of the preserves. Fold one side of dough over the filling, pressing the edges to seal. Place on the prepared baking sheet. Repeat until all the dough is used.

To cook dumplings: Bring a large pot of water to a rolling boil. Cook in batches of about 10 at a time, sitrring constantly, for about 10 minutes. Remove with a slotted spoon and drain on paper towels.

To serve: Place a few dumplings in a bowl. Spoon over melted butter and a teaspoon of sugar. Top with a tablespoon of sour cream. Drizzle with cherry syrup.

Couscous with Yogurt and Fruit

Serves 4

1 cup milk
1 tablespoon unsalted butter
¹/₄ teaspoon salt

²/₃ cup instant couscous
¹/₂ cup vanilla yogurt
2 tablespoons sugar
¹/₂ cup peeled and diced fresh fruit in
   season or whole berries
Sugar to taste

In a saucepan, combine the milk, butter, and salt and bring to a boil. Stir in the couscous, cover, and remove from the heat. Let stand until the liquid is absorbed, about 5 minutes. Fluff the couscous with a fork to separate the grains.

Stir in the yogurt and sugar and fold in the fruit. Sprinkle with sugar.

Butterscotch Apples with Sweet Noodles

Serves 8

¹/₂ cup raisins
1 cup unsalted butter
4 large tart apples, peeled, cored, and
   thinly sliced
1 teaspoon ground cinnamon
1 cup chopped walnuts
1 cup half-and-half
1 cup firmly packed light brown sugar
1 pound malfade

Place the raisins in a small bowl with hot water to cover. Let stand for 15 minutes. Drain.

In a large, deep skillet, melt the butter over medium heat. Add the apples, cinnamon, nuts, and raisins and sauté, turning as needed, until golden on both sides.

In a small saucepan, combine the half-and-half and brown sugar over low heat. Simmer, stirring, until the sugar is dissolved, then pour over apples. Continue to simmer until the apples are tender but not mushy and the sauce thickens.

Meanwhile, in a large pot, bring at least 4 quarts water to a rolling boil. Add 1 tablespoon salt. Add the pasta, stir to separate, and cook until *al dente*. Drain.

Transfer the pasta to a warm serving bowl. Pour the sauce over the pasta and toss carefully to combine.

Noodle Pudding with Nut Topping

Serves 8 to 10

Topping
²/₃ cup sugar
6 tablespoons unsalted butter, at room
   temperature, cut up
¹/₂ cup all-purpose flour
1 cup walnuts, finely chopped
¹/₂ teaspoon ground cinnamon

(continued)

½ pound medium egg noodles
3 tablespoons unsalted butter
1 cup cottage cheese
1 cup sour cream
½ cup sugar
½ teaspoon salt
Juice of ½ lemon
½ teaspoon ground cinnamon
½ cup raisins
3 eggs

Preheat the oven to 350°. Butter a 7½-by-12-inch baking dish.

Make the topping: Combine all the ingredients in a bowl. Crumble together with your fingers until a pebblelike consistency forms.

In a large pot, bring at least 4 quarts water to a rolling boil. Add 1 tablespoon salt. Add the pasta, stir to separate, and cook until *al dente*. Drain. Transfer to a large bowl and toss with the butter.

In a large bowl, using an electric mixer, beat together the cottage cheese and sour cream until smooth. Beat in the sugar, salt, lemon juice, and cinnamon. Fold in the raisins.

In another bowl, beat the egg until frothy. Combine the noodles with the cottage cheese mixture. Transfer to the prepared baking dish. Pour the eggs evenly over the top. Spread the topping evenly over the surface. Bake until set and the top is golden brown, about 1 hour. Serve hot.

Fruit-Filled Lasagna

Serves 6

Topping

$\frac{1}{4}$ cup granulated sugar
$\frac{1}{4}$ cup firmly packed brown sugar
$\frac{1}{2}$ cup old-fashioned rolled or quick-
   cooking oats
$\frac{1}{4}$ cup all-purpose flour
$\frac{1}{4}$ cup unsalted butter, cut up
$\frac{1}{4}$ teaspoon ground nutmeg
Pinch of salt

1 pound cream cheese, softened
$\frac{1}{2}$ cup sugar
$\frac{1}{2}$ cup half-and-half
2 eggs
4 lasagna noodles
One 21-ounce can apple or other fruit pie
   filling

Make the topping: Combine all the ingredients in a large bowl. Crumble together with your fingers until a pebblelike consistency forms.

Preheat the oven to 325°. Butter a 7$\frac{1}{2}$-by-11-inch baking dish.

In a bowl, using an electric mixer, beat together the cream cheese and sugar until light and airy. Beat in the half-and-half, and eggs briefly, just until the mixture is smooth.

Meanwhile, in a saucepan, bring at least 2 quarts of water to a rolling boil. Add 1 teaspoon salt. Add the pasta, stir to separate, and cook until *al dente.* Do not pour the noodles directly into a colander or they will stick together. Bring the pot to the sink and position over a colander. Run cold water into the pot as you pour the noodles out. Grab each one with your hands, shake gently, and place on a paper towel to blot excess moisture. (If necessary, keep moist under a lightly dampened towel until ready to fill.)

To assemble the lasagna, spread about one-third of the pie filling on the bottom of the prepared baking dish. Place 2 noodles on top. Spread half of the cream cheese mixture over the noodles. Spread on half of the remaining pie filling. Top with the remaining 2 noodles. Spread the remaining cheese over the noodles and then the remaining pie filling. Spread the topping evenly over the pie filling.

Bake until a knife inserted in the center comes out clean, about 50 minutes. Let stand for 15 minutes before cutting. Serve warm or cool.

INDEX

A

Alfabetini, 7
  and Zucchini Soup, 81-82
Alfredo Sauce, 51
  with Bacon, 52
Anchovies, 19-20
  Portuguese Green Noodles with, 239
Anellini, Tomato Soup with Meatballs and, 80-81
Angel Hair pasta, 2
  Curried Soup with, 84
  Grilled Vegetables with, 91-92
  Noodle Pancake with Grilled Shrimp Salad, 213-214
  Prawns Sambuca, 145-146
  Scallops and Champagne Cream Sauce with, 301
  Smoked Salmon and Dill in Cream Sauce with, 144
  Soft-Shell Crabs Over, 147-148
  Thai Noodle Salad, 209
Appetizers
  Calzoni, 61-62
  Capellini Frittata with Peas and Pancetta, 65
  Curried Chicken Egg Rolls with Yogurt Dipping Sauce, 70-71
  Fried Spaghetti, 72
  Meatballs Wrapped in Noodles, 61
  Melted Cheese Triangles, 71
  Nut Filled Pesto Rolls, 66
  Pasta Souffle, 62-63
  Pot Stickers, 69-70
  Red Snapper and Spinach Lasagna, 58-59
  Shells Stuffed with Chicken and Fennel, 64-65
  Shrimp Egg Rolls with Mustard Sauce, 69
  Spicy Pasta with Roast Long Island Duck, 60
  Spinach Wontons with Apricot Mustard Sauce, 63-64
  Sun-Dried Tomato Pasta Wheels, 59
  Toasted Ravioli with Pesto Cream Dipping Sauce, 66-67
  Vietnamese Spring Rolls, 68
Armenian Egg Noodles with Spinach and Cheese, 235
Artichokes, 96
  Penne with, and Pancetta, 305-306
  Radiatori with Shrimp and, in Parmesan Vinaigrette, 255-256
  Spirals with Shrimp and, 155
Arugula
  Penne with, and Tomatoes, 88
  Ziti with Shrimp and, 297
Asian noodles
  Salad with Spicy Peanut Sauce, 253
  see also Chinese noodles; Glass noodles; Ramen noodles; Soba noodles; Somen noodles
Asian seasonings, 202-204
Asparagus
  Linguine with, and Garlic Chicken Stir-Fry, 282
  and Pappardelle Pasta, 93
  Rigatoni with, 90
  Ziti with Orange Asparagus Sauté, 297-298
Auntie Sugar's Rock Shrimp and Langostino Marinara, 159-160
Avgolemono with Orzo, 83
Avocado
  Chicken and, with Spicy Tomato Salsa Over Linguine, 252-253
  Colorful Avocado Spirals, 94
  Spicy Duck with, 107

B

Bacon
  Alfredo Sauce with, 52
  Cappelletti Carbonara, 130-131
  Fusilli All'Arturo, 138
  Gemelli with Fava Beans and, 269
  see also Pancetta
"Badly Cut" Pasta with Eggplant and Tuna, 162-163
Baked Ziti with Meat, 288-289
Bay Shrimp Salad, 251
Beans
  Bow Ties with Black Beans and Cherry Tomatoes, 267-268
  Bucatini with Lima Beans, 272
  Chicken and Black Bean Salad Over Spirals, 271
  Chickpea and Pasta Soup, 77
  Ditalini with, 273-274
  Fiesta Pasta with Kidney Beans, 266-267
  Gaspacho Pasta with Cannellini Beans, 264
  Gemelli with Fava Beans and Bacon, 269
  Linguine with Beef and Black Bean Chili, 268
  Little Tubes and, 270-271
  Macaroni, Sausage, and Bean Soup, 79
  Orecchiette with Broccoli, Chickpeas, Onions, and Tomatoes, 262-263
  Orecchiette with Fava Beans and Sage, 273
  Orecchiette with Seafood, Rapini, and White Beans, 265
  Orzo pasta with Young Fava Beans in Cream and Curry Leaves, 263
  Pasta and Bean Soup, 86
  preparation, 272
  Rigatoni with Borlotti Beans and Sausage, 270
  substituting, 267
  Tagliatelle with Cannellini and Tomato Sauce, 268-269
  White Bean and Pasta Bake, 265-266
Bean Threads, Vegetables and, 219-220
Béchamel Sauce, 45
Beef
  Baked Ziti with Meat, 288-289
  Bourguignon with Pappardelle, 139-140
  Capellini with Basil, Tomatoes, and Sliced Grilled Steak, 136
  Dumplings for Soup: Kreplach Dough and Meat Filling, 236-237
  Linguine with, and Black Bean Chili, 268
  Marinated, and Pasta Salad, 250-251
  Spaghetti with Meat Sauce, 295
  Spicy Orange, with Glass Noodles, 210-211
  see also Meat
Beep Beep "Roadrunner" Pasta, 135
Beet and Spinach Pasta Rolls with Saffron Cream Sauce, 172-173
Bella Luna's Chicken Penne Pasta with Tomatoes, 106
Bell Peppers. see Peppers
Berry Medley with Noodles, 312

Black Pepper Fettuccine with Venison Sausage, Sun-Dried Tomatoes, Spinach, and Parmesan Herb Sauce, 140-141
Black and White Ravioli with Sage Butter, 175-177
Bow Ties
  with Black Beans and Cherry Tomatoes, 267-268
  New Wave, 277
  see also Farfalle
Bread crumbs, about, 20
Broccoli
  Orecchiette with, Chickpeas, Onions, and Tomatoes, 262-263
  Orecchiette with, in Saffron Vinaigrette, 257
  Penne with Chicken, Rosemary, and, 281
  Pine Nut Pesto, 49
  Rice Noodles with Almonds and, 215
  Spaghettini con Broccoli Siciliano, 89
  Turkey and, with Fusilli in Cream Sauce, 116
  Ziti with Dijon Chicken and, 108
Bucatini, 4
  with Lima Beans, 272
Butter, Clarified, 161
Butterscotch Apples with Sweet Noodles, 319

C

Cajun Pasta Salad, 244-245
Calamari
  Ink Fettuccine with, and Porcini Mushrooms Baked in Parchment Paper, 151-152
  Spaghetti with, in a Garlic, Pepper, and Spicy Olive Oil Sauce, 149-150
  see also Seafood
Calzoni, 61-62
Cannelloni, 7, 29, 35-36
  Crawfish, with Basil and Ricotta in Creole Tomato Sauce, 182-183
  with Salmon and Tomato Cream Sauce, 154
  Seafood, with Tomato and Lemon Parmesan Cream Sauce, 187-189
  Spinach, 175
Capellini, 3
  with Basil, Tomatoes, and Sliced Grilled Steak, 136
  with Chicken and Roasted Pepper Salsa, 111
  Frittata with Peas and Pancetta, 65
  Pasta alla E.M.I., 280
  Pescatore, 295-296
  with Snow Peas, 96
  with Super-Low-Fat Tomato Sauce, 284
Capers, 21
Cappelletti, 8, 37-38
  Carbonara, 130-131
  Lobster-Stuffed, in a Sherry Coral Sauce, 186-187
Carbonara, 50
Cavatappi, 5
  with Chicken, Tomato, and Leek Sauce, 121-122
  Marinated Beef and Pasta Salad, 250-251
Cavatelli, 9
  Primavera, 97
Caviar
  Chilled Soba Noodles with, and Oba, 206-207
  Pasta Quills with Beluga, and Chives, 152-153
  Ravioli of Salmon with Cabbage and, 146
  see also Seafood

Cheese, 18-19, 22
  Armenian Egg Noodles with Spinach and, 235
  Black Pepper Fettuccine with Venison Sausage, Sun-Dried Tomatoes, Spinach, and Parmesan Herb Sauce, 140-141
  Melted, Triangles, 71
  Spinach and Three-Cheese Ravioli with Roasted Tomato, Olive, and Basil Essence Sauce, 185-186
  Sweet, Triangles, 308
  see also Feta cheese; Goat cheese; Ricotta cheese
Chicken, 110
  in Aromatic Tomato Sauce with Perciatelli, 120
  and Avocado with Spicy Tomato Salsa Over Linguine, 252-253
  Bella Luna's, Penne Pasta with Tomatoes, 106
  and Black Bean Salad Over Spirals, 271
  Cacciatore with Rotelle, 119
  Capellini and Roasted Pepper Salsa with, 111
  Cavatappi, Tomato, and Leek Sauce with, 121-122
  Chinese Noodle Salad with Spicy Sesame Dressing, 220
  Crescent City Pasta, 112
  Curried, Egg Rolls with Yogurt Dipping Sauce, 70-71
  Curry Rice Noodles and Shrimp with, 221
  Egg Noodle Stir-Fry with, 215-216
  Fedelini Inverno, 116-117
  Fedelini with Pacific Rim, 109-110
  Fettuccine with, Herbed Onions, and Nuts in Cream Sauce, 123-124
  Garlic and Sun-Dried Tomatoes with, and Penne, 120-121
  Ham and, Lasagna, 181-182
  Indian Farfalle with Curried, 241
  Lasagna, 113
  Linguine with Asparagus and Garlic, Stir Fry, 282
  Orange Pasta Salad, 252
  Pasta Salad with Smoked, and Oven-Dried Tomatoes, 246
  Penne with, Broccoli and Rosemary, 281
  Poached, with Ratatouille Orzo Ragout, 118-119
  and Portabello Ravioli with Porcini and Sun-Dried Tomato Sauce, 179-181
  and Prosciutto Ravioli with Rosemary Oil, 177-178
  Radiatore and, in Tricolor Pepper Sauce, 122
  Randi's Bok Choy, Salad, 248
  Ruoti with Sweet-and-Sour, 290-291
  Santa Fe Fusilli, 114
  Shells Stuffed with, and Fennel, 64-65
  Smoked, and Pasta, 110-111
  Smoked, Penne, 115
  Spinach Cannelloni, 175
  Spinach Linguine with, Pesto, and Pine Nuts, 108-109
  and Tortellini Soup, 76
  Ziti with Dijon, and Broccoli, 108
  Ziti with, Pineapple, and Mint, 285-286
  Zuppa Maritata, 76
Chickpea and Pasta Soup, 77
Chili, Linguine with Beef and Black Bean Chili, 268

Chili-Peppers. see Peppers
Chilled Soba Noodles with Caviar and Oba, 206-207
Chinese Noodles, 198, 200-201
  with Asian Pesto, 207
  Salad with Spicy Sesame Dressing, 220
  Soup, 79-80
Chocolate
  Decadent Ravioli with Fudge Sauce, 315-316
  Magic Cookie Wontons, 317
  preparation, 317
Cinnamon, uses of, 314
Citrus Lobster Lasagna, 184-185
Citrus-Scented Orzo with Sesame Dressing, 258
Clams
  Linguine alla Vongole, 298
  Spaghetti with Asparagus, Pancetta and, 149
  see also Seafood
Classic Tomato Sauce, 42-43
Cold Noodles and Crabmeat in Peanut Sauce, 224
Colorful Avocado Spirals, 94
Coloring pasta, 39-40
Commander's Shrimp, 163
Conchiglie, 9
  Lemony, Salad, 245
Conchigliette, 6
  Soup, Crabmeat and, 85
Cookies, Magic Cookie Wontons, 317
Couscous, 234
  Herbed, Salad, 255
  Moroccan, 234-235
  Salad with Raspberry Vinaigrette, 256
  with Yogurt and Fruit, 318-319
Crab
  Cold Noodles and, in Peanut Sauce, 224
  Crabmeat and Conchigliette Soup, 85
  Crabmeat Fettuccine Primavera, 156
  Lo Mein Pasta Salad with Flash-Fried Soft-Shell, 249-250
  Soft-Shell, Over Angel Hair Pasta, 147-148
  see also Seafood
Crawfish, 147
  Cajun Pasta Salad, 244-245
  Cannelloni with Basil and Ricotta in Creole Tomato Sauce, 182-183
  Fettuccine, Creole Belle Pasta, 136-137
  New Orleans' Crawfish Pasta, 164
  Pasta Renaldo, 161-162
  and Tasso Pasta, 294-295
  see also Seafood
Creole Belle Pasta, 136-137
Crescent City Pasta, 112
Crispy Fried Noodles, 212-213
Crispy Tofu with Soba Noodles, 218-219
Curry
  Curried Chicken Egg Rolls with Yogurt Dipping Sauce, 70-71
  Indian Farfalle with Curried Chicken, 241
  Pasta with Young Fava Beans in Cream and Curry Leaves, 263
  Rice Noodles with Chicken and Shrimp, 221
  Soup with Angel Hair Pasta, 84
  Tonnarelli with, Vegetables, 282-283

D
Decadent Ravioli with Fudge Sauce, 315-316
Dessert
  Berry Medley with Noodles, 312
  Butterscotch Apples with Sweet Noodles, 319
  Couscous with Yogurt and Fruit, 318-319
  Decadent Ravioli with Fudge Sauce, 315-316
  Double Cherry Delight Dessert Dumplings, 318
  Festive Faralline, 313
  Fruit-Filled Lasagna, 321
  Heavenly Half Moons, 316
  Hot Honeyed Noodles with Bananas, 315
  Magic Cookie Wontons, 317
  Noodle Pudding with Nut Topping, 319-320
  Orange Almond Pastina Soufflé, 310-311
  Rich Roll-ups with Apricot Sauce, 311-312
  Sweet Blue Corn Ravioli Filled with Apples and Green Chili, 312-313
  Sweet Cheese Triangles, 308
  Sweet Lemon Stars with Lemon Cream Anglaise and Raspberry Coulis, 309-310
  Tagliatelle with Peaches, 314
Dilled Tomato Soup with Farfalline, 84
Ditalini, 7
  with Beans, 273-274
  Cajun Pasta Salad, 244-245
  Pork and Escarole Soup with, 74
  Zuppa Maritata, 76
Double Cherry Delight Dessert Dumplings, 318
Dough, preparation, 25-29
Duck, 60
  Spicy, with Avocado, 107
  Spicy Pasta with Roast Long Island, 60
Dumplings
  Double Cherry Delight Dessert, 318
  for Soup: Kreplach Dough and Meat Filling, 236-237

E
Egg Bow Ties and Wild Mushrooms in Herbed Broth, 100-101
Egg Noodles
  Armenian, with Spinach and Cheese, 235
  with Asparagus and Pork, 221-222
  Chinese Noodle Soup, 79-80
  Cold Noodles and Crabmeat in Peanut Sauce, 224
  Hungarian Goulash and Noodles, 240
  Marisa's Noodles, 238
  Meatballs Wrapped in Noodles, 61
  Portuguese Green Noodles with Anchovies, 239
  Stir-Fry with Chicken, 215-216
  Two Noodle Stir-Fry, 217, 217-218
Egg pasta, preparation, 24-31
Eggplant
  "Badly Cut" Pasta with, and Tuna, 162-163
  Gemelli with, and Tomatoes, 287-288
Egg Rolls
  Curried Chicken Egg Rolls with Yogurt Dipping Sauce, 70-71
  Shrimp, with Mustard Sauce, 69
  Wrappers, 200-201
Escarole
  Pork and, Soup with Ditalini, 74
  Soup, 80
  Spaghetti with Saffroned Onions, Sun-Dried Tomatoes and, 92-93

F

Farfalle, 9, 29
    Indian, with Curried Chicken, 241
    Turkey, Beef, and Mushroom Meatballs
        with, 142
    Turkey and Sausage with, 117-118
Farfalline, 6
    Dilled Tomato Soup with, 84
    Festive, 313
Fedelini, 3
    all'Ametriciana, 304
    Ham and Vegetable Noodle Salad with
        Peanut Sauce, 246-247
    Inverno, 116-117
    with Pacific Rim Chicken, 109-110
    with Shrimp and Snow Peas, 278
Feta cheese
    Tomato Linguine with Jumbo Shrimp,
        Scallops, Diced Leeks,and Saffron Cream,
        148-149
    see also Cheese
Fettuccine, 3, 16, 29
    alla Genovese, 99
    Black Pepper, with Venison Sausage, Sun-
        Dried Tomatoes, Spinach, and Parmesan
        Herb Sauce, 140-141
    with Chicken, Herbed Onions, and Nuts in
        Cream Sauce, 123-124
    Crabmeat, Primavera, 156
    Creole Belle Pasta, 136-137
    Fresh Spinach Fettuccine in Mussel Cream
        Sauce, 299
    Ink Fettuccine with Calamari and Porcini
        Mushrooms Baked in Parchment Paper,
        151-152
    with Light Alfredo Sauce, 285
    Lobster with Spinach Fettuccine, 151
    and Portabello Mushrooms with Balsamic
        Butter Sauce, 101-102
    with Potatoes and Tomatoes, 94-95
    Romanissimo, 139
    Spicy Sun-Dried Tomato Pesto with Shrimp
        and Scallops, 158-159
    Spinach Fettuccine with Smoked Salmon,
        Goat Cheese, Leeks, and Zucchini, 165-166
    Tagliatelle with Salmon, 289-290
    Tomato-Basil Pasta, 294
    with Truffles, 302
    Turkey and Spinach Fettuccine Casserole, 288
    with Zucchini, Pearl Onions, and
        Cardamom, 95
Fiesta Pasta, 266-267
Flavored pasta, 10, 39-40
French Fusilli with Mussels, 239-240
Fresh Spinach Fettuccine in Mussel Cream
    Sauce, 299
Fried Spaghetti, 72
Frittata
    Capellini, with Peas and Pancetta, 65
    Spinach and Pasta, 103
Fruit
    Filled Lasagna, 321
    see also Dessert
Fusilli, 9
    All'Arturo, 138
    French, with Mussels, 239-240
    with Fresh Herbs and Ricotta, 286

Pasta with Asparagus and Prosciutto in
    Balsamic Vinaigrette, 254
with Rapini and Sausage, 305
Santa Fe, 114
Turkey and Broccoli with, in Cream Sauce, 116

G

Garlic, 123
    and Olive oil (sauce), 48
    Roasted, 53
    and Sun-Dried Tomatoes with Chicken and
        Penne, 120-121
Gaspacho Pasta with Cannellini Beans, 264
Gemelli, 9
    with Eggplant and Tomatoes, 287-288
    with Fava Beans and Bacon, 269
    with Grilled Shrimp and Fruit Salsa, 259
    Spicy Cucumber Raita with, 277-278
Genovese Basil Pesto, 48
German Sautéed Cabbage and Noodles, 240-241
German Spaetzle, 237
Ginger, about, 247
Glass Noodles
    Sesame-Seared Scallops with Baby Bok choy
        and, Salad, 205-206
    Spicy Orange Beef with, 210-211
Gnocchi, 9, 231
    Cafè des Artistes, 228-229
    Potato, with Mushroom Sauce, 232
    White Truffle, 230-231
Goat cheese
    Greek Orzo with, 236
    Lemon Linguine with Rock Shrimp, Bay
        Scallops, Snap Peas, Plum Tomatoes, with,
        and Peppered Vodka Sauce, 150-151
    Ribbon Pasta with Rapini, Roasted Bell
        Peppers, Ripe Olives and, 90-91
    Spinach Fettuccine with Smoked Salmon,
        Leeks, Zucchini, and, 165-166
    see also Cheese
Goulash, Hungarian, and Noodles, 240
Greek Orzo with Goat Cheese, 236
Greek Pastitsio, 231-232
Grilled Scallops-Eggplant Ravioli, 173-175
Grilled Swordfish Medallions and Shrimp in a
    Roasted Yellow Tomato Sauce with
    Asparagus and Red Pepper over Penne
    Rigate, 164-165

H

Ham
    and Chicken Lasagna, 181-182
    Crawfish and Tasso Pasta, 294-295
    Penne with, in a Spicy Mixed Pepper Cream
        Sauce, 131
    Ravioli with Swiss Chard and Ham Hocks,
        189-191
    and Vegetable Noodle Salad with Peanut
        Sauce, 246-247
    see also Prosciutto
Heavenly Half Moons, 316
Herbed Couscous Salad, 255
Herbed and Ricotta Sauce, 54
Herb Linguine with Salmon, Cream, and
    Pistachios, 166
Herb Ravioli with Basil Oil and Tomato Coulis,
    168-171

Herbs, about, 20-21
Hot Honeyed Noodles with Bananas, 315
Hungarian Goulash and Noodles, 240

I

Indian Farfalle with Curried Chicken, 241
Ink Fettuccine with Calamari and Porcini
    Mushrooms Baked in Parchment Paper,
    151-152

J

Jalapeño Butter Sauce, 54
Japanese noodles, 198-199, 200-202
Japanese Shrimp and Pineapple with Cold
    Noodles, 206
Jewish Noodle Pudding, 238

K

Kasha, Russian Kasha with Mushrooms and
    Onions, 233

L

Lamb
    Greek Pastitsio, 231-232
    Ziti with Hearty Lamb Sauce, 138-139
Lasagna, 8, 193
    Beet and Spinach Pasta Rolls with Saffron
        Cream Sauce, 172-173
    Chicken, 113
    Citrus Lobster, 184-185
    fresh, 29
    Fruit-Filled, 321
    Frutti di Mare, 171-172
    Greek Pastitsio, 231-232
    Ham and Chicken, 181-182
    Lobster, 192
    with Lobster and Watercress, 196
    Nut Filled Pesto Rolls, 66
    Red Snapper and Spinach, 58-59
    Sun-Dried Tomato Pasta Wheels, 59
Leeks
    Cavatappi with Chicken, Tomato, and Leek
        Sauce, 121-122
    Lumache with, and Sausage Sauce, 126
Lemon
    Conchiglie Salad, 245
    Pepper Pasta, 103-104
    Sweet Lemon Stars with Lemon Cream
        Anglaise and Raspberry Coulis,
        309-310
Lemon Linguine with Rock Shrimp, Bay
    Scallops, Snap Peas, Plum Tomatoes, with
    Goat Cheese and Peppered Vodka Sauce,
    150-151
Lentils, 86
    Soup with Semi Di Melone, 85-86
Linguine, 3
    alla Cherrysela, 100
    alla Pescatore, 153-154
    alla Vongole, 298
    with Asparagus and Garlic Chicken Stir-Fry,
        282
    with Beef and Black Bean Chili, 268
    Chicken and Avocado with Spicy Tomato
        Salsa Over Linguine, 252-253
    Herb Linguine with Salmon, Cream, and
        Pistachios, 166

Lemon Linguine with Rock Shrimp, Bay
Scallops, Snap Peas, Plum Tomatoes, with
Goat Cheese and Peppered Vodka Sauce,
150-151
Pasta Jambalaya, 141
Saporiti, 144-145
Spinach Linguine with Chicken, Pesto, and
Pine Nuts, 108
Spinach Linguine with Ratatouille-Stuffed
Tomatoes, 97-98
with Sun-Dried Tomatoes, 103
Tomato Linguine with Jumbo Shrimp,
Scallops, Diced Leeks, Feta Cheese, and
Saffron Cream, 148-149
with Turkey, Tomatoes, and Olives, 114-115
Little Tubes and Beans, 270-271
Lobster
Citrus, Lasagna, 184-185
Lasagna, 192
Lasagna with, and Watercress, 196
Ravioli, 178-179
with Spinach Fettuccine, 151
Stuffed Cappelletti in a Sherry Coral Sauce,
186-187
and Vegetable Stew, 156-158
see also Seafood
Lo Mein Pasta Salad with Flash-Fried Soft-Shell
Crab, 249, 249-250
Long pasta, 2-3, 26-32
Low-fat cooking tips, 276
Lumache, 9
with Leek and Sausage Sauce, 126

M

Macaroni, 4
Sausage, and Bean Soup, 79
Magic Cookie Wontons, 317
Malfade, 4
Butterscotch Apples with Sweet Noodles, 319
Manicotti, 5, 29, 35-36
Marinated Beef and Pasta Salad, 250-251
Marisa's Noodles, 238
Meatballs
Farfalle with Turkey, Beef, and Mushroom
Meatballs, 142
Tomato Soup with Meatballs and Anellini,
80-81
Wrapped in Noodles, 61
see also Beef
Melted Cheese Triangles, 71
Mexican Pasta Bean Medley, 263-264
Mezzelune, 37
Moroccan Couscous, 234-235
Mortadella, 21
see also Sausage
Mostaccioli, 5, 16
Mother's Fresh Orecchiette with Rapini, 278-279
Mushrooms
Barley-Shaped Pasta Pilaf, 233-234
Egg Bow Ties and Wild, in Herbed Broth,
100-101
Fettuccine and Portabello Mushrooms with
Balsamic Butter Sauce, 101-102
Fettuccine with Truffles, 302
Poricini mushrooms, 21
Potato Gnocchi with Mushroom Sauce, 232
Roasted, Ragout, 190-191

Russian Kasha with, and Onions, 233
Shrimp and Shiitake Dijonaise, 160-161
Sun-Dried Tomato Ravioli with Wild, 194-195
White Truffle Gnocchi, 230-231
Wild, Broth, 75
Mussels
French Fusilli with Mussels, 239-240
Fresh Spinach Fettuccine in Mussel Cream
Sauce, 299
preparation of, 300
see also Seafood
My Pasta Sauce for 12 Hungry People, 55-56

N

Neapolitan Tomato Sauce, 43
New Orleans' Crawfish Pasta, 164
New Wave Bow Ties, 277
Noodle Pancake with Grilled Shrimp Salad,
213-214
Noodle Pudding with Nut Topping, 319-320
Nut-Filled Pesto Rolls, 66
Nuts
Asian Noodles Salad with Spicy Peanut
Sauce, 253
Cold Noodles and Crabmeat in Peanut
Sauce, 224
Fettuccine with Chicken, Herbed Onions, and
Nuts in Cream Sauce, 123-124
Ham and Vegetable Noodle Salad with
Peanut Sauce, 246-247
Noodle Pudding with Nut Topping, 319-320
Rice Noodles with Almonds and Broccoli, 49
toasting, 208
Vermicelli and Peanut Sauce Stir-Fry, 296
see also Pesto

O

Olive oil, 21
Garlic and, 48
Olives, 21-22
Orange
Almond Pastina Soufflé, 310-311
Festive Faralline, 313
Pasta with Pork Chops, 134
Pasta Salad, 252
Orecchiette, 9
alla Rosa, 153
with Broccoli, Chickpeas, Onions, and
Tomatoes, 262-263
with Broccoli in Saffron Vinaigrette, 257
with Fava Beans and Sage, 273
Mother's Fresh, with Rapini, 278-279
with Peas and Onions, 301
with Rapini and Sausage, 304
sauce for, 16
with Seafood, Rapini, and White Beans, 265
Shrimp, Genovese, 158
with Summer Tomato Sauce and Olives, 290
Orzo, 6
Avgolemono with, 83
Citrus-Scented, with Sesame Dressing, 258
Greek, with Goat Cheese, 236
Pasta with Young Fava Beans in Cream and
Curry Leaves, 263
Poached Chicken Breasts with Ratatouille,
Ragout, 118-119
Roasted Garlic, 298-299

P

Pad Thai, 208
Paglia and Fieno, 4, 127-128
Pancetta, 22
Capellini Frittata with Peas and, 65
Fedelini all'Ametriciana, 304
Penne with Artichokes and, 305-306
Spaghetti with Clams, Asparagus and, 149
see also Bacon
Pansotti, 8, 34, 36
Pappardelle, 4, 29
Asparagus and, 93
Beef Bourguignon with, 139-140
Pasta
Coloring, 39-40
Cooking, 13-14, 18, 32-33
Fresca, 11, 24-33
Machine, 24, 30-31
Purchasing, 11
Varieties of, 2-10, 13
Pasta alla E.M.I., 280
Pasta with Asparagus and Prosciutto in Balsamic
Vinaigrette, 254
Pasta and Bean Soup, 86
Pasta Jambalaya, 141
Pasta Provençale, 99-100
Pasta Quills with Beluga Caviar and Chives,
152-153
Pasta Roulade with Red Pepper Coulis, 193-194
Pasta Salad with Smoked Chicken and Oven-
Dried Tomatoes, 246
Pasta with Scallops and Champagne Cream
Sauce, 301
Pasta Soufflé, 62-63
Pasta with Yellow Summer Squash and Roasted
Garlic, 283
Pastina, Orange Almond, Soufflé, 310-311
Penne, 4, 16
with Artichokes and Pancetta, 305-306
with Arugula and Tomatoes, 88
Bella Luna's Chicken, with Tomatoes, 106
with Chicken, Broccoli, and Rosemary, 281
Chili-Pepper, Salad, 248-249
con Verdure, 281-282
Crawfish Pasta Renaldo, 161-162
Garlic and Sun-Dried Tomatoes with Chicken
and, 120-121
Grilled Swordfish Medallions and Shrimp in a
Roasted Yellow Tomato Sauce with
Asparagus and Red Pepper over, 164-165
with Ham in a Spicy Mixed Pepper Cream
Sauce, 131
Smoked Chicken, 115
with Tasso, Olives, Sun-Dried Tomatoes, and
Porcini, 130
in Tomato Broth with Cherry Pork Loin
Meatballs Topped with Hot Pepper
Coppa, 133
with Tomato and Fresh Basil, 91
Peppers
about Chili-Peppers, 67
Capellini with Chicken and Roasted Pepper
Salsa, 111
Chili-Pepper Penne Salad, 248, 248-249
Linguine alla Cherrysela, 100
Penne with Ham in a Spicy Mixed, Cream
Sauce, 131

Radiatore and Chicken in Tricolor,
   Sauce, 122
Ribbon Pasta with Rapini, Roasted Bell, Ripe
   Olives and Goat Cheese, 90-91
Sweet Blue Corn, Filled with Apples and
   Green Chili, 312-313
Perciatelli, 4, 16
   Chicken in Aromatic Tomato Sauce with, 120
Pesto
   Asian, 207
   Broccoli Pine Nut, 49
   Cream Dipping Sauce, 67
   Genovese Basil, 48
   Nut Filled, Rolls, 66
   Red, 49-50
   Shells with Scallops and Sun-Dried
      Tomato, 291
   Spicy Sun-Dried Tomato, 158-159
   Spinach, 49
   Spinach Linguine with Chicken, and
      Pine Nuts, 108-109
Poached Chicken Breasts with Ratatouille Orzo
   Ragout, 118-119
Polish Pierogi, 229-230
Porcini
   Penne with Tasso, Olives, Sun-Dried
      Tomatoes, and Porcini, 130
   Rigatoni with Sausage and Porcini, 128-129
Pork
   Crispy Fried Noodles, 212-213
   Egg Noodles with Asparagus and Pork,
      221-222
   and Escarole Soup with Ditalini, 74
   Hungarian Goulash and Noodles, 240
   Orange Pasta with Pork Chops, 134
   Pad Thai, 208
   Penne in Tomato Broth with Cherry Pork
      Loin Meatballs Topped with Hot Pepper
      Coppa, 133
   Pot Stickers, 69-70
   Rice Noodles with Pork and Shrimp,
      216-217
   Smothered Noodles, 225
   substitutions for, 135
   Two Noodle Stir-Fry, 217
Portuguese Green Noodles with Anchovies, 239
Potato
   Fettucine alla Genovese, 99
   Fettucine with Potatoes and Tomatoes, 94-95
Potato Gnocchi with Mushroom Sauce, 232
Pot Stickers, 69-70
Poultry. see Chicken; Duck; Turkey
Prawns Sambuca, 145-146
Primavera Sauce, 50-51
Prosciutto, 22
   Paglia and Fieno, 127-128
   Pasta with Asparagus and, in Balsamic
      Vinaigrette, 254
   Rigatoni alla Grappa, 127
   Shells with, Peas, and Mushrooms, 128
   Tortellini with, and Mesclun, 257-258
   see also Ham
Pudding
   Jewish Noodle Pudding, 238
   Noodle Pudding with Nut Topping, 319-320
Pumpkin Ravioli, 191-199
Puttanesca Sauce, 43

Q
Quadretti, 7
   Chickpea and Pasta Soup, 77

R
Radiatori, 9
   Beep Beep "Roadrunner" Pasta, 135
   and Chicken in Tricolor Pepper Sauce, 122
   with Shrimp and Artichokes in Parmesan
      Vinaigrette, 255-256
   Southwestern, 284
Ragout
   Poached Chicken Breasts with Ratatouille
      Orzo, 118-119
   Roasted Mushroom, 190-191
Raita, Spicy Cucumber, with Gemelli, 277-278
Ramen noodles, 199
   Randi's Bok Choy Chicken Salad, 248
Rapini
   Fusilli with, and Sausage, 305
   Mother's Fresh Orecchiette with,, 278-279
   Orecchiette with, and Sausage, 304
   Rotelle with Kielbasa and, 129
Ratatouille, Spinach Linguine with Ratatouille-
   Stuffed Tomatoes, 97-98
Ravioli, 8, 34-38
   alla Vodka, 183-184
   Black and White, with Sage Butter, 175-177
   Chicken-Portabello, with Porcini and Sun-
      Dried Tomato Sauce, 179-181
   Chicken-Prosciutto, with Rosemary Oil,
      177-178
   Decadent, with Fudge Sauce, 315-316
   Grilled Scallops-Eggplant, 173-175
   Herb, with Basil Oil and Tomato Coulis,
      168-171
   Lobster, 178-179
   Pumpkin, 191-199
   of Salmon with Cabbage and Caviar, 146
   Spinach and Three-Cheese, with Roasted
      Tomato, Olive, and Basil Essence Sauce,
      185-186
   Sun-Dried Tomato, with Wild Mushroom
      Filling, 194-195
   Sweet Blue Corn, Filled with Apples and
      Green Chili, 312-313
   Sweet Potato, in Wild Mushroom Broth, 75-76
   with Swiss Chard and Ham Hocks, 189-191
   Toasted, with Pesto Cream Dipping Sauce,
      66-67
Raviolini, 34, 36-37
Red Clam Sauce, 52-53
Red Pesto, 49-50
Red Snapper and Spinach Lasagna, 58-59
Red Wine Marinara Sauce, 47
Ribbon Pasta with Rapini, Roasted Bell Peppers,
   Ripe Olives, and Goat Cheese, 90-91
Ribbons, 3-4
Rice noodles, 199-200, 201
   with Broccoli and Almonds, 215
   Curry Rice Noodles with Chicken and
      Shrimp, 221
   Pad Thai, 208
   with Pork and Shrimp, 216-217
   Two Noodle Stir-Fry, 217
   see also Vermicelli
Rich Roll-ups with Apricot Sauce, 311-312

Ricotta cheese
   Fusilli with Fresh Herbs and, 286
   Herbed and, Sauce, 54
   Shells and Spinach and, 306
   see also Cheese
Rigatoni, 5
   alla Contadina, 303-304
   alla Grappa, 127
   with Asparagus, 90
   with Borlotti Beans and Sausage, 270
   sauce for, 16
   with Sausage and Porcini, 128-129
   Siciliana, 302
Roasted Garlic Orzo, 298-299
Roasted Mushroom Ragout, 190-191
Rotelle, 8, 16
   Chicken Cacciatore with, 119
   with Kielbasa and Rapini, 129
   New Orleans' Crawfish Pasta, 164
Rotini, 16
   Pasta Provençale, 99-100
   Pasta with Yellow Summer Squash and
      Roasted Garlic, 283
Roulade, Pasta, with Red Pepper Coulis,
   193-194
Roux, preparation, 44
Ruoti with Sweet-and-Sour Chicken, 290-291
Russian Kasha with Mushrooms and
   Onions, 233

S
Salad
   Bay Shrimp, 251
   Cajun Pasta, 244-245
   Chicken and Avocado with Spicy Tomato
      Salsa Over Linguine, 252-253
   Chicken and Black Bean, Over Spirals, 271
   Chili-Pepper Penne, 248-249
   Chinese Noodle, with Spicy Sesame
      Dressing, 220
   Citrus-Scented Orzo with Sesame
      Dressing, 258
   Couscous, with Raspberry Vinaigrette, 256
   Gemelli with Grilled Shrimp and Fruit
      Salsa, 259
   Ham and Vegetable Noodle, with Peanut
      Sauce, 246-247
   Herbed Couscous, 255
   Lemony Conchiglie, 245
   Lo Mein Pasta, with Flash-Fried Soft-Shell
      Crab, 249-250
   Marinated Beef and Pasta, 250-251
   Orange Pasta, 252
   Orecchiette with Broccoli in Saffron
      Vinaigrette, 257
   Pasta, with Smoked Chicken and Oven-Dried
      Tomatoes, 246
   Pasta with Asparagus and Prosciutto in
      Balsamic Vinaigrette, 254
   Radiatori with Shrimp and Artichokes in
      Parmesan Vinaigrette, 255-256
   Randi's Bok Choy Chicken, 248
   Tortellini with Prosciutto and Mesclun,
      257-258
Salmon
   Cannelloni with, and Tomato Cream Sauce,
      154-155

Herb Linguine with, Cream, and
Pistachios, 166
New Wave Bow Ties, 277
Orecchiette alla Rosa, 153
Ravioli of, with Cabbage and Caviar, 146
Spinach Fettuccine with Smoked, Goat
Cheese, Leeks, and Zucchini, 165-166
Tagliatelle with, 289-290
see also Seafood
Salsa Verde, 55
Santa Fe Fusilli, 114
Sauce, 14-16
Alfredo, 51
Basil Essence Sauce, 185-186
Béchamel, 45
Bolognese, 45-46
Carbonara, 50
Cream sauce, 16, 44
Fruit Salsa, 259
Garlic and Olive Oil, 48
Herbed and Ricotta, 54
Jalapeño Butter, 54
Lemon Vodka Sauce, 300
Mushroom Sauce, 232
Mustard Sauce, 69
My Pasta Sauce for 12 Hungry People, 55-56
Pesto Cream, 67
Primavera, 50-51
Red Clam, 52-53
Roasted Pepper Salsa, 111
Salsa Verde, 55
Sauce Bolognese, 45-45, 45-46
white, 53-54
white clam, 53-54
Yogurt Sauce, 70
Zucchini, 55
see also Tomato sauce
Sausage, 21, 132
Beep Beep "Roadrunner" Pasta, 135
Black Pepper Fettuccine with Venison,
Tomatoes, Spinach, & Sauce, 140-142
Cajun Pasta Salad, 244-245
Farfalle with Turkey and, 117-118
Fusilli with Rapini and, 305
Lumache with Leek and, Sauce, 126
Macaroni, and Bean Soup, 79
Orecchiette with Rapini and, 304
Pasta Jambalaya, 141
Rigatoni alla Contadina, 303-304
Rigatoni with Borlotti Beans and, 270
Rigatoni with, and Porcini, 128-129
Rotelle with Kielbasa and Rapini, 129
Spaghetti Pie, 131-132
Scallops
Grilled Scallops-Eggplant Ravioli, 173-175
Pasta with, and Champagne Cream
Sauce, 301
Sesame-Seared, with Baby Bok choy and
Glass Noodle Salad, 205-206
Shells with, and Sun-Dried Tomato Pesto, 291
Seafood
Auntie Sugar's Rock Shrimp and Langostino
Marinara, 159-160
Cannelloni with Tomato and Lemon
Parmesan Cream Sauce, 187-189
Capellini Pescatore, 295-296
Gnocchi Café des Artistes, 228-229

Grilled Swordfish Medallions and Shrimp in a
Roasted Yellow Tomato Sauce with
Asparagus and Red Pepper over Penne
Rigate, 164-165
Lasagna Frutti di Mare, 171-172
Lemon Linguine with Rock Shrimp, Bay
Scallops, Snap Peas, Plum Tomatoes, with
Goat Cheese and Peppered Vodka Sauce,
150-151
Linguine alla Pescatore, 153-154
Lo Mein, 222
Orecchiette with, Rapini, and White
Beans, 265
Pasta Jambalaya, 141
Red Snapper and Spinach Lasagna, 58
Shrimp Egg Rolls with Mustard Sauce, 69
Spicy Sun-Dried Tomato Pesto with Shrimp
and Scallops, 158-159
Tomato Linguine with Jumbo Shrimp,
Scallops, Diced Leeks, Feta Cheese, and
Saffron Cream, 148-149
Vermicelli with Tuna, Anchovies, and Capers,
286-287
see also specific seafood
Semi di melone, 6
Lentil Soup with, 85-86
Sesame-Seared Scallops with Baby Bok choy
and Glass Noodle Salad, 205-206
Shells, 9, 16
Lemony Conchiglie Salad, 245
with Prosciutto, Peas, and Mushrooms, 128
with Scallops and Sun-Dried Tomato Pesto, 291
Soup of Shrimp and, 83
and Spinach and Ricotta, 306
Stuffed with Chicken and Fennel, 64-65
Shrimp
Auntie Sugar's Rock, and Langostino
Marinara, 159-160
Bay, Salad, 251
Commander's, 163
Curry Rice Noodles with Chicken and, 221
Egg Rolls with Mustard Sauce, 69
Fedelini with, and Snow Peas, 278
Gemelli with Grilled, and Fruit Salsa, 259
Japanese, and Pineapple with Cold
Noodles, 206
Linguine Saporiti, 144-145
Noodle Pancake with Grilled, Salad, 213-214
Orecchiette Genovese, 158
Pad Thai, 208
Radiatori with, and Artichokes in Parmesan
Vinaigrette, 255-256
Rice Noodles with Pork and Shrimp,
216-217
and Shiitake Dijonaise, 160-161
Spirals with, and Artichokes, 155
Two Noodle Stir-Fry, 217
Ziti with, and Arugula, 297
see also Seafood
Smoked Chicken and Pasta, 110
Smoked Chicken Penne, 115
Smoked Salmon and Dill in Cream Sauce with
Angel Hair Pasta, 144
Smothered Noodles, 225
Soba noodles, 199
Chilled, with Caviar and Oba, 206-207
Crispy Tofu with, 218-219

Lo Mein Pasta Salad with Flash-Fried
Soft-Shell Crab, 249-250
Spicy Cold,, 214
Soft-Shell Crabs Over Angel Hair pasta, 147-148
Somen noodles, 198, 202
Japanese Shrimp and Pineapple with Cold
Noodles, 206
Soufflé
Orange Almond Pastina Soufflé, 310-311
Pasta Soufflé, 62-63
Soup, 78
Alfabetini and Zucchini, 81-82
Chicken, 78
Chicken and Tortellini, 76
Chinese Noodle, 79-80
Crabmeat and Conchigliette, 85
Curried, with Angel Hair Pasta, 84
Dilled Tomato, with Farfallini, 84
Escarole, 80
Lentil, with Semi Di Melone, 85-86
Lobster and Vegetable Stew, 156-157
Pasta and Bean, 86
Pasta shapes for, 6-7
Pork and Escarole, with Ditalini, 74
of Shrimp and Shells, 83
Sweet Potato Ravioli in Wild Mushroom
Broth, 75-76
Tagliolini, with Yogurt, 82
Tomato, with Meatballs and Anellini, 80-81
with Tubetti and Greens, 82
Zuppa Maritata, 76
Southwestern Radiatori, 284
Spaghetti, 2, 16
with Calamari in a Garlic, Pepper, and Spicy
Olive Oil Sauce, 149-150
with Clams, Asparagus, and Pancetta, 149
Fried, 72
Lemon Pepper Pasta, 103-104
with Meat Sauce, 295
Pasta alla E.M.I., 280
Pie, 131-132
with Saffroned Onions, Sun-Dried Tomatoes,
and Escarole, 92-93
Spinach and Pasta Frittata, 103
Spaghettini, 2
Asian Noodles Salad with Spicy Peanut
Sauce, 253
con Broccoli Siciliano, 89
with Veal, 137-138
with Winter Vegetables, 279-280
Spareribs with Noodles, 210
Spices, Asian, 202-204
Spicy Cold Soba Noodles, 214
Spicy Cucumber Raita with Gemelli, 277-278
Spicy Duck with Avocado, 107
Spicy Orange Beef with Glass Noodles, 210-211
Spicy Pasta with Roast Long Island Duck, 60
Spicy Sun-Dried Tomato Pesto with Shrimp and
Scallops, 158-159
Spinach
Cannelloni, 175
and Pasta Frittata, 103
Pesto, 49
Shells and Ricotta, with, 306
and Three-Cheese Ravioli with Roasted
Tomato, Olive, and Basil Essence Sauce,
185-186

Wontons with Apricot Mustard Sauce, 63-64
see also Fettuccine; Linguine
Spirals, 16
    Chicken and Black Bean Salad Over, 271
    Colorful Avocado, 94
    with Shrimp and Artichokes, 155
    White Bean and Pasta Bean Bake, 265-266
Spring Rolls, Vietnamese, 68
Squash, Pasta with Yellow Summer, and
    Roasted Garlic, 283
Squid, preparation, 223
    see also Seafood
Stuffed pasta
    preparation, 33-39
    shapes for, 7-8
Summer Tomato Sauce, 46
Sun-Dried Tomato
    with Black Pepper Fettuccine, Venison
        Sausage, Spinach, & Parmesan Herb
        Sauce, 140-141
    Pasta Wheels, 59
    Ravioli with Wild Mushroom Filling, 194-195
    see also Tomatoes
Sweet Blue Corn Ravioli Filled with Apples and
    Green Chili, 312-313
Sweet Cheese Triangles, 308
Sweet Lemon Stars with Lemon Cream Anglaise
    and Raspberry Coulis, 309-310
Sweet Potato Ravioli in Wild Mushroom Broth,
    75-76

T

Tagliatelle, 3-4, 29
    with Cannellini and Tomato Sauce, 268-269
    with Lemon Vodka Sauce, 300
    with Peaches, 314
    with Salmon, 289-290
Tagliolini, 4, 29
    Soup with Yogurt, 82
Tasso, Crawfish and Tasso Pasta, 294-295
Thai Fried Noodles, 211
Thai Noodle Salad, 209
Toasted Ravioli with Pesto Cream Dipping
    Sauce, 66-67
Tofu, Crispy Tofu with Soba Noodles, 218-219
Tomato-Basil Pasta, 294
Tomatoes, 19
    Bella Luna's Chicken Penne Pasta with, 106
    Black Pepper Fettuccine with Venison
        Sausage, Spinach, and, Parmesan Sauce,
        140-141
    Bow Ties with Black Beans and Cherry,
        267-269
    Capellini with Basil, Sliced Grilled Steak,
        and, 136
    Cavatappi with Chicken, and Leek Sauce,
        121-122
    Fettucine with Potatoes and, 94-95
    Garlic and Sun-Dried, with Chicken and
        Penne, 120-121
    Linguine with Sun-Dried, 103

Linguine with Turkey, and Olives, 114-115
Orecchiette with Broccoli, Chickpeas, Onions
    and, 262-263
Penne with Arugula and, 88
Penne with, and Fresh Basil, 91
Soup with Meatballs and Anellini, 80-81
Spaghetti with Saffroned Onions, Sun-Dried,
    and Escarole, 92-93
Spinach Linguine with Ratatouille-Stuffed,
    97-98
Sun-Dried, Pasta Wheels, 59
Tomato-Basil Pasta, 294
Tomato Linguine with Jumbo Shrimp, Scallops,
    Diced Leeks, Feta Cheese, and Saffron
    Cream, 148-149
Tomato sauce, 15-16
    Arrabbiata Sauce, 47
    Classic, 42-43
    Creole, 182-183
    Neapolitan, 43
    Puttanesca Sauce, 43
    Red Clam, 52-52
    Red Wine Marinara, 47
    Roasted Yellow, 164-165
    Spicy Tomato Salsa, 252-253
    Summer, 46
    Variation, 44
Tonnarelli, 4
    with Curried Vegetables, 282-283
tools, 11-12, 24-25, 30-31
Tortelli. *see* Ravioli
Tortellini, 8, 37
    Chicken and Tortellini Soup, 76
    with Prosciutto and Mesclun, 257-258
Tortiglioni
    Bay Shrimp Salad, 251
    Shrimp and Shiitake Dijonaise, 160-161
Truffles, 303
    Fettuccine with Truffles, 302
Tubetti, 7
    Little Tubes and Beans, 270-271
    Soup with, and Greens, 82
Tuna, "Badly Cut" Pasta with Eggplant and,
    162-163
Turkey
    and Broccoli with Fusilli in Cream Sauce, 116
    Farfalle with, and Sausage, 117-118
    Linguine with, Tomatoes, and Olives,
        114-115
    and Spinach Fettuccine Casserole, 288
    White Bean and Pasta Bake, 265-266
Two Noodle Stir-Fry, 217

U

Udon noodles, 198, 199, 201-202

V

Veal
    Hungarian Goulash and Noodles, 240
    Spaghettini with, 137-138
Vegetables

Angel Hair pasta with Grilled Vegetables 91-92
    and Bean Threads, 219-220
    Cavatelli Primavera, 97
    choosing, 280
    Lobster and Vegetable Stew, 156-158
    Orecchiette with Broccoli, Chickpeas, Onions,
        and Tomatoes, 262-263
    Pasta Provencale, 99-100
    Penne con Verdure, 281-282
    Ribbon Pasta with Rapini, Roasted Bell
        Peppers, Ripe Olives, & Goat Cheese,
        90-91
    Spaghettini con Broccoli Siciliano, 89
    Spaghettini with Winter Vegetables, 279-280
    Thai Noodle Salad, 209
    Tonnarelli with Curried Vegetables, 282-283
    see also specific vegetables
Vegetable Vermicelli, 102
Venison, Black Pepper Fettuccine with
    Venison Sausage, Tomatoes, Spinach, &
    Sauce, 140-141
Vermicelli, 3
    Commander's Shrimp, 163
    Crispy Fried Noodles, 212-213
    Pasta Souffle, 62-63
    and Peanut Sauce Stir-Fry, 296
    sauce for, 16
    Smothered Noodles, 225
    Spareribs with Noodles, 210
    with Tuna, Anchovies, and Capers, 286-287
    Vegetable Vermicelli, 102
Vietnamese Spring Rolls, 68
Vinegar, 254

W

Wagon Wheel pasta, Orange Pasta Salad, 252
White Bean and Pasta Bake, 265-266
White Truffle Gnocchi, 230-231
Wontons, 200-201
    Magic Cookie, 317
    Spinach, with Apricot Mustard Sauce, 63-64

Y

Yogurt
    Couscous with, and Fruit, 318-319
    Tagliolini Soup with, 82

Z

Ziti, 5, 16
    Baked, with Meat, 288-289
    with Chicken, Pineapple, and Mint, 285-286
    with Dijon Chicken and Broccoli, 108
    with Hearty Lamb Sauce, 138-139
    with Orange Asparagus Sauté, 297-298
    with Shrimp and Arugula, 297
Zucchini
    Alfabetini and, 81-82
    Fettuccine with, Pearl Onions, and
        Cardamom, 95
    Sauce, 55
Zuppa Maritata, 76